Ben Gook (ed.)
Libidinal Economies of Crisis Times

Ben Gook (Dr.) is a senior lecturer in Cultural Studies at the University of Melbourne. His research focuses on negative affects, psychoanalysis, social and cultural theory, as well as contemporary film.

Ben Gook (ed.)

Libidinal Economies of Crisis Times

The Psychic Life of Contemporary Capitalism

The editor and publisher acknowledge the generous support of the Alexander von Humboldt Stiftung and University of Melbourne for the printing and Open Access costs of this book.

Bibliographic information published by the Deutsche Nationalbibliothek
The Deutsche Nationalbibliothek lists this publication in the Deutsche Nationalbibliografie; detailed bibliographic data are available in the Internet at https://dnb.dnb.de/

This work is licensed under the Creative Commons Attribution 4.0 (BY) license, which means that the text may be remixed, transformed and built upon and be copied and redistributed in any medium or format even commercially, provided credit is given to the author.

Creative Commons license terms for re-use do not apply to any content (such as graphs, figures, photos, excerpts, etc.) not original to the Open Access publication and further permission may be required from the rights holder. The obligation to research and clear permission lies solely with the party re-using the material.

First published in 2024 by transcript Verlag, Bielefeld
© Ben Gook (ed.)

Cover layout: Kordula Röckenhaus, Bielefeld
Printed by: Elanders Waiblingen GmbH, Waiblingen
https://doi.org/10.14361/9783839456859
Print-ISBN: 978-3-8376-5685-5
PDF-ISBN: 978-3-8394-5685-9
ISSN of series: 2702-8968
eISSN of series: 2702-8976

Contents

Libido, Economy, Crisis

Ben Gook

This volume's authors propose that the libidinal has arisen again as a keyword in our times of crisis, from the economic to the ecological, the reproductive to the political, and on across the domains of everyday life. The book bears the mark of its time, the traumas of its birth: contemporary upheaval has multiplied while we have worked on it, and some of that is directly recorded here. Many contributors met in Berlin to discuss libidinal economy and crisis in late 2019, just a few weeks before COVID-19 entered the world system. I am belatedly compiling this collection in 2024, amid inflation, shortages, eco-catastrophes, genocides, and intractable wars. In the space between the Berlin conference and this book's release – in the rhythm and pace of crisis temporality – it has been hard to miss how the appetites, intensities, and desires of subjects in such times are monitored for signs of pathology and potentials for modulation or shaping. In essence, we have seen states and their annexes attempt to deal with the significant challenges presented by "mass psychology" in acute – and chronic – moments of instability. The past half-decade has only provided further evidence of the libido's psychosocial attunements, as well as the currency of thinking addressed to the passions and affections of subjects. Ultimately, "in times of crisis," as Frank O'Hara famously wrote, "we must all decide again and again whom we love."[1]

The recent crises are not unfamiliar topics in the history of psychoanalysis. War shaped Europe (and elsewhere) during Sigmund Freud's time, as did bouts of hyperinflation and goods shortages. If many of our contemporary crises are about the failing attachments to leading ideologies – forms of failing love, of disaffection – then they are also about murder, death, extinction. A deadly pandemic – the misnamed "Spanish flu" – deeply impacted the globe during the formative decades of psychoanalysis. In Jacqueline Rose's essay collection *The Plague*, she brings to our attention a detail of psychoanalytic history, often unremarked, that took on new significance a century later: in 1920, Freud's "favourite daughter," Sophie Halberstadt-Freud, died during the Spanish flu's fourth wave, after it had ravaged Europe for years and piled further disaster on top of WWI. Rose makes the case, following

---

1   Frank O'Hara, *Meditations in an Emergency* (New York: Grove Press, 1967), 3.

archival work by Ilse Grubrich-Simitis, that this experience of sudden loss and grief informed Freud's theorisation of the death drive. This theory was decisively added to *Beyond the Pleasure Principle* after Sophie's death.[2] It is worth remembering, too, that the title's "beyond" carries in German (*Jenseits*) the word's same English connotations – the hereafter, the afterlife, the other side – all of which take on a different complexion in times of mass death.

As Freud wrote the book, the vicissitudes of history – war, pandemic, inflation – scrambled many of his previous conceptualisations. In *Beyond*, he attempted to reconceive and speculate upon future directions in psychoanalytic thought.[3] It is also a text that sees Freud reflect on the notion of psychic trauma in connection with libido, even though these two theories – trauma theory and libido theory – are often seen as counterposed. As Eric Santner explains, however, the view of them as opposed is "highly misleading since libido is, at some level, the very substance of a wound correlative to the emergence of the human subject."[4] *Beyond the Pleasure Principle* thus becomes one of the few places where trauma and libido are thought

---

2   Jacqueline Rose, *The Plague* (London: Fitzcarraldo, 2023); Ilse Grubrich-Simitis, *Back to Freud's Texts: Making Silent Documents Speak* (New Haven: Yale UP, 1996). Frued also lost a beloved young grandson – Heinz, Sophie's child – to tuberculosis in 1923. A dissenting opinion on Sophie's death and *Beyond the Pleasure Principle* can be found in Ulrike May, "The Third Step in Drive Theory: On the Genesis of *Beyond the Pleasure Principle*," *Psychoanalysis and History* 17, no. 2 (2015): 250. May's fastidious comparison of manuscripts suggests it was not the death drive but its counterpart – Eros – introduced after Sophie's death. This thesis is no less fascinating or relevant.

3   This also includes the period of crisis (1910–1920) within the psychoanalytic community itself over technique, as Lacan discusses (*The Seminar of Jacques Lacan. Book II: The Ego in Freud's Theory and in the Technique of Psychoanalysis*, trans. Sylvana Tomaselli (Cambridge: Cambridge UP, 1988), 10–11). This crisis was marked by the declining efficacy of psychoanalysis and, in the same period, Freud's new structure: ego, super-ego and Id.

4   Eric L. Santner, *The Royal Remains: The People's Two Bodies and the Endgames of Sovereignty* (Chicago: University of Chicago Press, 2011), 69, 72–73. As Santner adds, "no doubt it was this effort that led him, for better or worse, to posit the existence of an autonomous death drive." Without wishing to derail the main discussion, we can also add that one connection between these two theories lies in the concept of "fixation." In libidinal terms, "fixations" develop if issues arise and are not expressed or dealt with properly during the affected stage of sexual development. This emerges in everyday conversation when someone is said to be "fixated" on a particular object – be it a person, idea, commodity, body part etc. In other words, a subject's libidinal energy is "stuck" at a particular psychosexual stage and will remain as such without intervention. This fixation can be a result of a traumatic experience, linking the theories of trauma and libido. Freud's theories can thus be said to suggest that the interplay of libidinal energy and traumatic experiences influences behaviours and mental states. These experiences can lead to fixations that impact our behaviours and the circulation of libidinal energy.

together, as Freud ventures to explain the traumas and libidinal investments – and libidinal investments in trauma – of a fraught period in European history.

What, we ask in this volume, are the virtues (and vices) of "libidinal economy" for thinking about the politics of desire in our present period, one marked by trauma as much as libidinal investment? The fortunes of "libidinal economy" have themselves risen in recent years. As various crises intersect, multiply and redouble, commentators have sought ways to make sense of the symptoms of subjective life in 21st-century crisis times. This reflects the growing sense that something "underlies all these intractable difficulties," "something fundamentally rotten in our social order": namely, "a deeper failure in the capitalist social formation."[5] Perhaps the catalyst here was the return to the *economic* amid the Global Financial Crisis (GFC) of 2007–8, which, in historical terms, happened soon after the affective intensity of the "west versus the rest" and the "war on terror" reactions to the 9/11 terrorist attacks in the US.[6]

After the GFC, heterodox economists and people working in critical finance studies have sought to think through the exuberance and "irrationalism" of the financial crash and its precipitates. The libidinal arose at this moment, too, as it had in an earlier phase of capitalist crisis (1960s and 70s), to consider how "we are libidinally galvanized to produce and consume the world rendered as a world of value," as Benjamin Noys puts it.[7] Beyond the moral categories of greed and envy common in media and political scapegoating of various actors in the GFC, critics have looked around for a model that can say something about subjectivity – forms of subjective investment – in neoliberalism. They arguably sought one distinct from the Foucauldian model of power and resistance that dominated critical approaches to the (early) neoliberal era, and which seems to have declining explanatory power in the (late) neoliberal era.[8] Libidinal economy is "founded on the notion of a desiring subject, which obeys a logic not of equanimity, good sense, and self-interest but unpredictability, profligacy, and indeed irrationality."[9] From this perspective, consumption, for example, is not seen as simply satisfying material or biological

---

5   Nancy Fraser and Rahel Jaeggi, *Capitalism: A Conversation in Critical Theory* (Cambridge: Polity, 2018), 4.

6   Notable here, throughout the 2010s, was the coexistence in many societies of the fallout from these two moments: the public austerity and private abundance of the post-GFC economic model plus the terrorist upsurge of the Islamic State movement, born of a reaction to the war on terror. Together, these generated shared moods of angst and uncertainty.

7   Benjamin Noys, "'We Are All Prostitutes': Crisis and Libidinal Economy," in *Credo Credit Crisis*, ed. Aidan Tynan, Laurent Milesi, and Christopher John Muller (London: Rowman & Littlefield International, 2017), 170.

8   For a helpful periodisation of neoliberalism: William Davies, "The New Neoliberalism," *New Left Review* 101 (2016): 121–34.

9   Ilan Kapoor et al., *Global Libidinal Economy* (Albany: SUNY Press, 2023), ix.

needs, but rather as an attempt to find solace for a deep sense of loss. Capital, for its part, is seen as something driven – cunning, seducing and beguiling in the service of unending accumulation for its own sake, even at the expense of cannibalising its very conditions of possibility. The libidinal economic approach, then, offers explanations for behaviour that seem counterintuitive in other terms.

In what follows, I outline Freud's understanding of libido before discussing its overlaps with, and distinctions from, related terms, such as desire and drive. I also address the two other key terms in this volume: economy and crisis. In opening the book, I ask what it means to speak about crisis and libido together, and how the signs of one are continually read in the other. I thus set out to furnish a scene that authors of subsequent chapters will enter and rework in their own fashion. While each chapter draws on diverse examples and theorists, some preceding the Freudian notions *per se*, the contributors all address one or more elements of this same knot in contemporary capitalism: libido, economy, crisis.

The libidinal as an expanded field

For Freud, "libidinal economy" names the energetic sexual exchanges – saving and spending, investing and divesting, occupying and transferring – that occur within the subject, and between subject and world. The "economy" here concerns a certain ordering and circulation of those exchanges within a closed yet expansive system. In its exchanges and worldliness, the libidinal economy is attuned to its environment – deeply intimate yet also external. Hence, the social surround enters the frame of the libidinal; graphs of surges and declines could practically be shown next to nightly reports about the fortunes of stock exchanges: "libido down 0.4 per cent today on news of floods affecting supply chains."

Jacques Lacan's infamous statement that "there's no such thing as a sexual relationship," amounts to a slogan for the psychoanalytic view of human sexuality as distinct from biology and anatomy – two realms it constantly subverts.[10] As Lacan indicates, following Freud to the letter, sexuality is not organised around anything stable, let alone a relation between biological sexes; human sexuality is nothing but its "out of placeness."[11] The libidinal is *unnatural*, bearing the rift of what we call culture from what we call nature. Essentially, the libidinal distinguishes *human* sexuality

---

10   Jacques Lacan, *The Seminar of Jacques Lacan. Book XX: Encore. On Feminine Sexuality: The Limits of Love and Knowledge*, trans. Bruce Fink (NY: Norton, 1999), 12. Lacan says here that this is the indisputable truth of what conditions analytic discourse.

11   Alenka Zupančič, *The Odd One in: On Comedy* (Cambridge: MIT Press, 2008), 207; Alenka Zupančič, *What Is Sex?* (Cambridge: MIT Press, 2017); Samo Tomšič, "No Such Thing as Society? On Competition, Solidarity, and Social Bond," *Differences* 33, no. 2–3 (2022): 51–71.

from nonhuman species reproduction. "Our sexual being results from a combination of the two [gender-sex or biology-culture], with an unruly surplus that exceeds both," Patricia Gherovici and Manya Steinkoler write, invoking the standard binaries.[12] The libidinal is de-natured – marked, more often than not, by its nonfunctional activity ("perversions"), contra the Darwinian functionalist view of species reproduction, and the pre-Darwinian religious view of spiritual and communal renewal via the sexual encounter. There is no natural pathway for human sexuality, but a constant finding of form – those path-finding and re-finding vicissitudes of drives, instincts, desires. Only the human creature produces streaming TV series called "Sex: Explained."[13]

Human sexuality is distinct from the unreflexive urges of the planet's procreating species, both animal and vegetal, by virtue of *the unconscious*.[14] This unconscious, Alenka Zupančič helps us to recall, is not the opposite of consciousness but refers "to an active and ongoing process, work of censorship, substitution, condensation and so on, and this work is itself intrinsic to sexuality (desire) and its deadlocks, rather than simply performed in relation to it."[15] Human sexuality goes beyond the sexual organs to sexualise sexual activity, endowing it with a surplus: sex is redoubled; sex becomes sexy.[16] The animal mates; the human has erotics. Put differently, human sexuality is sexualised in the constitutive interval that separates sexuality from itself. "The moment we try to provide a clear definition of sexual activity," Zupančič cautions, "we run into trouble."[17] We can see this in the paradox that, "the further sex

---

12   Manya Steinkoler and Patricia Gherovici, eds., *Psychoanalysis, Gender, and Sexualities: From Feminism to Trans** (London: Routledge, 2022), 6. Berlant (*Desire/Love* (Punctum, 2012), 58) writes that "ambivalence, anxiety, and other forms of sexual surplus are never fully absorbed into the managerial economy of gender identity."

13   Freud suggests that desire for knowledge is a form of sexual curiosity: some of the earliest theories children develop are about where babies come from and what sex is. Jamieson Webster: "For Freud, the question of knowledge was always a question of sexual curiosity, and sexuality, he suggests, never moves in straight lines, never moves this curiosity straightforwardly. Libido folds in on itself, or it simply exists as a series of folds, sometimes found in the form of a striving to know, to make something of itself, the object of discovery, one among many variations of autoeroticism, this folding as a folding back or in upon the self" (*Conversion Disorder: Listening to the Body in Psychoanalysis* (New York: Columbia UP, 2019), 31).

14   Challenges to elements of this position can be found in Luce Irigaray and Michael Marder, *Through Vegetal Being: Two Philosophical Perspectives* (NY: Columbia UP, 2016). And it is also worth pointing out that certain animals also display sexual "dysfunctions" from a purely reproductive standpoint.

15   Alenka Zupančič, "Biopolitics, Sexuality and the Unconscious," *Paragraph* 39, no. 1 (2016): 51.

16   Zupančič, *Odd*, 207.

17   Zupančič, 207. See also Zupančič, *What Is Sex?* She argues that in psychoanalysis, sex is a concept that captures a contradiction in reality not reducible to a secondary level (contradiction between established entities or beings), and is instead relevant to the ontological structuring of entities. It is presented as a twist or stumbling block of reality.

departs from the 'pure' copulating movement (that is to say, the wider the range of elements it includes in its activity), the more sexual it becomes."[18] In contemporary western culture at large, idiosyncratic kinks – loaded with singular significance – epitomise sex more readily than the straight up-and-down of family planning. This recognises that sexuality operates within the bounds of human meaning. This operation is encapsulated nowhere better than in the claim that an encounter was "just sex," which is inevitably followed by the defensive, negative statement that "it didn't mean anything."[19]

As a site of meaning, albeit sometimes disavowed, human sexuality is subject to an economy of ever-widening desires, routed through communicative systems, objectified in products, and offered in exchange: objects and techniques are discussed, debated and taken to market. Moreover, these varieties of exchange and debate can be intrapsychic: the human subject can distinctively analyse, reflect and act (or not) on their *drives*, which are precisely not fixed biological *instincts*. Human is she who, in her stressed dissatisfaction, buys a sex toy, or, alternatively, takes the same sum to a psychoanalyst for a session of the talking cure to straighten out her kinks in desire. In the analyst's rooms, the patient would stray from a narrow discussion of sexual activity and desires to all sorts of other freely associated topics (food, friends, work, death, pets).

The libidinal includes this expanded field, the full range of preoccupations, fixations and disruptions – clusters of thought, affect and practice – that enter the frame of human sexuality. If the libidinal is not always – indeed, only rarely – biologically reproductive, it can at least be considered generative of meaningful sociocultural reproduction. "Libido theory," Santner has suggested, is "from the start a special kind of social theory."[20] For Santner, if we are libidinal beings, desiring in a human sense, then this is because symbolic representation introduces a gap, separating humans from any directly "natural" life-process. Human enjoyment is entwined with the circulation of objects and the possibilities of language (explicitly in, say, erotic fiction, phone sex, flirtation; implicitly in other forms of cultural expression). Further, the symbolic – as the register of language, norms, and laws – is a mediator of social life, figured in the titles and entitlements that signify the subject, with the various "offices" in which people come to be invested, and referred to, in the world. Mother, student, refugee, board member, man, boss, banker – these symbolic representations constitute and populate the field of the Other or the social; this can be seen in how the worlds of sexual role-plays and pornography are rife with the taking on of a position or title to act out scenes of desire, often across lines of professional, familial and other social taboos (teacher, plumber, co-worker, doctor, therapist, step-sib-

18   Zupančič, *Odd*, 207.
19   Darian Leader, *Is It Ever Just Sex?* (London: Penguin, 2023), 6.
20   Santner, *Royal*, 73.

ling). The titles and roles in which we are invested are always subject to fluctuations, crises, and transformations, as are the objects they work with and through. Object attachments and investments are historically particular, including "the resistances that manifest when the objects in which we libidinally invest are imperiled."[21] We live in a time of unprecedented object abundance, as Baudrillard already pointed out in 1970, proliferating attachments to items that incite us to live by libidinally loaded practices related to object time – procuring, recycling, on-selling, hoarding, destroying.[22]

These fluctuations in the symbolic – and attendant object world – fundamentally affect how human beings relate to themselves and others. Santner draws from Lacan, for whom the subject's libidinal investments are shaped by its relationship to language and the symbolic order, structuring the subject's desires and shaping their sense of self. In Lacan's theory, the subject's libidinal economy is in constant flux, as desires and investments shift and change over time. In this sense, "libidinal economy" is used to explain the dynamics of how people direct their energy towards certain things, and how this shapes their experiences of pleasure and desire. So when Santner writes that libido theory is a special kind of social theory, he indicates that it tries to account for how historical forms of life have come to terms with the funda-

---

21   Earl Gammon, "Narcissism, Rage, Avocado Toast," in *Clickbait Capitalism: Economies of Desire in the Twenty-First Century*, ed. Amin Samman and Earl Gammon (Manchester: Manchester UP, 2023), 23.

22   Jean Baudrillard, *The Consumer Society: Myths and Structures* (London: Sage, 1998). See the opening paragraph of this 1970 text: "all around us today [is] a kind of fantastic conspicuousness of consumption and abundance, constituted by the multiplication of objects, services and material goods, and this represents something of a fundamental mutation in the ecology of the human species. Strictly speaking, the humans of the age of affluence are surrounded not so much by other human beings, as they were in all previous ages, but by *objects*. Their daily dealings are now not so much with their fellow men, but rather – on a rising statistical curve – with the reception and manipulation of goods and messages. This runs from the very complex organization of the household, with its dozens of technical slaves, to street furniture and the whole material machinery of communication; from professional activities to the permanent spectacle of the celebration of the object in advertising and the hundreds of daily messages from the mass media; from the minor proliferation of vaguely obsessional gadgetry to the symbolic psychodramas fuelled by the nocturnal objects which come to haunt us even in our dreams. The two concepts 'environment' and 'ambience' have doubtless only enjoyed such a vogue since we have come to live not so much alongside other human beings – in their physical presence and the presence of their speech – as beneath the mute gaze of mesmerizing, obedient objects which endlessly repeat the same refrain: that of our dumbfounded power, our virtual affluence, our absence one from another.... We live by object time: by this I mean that we live at the pace of objects, live to the rhythm of their ceaseless succession.... Objects are neither a flora nor a fauna. And yet they do indeed give the impression of a proliferating vegetation" (25).

mental impasses plaguing human flourishing and the imbrication of these impasses with the distinctive forms of human sexuality.

The cultural, the symbolic, the exchanged are lodged in our sexuality, rattling in our unconscious, and thereby inseparable from any supposedly pure, innate, pre-social human appetites or drives. As Cornelius Castoriadis observed, the human psyche has been defunctionalised: representational pleasures dominate over organ pleasures, and its representational spontaneity is not at the mercy of an ascribable end.[23] This is not esoteric theory but very public knowledge and practice: highly ranked on porn site search lists are beloved figures of popular culture and its fictions (deepfaked musicians, actor lookalikes, eroticised superheroes, game characters), or current events ("tennis skirt" during Grand Slams, "military uniform" as wars begin, "robots" during the recent discourse around AI and automation).[24] There is a complex psychic work here around imagination and fantasy, as people test out the feeling and sensations of other symbolic positions and turn "misery and oppression into a temporary and complex source of pleasure."[25] These sites also play host to all the libidinal energies around taboos, symbolic power, social domination and sexual control that can, at once, unsettle, undo and maintain hierarchies of social incommensurability: the fetishised figures of social abjection and hate, the transgression of otherwise off-limits interactions, the denigrated-cum-desired others of socio-political enmity, the full libidinal load of hate speech and its fantasmatic underside.[26]

Confronted with the sexual surfeit of the online world, all this may appear like some decadent 21st century diffusion of eroticism. It has become this in the late-modern fever dreams of religious zealots and QAnon conspiracists, fixated on the psychosexual antics of some roving band of world-ending perverts connected via secret social networks. But none of this is especially new. Freud himself points out in how many directions sexuality spreads. In *Mass Psychology*, he writes that we can begin from a basic premise:

> libido is an expression taken from the theory of emotions. It is how we refer to the energy (considered a quantitative value, albeit currently unmeasurable), of those drives that have to do with everything that can be brought together under the word "love." The core of what we call love is, of course, what is commonly called love and what the poets sing about: sexual love with the goal of sexual union.[27]

23   Cornelius Castoriadis, *The Imaginary Institution of Society* (Cambridge: Polity, 1987), 314–15.

24   PornHub's regular "Insights" reports are troves of this information. They also now employ a "sexual wellness" team, who comment on the respective "top search terms" each year.

25   Leader, *Is It?*, 241.

26   Avgi Saketopoulou, *Sexuality beyond Consent: Risk, Race, Traumatophilia* (NY: New York UP, 2023).

27   Sigmund Freud, *The Standard Edition of the Complete Psychological Works of Sigmund Freud*, 24 vols. (London: Hogarth Press, 1953), XVIII: 90–91, translation altered. Hereafter *SE*. This book

Freud here encapsulates how he understands libido, including the economics of its quantity and organisation. Libido refers to the energy behind human drives that pertain to "love." If libido is a *measure* of sexual excitation, then here it is the potentially *quantifiable* energy of love-related instincts. It transforms somatic sexual energy into psychical energy, specifically for sexual instincts. In Freud's energetics of love, libidinal energy accumulates and when it reaches a certain threshold, it becomes psychical and desires or wishes result.[28] Libido, he goes on to say, encompasses different forms of love:

> we do not separate from [libido] the other things that share the name of love: self-love, on the one hand, and on the other, parental and infant love; friendship; general love of humanity; and even dedication to concrete objects or abstract ideas. Our justification is that psychoanalytic investigation has taught us that all these urges are expressions of the same drives that push the sexes toward sexual union. Though in other circumstances, they may be pushed away from that sexual goal or hindered in its attainment, they always preserve enough of their original essence for their identity to remain recognisable (self-sacrifice, striving for greater closeness).[29]

The same instincts that drive sexual union can be expressed by ostensibly different forms – other wishes and desires – and remain recognisable despite being redirected or hindered in their attainment. Freud believed humans to be driven by both external and internal stimuli, which include sexuality as well as vital needs such as hunger or thirst. As we see, these drives create desires and impulses that accumulate psychical "energy" that needs to be discharged through activity. If these desires are not satisfied, it can lead to tension and unpleasure; libido is thus linked as much to unpleasure as to pleasure. As he encapsulated all the above at one point: libido is "the dynamic manifestation" of the sexual instinct "in mental life."[30] It is also worth noting that at a certain level of abstraction, including in the above passages, the libido is ungendered – although, as Lauren Berlant writes, when this unfolds in the world, "each gender is associated with particular forms of representing and processing the

---

is often called *Group Psychology*, but Freud's term *Massen* (in German) tied it into the moment of mass and crowd psychology, hence why some choose to retain that more direct translation.

28   Bennett comments, "the links between energetics and economics are more literal than analogical, as demonstrated by the pivotal role of the steam engine in generating the wealth of the Industrial Revolution – and providing Jung with a model of the mind" (*The Currency of Desire: Libidinal Economy, Psychoanalysis and Sexual Revolution* (London: Lawrence & Wishart, 2016), 33). But it is more complicated than Bennett describes, see: Vladimir Safatle, "Death, Libido, and Negative Ontology in the Theory of Drives," in *Sexuality and Psychoanalysis: Philosophical Criticisms*, ed. Jens de Vleminck and Eran Dorfman (Leuven: Leuven UP, 2010), 63–65.

29   Freud, *SE*, XVIII: 90–91, translation altered.

30   Freud, *SE*, XVIII: 244.

ambivalent pressures of the drive's energy."[31] Clearly Freud's concept of psychical energy has theoretical and empirical complications, some of which saw him, in his typical manner, continue to rework it in his thinking. Still, it persistently brings forward questions about the *intensity* of desires and impulses, and their inhibition or release.[32]

Freud's concept of libidinal economy also refers to a certain circulation of value within the psychical apparatus, specifically in the sphere of sexual instincts. The "economic problem" for Freud is precisely about the rise and fall of intensities in response to the world and its psychic representation.[33] While Carl Jung, Freud's onetime ally and long-time foe, expanded libido to encompass *all* forms of psychical energy, Freud resisted this "monistic" move and focused it on sexual instincts.[34]

---

31   Berlant, *Desire*, 42. Freud (*SE*, XIX: 258) underlines, in one of his more lucid remarks on the topic, that gendering is not fixed and binary: "the majority of men are ... far behind the masculine ideal and ... all human individuals, as a result of their bisexual disposition and of cross-inheritance, combine in themselves both masculine and feminine characteristics, so that pure masculinity and femininity remain uncertain theoretical constructions of uncertain content."

32   Critics of the libido theory include Karen Horney, who, in *New Ways in Psychoanalysis* (London: Routledge & Paul, 1939), draws on her clinical material to pose some of the strongest challenges to Freud's theory. She considers it an unsupported cornerstone of psychoanalysis, while also holding that it afforded insights into human behaviour. Horney criticised how Freud's theory attributed most of human behaviour, personality or character to sexual instincts. She challenges Freud's assumption that all bodily sensations of pleasure are sexual, and that various character traits and attitudes are derived from sexual drives or their frustration. She also questions Freud's concepts of sublimation, aim-inhibition, and reaction-formation, which imply that non-sexual phenomena are expressions of desexualised libido. Horney counterposed the libido theory to her theory of anxiety and safety, putting the environment and its challenges at the centre: neurotic tendencies are driven not only by the pursuit of satisfaction but also by the need for safety against anxiety. For example, feelings of helplessness towards a hostile world shape defensive attitudes. These defensive strategies, termed "neurotic trends," are seen as attempts to cope with an unreliable and threatening environment. She saw the libido theory as a dead end in therapy, as the prevailing biological factor meant it could not be ultimately challenged or changed. Fundamentally, she did not see the drive to fulfill primary, biologically given needs as being powerful enough to exert a decisive influence on the subject's personality and – hence – entire life. While she underplays the environmental elements of Freud's theory, there is a force in her argument, particularly around the often unsubstantiated claims about how sexual problems are at the bottom of all emotional problems and neurotic behaviour. (There are some pretty sexually satisfied neurotics, she notes; and some pretty sexually unsatisfied people who show no neurosis.) In 1940s America, Horney saw more repression of hostility than sexual repression, generating the proliferation in neurotic anxiety since that era, perhaps reflecting the cultural shift to a more competitive culture. This urges some caution in the approach to the libidinal economy, particularly if deployed in a reductive and ahistorical manner.

33   Lauren Berlant, *On the Inconvenience of Other People* (Duke UP, 2022), 179n16.

34   Freud, *SE*, XVIII: 53.

Yet Freud did not hold to narrow conceptions of the sexual, libido or love. As we saw above, the psychoanalytic understanding takes us beyond typical versions of sexual instincts and desires, encompassing regular cultural expressions of love for friends and kin, up through love for cultural objects and political projects. Hence, to be more precise about the primary claim for human sexual distinctiveness with which I started: the Freudian libido differs from biological instincts in its undefined *object* (i.e., not simply the partner of the opposite sex), *aim* (i.e., not simply involving genital organs and coitus for reproduction), variable modalities of *satisfaction* (i.e., perversions), and ability to derive satisfaction from diverse *activities* (i.e., an expanded concept).[35] It thus encompasses a range of excitations and activities beyond genital sexuality – and beyond intercourse, which Freud largely sets aside in his discussion of sexuality. For instance, even in Freud's first edition of *Three Essays on Sexuality*, a relatively early text in dialogue and dispute with sexologists around the turn of the century, he focused on the so-called perversions from the biological objects and aims. In the three essays, Freud exhibits the great diversity in the choice of sexual objects and activities, and largely undermines the distinction between "perverse" and "normal" sexuality.[36] The libido is constituted by adoption, adaptation, diversion and redirection – a series of perversions from any straight path.

Freud's theory of sexuality suggests a fundamental conflict derived from the self's formation in a social environment: from the start, the sexual drives come up against conventional morality, which wants to have a say over the self's configuration. Developmentally, human sexuality goes through a complex and precarious evolution before being organised under genitality as a notionally fixed, final and socially sanctioned instinct. The child is formed as an amalgam, with biological, emotional and mental elements interacting with personal-familial and more general social contexts. Where this can be typically seen as "unfolding" into the future self, Freud construed his theorisation of sexuality analeptically: "as a back formation, a hypothesized antecedent, a precondition derived to account for actual adult sexuality."[37] So, infancy is understood via adulthood, normalcy via perversion. The "final"

---

35 For an up-to-date set of reflections on Freud, gender, and queer theory, see Steinkoler and Gherovici, *Psychoanalysis, Gender, and Sexualities*. In the current chapter, I leave the question of sexual difference largely to one side as it – evidently – can fill an entire volume or small library, and others remain better placed to discuss its considerable conceptual history and trajectory.

36 Sigmund Freud, *Three Essays on the Theory of Sexuality: The 1905 Edition*, trans. Ulrike Kistner (London: Verso, 2017).

37 Jeri Johnson, "Introduction," in *The Psychology of Love*, by Sigmund Freud (London: Penguin, 2006), x–xi. As Adrian Johnston has argued, two temporal modes are at work in Freud: one emphasises the past's dominance over the present, and another highlights the retroactive influence of the present on the past. For Johnston, there is a constitutive antagonism between

adult form of sexuality – forged in that biological, emotional, mental, familial and social idiosyncrasy – exists in (normative) tension with pervasive perversions. This rocky path to adult sexuality introduces the nonfunctional fixations and preoccupations that lead to symptom formation among neurotics and other patients; indeed, a foundational observation for psychoanalysis came in noticing that the symptoms could become so invested with libidinal charge that they constituted, for some patients, their entire sexual activity. In other words, Freud's analysis of the neuroses revealed that symptoms often involve displaced and modified sexual wishes – and these are at the heart of the subject's libidinal economy.

These displaced and modified wishes help furnish the realms of fantasy life. As Freud's work develops, he increasingly focuses on fantasy, where, as John Forrester writes, "love, envy, infatuation, hate and that very strong emotion, disgust, come into play to shape our practices and attitudes."[38] In fact, Forrester adds, "sexuality is largely all in the mind; there is no such thing as a sexual act without fantasy."[39] So fantasy is not just an (imagined) alternative to sex but a condition for arousal. Fantasising develops early in life and is intertwined with identity and symbolic processes. Fantasy, Darian Leader writes, "is a profoundly symbolic process, and the way it allows us to be others and shift identities is central to the sexual experience."[40] In its symbolic processes and identity work, it sustains the scenario that grants access to pleasure; this is the setting for enacting desire, in which one acts as well as spectates, being both *in* and *of* the story. During intimate moments, individuals often imagine their partner as someone else, highlighting a symbolic disconnection even in moments of physical connection. This, too, is what Lacan meant with his slogan about the lack of sexual relation.[41] After all, this possibility – the ability to separate oneself

---

temporal orders in the psyche – and he locates there the source of the drive's failure and frustration (covered in the next section), as well as the psyche's motive force. See his *Time Driven: Metapsychology and the Splitting of the Drive* (Evanston: Northwestern UP, 2005).

38   John Forrester, *Freud and Psychoanalysis: Six Introductory Lectures*, ed. Lisa Appignanesi (Cambridge: Polity, 2023), 74–75.

39   Forrester, *Freud and Psychoanalysis*, 74–75.

40   Leader, *Is It?*, 183. This is also an element of its usefulness for social theory, as I will touch on again in the closing chapter.

41   Sexologist and psychoanalyst Bernard Apfelbaum adds intriguing comments here about sexual culture from a different psychoanalytic standpoint: "The paradox is that sex is perhaps among the most nonintimate of human activities, yet, at least in the West, it is idealized as the ultimate form of intimacy and even as the best form of communication…. Not only is sex often solitary, such as masturbation, but sex partners typically are silent and are likely to resent it when the silence is broken, unless it is by expressions of desire and pleasure. 'Sex talk,' when it does occur, is highly stylized – limited to flattery and encouragement. When the real partner is not responsive in this way, we are likely to turn to a mental picture of someone who is…. I would say that the most direct acknowledgement of sex as nonintimate and even as coercive is in our use of profanity, at least in English. Thus, the English word 'fuck' is our

from the immediate environment, moment and others – has long been taken as distinguishing the human: Freud, in the psychoanalytic articulation, sees these human possibilities unfolding in libidinal development. These developments, in brief, include the infant's separation from oceanic oneness, moving into autoeroticism to, ideally, some form of relative independence, including all the play of imagination along the way. In other words, psychoanalysis shows that the human sexual instinct is closely linked to ideas or fantasies that shape its form, undergird its meaning and unfurl a set of appealing dispositions and objects. Sex, in this view, is a complex interplay of personal and social elements, encompassing history, socialisation, and a range of emotions and experiences beyond mere pleasure.

The libido, we have so far established, names how sexuality incorporates symbolic components. These are not superfluous but intrinsic to this sexuality. The libidinal – and its economy – is thus a uniquely human phenomenon. To understand it, we must look beyond the evolutionary and naturalistic logics that can govern our view of sex, and the limited domain they give to "the sexual." It is not a brute matter of physical attraction or repulsion, pleasure or unpleasure, but rather a complex interplay between conscious and unconscious desires, necessarily embedded in sociability across the full range of interpersonal and symbolic bonds. Sex is here more than the physical act, instead connected with other psychic and social functions, such as alleviating anxiety or caught up in interpersonal or social power dynamics. In its most dynamic form, the libidinal economy can be seen as an unfolding dialogue between the individual and the collective – or, put differently, the interplay between idiosyncrasy and ideology. Anthropologists, sexologists and psychologists each in their way describe the culturally specific but deeply varied sexual practices that happen in human societies. This interplay shows how human sexuality evolves "culturally" rather than "biologically." The distinctly human – and, at the same time, surprisingly structural and supra-human – quality of the libidinal means it is also a source of great ambiguity and ambivalence. It is both an engine of social life and a disruptive force; it takes us towards the norms of our culture, and it challenges us to break them. So despite its imbrication in often compelling social logics, libido can also sometimes be seen as a form of playfulness, an expression of "perversity" leading to creativity and exploration.

The libidinal is a field of both subjective organisation and profound disorganisation, collectivity and nihilism.[42] The "erotic" has ancient senses of a heightened feeling of one's personality ("I am more myself than ever before!," as Anne Carson writes

---

most emphatic way to express one-sidedness or being cheated. When we want to find the strongest way of saying someone has been used, we say that he or she has been fucked or screwed" ("Sexuality: Intimacy or Illusion?," in *Sexology*, ed. Wolf Eicher et al. (Berlin, Heidelberg: Springer, 1988), 229–30).

42   Jamieson Webster, *Disorganisation & Sex* (Brussels: Divided Publishing, 2022).

of *Eros*) and the contrary feeling of losing oneself, becoming the site of potential dis-integration, both physical and emotional: *Eros* is the "melter of limbs" for Sappho.[43] The tendency to heightened and ecstatic states explains why sexual pleasure can be caught up in the appeals to be a form of wellness, an escape – however quickly we sharpen our critical knives around this point – from the crisis-ridden social field to quiet, private enjoyment. (I return to this in the closing chapter of this volume.) It can also cement libidinal identifications that form social bonds and communities. In the form of sublimations, libidinal energy can be a powerful and transformative force, and various revolutionary movements and thinkers have sought to harness this aspect of psychic and bodily energy. It can equally be channelled into the work of generating hate campaigns and violence, underwriting communities that oper-ate in modalities or orders of enjoyment constituted by, for example, supremacist violence.

This is how, to recall Santner again, the libidinal can be a key element in a social theory, including Freud's own. Libidinal economy is fundamental for understand-ing how people come to identify with groups, as explored in Freud's *Mass Psychology*: "We shall try adopting the premise," Freud writes, "that love relationships (or, indif-ferently expressed, emotional ties) ... constitute the essence of the group mind."[44] Freud claims that social bonds are constituted by the push and pull of subjective in-vestments that run horizontally and vertically, generating a sense of cohesion that proves durable if not permanent. People will have their idiosyncrasies, their minor variations, from the libidinal economy and the associated political fantasies.[45] Still, a sort of regularity insists in the economy and fantasies, tied as they are to a culture or subculture anchored in the symbolic order, that locus of authority for prevailing norms, ideologies and sociohistorical understandings. The language of particular orders – nations, for example – demonstrate the potential for attachment, attrac-tion, organisation, repulsion and binding that can bring people together around os-

---

43   Carson and Sappho are invoked in William Mazzarella, *The Mana of Mass Society* (Chicago: University of Chicago Press, 2017), 5.

44   Freud, *SE*, XVIII: 91, translation altered. On the following page, Freud adds: "We base our ex-pectation on two fleeting thoughts. First, a group is clearly held together by a power of some kind: and to what power could this feat be better ascribed than to Eros, which holds the world together? Second, if an individual gives up his distinctiveness in a group and lets its other members influence him by suggestion, it gives one the impression that he does it because he feels the need to be in harmony with them rather than in opposition to them – so that perhaps after all he does it *'ihnen zu Liebe'*" (92, translation altered). The concluding German phrase here literally means "for the love of them," or idiomatically "for their sake," intimating love's self-sacrifice.

45   In this paragraph, I echo the helpful summary in Derek Hook, "Fanon and Libidinal Econ-omy," in *Re(Con)Figuring Psychoanalysis: Critical Juxtapositions of the Philosophical, the Sociohis-torical and the Political*, ed. Aydan Gülerce (London: Palgrave Macmillan, 2012), 165.

tensibly stable sites of identification. A libidinal economy substantiates a community, working to establish fundamental social ties necessary for any coherent social group, as people gather around shared rituals, objects, ideas and people. "This description," as Derek Hook puts it, "informs a provisional definition of libidinal economy as a force-field of affects; a set of regular patterns and distributions of libido underwritten by a symbolic frame; which entails relations of passionate attachment and exclusion; that affirms types of group identification and holds certain social formations in place."[46] This understanding prepares the ground for the critique of libidinal economy, removing it from any conception of spontaneous erotics or pure reproduction to the concept of a social ordering and disordering.

Intensified zones of attachment: desires and drives

As noted above, Freud's writings on libido suggest that libidinal energy *circulates*. It entails both movement within the subject (affect or feeling), as well as social circulation (implication, complicity in shared objects, ideals, emotions and so on). We might understand this social circulation to constitute *desire*. This term again takes us beyond the superficially sexual: it is "socialised sexuality," indicating the move towards social interaction of the drives, their sublimation via exteriorisation in the social circuit of desire, transforming and binding drives into investments in objects.[47] "Desire" is one of the Latin meanings of the term "libido," and one that likewise signals something predominantly human and *driven* yet linked with a social order. In everyday English, "desire" can feel less tangled in bed sheets than "libido," yet they both intimate a sexualised relation to some ostensibly external and concretised aim (such as objects, wealth, partners, status, politics). Lacan, in his seminar on desire and its interpretation, suggests it is central to understand that we desire to desire in

46   Hook, 165.

47   Bernard Stiegler, "Nanomutations, Hypomnemata and Grammatisation," Ars Industrialis, 2006. It is worth quoting Stiegler in full here: "desire is not sexuality, it is not 'completely' sexuality, it is only 'partially' sexuality: desire is socialised sexuality, i.e., always already transindividuated.... If desire was nothing but sexuality, it would be only drive: sexuality is based in the drives. Sexed animals also have a sexuality. But it is desire, constitutive of the process of psychic and collective individuation as such, that binds the drives, that is, that denatures them." For Stiegler, this re-/de-functionalisation and transindividuation is induced by technicity. For his most sustained discussion of the contemporary libidinal economy via a critique of Luc Boltanski, Ève Chiapello and Herbert Marcuse, see *The Lost Spirit of Capitalism* (Cambridge: Polity, 2014).

accordance with what we believe others (and the symbolic order) want from us: "this desire is the central, pivotal point of the entire economy we deal with in analysis."[48]

It is a pivotal point that carries ambiguities and enigmas. In an earlier seminar, Lacan writes, "desire, a function central to all human experience, is the desire for nothing nameable. And at the same time this desire lies at the origin of every variety of animation."[49] Lacan will take this ambiguity into his distinction between desire and drive: desire aims to obtain the object (but is inhibited), whereas drive's goal – and the enjoyment obtained – is ceaseless looping and repetition. The closeness of these processes can be heard in our everyday reference to "insatiable desires." Even when ostensibly fulfilled, desire cannot deliver on its promise: desire, in fact, names this principle of negativity; it is the activity of "repeating pleasure by finding substitutes for a lost or unstable object."[50] The libidinal economy is sustained by

---

48   Jacques Lacan, *The Seminar of Jacques Lacan. Book VI: Desire and Its Interpretation*, trans. Bruce Fink (Medford, MA: Polity, 2019), 480–81.

49   Lacan, *SII*, 223. We can also refer to Lacan's distinction between desire, demand and need, a technical discussion I will confine to a footnote to avoid derailing the main discussion. The baby's cry is the singular example here: the hungry infant's cry is not merely operative as an instinct but works in a system of signs (a linguistic structure, even before language appears for the child); the infant is born into helplessness and cannot feed itself, so it demands (vocally) another (the caregiver) to act. The caregiver participates in shaping the links between needs and their socially mediated significance (demands). This enlistment of another, which adds a surplus of care to the need, introduces a doubling: not just a need but a demand for love; as the child grows, which includes the growing vocabulary that marks entry into language and social intercourse, and as they more directly express hunger, specific items offered in response carry the weight of meaning (something more than basic nourishment – a little treat, a token of love). Every demand, then, is a demand for love. This demand for love eclipses its function (need). Desire appears here: hunger (as need, as vital and unavoidable requirement) can be satisfied, but love's cravings are insatiable, always leaving a leftover (desire). In the seminar on transference, Lacan considers Freud's theory of libidinal organisation and development – "the migration of the libido to the erogenous zones" (209) – as types of demand. Oral: demand by the subject (to the Other) to be fed. Anal: demand by/from the Other (parental discipline). Genital: desire eclipses the demand of the prior, pre-genital stages. (See Jacques Lacan, *The Seminar of Jacques Lacan. Book VIII: Transference*, trans. Bruce Fink (Cambridge: Polity, 2015), sec. XIV–XV.) It is worth recalling that the Other begins a process of decoding-encoding of needs and demands as they are translated into dialogic demands (the initiation into and continual triangulation through the symbolic order). While the above account assumes reciprocity, the look or object can be withheld, eliciting feelings of privation. One final point: Darian Leader suggests, in an unorthodox fashion, that "the Lacanian use of the term 'desire' is actually closer to that of [Erich] Fromm and Karen Horney than it is to Freud, indexing less a repressed chain of signifiers linked to loss than a positive aspiration that the subject may have felt forced to give up or relinquish due to an appropriation of the Other's demand" (*Jouissance: Sexuality, Suffering and Satisfaction* (Cambridge: Polity, 2021), 63). This can indeed be read in the preceding outline of Lacan's terms.

50   Berlant, *Desire*, 36.

fantasies of full enjoyment that conceal the impossibility of the drives from the subject; enjoyment is extracted from this process of containment in the very failures and thwartings of desire. These fantasies of complete satisfaction, which work as transcendental conditions of possibility for the subject's libidinal economy, depend on external impediments that serve as alibis for the drive's failure – a "perpetual frustration machine."[51]

Desire – in its animation, in its libidinal disposition – pulls subjects towards objects and the possibilities they seem to contain. Desired objects constitute the attachments that enable this transient stabilisation in the subject. This is transient for the divided subject because desire always operates with and beyond these objects, aiming to destroy and preserve them. Berlant suggests subjects deal with the "organization of the drives into object-anchored desires, orientations, and styles of relating."[52] Desire, for Berlant, describes "a state of attachment to something or someone, and the cloud of possibility ... generated by the gap between an object's specificity and the needs and promises projected onto it."[53] The objects of desire are not a thing (a commodity, a person, a situation) but fantasmatic investments that seem to proffer traction, a sense of stability in one's being, a healing of the foundational rift. They are constitutively misrecognised objects ("desire has bad eyesight") that do not express "who you are" but speak of what you need to anchor yourself.[54] Echoing Freud's description of the drive, Berlant writes, "desire visits you as an impact

---

51   Johnston, *Time Driven*, xxxi. This fits very well with capitalism, as Luc Boltanski and Ève Chiapello point out, summarising a prominent line of critique: "The illusory character of the liberation held out by capitalism thanks to the market in goods can ... be denounced. Particularly in Marx's work, we find ... one of the bases right up to the present day for the denunciation of what has been called the 'consumer society' since the 1960s, to which the development of marketing and advertising would give new vigour. It runs as follows: seemingly free, consumers are in fact completely in the grip of production. What they believe to be their own desires, emanating from their autonomous will as unique individuals, are, unbeknown to them, the product of a manipulation whereby the suppliers of goods enslave their imagination. They desire what they are led to desire. Supply subordinates and determines demand – or, as Marx puts it, '[p]roduction thus not only creates an object for the subject, but also a subject for the object'. Given that the supply of goods through which profit is created is, by its very nature, unlimited in a capitalist framework, desire must be constantly stimulated so that it becomes insatiable" (*The New Spirit of Capitalism* (London: Verso, 2005), 427).
52   Berlant, *Desire*, 69.
53   Berlant, 6.
54   Berlant, 76. As Berlant writes elsewhere: "intersubjectivity is impossible. It is a wish, a desire, and a demand for an enduring sense of being with and in x and is related to that big knot that marks the indeterminate relation between a feeling of recognition and misrecognition. [R]ecognition is the misrecognition you can bear, a transaction that affirms you without, again, necessarily feeling good or being accurate (it might idealize, it might affirm your monstrosity, it might mirror your desire to be minimal enough to live under the radar, it might feel just right, and so on)" (*Cruel Optimism* (Durham: Duke UP, 2011), 26).

from the outside, and yet, inducing an encounter with your affects, makes you feel as though it comes from within you." So your objects are not objective; others probably struggle to "see" what you see in them; they are "things and scenes that you have converted into propping up your world, and so what seems objective and autonomous in them is partly what your desire has created and therefore is a mirage, a shaky anchor."[55] Similarly, Stiegler suggests that the "mutability of instincts" – the move from animality to humanity – is the name for the passage of desire, economising on the satisfaction of the drive: libidinal "energy is produced by an economy," he writes, "through which the drive becomes an energy invested in objects that are highly variable, and are so because they are fantasies, that is, supports of the projection of what does not exist: the singular, that is, incalculable, object."[56]

The space of love – amorous and familial, returning us to the love-libido pair – is conventionally seen as a relation where singular and desirable objects have been found, alongside the fantasies of belonging, intimacy and reciprocity. "Love is the embracing dream in which desire is reciprocated," Berlant suggests. "Rather than being isolating, love provides an image of an expanded self, the normative version of which is the two-as-one intimacy of the couple form."[57] In the romantic ideal, desire leads to love, "which will make a world for desire's endurance," Berlant suggests. Whether normative or not, desire and love name "intensified zones of attachment" to particular objects, people, things.[58] This intensity can be apparently organ-

---

55   Berlant, *Desire*, 6.

56   Stiegler, *Lost Spirit*, 57.

57   Berlant, *Desire*, 6. Søren Kierkegaard, in his influential work on anxiety, also refers to the role of sexuality in leading into the social. For Kierkegaard, "sex is significant," the existential psychologist Rollo May summarises, "because it stands for the problem of *individuation and community*. In Kierkegaard's culture as well as in ours, sex is often the clearest fulcrum of the problem of being a self – e.g., having individual desires, urges, yet being in expanding relationships with others. The complete fulfillment of these desires involves other persons. Sex may thus express this individuality-in-community constructively (sex as a form of interpersonal relatedness), or it may be distorted into egocentricity (pseudo-individuality) or into mere symbiotic dependence (pseudo-community)" (*The Meaning of Anxiety*, Rev. ed. (NY: Norton, 1977), 45).

58   Berlant, *Desire*, 18. Berlant (106) writes later in the same book, "The fantasy, which is at the heart both of popular culture [e.g., the romantic comedy] and Lacanian psychoanalysis, is that love is the misrecognition you like, can bear, and will try to keep consenting to. If the Other will accept your fantasy/realism as the condition of their encounter with their own lovability, and if you will agree to accept theirs, the couple (it could be any relation) has a fighting chance not to be destroyed by the aggressive presence of ambivalence, with its jumble of memory, aggressive projection, and blind experimentation. This is not a cynical bargain, but the bargain that fantasy enables for any subject to take up a position in a sustained relation." Lovers are, hence, mutual fantasisers. There is no sexual relation – just fantasy scenes that are multiple exposures. These scenes could be beautiful or unlikely in their composition or comfortably skeuomorphic in their imitation of archaic scenes.

ising (as in romance, which disavows erotic ambivalence) or deeply disorganising (as in experiences of honest erotic ambivalence, antagonism or anxiety). The singular Freudian lesson may be that the libidinal economy features double bookkeeping: on one side, of love (caring, confirming, giving, receiving), which is bound up with, on the other, an economy of aggression, constantly threatening the fragile experience of love-as-stability.[59] Idealisation, aggression, melancholia, perversions, masochism, fetishism – all these signature states in psychoanalytic thought are, as Berlant puts it, "integral to the ordinary career of desire, as it struggles and fails continuously to find ideal objects on which it can rest."[60] The foundational normality of "perversions" can again be seen in this: within the circulation of desire, *failure* or *pain*, which we might spontaneously associate with unpleasure, produce their own pleasures.

Freud introduced the drive to "get a grip on the internal sources of excitement that the organism cannot escape."[61] The drive is a *hypothesis* in psychoanalysis, and its object is obscure and subject to doubt. It is neither nature nor culture but exists as a third domain that challenges the nature-culture dichotomy. As Samo Tomšič encapsulates it, the drive is seen as a limit-notion between the psychic and the somatic, representing stimuli from within the body and imposing a demand for work on the psyche: "the Freudian notion of the drive strives to grasp and explain first and foremost the bodily experience of the dynamic of representation and significa-tion."[62] Epistemologically, the drive serves as a border between the natural and human sciences, representing the connection between the symbolic and the biological. Experientially, drives might be felt as urges – hardwired, species-bound biological mechanisms with external triggers. The drive – as encapsulated in the libidinal – puts "pressure on the individual" to move from the infant's omnipotent sensual autonomy to a relation with the world, as we saw in Freud's understanding of sexual development.[63] In all of this – libido theory, the drive and so on – the disciplinary expansiveness of Freud's endeavour is clear. This conceptual field is situated at the crossroads of many areas of inquiry, marked by a refusal to choose between biological and human sciences – dealing as much with energetics as with hermeneutics, literature as much as anatomy.[64] Unsurprisingly, then, his foundational theory of the libidinal – a stand-in for a theory of love – itself encompasses these fields, continually ranging across them. At bottom, however, the libidinal economy names the organisation of drives, affects, and fantasies that animate human life and its forms of

---

59   Berlant, 25.

60   Berlant, 43.

61   Safatle, "Death, Libido," 63.

62   Samo Tomšič, *The Labour of Enjoyment: Towards a Critique of Libidinal Economy* (Cologne: August Verlag, 2019), 67. See Freud, *SE*, XIV: 121–122.

63   Berlant, *Desire*, 19.

64   John Forrester, *Language and the Origins of Psychoanalysis* (London: Palgrave Macmillan, 1980).

collectivity. Equally, each one of these terms – drives, affects, fantasies – also names a disorganising and mortifying element of human life. Such are the ambivalences of the psychoanalytic conceptual field.

Libido, in this economy

We are yet to fully address another key term here. "The economic," Freud ominously writes, "leads us to one of the most important, but unluckily one of the most obscure, regions of psychoanalysis."[65] This obscurity is in no small part related to the mixed and varied connotations of "economy" and "economics" in everyday language.[66] At this level, it often refers to the familiar contemporary domain that *economists* study – transactions, markets, exchange, investments, currency, price, value, labour, capital and so on. These categories and practices are integral to the operations of social production and reproduction that a given economy represents: all economies are forms of provisioning. "Economy" carries senses of being prudent ("economising") as well as the "organization of parts of a whole, an arrangement of resources, or an internal ordering."[67] Such ordering and organisation is clear in the case, for example, of "home economics," which includes financial questions but also those of nutrition, cleaning, maintenance and so on. This links to the Greek understanding of *Oikos* as ordering the household. In Freud's tongue, the German term for economy, *Wirtschaft*, stems from the metaphor of an innkeeper (*der Wirt*). It thereby carries historical connotations of running an economic entity (either an "inn," or a "public house" in English) and the sociability it carries with it, hence a certain socioeconomic ordering too.[68]

These senses of economy – organisation, arrangement, ordering, distribution – are those most often invoked in psychoanalysis when people speak of the psychic or libidinal economy. For example, Lacan will note that living beings exist because of an internal organisation that limits the free flow of energy from outside forces, allowing a psychic reality – or a psychic household (*psychischen Haushalt*) in Freud's terms – to exist.[69] Yet this reality is, as Freud would suggest, one in which the ego is not master of the house or, indeed, the keeper of the inn – the libidinal haunts this

65   Freud, *SE*, XVI: 355.
66   Yahya M. Madra and Ceren Özselçuk, "Economy/Oikonomia," in *The Marx through Lacan Vocabulary: A Compass for Libidinal and Political Economies*, ed. Christina Soto van der Plas, Edgar Miguel Juárez-Salazar, and Carlos Gómez Camarena, The Lines of the Symbolic (NY: Routledge, 2022).
67   Madra and Özselçuk, 63.
68   Frédéric Langer, "Economy," in *Dictionary of Untranslatables: A Philosophical Lexicon*, ed. Barbara Cassin et al. (Princeton UP, 2014), 243.
69   Lacan, *SII*, 60.

house, along with some other unruly guests, randomly turning the taps on and off, bashing on the walls, all upsetting any push to utterly rational organisation.

The economic is one of Freud's metapsychological standpoints, the others being the topographic (different levels – unconscious, preconscious, conscious) and dynamic (interacting conflicts). The metapsychology also includes the spatial-structural (ego, id, superego) and genetic (developmental processes) as key elements. Together, these offer those principles, fundamental ideas and theories of psychoanalytic conceptual models that abstract from consciousness and reality. Freud's restless formulations, his endless revisions of his metapsychology, hint at how difficult it is to demonstrate anything conclusively at this level.[70] Within this generally complex space of axioms and hypotheses, the "economic" hypothesis is among the most challenging to orient ourselves within. Above all, however, the economic standpoint conditions elements of the others. It assumes a fixed distribution of psychic resources and processes of transfer between different components. This "economic determinism," as Anna Kornbluh half-jokingly calls it, is evident in Freud's works from beginning to end, with the notion of psychic resources and organisation – an economy – being consistent throughout.[71] So to risk a simplification of this obscure region: the economy in Freud refers to the idea that psychical processes are related to a definable flow and distribution of instinctual (drive) energy. Hence, the economic standpoint focuses on the attachment of energy, and the variations, movement, and conflicts of these attachments as they occupy different positions.

In English, all this has been further obscured by translations. Freud noted his dislike for the standard English translation of *Besetzung* as "cathexis," and *besetzen* as "cathect," because they are abstruse terms chosen by translator James Strachey from Greek. *Besetzung* and *besetzen* draw on a more everyday terminology of activity in German, with the verb primarily meaning "to occupy," as one does a toilet cubicle, Paris during the war or a squat in east Berlin. Its noun form (*Besetzung*) also has connotations of grouping, occupying and organising – such as casting cultural productions (on screen or stage), filling a job vacancy, or orchestrating musical composition, as well as the military uses that also carry senses of mobilising, actively taking over and using something or someone. "Investment" is one alternative translation to cathexis – and one more favourably viewed by Freud. Kornbluh sees this

---

70   Freud's theory formation is procedural and prone to self-revision. This has led to unedifying debate and inflexible position-taking by scholars, who often focus on how one theory supersedes others when they are, in fact, complementary. Moving procedurally and reflexively, "later stages of his thought processes do not do away with the earlier ones. The first drive theory (sexual vs. self-preservative drives) is not invalidated by the second (narcissism theory), any more than the third drive theory (death drive vs. Eros) replaces the preceding ones" (May, "The Third Step," 260).

71   Anna Kornbluh, *Realizing Capital: Financial and Psychic Economies in Victorian Form, Realizing Capital* (NY: Fordham UP, 2014), 138

less positively, arguing that, while sidelining the Greek esotericism of Strachey, this translation reduces the intricacy of Freud's work by portraying the psychoanalytic subject as a typical bourgeois agent of finance, or the *Kleinbürger* anxiously seeking returns on investment. This sense has permeated English-speaking culture, where one might "invest" in an outcome or person or idea, ostensibly indicating an emotional implication rather than a pecuniary one. For Kornbluh, *besetzen* should be seen in the context of an economy – as above, indicating a household, an *Oikos*, or even a *Wirtschaft* – as arranging and orchestrating resources, thereby better capturing the everyday, ubiquitous process of organising, as well as recruiting and putting something to use (such as a bathroom, a vacant apartment or a Hollywood actor).[72]

All this translational arcana is relevant insofar as making this adjustment in translation and semantics helps us notice that Freud's (libidinal) economics and capitalist economics are analogical. There is no grounding between the two systems; Freud refuses to *overlay* psychic and capitalist economies, a tendency elsewhere visible in economic psychologism.[73] Freud's psychoanalytic approach differs from this contemporaneous Victorian psychological tradition in that it does not view "psychic economy" as a natural object and does not see capital as the unique and adequate signifier of desire. Freud's refusal to overlay the psychic and social economies derives, as Kornbluh explains, from the "metaleptic inconsistency" of the economic in his theory. In these narratological terms, the metalepsis concerns the breach between levels or layers of narrative, the inconsistent substitutions and displacements, and the incomplete shuffling of one figure into another.[74]

Despite the torment of working with figurative and analogical language, Freud believed that all sciences, including psychoanalysis, require such language to describe and understand the processes they study. He argued that only through such analogies could one develop hypotheses to gain a deeper understanding of psychic life. Therefore, figurative language – the same word used in several senses – is essential in psychoanalysis, just as in other endeavours, even when these figures break down.[75] For example, Freud's clinical encounters with hysteria and obsession encouraged a "quantitative conception" of psychic energy. He borrowed the vocabulary and relationships of the socioeconomic system to offer an interpretive procedure for dynamics in the psyche – a system and process then in scientific construction. The Freudian *economic* standpoint thus forged a structure for the libido theory as that theory emerged.[76] It was a set of figurative expressions to help make psychoanalysis

---

72   Kornbluh, 144–45. See also Darius Gray Ornston, "The Invention of 'Cathexis' and Strachey's Strategy," *International Review of Psychoanalysis* 12 (1985): 391–98.

73   Kornbluh, *Realizing Capital*, 144.

74   Kornbluh, 154.

75   Kornbluh, 139–40.

76   Kornbluh, 144.

known – "just as the psyche commissions successive figurative expressions to make itself known."[77] Put differently, should we be surprised that in the clinic of the unconscious, linguistic symbols and analogies emerge to account for what is going on in that "other scene," as Freud dubbed the unconscious?

Freud's concept of "the economic" thus refers to a way of seeing – a metapsychological standpoint and a figurative language that analysts can use to describe and understand the psyche. Still, Freud was cautious and sceptical when discussing the concept of "psychic economy," warning that it was only a vague expression, such that he was constantly qualifying his statements with self-reflexive confessions and roundabout adverbial phrasing (*sozusagen*, so to speak, *sogennante*, so-called). As Kornbluh advises, we should remember Freud's qualified, halting formulations when evoking this concept today. By resisting this slippage between the two fields, psychoanalysis offers no immediate insights into economics, nor does it support the desirous theory of value in the economics of marginal utility, nor, worse, does it naturalise capitalism.[78] Freud is not (only) unthinkingly repeating ambient discourses (or, stronger, ideologies) of economy but, rather, knowingly and tentatively putting them to work, offering an "economy that knows itself as figure."[79] If Freud never entirely settled into the economic metaphor, then this contrasts with our ease in casually combining the libidinal and the economic – and this self-awareness is a signal lesson from Freud's more uneasy figuration.

In all this, we can see that Freud typically uses "economy" with a view toward psychic organisation in the sense of parts-whole relations (a micro and macroeconomics), while nevertheless drawing on the term's rich semantics. This is how he comes to formulate "economy" in various ways. As Kornbluh argues, this variation in formulation performs "the essential deferral of the grounding of economy: there is no given economy; no hypostatized – or literally capitalized – Economy."[80] By multiplying figures and formulations, a unique perspective on economy emerges, highlighting its openness, polyvalence, and antagonism: not poised equilibrium but vacillating disequilibrium. Freud's figures, such as the household and drive, signify economy differently and create a new – alternative – way of reading and understanding it. Economy and subject, both are divided from themselves.

One implication of Freud's economic figures is that, like the monetary economy, the psyche too can be seen as a system of symbolic substitution without end.[81] In money economies, this substitution can be seen as currency symbolising "value" or paper substituting for precious metal; in exchange societies, this is clearly the

---

77   Kornbluh, 147.

78   Kornbluh, 142. Cf. Bennett, *Currency*.

79   Kornbluh, *Realizing Capital*, 155.

80   Kornbluh, 20.

81   Kornbluh, 147–48.

case with prices, a continuous operation of inscribing into number – equivalences – for exchange. In psychoanalysis, meanwhile, the Rat Man case is the classic, rich demonstration of symbolic substitution. In this case, Freud details his man's associations of "rats" with manifold things: torture, authority, vermin, filth, offspring, penises, money, loans, debts, and compound interest. Freud even notes that the patient is "accumulating" (*hinzuraten*) associations, while paying for the analytic exchange with "rats," and receiving yet more rats in return. Freud concludes that the Rat Man, unable to outrun the steadily breeding vermin of his unconscious, "had coined a regular rat currency" – a neurotic mental economy of associations with proliferating signifiers and ratty images.[82] For Freud, the neurotic's symptom – with the Rat Man being the neurotic *par excellence* – is "the outcome of a conflict which arises over a new method of satisfying the libido."[83] Every symptom-as-substitution enjoins a conflict resolution that carries enjoyment and suffering, a libidinal economy of pain and pleasure, satisfaction and dissatisfaction.

If this produces an "obscure region" – likewise indicated in my own hesitations and doubling back in the preceding account – the strength of this thinking of the economic lies in the absence of a straightforward explanatory approach and the lack of a single (unified) dominant concept.[84] What is more, the tendency to naturalise "economy" in both critique and everyday life – to take it at face value, to fetishise or reify it, to miss its symbolic-fantasmatic construction and, thus, plasticity – is to miss its essentially *political* character. Any economic form must be designed, planned, and made, a fact often more tangible at the everyday household level than the global level. Any form of economy will be contested and will be beset with antagonisms – something, again, more immediately felt at home than in the ordinary, yet remote, run of transnational trade: household economies, after all, also run hot with trade and class wars, decision-making cores and powerless peripheries.[85] A libidinal economy, as Freud helps us recognise, is no different from this in its conflicts and stability pacts, its bargains and contracts. The complexity and versatility of Freud's economic imagery reveal the fundamental conflict inherent in any economy and the "referential unreliability" at the heart of economic relations.[86] This reminds us of Althusser's claim that psychoanalysis and Marxism share their status as conflictual sciences: conflict is their home ground, where they have an advantage

82   Freud, *SE*, X: 213–214.

83   Freud, XVI: 358.

84   Kornbluh, *Realizing Capital*, 154.

85   My point here is not the neoliberal one that national economies can be metaphorised as household economies (and, hence, the need for an austere watch over income and debts); the shift in scale – a shift that includes, for example, the role of the state in money creation – makes this metaphor economically nonsensical even as it has functioned that way politically over recent decades. My point is the obverse.

86   Kornbluh, *Realizing Capital*, 154–55.

over other approaches.[87] Arguably, this accounting for unreliability, conflict and political construction makes the critique of libidinal economy come to the fore in crisis periods. If the libidinal economy is always subject to fluctuations and crises, depending on the subjective situation just as much as historical and social context, then psychoanalysis is the science that tries to understand and intervene – both clinically and culturally – in this crisis-ridden economy.

Crises in / of libido

If recent decades have repeatedly shown that capitalist societies are crisis-prone in their own terms, then what of the libido? Does it find itself amid crisis too? To speak of crisis and libido is to open two vistas: first, the crisis *of* libido (i.e., what happens when libido itself precipitates a subjective *and* social crisis) and, second, the libidinal *in* crisis (i.e., what happens to the libido in moments of social crisis). In both views, libido and sexuality are taken as either symptom (surface expression or temporary resolution of a deeper crisis) or cure (path of return from crisis).

The crisis *of* libido was historically notable in Freud's case studies. Each patient arrived at his consulting room in the middle of a certain libidinal upheaval. This apparently errant sexual functioning enabled psychoanalysis to map the very *nonfunctional* nature of desire I have been outlining.[88] Freud distinguishes his method of psychoanalytic treatment, which involves the *verbalisation* of unconscious fantasies and desires, from the medical practices that rely on physical interventions, such as the injections, or hypnotism, that he had previously attempted. He suggests that speech is the only way to access and modify the libidinal economy of the patient, and to address the problems of the flesh rooted in the symbolic order. This discovery suggested and presaged a social shift subsequently nominalised as "Freudian" but really only captured in his writing – that is, in his attempted theorisations of what was abroad in Vienna and elsewhere. Put differently, although Freud is regularly taken to be the prime mover in modern sexuality – if not the villain for instigating a new social dis-ease around sex (and gender) – he was instead the theorist and stenographer of a shift already under way. It becomes increasingly clear that where once

---

87   Louis Althusser, "On Marx and Freud," trans. Warren Montag, *Rethinking Marxism* 4, no. 1 (1991): 17–30. The second formulation is paraphrased from Mladen Dolar, "Freud and the Political," *Theory & Event* 12, no. 3 (2009).

88   The insights of psychoanalysis merge "with the scientific proof brought about by William Masters and Virginia Johnson whose guide to sexuality was in fact a guide to sexual dysfunction. Its title, *Human Sexual Inadequacy* (1970), meant that what sex amounts to, for humans, was something … fundamentally inadequate" (Patricia Gherovici and Manya Steinkoler, "Introduction," in *Psychoanalysis, Gender, and Sexualities: From Feminism to Trans**, ed. Manya Steinkoler and Patricia Gherovici (London: Routledge, 2022), 17).

there was a *sort of* organisation tenuously held together as we enter maturity yet rife with symptoms, now only *disorganisation* and perplexity can be found.[89]

The crisis of libido here equally pointed to the libidinal *in* crisis. The crisis of imperial bourgeois patriarchy – and attendant sexual mores – presented itself in Freud's rooms and took its place on the couch, speaking through the patient's utterances and hesitations. Freud's early "hysterics" lived out a crisis-ridden relation to sexuality, while the later war neuroses of young men also expressed crisis-stamped suffering. "Hysteria is never just a personal problem," Zupančič reminds us, "it is a problem of a *certain structuring* of power and social links."[90] While the hysteric is part of the formation she denounces, her subjective position makes the problem perceptible – and impossible to ignore.[91] So "the problem of the hysteric is almost always our problem too, whether we care to hear about it or not – not simply because she makes it our problem but because the problem actually exists independently of her, 'objectively.'" That is to say that "hysteria is a subjectivation of that problem, not simply a 'subjective problem.'"[92]

While the analytic technique afforded space and time for these symptoms to speak and emerge socially, these subjects – as subjectivations of structural problems – pushed Freud to go beyond the quasi-utilitarian pleasure principle and establish new clinical techniques and notions. Freud developed his theory of the sexual as constitutively problematic after he found that revealing the sexual meaning behind symptoms and the unconscious – the psychic economy – did not solve the problem.[93] So the clinical encounter with the libidinal demands new practices and responses from Freud as he also encounters, through his patients, a broader social crisis, perhaps one that can only be tended to and, at best, staunched in the clinic. Here, we see the crisis enter the libido, which becomes faulty, short-circuits, or just generally misfires by normative standards, producing an array of discontents, both localised in the patient and abroad in the culture.

---

89   Webster, *Disorganisation & Sex*. This perplexity may be something that cannot ultimately be fixed: "from the Kamasutra to today's sex-help books, the assumption is that if only we could do it right, it would not be a problem" (Gherovici and Steinkoler, "Introduction," 21). The wryly titled bestseller *Joy of Sex* – a riff on the *Joy of Cooking* – seemed to offer double pleasure: joy in sexual mastery and sexual enjoyment itself.

90   Alenka Zupančič, *Let Them Rot: Antigone's Parallax* (NY: Fordham UP, 2023), 82.

91   The hysteric might be a killjoy in Sara Ahmed's sense: someone – often a "feminist," often an "angry woman of colour" – who gets in the way, who disrupts the happiness of others, particularly when that happiness is not something they can agree upon. The killjoy interrupts the flow of positive affect and emotion, while becoming a locus of other affects – irritation, anger, fear – for speaking up and out about what is not working (*The Cultural Politics of Emotion*, 2nd ed. (Edinburgh: Edinburgh UP, 2014), 224–25).

92   Zupančič, *Let Them Rot*, 82.

93   Zupančič, *What Is Sex?*, 8.

The libidinal is still today taken to be a barometer of social health, especially among young women, the demographic from which many of Freud's hallmark cases were drawn. Today, we find assiduous attention paid to the erotic lives of adolescents and young adults, often as a proxy for diagnosing the health of contemporary societies. Commentators regularly ask, "is this generation having more or less sex than their predecessors." At the same time, millions tune into TV streaming series such as *The Sex Lives of College Girls* (2021–), the shamelessly yet ironically titled teen drama first seen on HBO Max; or *Sex Education* (2019–23), the knowing series created for Netflix about high school students and their sexual misadventures; or *How to Have Sex* (2023), the film about British teenage girls and their rites-of-passage holiday abroad. We realise there is a neuralgic point here as the alternately prurient and prudish discussions of "the young" are deeply variable from one day to the next: a report on the "sex recession" among today's youth is often followed by reporting on epidemics of outrageous, promiscuous adolescent sexual behaviour; more recently, the latter panic has focused on the casual sexual encounters brokered by phone apps.[94] Elsewhere, alongside the often proudly sex-positive streaming series, some have contemplated the contemporary hatred of sex and the sexlessness of a whole era of blockbuster cinema.[95]

Suggesting a crisis of non-relationality, these diagnoses come from different points on the political spectrum, from leftist queer theorists to conservative broadsheet columnists, as well as their unlikely convergences. In the *NY Times*, Catholic commentator Ross Douthat cited a leftist article on sexlessness in Hollywood cinema and TV but gave it the longstanding conservative *Kulturpessimismus* twist: "everyone should be rooting for the cinema of desire. For artistic reasons, yes – but also for the sake of the continuation of the human race." Douthat ultimately concluded:

---

94   The suggestively economic term "sex recession" entered public discussions via Kate Julian, "Why Are Young People Having So Little Sex?," *The Atlantic*, November 13, 2018. For some of the research around this: Peter Ueda et al., "Trends in Frequency of Sexual Activity and Number of Sexual Partners Among Adults Aged 18 to 44 Years in the US, 2000–2018," *JAMA Network Open* 3, no. 6 (2020): e203833; Jean M. Twenge, "Possible Reasons US Adults Are Not Having Sex as Much as They Used To," *JAMA Network Open* 3, no. 6 (2020): e203889. See the opening of Lauren Berlant, "Starved," *South Atlantic Quarterly* 106, no. 3 (2007): 433–44: Berlant notes that Susie Orbach, in the early 2000s, was reporting an epidemic of celibacy. In the two decades since, we have also seen attention paid to apparent trends in asexuality and conscious singleness. And on the pervasive figures of youth and how they come to signify – in crisis talk and moral panics – anxieties about the future, see Steven Threadgold, "Figures of Youth: On the Very Object of Youth Studies," *Journal of Youth Studies* 23, no. 6 (2020): 686–701.

95   Oliver Davis and Tim Dean, *Hatred of Sex* (Lincoln: University of Nebraska Press, 2022); Gila Ashtor, *Homo Psyche: On Queer Theory and Erotophobia* (NY: Fordham UP, 2021); Raquel S. Benedict, "Everyone Is Beautiful and No One Is Horny," *Blood Knife*, February 14, 2021.

"we'll know we're actually escaping stagnation when the cinema of desire returns."[96] Here the cultural, libidinal and economic are deeply attuned – and can be read off one another. Other commentators wring their hands about the "epidemic of loneliness" and how sex lives are involved, intimating an era of libidinal crisis. A decline in sex, partnership, and cohabitation is apparently causing negative physical, mental, and social health impacts; ergo, those who can have more sex should do so as an act of social solidarity.[97] In such accounts, a skim of social survey statistics about sexual activity becomes the occasion for deep concern about contemporary social bonds. In these diagnoses of cultural and social crisis, we find the sexual foregrounded, with its symptomatology and pathologies holding civilisational significance. Such reflections can evoke the dread of *aphanisis*, a concept coined by Ernest Jones in 1927 to describe the disappearance of sexual desire and enjoyment.[98] For Jones, the singular human fear was not castration but the loss of desire, as the fading of the libidinal became the "disappearance" (the Greek meaning of *aphanisis*) of the human subject. Wanting nothing, lacking appetite, the subject would disappear – and the realm of social meaning and bonds with it, sinking into a permanently sexless inertia, an image of anhedonia. These scenarios may haunt us because, as psychoanalysis suggests, people can resist pleasure as much as suffering; they also worry that pleasures are culturally forbidden, or might make us uncomfortably dependent, or might overwhelm us.

So while they may be ambient today, these fears about the decline of sexual pleasure are old news, probably as old as human sexuality. Wilhelm Reich intervened at this level almost a hundred years ago in his pamphlet "Politicizing the Sexual Problem of Youth." This tract precipitated his expulsion from the German Communist Party, despite – or because – of its popularity with its intended audience (i.e.,

---

96   Ross Douthat, "What the 2020s Need: Sex and Romance at the Movies," *The New York Times*, March 20, 2021.

97   Magdalene J. Taylor, "Have More Sex, Please!," *The New York Times*, February 13, 2023. We might also put this in the context of flagging reproduction rates in wealthy economies and panics about overpopulation in climate change discussions.

98   Ernest Jones, *Papers on Psycho-Analysis*, 5th ed. (London: Maresfield, 1977), 440: "the total, and of course permanent, extinction of the capacity (including opportunity) for sexual enjoyment." For Jones, castration anxiety mattered insofar as the male feared losing the capacity for sexual pleasure, a dread that was not exclusive to men, and manifested in women as the fear of desertion or separation. Constance Debré's recent autobiographical novel *Playboy* (trans. Holly James, South Pasadena: Semiotext(e), 2024, part 2, ch 23), which recounts her exploration of a new life and new desires or renewed desires and a renewed life, illustrates this in one short chapter, the entirety of which is the following: "I'm so scared of not being able to come. It's terrifying how much it terrifies me. I don't know what I'd do with the emptiness. That's why you have to be tough, you have to keep your body strong. To get through the fear. Fear of desire, fear of love, all the fears. Then everything will be OK."

young, would-be communists).[99] Here, at least, the analysis was upfront in naming capitalism and patriarchal authoritarianism as culprits in matters of love and
sexuality.[100] Meanwhile, during a contemporaneous lecture series in Frankfurt in
1931 and 1932, Karl Mannheim commented that "the economy provides the framework, but the erotic problem, as asceticism shows, is the one most central to humankind." Mannheim's litany of ills is familiar nine decades later: "everyone knows
– because everyone talks about it – that the family is in crisis; that sexuality is in
crisis; that the frequency of divorce is a problem; that there is talk of an uprising
for women, an uprising of youth." After an aside, he continues the list of what everyone knew in the early 1930s: "that one can speak of a reproductive strike; that
widespread psychic immiseration is being traced to the family (psychoanalysis); that
there is hope of forming an altogether new human being." The family for Mannheim
is the focal point of the lecture series, taking it as an institution in flux yet a distinct
and autonomous human field, organised around erotic relations. The various family formations, alongside related social practices that sustain those forms, including celibacy and prostitution, are solutions to the central tensions here, while "every solution creates its distinctive sense of the body [*Köpergefühl*, bodily feeling]."[101]
Mannheim is not a figure typically featured in the libidinal economic literature. Still,
he was conversant with psychoanalysis, including contemporaries Erich Fromm and
Karen Horney, plus Frankfurt *bête noire* to Theodor Adorno, Herbert Marcuse and
Max Horkheimer – and most likely Reich, who sat at the confluence of those critical and psychoanalytic currents. Mannheim's enmities and allies aside, what we
see here is another concerted grappling with the "psychic productive forces," in his
phrase, that had entered crisis alongside liberal capitalism in this period, pushing
even figures such as Mannheim to turn towards an answer rooted in something like
a critique of libidinal economy.

99   Wilhelm Reich, *Sex-Pol: Essays, 1929–1934*, ed. Lee Baxandall (London: Verso, 2012). Writ-
     ing from within and against the Soviet project, see Alexandra Kollontai, *Selected Writings of
     Alexandra Kollontai*, trans. Alix Holt (Westport: Lawrence Hill, 1978)
100 The analysis fell into a temporal trap: if Freud is arguably guilty of positing the fantasy of
     an "unimpeded, (re)naturalized libidinal economy ... projected back into a distant historical
     past, a mythical period preceding the emergence of socially imposed instinctual renuncia-
     tion," then in Reich's Freudo-Marxism, "this fantasy of a final, exhaustive satisfaction ... is pro-
     jected into an ever-receding future" (Johnston, *Time Driven*, xxxiv). For Stiegler, both tempo-
     ralities are at work in Marcuse, who "believed in the possibility of unearthing a golden age of
     the libido, which it would be a matter of recovering through revolutionary struggle, a golden
     age in which the pleasure principle would dominate the reality principle, where the 'instincts'
     would be 'liberated'" (*Lost Spirit*, 3).
101 Cited from lectures and contextualised in David Kettler and Volker Meja, *Karl Mannheim
     and the Crisis of Liberalism: The Secret of These New Times* (New Brunswick: Transaction, 1995),
     124–25.

In general, what sort of morphology can be proposed between the crisis in and of the libido? To what extent does the libido register, like the spinning dials of an aircraft in freefall, the presence of crisis, the atmospheres and pressures of a failing economy or social formation? And to what extent does the libido produce or play a role in crisis conditions? These questions already hint at the response – the answer is not one or the other but both. The understandings of libido *in* and *of* crisis speak to, for and about each other. Indeed, this was already the procedure Freud undertook as he expanded from individual case studies to cultural criticism: for example, dismantling popular (and sexological) understandings at the outset of his *Three Essays on Sexuality* from 1905, or addressing psychosocial sexual emergencies in "'Civilized' Sexual Morality and Modern Nervous Illness" from 1908, or, again, intimating in his early hysterics the libidinal economy of a turn-of-the-century Europe navigating its way to a changed sexual and gender order.[102] A year after the crisis-stamped *Beyond the Pleasure Principle*, Freud published *Mass Psychology and the Analysis of the Ego*, offering an account of the libido in group formation – its role in institutions, collectives, cultures as they are composed and decomposed – and opening onto a libidinised social theory. Étienne Balibar has reminded us that *Mass Psychology* is written during the crisis of the Austro-Hungarian empire, including the war that helped bring it down.[103] As such, Freud metonymically names this crisis-ridden state via his focus on the army and church – the two key models for a libidinal linking structure in his text and, as we know, the two great apparatuses in Althusser's work on ideology.

If Karl Marx saw individuals as embodiments or bearers of economic relations and capitalism's abstractions, then Freud sees individuals as manifesting structural dysfunction and contradiction within society. An individual's symptoms are not separate from the social context. Their suffering reflects a truth about the socioeconomic condition: "the political weight of psychoanalysis, at least in its Freudo-Lacanian guise," Tomšič writes, "consists in the effort of organising the subject's thoughts and actions around an attempt to work on the structure that conditions their illness."[104] Beyond the continuing case studies of psychoanalysis – similarly published today to record the libidinal status quo as overheard in the clinic – we can also look to cultural, political and social life for contemporary forms of libidinal upheaval amid crisis. This is the task the authors undertake in the following chapters: a contribution to the critique of libidinal economy.

---

102   Freud, *Three Essays*; Freud, *SE*, IX: 177–204. See Claudia Leeb, "The Hysteric Rebels: Rethinking Radical Socio-Political Transformation with Foucault and Lacan," *Theory & Event* 23, no. 3 (2020): 607–40.

103   Étienne Balibar, *Spinoza, the Transindividual*, trans. Mark G. E. Kelly (Edinburgh: Edinburgh UP, 2020), 172–173.

104   Tomšič, *Labour*, 16–17.

References

Ahmed, Sara. *The Cultural Politics of Emotion*. 2nd ed. Edinburgh: Edinburgh UP, 2014.

Althusser, Louis. "On Marx and Freud." Translated by Warren Montag. *Rethinking Marxism* 4, no. 1 (1991): 17–30. https://doi.org/10.1080/08935699108657950.

Apfelbaum, Bernard. "Sexuality: Intimacy or Illusion?" In *Sexology*, edited by Wolf Eicher, Götz Kokott, Hermann-J. Vogt, Volker Herms, and Reinhard Wille, 229–33. Berlin, Heidelberg: Springer, 1988.

Ashtor, Gila. *Homo Psyche: On Queer Theory and Erotophobia*. NY: Fordham UP, 2021.

Balibar, Étienne. *Spinoza, the Transindividual*. Translated by Mark G. E. Kelly. Edinburgh: Edinburgh UP, 2020.

Baudrillard, Jean. *The Consumer Society: Myths and Structures*. London: Sage, 1998.

Bennett, David. *The Currency of Desire: Libidinal Economy, Psychoanalysis and Sexual Revolution*. London: Lawrence & Wishart, 2016.

Berlant, Lauren. *Cruel Optimism*. Durham: Duke UP, 2011.

———. *Desire/Love*. Punctum, 2012.

———. *On the Inconvenience of Other People*. Duke UP, 2022.

———. "Starved." *South Atlantic Quarterly* 106, no. 3 (2007): 433–44. https://doi.org/10.1215/00382876-2007-002.

Boltanski, Luc, and Ève Chiapello. *The New Spirit of Capitalism*. London: Verso, 2005.

Castoriadis, Cornelius. *The Imaginary Institution of Society*. Cambridge: Polity, 1987.

Davies, William. "The New Neoliberalism." *New Left Review* 101 (2016): 121–34.

Davis, Oliver, and Tim Dean. *Hatred of Sex*. Lincoln: University of Nebraska Press, 2022.

Dolar, Mladen. "Freud and the Political." *Theory & Event* 12, no. 3 (2009). https://doi.org/10.1353/tae.0.0085.

Douthat, Ross. "What the 2020s Need: Sex and Romance at the Movies." *The New York Times*, March 20, 2021. https://www.nytimes.com/2021/03/20/opinion/sunday/sex-romance-movies.html.

Forrester, John. *Freud and Psychoanalysis: Six Introductory Lectures*. Edited by Lisa Appignanesi. Cambridge: Polity Press, 2023.

———. *Language and the Origins of Psychoanalysis*. London: Palgrave Macmillan, 1980.

Fraser, Nancy, and Rahel Jaeggi. *Capitalism: A Conversation in Critical Theory*. Cambridge: Polity, 2018.

Freud, Sigmund. *The Standard Edition of the Complete Psychological Works of Sigmund Freud*. 24 vols. London: Hogarth Press, 1953.

———. *Three Essays on the Theory of Sexuality: The 1905 Edition*. Translated by Ulrike Kistner. London: Verso, 2017.

Gammon, Earl. "Narcissism, Rage, Avocado Toast." In *Clickbait Capitalism: Economies of Desire in the Twenty-First Century*, edited by Amin Samman and Earl Gammon, 21–40. Manchester: Manchester UP, 2023.

Gherovici, Patricia, and Manya Steinkoler. "Introduction." In *Psychoanalysis, Gender, and Sexualities: From Feminism to Trans**, edited by Manya Steinkoler and Patricia Gherovici. London: Routledge, 2022.

Grubrich-Simitis, Ilse. *Back to Freud's Texts: Making Silent Documents Speak*. New Haven: Yale UP, 1996.

Hook, Derek. "Fanon and Libidinal Economy." In *Re(Con)Figuring Psychoanalysis: Critical Juxtapositions of the Philosophical, the Sociohistorical and the Political*, edited by Aydan Gülerce, 164–83. London: Palgrave Macmillan, 2012.

Horney, Karen. *New Ways in Psychoanalysis*. London: Routledge & Paul, 1939.

Irigaray, Luce, and Michael Marder. *Through Vegetal Being: Two Philosophical Perspectives*. NY: Columbia UP, 2016.

Johnson, Jeri. "Introduction." In *The Psychology of Love*, by Sigmund Freud. London: Penguin, 2006.

Johnston, Adrian. *Time Driven: Metapsychology and the Splitting of the Drive*. Evanston: Northwestern UP, 2005.

Jones, Ernest. *Papers on Psycho-Analysis*. 5th ed. London: Maresfield, 1977.

Julian, Kate. "Why Are Young People Having So Little Sex?" *The Atlantic*, November 13, 2018. https://www.theatlantic.com/magazine/archive/2018/12/the-sex-recession/573949/.

Kapoor, Ilan, Gavin Fridell, Maureen Sioh, and Pieter de Vries. *Global Libidinal Economy*. Albany: SUNY Press, 2023.

Kettler, David, and Volker Meja. *Karl Mannheim and the Crisis of Liberalism: The Secret of These New Times*. New Brunswick: Transaction, 1995.

Kollontai, Alexandra. *Selected Writings of Alexandra Kollontai*. Translated by Alix Holt. Westport: Lawrence Hill, 1978.

Kornbluh, Anna. *Realizing Capital: Financial and Psychic Economies in Victorian Form. Realizing Capital*. NY: Fordham UP, 2014.

Lacan, Jacques. *The Seminar of Jacques Lacan. Book II: The Ego in Freud's Theory and in the Technique of Psychoanalysis*. Translated by Sylvana Tomaselli. Cambridge: Cambridge UP, 1988.

———. *The Seminar of Jacques Lacan. Book VI: Desire and Its Interpretation*. Translated by Bruce Fink. Medford, MA: Polity, 2019.

———. *The Seminar of Jacques Lacan. Book VIII: Transference*. Translated by Bruce Fink. Cambridge: Polity, 2015.

———. *The Seminar of Jacques Lacan. Book XX: Encore. On Feminine Sexuality: The Limits of Love and Knowledge*. Translated by Bruce Fink. NY: Norton, 1999.

Langer, Frédéric. "Economy." In *Dictionary of Untranslatables: A Philosophical Lexicon*, edited by Barbara Cassin, Emily Apter, Jacques Lezra, and Michael Wood, 243–45. Princeton UP, 2014.

Leader, Darian. *Is It Ever Just Sex?* London: Penguin, 2023.

———. *Jouissance: Sexuality, Suffering and Satisfaction*. Cambridge: Polity, 2021.

Leeb, Claudia. "The Hysteric Rebels: Rethinking Radical Socio-Political Transformation with Foucault and Lacan." *Theory & Event* 23, no. 3 (2020): 607–40. https://doi.org/10.1353/tae.2020.0037

Madra, Yahya M., and Ceren Özselçuk. "Economy/Oikonomia." In *The Marx through Lacan Vocabulary: A Compass for Libidinal and Political Economies*, edited by Christina Soto van der Plas, Edgar Miguel Juárez-Salazar, and Carlos Gómez Camarena. The Lines of the Symbolic. NY: Routledge, 2022.

May, Rollo. *The Meaning of Anxiety*. Rev. ed. NY: Norton, 1977.

May, Ulrike. "The Third Step in Drive Theory: On the Genesis of *Beyond the Pleasure Principle*." *Psychoanalysis and History* 17, no. 2 (2015): 205–72. https://doi.org/10.3366/pah.2015.0170.

Mazzarella, William. *The Mana of Mass Society*. Chicago: University of Chicago Press, 2017.

Noys, Benjamin. "'We Are All Prostitutes': Crisis and Libidinal Economy." In *Credo Credit Crisis*, edited by Aidan Tynan, Laurent Milesi, and Christopher John Muller, 169–84. London: Rowman & Littlefield International, 2017.

O'Hara, Frank. *Meditations in an Emergency*. New York: Grove Press, 1967.

Ornston, Darius Gray. "The Invention of 'Cathexis' and Strachey's Strategy." *International Review of Psychoanalysis* 12 (1985): 391–98.

Raquel S. Benedict. "Everyone Is Beautiful and No One Is Horny." *Blood Knife*, February 14, 2021. https://bloodknife.com/everyone-beautiful-no-one-horny/.

Reich, Wilhelm. *Sex-Pol: Essays, 1929–1934*. Edited by Lee Baxandall. London: Verso, 2012.

Rose, Jacqueline. *The Plague*. London: Fitzcarraldo, 2023.

Safatle, Vladimir. "Death, Libido, and Negative Ontology in the Theory of Drives." In *Sexuality and Psychoanalysis: Philosophical Criticisms*, edited by Jens de Vleminck and Eran Dorfman. Leuven: Leuven UP, 2010.

Saketopoulou, Avgi. *Sexuality beyond Consent: Risk, Race, Traumatophilia*. NY: New York UP, 2023.

Santner, Eric L. *The Royal Remains: The People's Two Bodies and the Endgames of Sovereignty*. Chicago: University of Chicago Press, 2011.

Steinkoler, Manya, and Patricia Gherovici, eds. *Psychoanalysis, Gender, and Sexualities: From Feminism to Trans**. London: Routledge, 2022.

Stiegler, Bernard. "Nanomutations, Hypomnemata and Grammatisation." Ars Industrialis, 2006. https://web.archive.org/web/20231002204230/https://arsindustrialis.org/node/2937.

———. *The Lost Spirit of Capitalism*. Cambridge: Polity Press, 2014.

Taylor, Magdalene J. "Have More Sex, Please!" *The New York Times*, February 13, 2023. https://www.nytimes.com/2023/02/13/opinion/have-more-sex-please.html.

Threadgold, Steven. "Figures of Youth: On the Very Object of Youth Studies." *Journal of Youth Studies* 23, no. 6 (2020): 686–701. https://doi.org/10.1080/13676261.2019.1636014.

Tomšič, Samo. "No Such Thing as Society? On Competition, Solidarity, and Social Bond." *Differences* 33, no. 2–3 (2022): 51–71. https://doi.org/10.1215/10407391-1012 4676.

———. *The Labour of Enjoyment: Towards a Critique of Libidinal Economy*. Cologne: August Verlag, 2019.

Twenge, Jean M. "Possible Reasons US Adults Are Not Having Sex as Much as They Used To." *JAMA Network Open* 3, no. 6 (2020): e203889. https://doi.org/10.1001/ja manetworkopen.2020.3889.

Ueda, Peter, Catherine H. Mercer, Cyrus Ghaznavi, and Debby Herbenick. "Trends in Frequency of Sexual Activity and Number of Sexual Partners Among Adults Aged 18 to 44 Years in the US, 2000–2018." *JAMA Network Open* 3, no. 6 (2020): e203833. https://doi.org/10.1001/jamanetworkopen.2020.3833.

Webster, Jamieson. *Conversion Disorder: Listening to the Body in Psychoanalysis*. New York: Columbia UP, 2019.

———. *Disorganisation & Sex*. Brussels: Divided Publishing, 2022.

Zupančič, Alenka. "Biopolitics, Sexuality and the Unconscious." *Paragraph* 39, no. 1 (2016): 49–64. https://doi.org/10.3366/para.2016.0183.

———. *Let Them Rot: Antigone's Parallax*. NY: Fordham UP, 2023.

———. *The Odd One in: On Comedy*. Cambridge: MIT Press, 2008.

———. *What Is Sex?* Cambridge: MIT Press, 2017.

Axioms of Libidinal Economy

Benjamin Noys

The problem or question of libidinal economy is rarely confronted in its radical form. Libidinal economy refers to the fusion of the libido, in the sense of sexual energy or the drive, with economy, either in the specific sense of a sector of human activity concerned with the production and consumption of goods or in the more metaphoric or general sense of calculation and production across all activities. This chapter explores various modes and conceptions of this fusion between the libido and the economic and the issues that arise from it. My argument is that in the thinking of libidinal economy, there is a tendency to isolate certain elements of libidinal economy, treat them as acceptable or unacceptable, and then praise or reject them. In doing so, while often claiming to be beyond good and evil in a Nietzschean fashion,[1] the discourse of libidinal economy repeats a moralism that judges or proposes we distinguish between a good and bad libidinal economy. It is not that we should not make ethical or moral judgements, or analyse the ethical and moral dimensions of libidinal economy, but that these judgements are left abstract and generate a potentially infinite task of separating good libidinal economy from bad. While claiming to transcend the moral and ethical, or at least reconsider them in terms of libidinal economy, such discourses remain with an unthought moral and ethical dimension. The aim here is to confront the fundamental axioms of libidinal economy as a discourse to gauge how this problem is generated and to seek ways beyond the limits of libidinal economy.[2]

To begin, we can identify the axioms of libidinal economy and, in particular, their connection. These axioms are:

1. Every economy is libidinal.
2. Every libido is economic.

---

1   Friedrich Nietzsche, *Beyond Good and Evil*, trans. R. J. Hollingdale (London: Penguin, 1973).
2   See also Benjamin Noys, "'We are All Prostitutes': Crisis and Libidinal Economy," in *Credo Credit Crisis: Speculations on Faith and Money*, ed. Aidan Tynan, Laurent Milesi, and Christopher John Müller (London: Rowman and Littlefield, 2017).

We can, first, reject one or both of these axioms. In a sense, this is to rule out libidinal economy altogether. For axiom one, we could deny that the economy is a matter of libido, arguing instead that it is a matter of labour, a matter of prices setting values, a human organisation of exchange, and so on. In this way, the question of libidinal economy, as something that concerns us in the world, does not seem to arise. The economy might be many things and cause many problems, but it would not be libidinal. I would imagine this is quite a rare position, but by no means impossible. The denial of axiom two suggests that the libido is not economic. This can go along with an acceptance of axiom one, in which we could say that, while the economic is libidinal, our libido is not exhausted by the notion of the economic. Such a position involves rejecting Freud's argument that the libidinal drive can be analysed in mechanical and quantitative form.[3] While the economic can be infused with desire, this does not mean the reverse, so our desire is protected from the economic. This has been and probably still is a remarkably common position. Such arguments begin with Jung, who believed the libido was not a quantitative sexual force but generalised psychic energy.[4] The libido is desexualised and de-mechanised at the same time. These arguments often take a vitalist form,[5] in which the desire or drive is regarded as a living force beyond calculation, the mechanical, and the economic.

This already compressed sketch might suggest that the acceptance of libidinal economy is less common and more complex than we might usually assume. Part of our position as jaded post-Freudian subjects is the cynical acceptance that libido drives everything as a matter of course. On closer examination, however, this cynicism often breaks into a more romantic celebration of freedom or excess, libidinal or not, against the economic. In a sense, we do not have libidinal economy, but libido versus economy in which our desires exceed the economic constraints, "beneath the cobblestones the beach," as the slogan of May '68 had it. This is despite Foucault's well-known dismantling of the "repressive hypothesis."[6] Foucault would target D. H. Lawrence as the figure of a cosmogenic Eros, in his novel *The Plumed Serpent* (1926), where Lawrence valorised sex against sexuality.[7] While the terms have been updated, we often remain clearly within this posing of sex as a force against

3   Lawrence Birken, "Freud's 'Economic Hypothesis': From *Homo Oeconomicus* to *Homo Sexualis*," *American Imago* 56, no. 4 (1999).

4   Carl Gustav Jung, *Symbols of Transformation*, ed. Gerhard Adler, trans. R. F. C. Hull (Princeton: Princeton UP, 1977).

5   Ludwig Klages, *Of Cosmogonic Eros*, trans. Mav Kuhn (Munich: Theoin Publishing, 2018). See also Nitzan Lebovic, *The Philosophy of Life and Death: Ludwig Klages and the Rise of a Nazi Biopolitics* (NY: Palgrave Macmillan, 2013), 111–153.

6   Michel Foucault, *The History of Sexuality. Volume One*, trans. Robert Hurley (NY: Pantheon, 1978), 15–49.

7   Foucault, *The History of Sexuality*, 157.

the constraints of a libidinal economy. This is recast after Foucault in the vitalist dimension of desire as resistance, which was the innovation of Gilles Deleuze.[8] In this case, there is a "good" libido of cosmic excess and a "bad" libido restricted in its flow to the economy's limits, to use Freud's hydraulic metaphor.[9] The slogan of libido versus libidinal economy would be another May '68 slogan, "enjoy without shackles," as Alain Badiou has identified.[10]

Again, these are ethical or moral critiques, which play the two axioms against each other, but mainly rest on repressing or denying axiom two. The difficulty of every libido being economic is that it seems to foreclose the space of critique of the capitalist economy. Libidinal economy would lose its critical edge and, even worse, it would seem as if either the economic has colonised the psyche or, worst of all, the psyche was always "capitalist" or economic. This is the point made in Freud's metaphor from *The Interpretation of Dreams*, in which our unconscious wish is "the capitalist who provides the psychical outlay for the dream."[11] What if this was not a metaphor? What if our desire was a capitalist investing in dreams and symptoms and anything or everything else? What if we were capitalist subjects in a very literal and libidinal sense? At this point, the critical value of libidinal economy would seem to collapse. We might even seem to have returned to a justification of capitalist society as consonant with a fundamentally "selfish" libidinal drive. Capitalist economy would be the fulfilment of libidinal economy.[12]

This is the risk. The threat of Freud's model of the unconscious as sexual through and through, and economic or mechanical through and through, was the ending of the romantic unconscious. Hence the difference between Freud and all the various vitalisms, and the hostility of virtually all other forms of the unconscious to that argued by Freud. I have already suggested the opposition of Jung, Klages, and Lawrence. However, we can trace a general stream, or better an overflowing torrent, of vitalist conceptions of the unconscious that have tried to override Freud's "mechanical" unconscious. The scandal was not so much that the unconscious was sexual, which was beginning to be accepted by various vitalists and is at the heart

8   Gilles Deleuze, *Foucault*, trans. and ed. Séan Hand (London: Athlone, 1987).

9   Sigmund Freud, *The Three Essays on the History of Sexuality. The 1905 Edition*, trans. Ulrike Kistner, ed. and intro. Philippe Van Haute and Herman Westerink (London: Verso, 2016), 38.

10   Alain Badiou, "The Caesura of Nihilism," in *The Adventure of French Philosophy*, trans., ed., and intro. Bruno Bosteels (London: Verso, 2012).

11   Sigmund Freud, *The Interpretation of Dreams*, trans. and ed. James Strachey (London: Penguin, 1976), 714. For a discussion of this metaphor, see Samo Tomšič, *The Capitalist Unconscious* (London: Verso, 2015), 108–110. See also Samo Tomšič, *The Labour of Enjoyment: Towards a Critique of Libidinal Economy* (Cologne: August Verlag, 2019).

12   For a discussion of forms of socialist libidinal economy, see Keti Chukurov, *Practicing the Good: Desire and Boredom in Soviet Socialism* (Minneapolis: e-flux, 2020).

of Lawrence's vision. We could again turn to Foucault's analysis of sexuality, especially of "the perverse implantation" at the end of the 19th century,[13] to suggest an
increasing sexualisation of the notion of life itself. As we have seen with Lawrence,
this sexualisation is accepted, but only on the condition of opposing sex to sexuality.
If the vitalist does not simply desexualise or pan-sexualise the libido, as in Jung, they
oppose sex as a vital force to the limits of sexuality and the economy.

The real scandal is not that the unconscious is sexual but that it might be mechanical (or economic). The problem was not sex per se but sex as economy or mechanism. If sex or sexuality could be analysed scientifically as a quantitative and mechanical phenomenon, then it would lose its sense of romantic opposition. The Romantic unconscious of the "divinities of the night" and the "primordial will," as Lacan
noted,[14] would be replaced by Freud's machinic unconscious. In this sense, we could
say the true inheritors of Freud were the abstract vision of humans as comedic machines found in Wyndham Lewis,[15] or the bitter vision of sexuality as mechanical
performance in T. S. Eliot's "The Wasteland" (1922). In Eliot's poem, the aftermath of
a unsatisfactory sexual encounter, amounting to a rape, is recounted:

> Her brain allows one half-formed thought to pass:
> "Well now that's done: and I'm glad it's over."
> When lovely woman stoops to folly and
> Paces about her room again, alone,
> She smooths her hair with automatic hand,
> And puts a record on the gramophone.[16]

In this misogynistic vision, the female body is an automatic machine dispensing
sexuality in a detached fashion, even as an unwilling partner. The sexual drive is correlated with the turning gramophone record or the machinic "throbbing" of the taxi
engine earlier in the scene.[17] Eliot and Lewis still belong to the romantic reaction,
despite themselves, as they can only register this mechanical vision of sexuality as

---

13   Foucault, *The History of Sexuality*, 36–49.

14   Jacques Lacan, *The Four Fundamental Concepts of Psycho-Analysis*, ed. Jacques-Alain Miller,
      trans. Alan Sheridan (Harmondsworth, UK: Penguin, 1977), 24. On the rejection of the me-
      chanical unconscious by vitalists, see Lebovic, *The Philosophy of Life and Death*, 53; Benjamin
      Noys, "Vital Texts and Bare Life: The Uses and Abuses of Life in Contemporary Fiction," *Coun-
      terText* 1, no. 2 (2015): 172.

15   Wyndham Lewis, *Wild Body* (London: Penguin, 2004). On Lewis's libidinal economy, see
      Fredric Jameson, *Fables of Aggression: Wyndham Lewis, The Modernist as Fascist* (London: Verso,
      2008).

16   T. S. Eliot, *Collected Poems 1909–1962* (London: Faber and Faber, 1963), 72. See also Charles Fer-
      rall, *Modernist Writing and Reactionary Politics* (Cambridge: Cambridge UP, 2009), 88.

17   Eliot, *Collected Poems*, 71.

an object of aggression and disgust. In that sense, the scandal of Freud's discovery remains hard to accept.

The work of Herbert Marcuse is another sign of the tension over the concept of the libido as economic, this time on the left, as he tried to recover libido against libidinal economy.[18] This involved disputing Freud's vision of mechanical sexuality, especially in the form of the death drive. To save libido, it must be identified with the "binding" of Eros and seen as a constructive drive, a "self-sublimation in lasting and expanding relations."[19] This possibility of the drive, mutilated and violated by capitalist society, can then be reconstructed as a point of dis-adaptation and so of the critique of capitalist society as long as we resist the mechanical vision of unbinding the death drive. The binding of Eros to the death drive threatens this project of a "non-repressive development" as "the brute fact of death denies once and for all the reality of non-repressive existence."[20] Marcuse then reinterprets the death drive to argue that in the form of the Nirvana principle – reducing tension to zero – it can be seen as a state of gratification, while failing the reach that state leaves the death drive as an instinct of destruction.[21] So we have a splitting of the two drives and then a splitting in the death drive itself to save good libido.

Certainly, Marcuse would become more pessimistic in his conclusions, suggesting, in *One-Dimensional Man*,[22] the capacities of capitalism to absorb and profit from libidinal opposition. In this case, harnessing the desire for destruction could lead to "the supreme risk, and even the fact of war would meet, not only with helpless acceptance, but also with instinctual approval on the part of the victims."[23] This pessimism is justified by the death instinct, which is treated as a negative force of destruction against the constructive possibilities of Eros. Again, the death drive threatens to emerge as the "bad" drive of destruction, and Marcuse leaves the utopian hope to resist such a drive to the least integrated in the one-dimensional society.[24] In both cases, the difficulty does not simply lie in the death drive hypothesis but also in the intimate identification of the death drive with the life drive. This is why Marcuse's thought proved vulnerable to those reconstructions of Freud that noted the complete identification of Eros and the death drive.[25] The dualism of drives, or the splitting of the drive, is necessary to maintain the distinction between good and bad libido.

---

18   Hebert Marcuse, *Eros and Civilisation: A Philosophical Inquiry into Freud* (London: Abacus, 1972).

19   Marcuse, *Eros and Civilisation*, 157.

20   Marcuse, *Eros and Civilisation*, 162.

21   Marcuse, *Eros and Civilisation*, 165.

22   Herbert Marcuse, *One-Dimensional Man: Studies in the Ideology of Advanced Industrial Society* (1964; reis., London: Routledge, 2002).

23   Marcuse, *One-Dimensional Man*, 82.

24   Marcuse, *Eros and Civilisation*, 222–237.

25   Jean Laplanche, *Life and Death in Psychoanalysis*, trans. Jeffrey Mehlman (Baltimore: The Johns Hopkins UP, 1985).

If there is only one drive, if it is sexual, and if it is entropic, then we have the mechanical vision of the libido as economic. This is the Freudian vision, which remains the core of Freud's original monist vision, despite his turn to speculative dualism.[26] The death drive, which proves so hard for Freud to distinguish from the life drive, is better thought of not as a separate drive but as a process of unbinding within that singular drive. The result retains negativity and conflict, but within the form of the drive treated still as subject to mechanical and quantitative analysis. It is the difficulty with and resistance to this vision we have been tracing.

The resistance to Freud's vision can continue even if we maintain the fusion of the drives and identify the death drive as an entropic effect of unbinding. In this case, Marcuse can be inverted and resistance located on the side of death drive as the instance of excess and what is "beyond" not only the pleasure principle but also the economic. It is the unbinding and entropic form of the death drive that promises to undo the economy of the libido and the economy as libidinal. In this case, we would not have a restricted economy, in which the drives were bound together, but the death drive as excess or general economy, to use Bataille's terms.[27] This celebrates the death drive as excess, a point of negativity, and a factor that cannot be economically integrated. Jean Baudrillard's *Symbolic Exchange and Death* would probably be the most definitive version of the position,[28] although traces of it remain in Lacanian approaches.[29] Whether we consider the excess of Eros or the excess of Thanatos, what appears to be at stake is the difficulty of accepting the libidinal melding with the economic. The trauma of accepting axiom two (the libido is economic) is the threat that axiom one (the economic is libidinal) will come to supplant the libido – and the fusion of libidinal economy will be, finally, economic.

So far, we have focused on the difficulty of accepting axiom two – that the libidinal is economic. If this is difficult, so is the scandal disguised in the acceptance of axiom one – the economy is libidinal. While I have suggested this is more readily accepted, the consequences too are often limited. If the economy is libidinal, this does not only mean that the economy expresses our wishes and whims, especially our sexual desires; it does not only mean that "sex sells," it does not only mean that money is "sexy," it means that the economy is, fundamentally, an exchange of bodies. Money, as the general equivalent, is merely a representative for the exchange of bodies, as the economy is libidinal at base. This point is Sade's and is made again by

---

26   Sigmund Freud, *Beyond the Pleasure Principle and Other Writings*, trans. John Reddick, intro. Mark Edmundson (London: Penguin, 2003).

27   Georges Bataille, *The Accursed Share, Volume One*, trans. Robert Hurley (NY: Zone Books, 1988).

28   Jean Baudrillard, *Symbolic Exchange and Death*, trans. Iain Hamilton Grant, intro. Mike Gane (1976; reis., London: Sage, 1993).

29   Lee Edelman, *No Future: Queer Theory and the Death Drive* (Durham: Duke UP, 2004); Slavoj Žižek, *Living in the End Times* (London: Verso, 2010), 77.

Pierre Klossowski.[30] It would seem to fuse the libidinal and the economic with no reserve, identifying the economy itself as libidinal. In this case, critique dissolves, or it would be limited to pointing out that we disguise this exchange of bodies with an exchange of money and would be "better off" revealing the properly libidinal form of economy.

In practice, however, the critical form can still be retained. This is evident in the work of Pierre Klossowski. Not only can we reveal the true libidinal flows and abandon all the disguises and misdirections of the actual economy, but this economy of desire also exceeds the civilised and discrete forms of the actual economy. In Klossowski, this is achieved by pitting Fourier's playful visions of libido as play against Sade's "serious" vision of libido as court masque. Fourier takes libido as a new principle of flux and flow that exceeds the limits of economy, while Sade, for all his bravado, remains within an economic vision of exchange and trade, if not of the violent subjugation of bare life.[31] Similarly, Klossowski had previously chided Sade for not being able to accept the "innocence of becoming" suggested by Nietzsche.[32] Sade remained too attached to what he transgressed. As an atheist who demanded male and female victims dress as nuns and priests to be violated, Sade proved his disregard for religious norms but also gained enjoyment from the transgression of those norms. Klossowski, as a heterodox Christian, finds the flow of souls in Nietzsche and Fourier – in which identity disintegrates into an exchange of souls or "breaths"[33] – to be the economy beyond libidinal economy. In a typical criticism, Sade's vision of the true economy of the violent exchange of bodies is found to be transgressive and too attached to what it transgresses. To depart the economy via the libidinal, it is not enough to dissolve the economic into the libidinal, but the principle of identity itself, on which the economic depends for calculation, must be dissolved.[34]

Once again, we have a good and bad libidinal economy. The bad libidinal economy of the world around us, in which exchange is really libidinal, and the good libidinal economy, which dissolves economy into pure flux. What is more challenging to concede is that we just have libidinal economy. In this case, the economy and the

---

30   Marquis De Sade, *The 120 Days of Sodom or the School of Libertinage*, trans. and intro. Will Mc-Morran and Thomas Wynn (London: Penguin, 2016); Pierre Klossowski, *Living Currency*, ed. Daniel W. Smith, Nicolae Morar, and Vernon W. Cisney (London: Bloomsbury, 2017).

31   Theodor Adorno and Max Horkheimer, *Dialectic of Enlightenment: Philosophical Fragments*, ed. Gunzelin Schmid Noerr, trans. Edmund Jephcott (Stanford: Stanford UP, 2002).

32   Pierre Klossowski, *Sade My Neighbour*, trans. Alphonso Lingis (Evanston, IL: Northwestern UP, 1991), 34.

33   Pierre Klossowski, *The Baphomet*, trans. Sophie Hawkes and Stephen Sartarelli (Hygiene, CO: Eridanos Press, 1988). See also Ian James, "Evaluating Klossowski's *Le Baphomet*," *Diacritics* 35, no. 1 (2005).

34   Vincent Descombes, *Modern French Philosophy*, trans. L. Scott-Fox and J. M. Harding (Cambridge: Cambridge UP, 1998), 183.

libidinal are coterminous. What we buy and sell belongs to bodies, or they are part-bodies or, in Freudian or Kleinian terminology, part-objects.[35] In this case, the exposure simply reveals the situation as it is, in which the libidinal and the economic are fused in all forms of exchange, identitarian or not. The division or dissolution of identity is not a cause for celebration as a principle of resistance or escape but another incitement to further calculability and economic activity. The world of the economic, or the world of capitalism, which is the world subject to the economic as final imperative,[36] is a world of the commodity as a series of part-objects. It is for this reason, among others, that Gilles Deleuze offers such apt descriptions of the psychic landscape of high capitalism.[37] Deleuze plays the part-objects against any totalisation by suggesting they constitute a multiplicity.[38] This will later form the basis of the libidinal description that opens *Anti-Oedipus*, cowritten with Félix Guattari, in which the part-object becomes identified with the economic forms of the capitalist machine.[39] We live in a world of part-object or, if we prefer, what Lacan called *lathouses*,[40] in which the part-object is also a technical object or gadget.

We might be familiar with the joy sparked by the act of purchasing, in which what we purchase is somehow not particularly relevant. This might be seen as the act of the collector. In his discussion of book collecting, Walter Benjamin remarks on the "thrill of acquisition" experienced by the collector and the "non-reading of books" characteristic of collectors.[41] Similar instances abound in contemporary life, of music unplayed or "watch lists" left unwatched. Such unused objects are often experienced as objects of shame. In board gaming, "a shelf of shame" is a shelf of unopened games, especially when they are still wrapped in shrink. The prophylactic of shrink suggests this is the safe sex of purchasing. What "sparks joy," in this case, is the purchase, not the object, hence perhaps why we accumulate so many objects that do not spark joy and yet which we find so hard to throw out. They are past loves, or past lovers. Accumulated objects are accumulated stale libido. This, in part, is the

---

35   Melanie Klein, *The Selected Melanie Klein*, ed. Juliet Mitchell (Harmondsworth, UK: Penguin, 1986), 84–94.

36   Georg Lukács, *History and Class Consciousness*, trans. Rodney Livingstone (London: Merlin, 1971).

37   See Benjamin Noys, "'Love and Napalm: Export USA': Schizoanalysis, Acceleration, and Contemporary American Literature," in *Deleuze and the Schizoanalysis of Literature*, ed. Ian Buchanan, Tim Matts, and Aidan Tynan (London: Bloomsbury Academic, 2015).

38   Gilles Deleuze, *Proust and Signs*, trans. Robert Howard (London: Allen Lane, 1973), 109–110.

39   Gilles Deleuze and Félix Guattari, *Anti-Oedipus*, trans. Robert Hurley, Mark Seem, and Helen R. Lane (Minneapolis: University of Minnesota Press, 1983).

40   Jacques Lacan, *The Seminar, Book XVII, The Other Side of Psychoanalysis*, trans. Russell Grigg (NY: Norton, 2007), 150–163.

41   Walter Benjamin, "Unpacking My Library," in *Illuminations*, ed. and intro. Hannah Arendt, trans. Harry Zohn (NY: Schocken Books, 1968), 60, 62.

libidinal economy of contemporary capitalism as an economy of part-objects, gadgets, and now, of course, digital objects. Digital objects are supposed to solve the problems of physical storage, evident in the multiplication of storage solutions and storage services – but these digital objects rapidly become another storage problem in turn.

We can conclude that we are reluctant to take libidinal economy seriously. It is difficult to think or sustain axiom one (every economy is libidinal) or two (every libido is economic). However, the fusion of these two axioms is perhaps most difficult. This just is libidinal economy. The two-word phrase condenses the fact that the libido is economic and the economic is libidinal. I would say this accounts for the scandal of Jean-François Lyotard's book *Libidinal Economy* (1974), which might be the closest attempt to think this fusion.[42] The scandal can be overstated, and Lyotard's references to the book as evil and bought at the cost of agonies to his soul suggest his religious background and a tendency to self-dramatisation.[43] Perhaps the only way to write a book called "libidinal economy" is through a hyperbole that tries desperately to fuse the two axioms. Lyotard's book is far from the enumerative passions of Sade, what Adorno called "mechanical ballets,"[44] but somewhat closer to the transgressive anguish of Georges Bataille, although with a non-tragic pathos, yet not as light as Klossowski's exchange of souls.

Still, in many ways, Lyotard's book, in itself, does not matter. What matters is the problem it points to: fusing the two axioms to as great an extent as possible. All economics becomes libidinal, not just capitalist economy. The book treats high mercantilism – the economy as a war over silver, as a zero-sum game of maximising exports at the expense of other states – as another instance of libidinal satisfaction.[45] If all instances of the economy are flattened into libidinal instances, then the same is true of the experience of subjectivity and the unconscious. The book's notorious opening presents the libidinal model of the subject as flayed body, which constitutes a libidinal band or Moebius strip.[46] In Lyotard's libidinal economy, there is no room for depth, as all is a surface on which libidinal intensities pass, occasionally cooling to form representations and the world around us as one of relative stability. While developing from the energetics of Freud, this is now radicalised by Nietzsche's critique of depth, in which "there is no 'being' behind doing, acting, becoming; 'the doer'

---

42 Jean-François Lyotard, *Libidinal Economy*, trans. Iain Hamilton Grant (1974; reis., London: Athlone, 1993).

43 Jean-François Lyotard, *Peregrinations: Law, Form, Event* (NY: Columbia UP, 1988), 13.

44 Theodor Adorno, *Quasi una Fantasia: Essays on Modern Music*, trans. Rodney Livingstone (London: Verso, 1992), 173.

45 Lyotard, *Libidinal Economy*, 188–200.

46 Lyotard, *Libidinal Economy*, 1–5.

is merely a fiction imposed on the doing."[47] In this case, the "doing" is done by the libidinal intensity, and the idea of depth and subjectivity is mere fiction. The result is a world without psychic interiority and neurosis, as there is no space for anguished negotiation between the inner and outer worlds, as we find in Klein or Winnicott.[48]

This collapsing of space into a monism of libidinal intensity falters, however, on the issue of "cooling" and of how and why these intensities should ever appear as mere "representations." In fact, it might be that the libidinal intensities are more apparently fictions and instantiate a sort of depth that could be displaced by language.[49] The production of libidinal economy as a fusion immediately seems to result in the project's termination. Lyotard would retreat from this monistic model to problems of language and the limit inspired by Kant.[50] In fact, *Libidinal Economy* received relatively little discussion or critique.

One of the few substantial criticisms from the time was that made by Guy Lardreau and Christain Jambet in their book *L'Ange* (1976).[51] Lardreau and Jambet violently rejected Lyotard's libidinal "leftism" and any foundation of radical politics on sexuality. Instead, they celebrated the angelic and chaste experience of early Christian monasticism and the Chinese cultural revolution. These monastic and celibate revolutionaries

> invert every accepted form of value, renounce all inheritance, refuse any loyalty to family and familiarity, deny the body, reject sexual difference and desire, affirm the all-or-nothing simplicity of redemption, pursue a heroic anonymity, adopt a permanent posture of self-criticism, embrace the most severe forms of frugality and discipline.[52]

The implication is that the fusion of libido and economy cannot be sundered by selecting a good libido from bad, only by the absolute and intransigent rejection of sexuality. This puritanical position was not taken up, and it skirted being a fantas-

---

47   Friedrich Nietzsche, *On the Genealogy of Morals*, trans. Douglas Smith (Oxford: Oxford UP, 2008), 29.

48   Klein, *The Selected Melanie Klein*; D. W. Winnicott, *Playing and Reality* (London: Routledge, 2005).

49   Geoffrey Bennington, *Lyotard: Writing the Event* (Manchester: Manchester UP, 1988), 46.

50   Jean-François Lyotard, *The Differend: Phrases in Dispute*, trans. George Van Den Abbeele (Minneapolis: University of Minnesota Press, 1983).

51   Guy Lardreau and Christian Jambet, *L'Ange. Ontologie de la révolution, tome 1: pour une cynégétique du semblant* (Paris: Grasset, 1976). See also, Peter Hallward, "Reason and Revolt: Guy Lardreau's Early Voluntarism and Its Limits," *Radical Philosophy*, no. 190 (2015).

52   Peter Hallward, "Fallen Angel: Guy Lardreau's Later Voluntarism," *Radical Philosophy*, no. 203 (2018): 45.

matic projection. The necessity to violently reject sexuality to retain the possibility of revolution did, however, indicate the intrinsic difficulties of libidinal economy.[53]

The extremity of this response usefully indicates the extremity of Lyotard's project. It is telling in both cases, for Lyotard and for Lardreau and Jambet, that they would move from these positions to the problem of ethics. Ethics indicates, we could say, the limits of the project of libidinal economy.[54] This is not to dismiss ethics or the ethical as a concern about the libidinal – far from it. Instead, my point is that the extreme moralisms that resulted from the project of libidinal economy prevented the integration and concern with the ethical as central to the problem of libidinal economy. The fusion of libido and economy that seems to leave no point of critique, or the rejection of sexuality as corrupted in favour of absolute revolution, dissolve the space of the ethical as a socio-political space formed out of relations of domination, resistance, and freedom. Instead of this vision of the ethical life associated with Hegel,[55] we find a detached and injunctive ethics that constantly struggles with the impossible limit of complete libidinal identification or absolute revolution. This is, as Hegel recognised, the problem of the ethical misrecognised and instead turned into fiat and injunction. It results in a political moralism that Hegel associated with the political thinking of Kant and Fichte.

The history we have reconstructed out of the axioms of libidinal economy has been a history of this kind of moralism of the injunction. The turn to Kant as a refuge after libidinal extremism only serves to disguise the continuity of modes of Kantian thinking and moralism. In this case, ethics becomes fractured and separated from its social forms, partially as libido's distinctiveness becomes dissolved – as we saw with Lyotard it may be that everything is libidinal or equally nothing if the libidinal is treated simply as a mode of speaking. This does not mean dismissing the problematic of libidinal economy or simply replacing it with some new form of Kantian ethics. Instead, the impasse we have traced in libidinal economy offers an opportunity to rethink these questions. We have often seen the project abandoned altogether or its softening into an acceptance of the libidinal that struggles to produce libidinal economy as a conceptual or theoretical form.

We see the fragmentation and tensions in Michel Foucault. The aim of Foucault's project was, in many ways, to end talking in terms of sex, yet his project licensed and

---

53   See Benjamin Noys, "'The End of the Monarchy of Sex': Sexuality and Contemporary Nihilism," *Theory, Culture & Society* 25, no. 5 (September 2008).

54   We could note the turn in Foucault away from the project concerned with sexuality and power and towards a concern with sexuality and ethics. See Benjamin Noys, "Crisis and Transition: The Late Foucault and the Vocation of Philosophy," ed. Gavin Walker, *South Atlantic Quarterly* 121, no. 4 (2022),

55   G. W. F. Hegel, *Elements of the Philosophy of Right*, ed. Allen W. Wood (Cambridge: Cambridge UP, 1991).

proliferated the categories he claimed to have surpassed.[56] Notably, Foucault also turned to ethics and subjectivity in his late work – parallel to, if not in advance of, those made by Lyotard and Lardreau and Jambet. Again, the difficulty I am pointing to is not the turn to ethics and subjectivity but the fracture in Foucault's project between his histories of institutions and powers and his new history of ethics and subjectivity. It appears that what we cannot think is precisely what Hegel meant by ethical life (*Sittlichkeit*): the problem in modernity of thinking freedom through the relation of subjectivity to institutional forms of power.[57] The fracture of Foucault's history of sexuality suggests the difficulty of an ethical relation to libidinal economy formed through the relationship between subjectivity and institutional forms, not the least of which is the capitalist economy itself. In fact, the tendency of Foucault to treat capitalism as a plural moment, one institutional form among others, or as another mode of governmentality, is one sign of the difficulty his project has in grasping the contemporary form of capitalist totality.[58]

These various endpoints do not, I think, indicate the end of the problematic of libidinal economy but from where we must start thinking. This is not to say that the problem of libidinal economy should be accepted as it was. However, a confrontation with its scandal can remind us that, while we might pride ourselves on our acceptance of sexuality as diverse and plural, we often remain constrained in our thinking and prone to repeat political moralisms. The ethical difficulties of sexuality, signalled in Hegel's text but not fully developed,[59] remain for us, especially in the tension between modes of liberation and new forms of repression. The gains of the sexual revolution, as it was called, must be defended and deepened, especially in the face of reactionary calls to new modes of repression and normativity. At the same time, the political and institutional questions of sexuality and libido, particularly concerning the state and capital, remain pressing problems to be thought and analysed. In the end, the extremism of libidinal economy might be regarded as a block to thinking these problems. However, abandoning libidinal economy has too often led to assumed consonances between libido and liberation or between libido and repression that do not hold up to examination. The fact that libidinal economy remains a battleground is evident, from the misogyny of the "incel movement" to the transphobia of the public sphere, to select only two examples of reactionary currents.[60] In response, we should not abandon libidinal economy but insist on engaging with the

56   See Noys, "The End of the Monarchy of Sex."

57   Gillian Rose, *Hegel Contra Sociology* (London: Verso, 2009).

58   Michel Foucault, *The Birth of Biopolitics: Lectures at the Collège de France, 1978–79*, ed. Michael Senellart, trans. Graham Burchell (Basingstoke: Palgrave Macmillan, 2008).

59   Jacques Derrida, *Glas*, trans. David Wills and Geoffrey Bennington (Minneapolis: University of Minnesota Press, 2021).

60   On incels, see Benjamin Noys, "He's just Not that into You: Negging and the Manipulation of Negativity," *Manipulations/Platform* (2015), https://web.archive.org/web/20151108100033/

ethical as the socio-political problem of living together, with libido as the formation of relations, and with the possibilities of necessary and further liberation.

References

Adorno, Theodor. *Quasi una Fantasia: Essays on Modern Music*. Translated by Rodney Livingstone. London: Verso, 1992.

Adorno, Theodor, and Max Horkheimer. *Dialectic of Enlightenment: Philosophical Fragments*. Edited by Gunzelin Schmid Noerr. Translated by Edmund Jephcott. Stanford: Stanford UP, 2002.

Badiou, Alain. "The Caesura of Nihilism." In *The Adventure of French Philosophy*, translated, edited, and introduced by Bruno Bosteels, 53–66. London: Verso, 2012.

Bataille, Georges. *The Accursed Share, Volume One*. Translated by Robert Hurley. NY: Zone Books, 1988.

Baudrillard, Jean. *Symbolic Exchange and Death*. Translated by Iain Hamilton Grant. Introduction by Mike Gane. London: Sage, 1993.

Benjamin, Walter. "Unpacking My Library." In *Illuminations*, edited and introduced by Hannah Arendt. Translated by Harry Zohn, 59–67. NY: Schocken Books, 1968.

Bennington, Geoffrey. *Lyotard: Writing the Event*. Manchester: Manchester UP, 1988.

Birken, Lawrence. "Freud's 'Economic Hypothesis': From *Homo Oeconomicus* to *Homo Sexualis*." *American Imago* 56, no. 4 (1999): 311–330. https://doi.org/10.1353/aim.19 99.0017

Chukurov, Keti. *Practicing the Good: Desire and Boredom in Soviet Socialism*. e-flux, 2020.

Deleuze, Gilles. *Proust and Signs*. Translated by Robert Howard. London: Allen Lane, 1973.

———. *Foucault*. Translated and edited by Séan Hand. London: Athlone, 1987.

Deleuze, Gilles, and Félix Guattari. *Anti-Oedipus*. Translated by Robert Hurley, Mark Seem, and Helen R. Lane. Minneapolis: University of Minnesota Press, 1983.

Derrida, Jacques. *Glas*. Translated by David Wills and Geoffrey Bennington. Minneapolis: University of Minnesota Press, 2021.

Descombes, Vincent. *Modern French Philosophy*. Translated by L. Scott-Fox and J. M. Harding. Cambridge: Cambridge UP, 1998.

Edelman, Lee. *No Future: Queer Theory and the Death Drive*. Durham: Duke UP, 2004.

Eliot, T. S. *Collected Poems 1909–1962*. London: Faber and Faber, 1963.

Ferrall, Charles. *Modernist Writing and Reactionary Politics*. Cambridge: Cambridge UP, 2009.

---

http://www.manipulations.info/hes-just-not-that-into-you-negging-and-the-manipulatio
n-of-the-negativity/ .

Foucault, Michel. *The History of Sexuality. Volume One*. Translated by Robert Hurley. NY: Pantheon, 1978.

———. *The Birth of Biopolitics: Lectures at the Collège de France, 1978–79*. Edited by Michael Senellart. Translated by Graham Burchell. Basingstoke: Palgrave Macmillan, 2008.

Freud, Sigmund. *The Interpretation of Dreams*. Translated and edited by James Strachey. London: Penguin, 1976.

———. *Beyond the Pleasure Principle and Other Writings*. Translated by John Reddick. Introduction by Mark Edmundson. London: Penguin, 2003.

———. *The Three Essays on the History of Sexuality. The 1905 Edition*. Translated by Ulrike Kistner. Edited and introduction by Philippe Van Haute and Herman Westerink. London: Verso, 2016.

Hallward, Peter. "Reason and Revolt: Guy Lardreau's Early Voluntarism and Its Limits." *Radical Philosophy*, no. 190 (2015): 13–24.

Hallward, Peter. "Fallen Angel: Guy Lardreau's Later Voluntarism." *Radical Philosophy*, no. 203 (2018): 43–60.

Hegel, G. W. F. *Elements of the Philosophy of Right*. Edited by Allen W. Wood. Cambridge: Cambridge UP, 1991.

James, Ian. "Evaluating Klossowski's *Le Baphomet*." *Diacritics* 35, no. 1 (2005): 119–135. https://doi.org/10.1353/dia.2007.0013

Jameson, Fredric. *Fables of Aggression: Wyndham Lewis, The Modernist as Fascist*. London: Verso, 2008.

Jung, Carl Gustav. *Symbols of Transformation*. Edited by Gerhard Adler. Translated by R. F. C. Hull. Princeton: Princeton UP, 1977.

Klages, Ludwig. *Of Cosmogonic Eros*. Translated by Mav Kuhn. Munich: Theoin Publishing, 2018.

Klein, Melanie. *The Selected Melanie Klein*. Edited by Juliet Mitchell. Harmondsworth, UK: Penguin, 1986.

Klossowski, Pierre. *The Baphomet*. Translated by Sophie Hawkes and Stephen Sartarelli. Hygiene, CO: Eridanos Press, 1988.

———. *Sade My Neighbour*. Translated by Alphonso Lingis. Evanston, IL: Northwestern UP, 1991.

———. *Living Currency*. Edited by Daniel W. Smith, Nicolae Morar, and Vernon W. Cisney. London: Bloomsbury, 2017.

Lacan, Jacques. *The Four Fundamental Concepts of Psycho-Analysis*. Edited by Jacques-Alain Miller. Translated by Alan Sheridan. Harmondsworth, UK: Penguin, 1977.

———. *The Seminar, Book XVII, The Other Side of Psychoanalysis*. Translated by Russell Grigg. NY: Norton, 2007.

Laplanche, Jean. *Life and Death in Psychoanalysis*. Translated by Jeffrey Mehlman. Baltimore: The Johns Hopkins UP, 1985.

Lardreau, Guy, and Christian Jambet. *L'Ange. Ontologie de la révolution, tome 1: pour une cynégétique du semblant.* Paris: Grasset, 1976.

Lebovic, Nitzan. *The Philosophy of Life and Death: Ludwig Klages and the Rise of a Nazi Biopolitics.* NY: Palgrave Macmillan, 2013.

Lewis, Wyndham. *Wild Body.* London: Penguin, 2004.

Lukács, Georg. *History and Class Consciousness.* Translated by Rodney Livingstone. London: Merlin, 1971.

Lyotard, Jean-François. *The Differend: Phrases in Dispute.* Translated by George Van Den Abbeele. Minneapolis: University of Minnesota Press, 1983.

———. *Peregrinations: Law, Form, Event.* NY: Columbia UP, 1988.

———. *Libidinal Economy.* Translated by Iain Hamilton Grant. London: Athlone, 1993. First published 1974 by Les Éditions de Minuit.

Marcuse, Hebert. *Eros and Civilisation: A Philosophical Inquiry into Freud.* London: Abacus, 1972.

———. *One-Dimensional Man: Studies in the Ideology of Advanced Industrial Society.* London: Routledge, 2002.

Nietzsche, Friedrich. *Beyond Good and Evil.* Translated by R. J. Hollingdale. London: Penguin, 1973.

———. *On the Genealogy of Morals.* Translated by Douglas Smith. Oxford: Oxford UP, 2008.

Noys, Benjamin. "'The End of the Monarchy of Sex': Sexuality and Contemporary Nihilism." *Theory, Culture & Society* 25, no. 5 (September 2008): 104–122. https://doi.org/10.1177/0263276408095218

———. "He's just Not that into You: Negging and the Manipulation of Negativity." *Manipulations/Platform.* 2015. https://web.archive.org/web/20151108100033/http://www.manipulations.info/hes-just-not-that-into-you-negging-and-the-manipulation-of-the-negativity/.

———. "Vital Texts and Bare Life: The Uses and Abuses of Life in Contemporary Fiction." *CounterText* 1, no. 2 (2015): 169–185. https://doi.org/10.3366/count.2015.0016

———. "'Love and Napalm: Export USA': Schizoanalysis, Acceleration, and Contemporary American Literature." In *Deleuze and the Schizoanalysis of Literature*, edited by Ian Buchanan, Tim Matts, and Aidan Tynan, 175–189. London: Bloomsbury Academic, 2015.

———. "'We are All Prostitutes': Crisis and Libidinal Economy." In *Credo Credit Crisis: Speculations on Faith and Money.* Edited by Aidan Tynan, Laurent Milesi, and Christopher John Müller, 169–184. London: Rowman and Littlefield, 2017.

———. "Crisis and Transition: The Late Foucault and the Vocation of Philosophy." Edited by Gavin Walker. *South Atlantic Quarterly* 121, no. 4 (2022): 675–691. https://doi.org/10.1215/00382876-10066385.

Rose, Gillian. *Hegel Contra Sociology.* London: Verso, 2009.

Sade, Marquis De. *The 120 Days of Sodom or the School of Libertinage*. Translated and introduced by Will McMorran and Thomas Wynn. London: Penguin, 2016.

Tomšič, Samo. *The Capitalist Unconscious*. London: Verso, 2015.

———. *The Labour of Enjoyment: Towards a Critique of Libidinal Economy*. Cologne: August Verlag, 2019.

Winnicott, D. W. *Playing and Reality*. London: Routledge, 2005.

Žižek, Slavoj. *Living in the End Times*. London: Verso, 2010.

"Out of Your System": After Lyotard's Libidinal Set-Ups

Julie Gaillard

In lieu of an introduction, let me start with an image. The scene is in France, in the city centre of a provincial metropolis, on a Saturday afternoon. A pedestrian shopping street is filled with a human tide massed for a day of shopping and leisure. Like every Saturday for a few weeks, this dense, uniform crowd of shoppers and onlookers is interrupted by another bright yellow stream gushing onto the avenue. These two streams form two perpendicular axes, the bright yellow stream segmenting the other axis in two black halves. And yet, by some optical mystery, these two halves seem to continue swarming as one, inexorable, continuous flow. How? Of course, large contingents of police in full riot gear and agents of the anti-crime brigades[1] strictly contain the bright yellow stream. Business can go on as usual amid the sound of grenades and the stench of tear gas. Why is it, though, that this stream of shoppers and passers-by seems to keep swarming undisturbed, when, sometimes three or four metres away, demonstrators are held at gunpoint, chased, held down, beaten, strangled, injured?

This image of two streams – the uniform dark stream of continuation, the yellow stream of disruption – will serve as a backdrop, not to address the Yellow Vests movement in itself but to assess the relevance of Jean-François Lyotard's libidinal economic framework for the 21st century. How helpful is this framework for understanding how the capitalist machinery organises flows and libidinal investments? What insights can it offer for reconsidering the conditions of possibility for a revolution of these arrangements of desire (or, to use a more appropriately Lyotardian term, of these libidinal set-ups)? Indeed, what about a wholesale revolution of the system? Finally, in reassessing the relevance of the libidinal framework today, what can be learned from Lyotard's own reassessment of his work?

Within the context of this volume, which sets out to enquire about the relevance of the libidinal economic framework in crisis times, it seems opportune to observe the trajectory of this framework across the works of one of its notorious theorists –

---

1   A section of the French national police, in Paris and other cities, dressed in civilian clothing, often moving on foot or in unmarked cars, and stopping people for street or "public order" offences and identity checks. These brigades have earned a negative reputation for their disproportionate use of provocation and violence against minorities and during demonstrations.

who, just as notoriously, abandoned the libidinal approach in favour of a pragmatics of phrases, in *The Differend* (1983) and onwards. By the 1980s, Lyotard deemed the
libidinal approach he developed in the 1970s as a "metaphysics of forces."[2] *Libidinal
Economy* (1974) was discarded as "my book of evilness" ("*mon livre méchant*")[3] and affect reframed as "affect-phrase."[4] Upon closer inspection, this opposition between
the two frameworks is not as clear-cut as usually assumed. Traces of the libidinal often resurface in Lyotard's late prose, coexisting alongside other frameworks in more
than one text.[5] Through a journey across three texts bridging the earlier and later
periods of Lyotard's works, I will contend that he did not entirely reject the libidinal framework, but rather reserved its application for an original thinking of "the
system."

Over time, Lyotard's initial transposition of the Freudian energetic model to socioeconomic set-ups evolves to make room for a generalised conceptualisation of
the system. This shift situates Freudian libidinal economy in continuity with systemic models present in modern physics and evolutionary biology, as well as political
economy. As we shall see, libidinal economy is not merely replaced with the phrastic
framework and a thinking of infancy and unconscious affect; the libidinal framework persists, albeit in a secondary way, providing for a description of the forces
that drive "the system," and coexisting alongside this later framework to allow for a
thinking of the system's links with the question of terror.

1968: "March 23"

In August 1971, three years before publishing *Libidinal Economy*, Lyotard wrote an introduction to a book he never completed. Lyotard intended it to be a "history" of
the Movement of March 22, a leftist movement generally considered one of the first

---

2   Jean-François Lyotard, "Emma: Between Philosophy and Psychoanalysis," trans. M. Sanders
     with R. Brons and N. Martin, in *Lyotard: Philosophy, Politics and the Sublime*, ed. Hugh Silverman
     (NY: Routledge, 2002), 34.

3   Jean-François Lyotard, *Peregrinations: Law, Form, Event* (NY: Columbia UP, 1988), 13.

4   Jean-François Lyotard, "The Affect-Phrase (From a Supplement to The Differend)," trans. Keith
     Crome, in *The Lyotard Reader and Guide*, ed. Keith Crome and James William (Edinburgh: Ed-
     inburgh UP, 2006).

5   For instance, in 1994, two major works of Lyotard's earlier "libidinal period" were reprinted
     with Galilée, both augmented with new prefaces by the author; in tone these are far from
     solely retrospective, let alone apologetic: *Dérives à partir de Marx et Freud* (partly translated
     as *Driftworks*), and *Des dispositifs pulsionnels* ("Libidinal Set-Ups"), originally published in 1973
     and 1974 respectively. Neither of these books has been published extensively in English, but
     selected essays have been translated and collected in *Driftworks*, ed. Richard McKeon (Los
     Angeles: Semiotext(e), 1984) and *Political Writings*, trans. and ed. Bill Readings with Kevin
     Paul Geiman (London: University College London, 1993).

student revolts of the year 1968 that led to the events of May.[6] Lyotard begins by locating his interest in the movement in its generalised critique of representation in
the socio-political field – a critique not reserved for institutionalised forms of politics only, such as the party or the union, but understanding "politics" in the broadest
sense, traversing all spheres of life and social activity. While Lyotard distances himself from what he considers to be the movement's naïve ideal of a life beyond any
form of mediation and representation, governed only by spontaneity, immediacy,
and autonomy, he applauds the movement's critical power. He perceives this precisely as an invitation to "get beyond the opposition between spontaneity and mediation, between the masses and the apparatus, between life and the institution,"
and develop new critical weapons. And he adds, "With Freud (but not with Marcuse
or Reich), one can begin to perceive and roughly sketch out that 'beyond' that Marx
left undeveloped."[7] To take up this challenge, Lyotard turns to Freud to elaborate a
thought of the institution as an energetic system, and to find in his libidinal economy an alternative to the symbolic and semantic models put forward by structural
linguistics. These, to Lyotard, did not allow thinking the event's force, or – which
amounts to the same thing – thinking the event as force.[8]

In the early economic model developed in the *Project for a Scientific Psychology*
(1895), Freud describes the psychic apparatus as a regulator of energies that captures (channels or represses) the unbound energies of the drives. Likewise, Lyotard
proposes considering socioeconomic institutions according to an energetic model:

> One can imagine any society as an ensemble of persons ruled by a system whose
> function would be to regulate the entry, the distribution, and the elimination of
> the energy that this ensemble spends in order to exist. "Objects" ... would be spec-
> ifications, concretions of this energy; institutions would be operators that make
> this energy usable by the ensemble, make it circulate within. The institution, far
> from being only what presents itself as such to the observer, would in general be
> any stable formation, explicit or not, transforming incoming energy into bound
> energy within a given field of the circulation of objects.[9]

---

6   On March 22, 1968, students occupied the administrative building of Université Paris Nan-
    terre in protest of the arrest of six activists against the Vietnam War. The "Movement of March
    22," a spontaneist movement using direct action methods and refusing institutionalisation,
    was founded three days later. Lyotard's text was published under the title "*Le 23 Mars*" ("March
    23") in the 1973 collection *Dérives à partir de Marx et Freud* (Paris: Galilée, 1994), 107–115, and
    was included in the English volume of Lyotard's *Political Writings*.

7   Lyotard, "March 23," 63.

8   Lyotard, "March 23," 64.

9   Lyotard, "March 23," 63.

Lyotard defines societies as being governed by such systems (economic systems of exchange, social institutions), which are designed to capture, transform, or eliminate energies. Capitalism is but one such system of regulation. It has the property of being "structured as a regulator of growth."[10] Capitalism allows, in principle, the introduction and elimination of ever-increasing quantities of energy.

In this context, Lyotard proposes defining an event as "the impact, on the system, of floods of energy such that the system does not manage to bind and channel this energy."[11] In the case of the capitalist system, Lyotard ascribes such a failure to process incoming energies to two possible configurations. The first configuration involves the capitalist system's friction with "precapitalist social regions," such as religion, family, or labour, which the system fails to integrate because they are incompatible with its principle of exchange value.[12] Lyotard immediately notes that this configuration no longer seems decisive at the end of the 20th century, when capitalism has largely made these institutions obsolete.

The second configuration is internal to the system and occurs when the incoming energy no longer lets itself be "captured, bound or circulated in the 'objects' of the system."[13] The cause of this failure to bind incoming energies can lie either in an overload of energies, or in a defect of the regulatory system itself. Crises of overproduction, where the quantities of incoming energy are too significant to be processed by the system, are an example of a crisis induced by an energy overload. Lyotard notes that while they can gravely endanger the system, such crises ultimately reinforce it. Analysing them "provides the system with the chance to improve its capacity to bind energy."[14] However, next to this quantitative order of events, Lyotard notes the existence of "a much more enigmatic, qualitative order of events."[15] In these, the failure to channel incoming energies does not come from an overabundance of these energies, but from the qualitative incapability of the regulating system itself – which used to function perfectly until, inexplicably, it no longer did.

In drawing an analogy between the libidinal economy laid out by Freud and his own energetic account of social regulation, Lyotard reintroduces the libidinal within socioeconomic mechanisms, and posits that any social system is underpinned by a position of desire. He writes, "the objects that appear within the system are set up so that desire ... is fulfilled in their production and in their destruction."[16] Describing the energetic system that regulates societies as a system that channels libidinal

10   Lyotard, "March 23," 64.
11   Lyotard, "March 23," 64.
12   Lyotard, "March 23," 64.
13   Lyotard, "March 23," 64.
14   Lyotard, "March 23," 65.
15   Lyotard, "March 23," 65.
16   Lyotard, "March 23," 65.

fluxes into objects allows Lyotard to elaborate an explanation for this second qualitative order of events: it is "an inexplicable mutation in the position of desire," whereby desire can no longer be fulfilled or repressed in the objects that used to channel it.[17] The institution, as a regulating system, mysteriously becomes unable to bind and process the incoming energy. Although the system used to function perfectly, it suddenly became obsolete.

May '68 is an event according to all three configurations. A symptom of crises in universities and society at large, this anti-institutional movement, by attempting to propose solutions, is also bound to become an institution itself and thus contribute to regulating energies. To Lyotard, the specificity and import of the movement of March 22 does not lie in its political impact – whereby it is bound to reinforce the system – but precisely in its anti-political work and unbinding potentialities: "it owes its proper dimension to the space that it has created, even though it is minimal and violated by ideologies, for a mutation in the relationship between what is desired and what is given, between potential energy and the social machinery."[18] May '68, to a certain extent, disrupted how the system channelled energies and involved a qualitative mutation in the position of desire, which had the potential to make the system obsolete. As an event, it opened the possibility of undoing the system; even the possibility of its collapse, Lyotard dares to say (with considerable precautions).

This utopian revolutionary opening, afforded by the unbinding work of the death drive, is immediately obfuscated by the weight of ideologies, and a certain sense of discomfort can be felt throughout the text of Lyotard's incomplete introduction. When he participated in the Movement of March 22, Lyotard had already left *Socialisme ou Barbarie*. He had dedicated twelve years of his life to this radical Marxist group and had, by 1968, lost faith in the revolutionary destiny of the proletariat and a global alternative to the capitalist system.[19] "March 23" and other texts of the period seek to develop an alternative to the Marxist framework's perceived loss of relevance for the late 20th century – and perhaps save the idea of a revolution. The texts bear the trace of this tenacious scepticism. While this theory shows that a mutation in the position of desire is necessary for a revolution of the system, it fails to identify possible causes for such a mutation, let alone strategies to precipitate it. Eventually,

---

17   Lyotard, "March 23," 65.

18   Lyotard, "March 23," 65.

19   In his new preface to the 1994 re-edition of *Dérives à partir de Marx et Freud* with Galilée (9–10), Lyotard bears witness to this uncomfortable gap between his intimate theoretical conviction and his active participation to the movement. It is in his tribute to Pierre Souyri titled "A Memorial for Marxism" that Lyotard accounts in most detail for this progressive loss of faith in the Marxist framework for "understanding and transforming the new direction taken by the world after the Second World War," and his *différend* with his Marxist friends: "A Memorial for Marxism," trans. Cecile Lindsay, in *Peregrinations: Law, Form, Event* (NY: Columbia UP, 1988), 45–75.

Lyotard will renounce the revolutionary perspective to adopt a position favouring "resistance." The libidinal framework is not discarded with this shift but rather reassessed and recast within a broader evolutionary perspective to produce an original and powerful theory of "the system."

Globalisation: "Déluge Warning"

In December 1993, Lyotard wrote a new preface for the third edition of *Des Dispositifs Pulsionnels*,[20] 20 years after the collection was first published. Titled "*Avis de Déluge*" ("Déluge Warning"), the new preface reassesses and reinvests in the libidinal framework that Lyotard had seemingly set aside for almost two decades. The notion of libidinal set-up relied on an analogy: Lyotard transposed Freud's metapsychology to social and representational systems. By recontextualising Freud's economic hypothesis within the history of ideas, showing its indebtedness to modern physics and evolutionary biology, and reminding his readers of the historic filiation of evolutionary biology and liberal economics, Lyotard suggests that this transposition is not to be entirely discarded as a theoretical *coup de force*. On the contrary, by representing the psychic apparatus according to the model of an energetic system, "Freud did more than a comparison. He grafted the dynamics that affect souls directly onto those of 'inert' living or social bodies."[21]

Freud's theories are marked by the physical understanding of human physiology that prevailed in the German-speaking world in the 19th century. The model of the psychic apparatus developed in the *Project for a Scientific Psychology* is indebted to the psychophysical research in stimulus-response undertaken by Gustav Fechner and Ernst Weber; the hypothesis of the death drive developed in 1920 in *Beyond the Pleasure Principle* accounts for the principle of entropy formulated in the second law of thermodynamics.[22] Lyotard notes that, in applying the systemic hypothesis to the living, Freud also drew inspiration from Charles Darwin and Herbert Spencer. They, in turn, derived their inspiration from the first theoreticians of eco-

---

20   Jean-François Lyotard, "Avis de Déluge," in *Des dispositifs pulsionnels* (Paris: Galilée, 1994). All translations are mine. The second edition of this volume appeared with Christian Bourgois in 1980.

21   Lyotard, "Avis de Déluge," 11.

22   See Jessica Tran The, Pierre Magistretti, and François Ansermet, "The Epistemological Foundations of Freud's Energetics Model," *Frontiers in Psychology* 9 (October 2018); Jessica Tran The et al., "From the Principle of Inertia to the Death Drive: The Influence of the Second Law of Thermodynamics on the Freudian Theory of the Psychical Apparatus," *Frontiers in Psychology* 11 (February 2020). Lyotard mentioned Fechner and Weber's psychophysics and the import of thermodynamics in "Avis de Déluge," 9 and 11, respectively.

nomic liberalism, Thomas Malthus, Adam Smith, and David Ricardo.[23] Demographics, economics, evolutionary biology, psychophysics – Lyotard describes how a systemic worldview based on mechanical flow, energy exchange and regulation, performativity,[24] and adaptation takes precedence across all fields in the natural and human sciences in the late 18th and 19th centuries. As a result, living beings and societies are regarded as part of a continuum of material systems designed to transform energy and regulate its input and output to optimise its relations with its environment, integrated in an evolutionary perspective.[25] "All matter," writes Lyotard, "is energy concretized in a system. Some systems are enormous, such as the galaxies; others, such as unicellular terrestrial beings, are miniscule." He adds that "all are subject to the principle of entropy: when incoming energy runs out, internal differentiation can no longer be sustained, and the system disappears ... in chaos."[26] Like all systems, human communities risk decomposing and dying if they are no longer supplied with energy; they also seek to optimise their performance to delay this moment.

From unicellular beings to posthuman computers, Lyotard now regards evolution as one long, continuous history of complexification, of which the human psyche is but one stasis – a complexification that, in *Postmodern Fables* (1997), he imagines will continue until "the big solar explosion" destroys the earth in four billion years.[27] Within this picture, the capitalist set-up of liberal democracies is no longer one among various ways to regulate the energies necessary for the system and to control potentially unsettling events, as was the case in Lyotard's earlier descriptions: rather, it is now considered the latest and most up-to-date organisational form of an ever complexifying energetic system. As opposed to other forms of social organisation, this system can always adapt: "it is programmed to capture new sources of natural energy" and optimise the productivity of human labour.[28] Lyotard now views this form of organisation as irreversible: all crises are occasions

---

23   Darwin's influence on Freud as well as the influence of the liberal economists on Darwin has been widely studied. See, for instance, Lucille B. Ritvo, *Darwin's Influence on Freud: A Tale of Two Sciences* (New Haven: Yale UP, 1990); Silvan S. Schweber, "Darwin and the Political Economists: Divergence of Character," *Journal of the History of Biology* 13, no. 2 (1980).

24   In *The Postmodern Condition*, Lyotard defines "performativity" as "the optimisation of the global relationship between input and output," that is, a principle according to which the system constantly improves its performance/efficiency. This, he states, is "the true goal of the system" and the only alternative to entropy: Jean-François Lyotard, *The Postmodern Condition: A Report on Knowledge*, trans. Geoff Bennington and Brian Massumi (Minneapolis: University of Minnesota Press, 1984), 11–12.

25   Lyotard, "Avis de Déluge," 9.

26   Lyotard, "Avis de Déluge," 11.

27   Jean-François Lyotard, "A Postmodern Fable," in *Postmodern Fables*, trans. Georges Van Den Abbeele (Minneapolis: University of Minnesota Press, 1997).

28   Lyotard, "Avis de Déluge," 12.

to improve its efficiency. In this updated framework, the possibility of a sudden "qualitative" mutation of the regulatory system – the possibility of a revolution – seems to have disappeared.

It could seem that the libidinal framework has been entirely diluted, even liquidated, within this predominantly mechanistic panorama. However, if Lyotard elaborates an energetic theory of "the system" that governs the West, shedding light on the ideological roots that underlie its functioning (such as input/output optimisation, efficiency, and competitiveness), he also theorises the crucial contribution made by Freudian thought for understanding the unconscious motives that drive this system. Indeed, "with the hypothesis of the drives, Freud complicates the mechanistic picture" inherited from Fechnerian psychophysics.[29] Freud postulates that the channelling of energetic flows is not a simple matter of engineering but that it is rushed by the anxiety about flooding the system. As opposed to the external energies that are fed into mechanical systems according to a model of input–output (or stimulus–response), the source of the drive is not external but internal; it is not intermittent but constant, and can only be attested through its psychic effects, as it activates representations. The psychic apparatus is designed to regulate and transform these internal energies. It builds barriers to avoid the self becoming submerged by the constant thrust of the drives: "the psychic apparatus supports itself by repressing a threatening overflow."[30]

Lyotard associates this erratic overflow of energies with the polymorphous perversity defined by Freud in his 1905 *Three Essays on the Theory of Sexuality*. This perversity is characteristic of infantile sexuality, before the Ego is formed and defence mechanisms set in, before the *infans* gradually learns to channel libidinal flows towards specific outlets rather than others. And as we shall see, this turn to infantile sexuality will allow Lyotard to connect the libidinal framework developed in the 1970s with a thinking of affect (or *infantia*) based on a model of primary repression developed in other texts after *The Differend*. The philosopher notes that Eros (the principle of organisation, cohesion, and complexification) and the death drive (which tends to bring the living back to an anorganic state by suppressing all tensions) are two regimes according to which the tension occasioned by this overflow of energies can be solved. As mentioned earlier, Freud's 1920 formulation of the death drive accounts for the principle of entropy formulated with the second law of thermodynamics: Eros and the death drive are *mutatis mutandis* psychoanalytical names for negentropy and entropy. Emphasising the structural similarities of Freud's theory of the psychic apparatus with principles governing other systemic organisations, Lyotard postulates that any activity regulating the energetic flows within a system

---

29   Lyotard, "Avis de Déluge," 9.

30   Lyotard, "Avis de Déluge," 10: "Le dispositif psychique se soutient de refouler un débordement menaçant."

is based on repressing an anxiety: namely, the system's submersion under a déluge of undifferentiated energy.

This provides Lyotard with a framework to describe the situation of the West at the turn of the millennium:

> [After the crisis of 1929], it became obvious that global capitalism had to find remedies to so-called overproduction other than speculation, unemployment, totalitarianisms, and, ultimately, the massacre of about sixty million human beings. After its reconstruction, the system worked, euphoric about its growth, oblivious of its crimes. But now it finds itself confronted with the turn of the millennium; and for a long time, with a double, deadly threat: the necessity of integrating and employing the potential energies localised in the Third World and in what is left of the Second after the collapse of the Soviet empire, on the one hand; and on the other hand, the urgency of solving the question, this time internal, of employment within the so-called developed regions of the world, where technoscientific development makes an ever-increasing proportion of the traditional human workforce once and for all useless. All it needs is brains and fingers skilled with the keyboard.
> Here again is the anxiety of an outpouring of undifferentiated energy ... All barriers built against this rising tide bear the mark of *this* anxiety: foreigners, nobodies, pariahs, anything that proliferates, has no home, no job ... is filtered, repressed, sometimes foreclosed.[31]

Thirty years later, this diagnosis continues to resonate cruelly with the realities of the necropolitical governance prevalent in Western countries. By shedding light on the scientific and ideological roots of a systemic vision of the world, Lyotard develops a framework that allows us to account for the obsession with flows and performativity that drives the West and serves as a justification to turn the lives of billions of human beings, in what is now called the Global South and in increasing fractions of Western countries, into disposable energies.

This theoretical framework goes beyond the libidinal, properly speaking, and mobilises what Lyotard calls a global "political economy of forces."[32] However, it includes and builds on an analysis of the capitalist libidinal economy. It allows us to see how capitalist liberalism is sustained by a lifting of inhibitions and a liberation of libidinal flows – on the condition, Lyotard emphasises, "that these put the system to work (*fassent travailler le système*)" and increase its performativity.[33] Everything that escapes the law of the exchange – the absolute, the Law, the erratic flow of energies that threaten to overflow, death, infancy – is foreclosed. Before further exploring

---

31   Lyotard, "Avis de Déluge," 12.
32   Lyotard, "Avis de Déluge," 13.
33   Lyotard, "Avis de Déluge," 13.

the consequences of the challenges outlined by Lyotard and questioning their relevance today, I will turn to one last text, where Lyotard explores the link between the capitalist system's libidinal economy and the question of terror and totalitarianism.

"The system" and the question of terror: "Survivor"

In 1988, the Goethe Institute in Paris invited Lyotard to speak about the works of Hannah Arendt.[34] Lyotard titled his lecture "Survivor" (*Survivant*); he devoted the end of this intervention to considering Arendt's treatment of totalitarianism, in a way that unexpectedly brings Freud's economic framework into play.

In *Between Past and Future* (first published in 1961), Arendt compares the organisation of the totalitarian system to the structure of an onion.[35] Unlike the pyramidal structure of authoritarianism, or the structure of tyranny, which places the ruler above everyone else, totalitarianism is organised in concentric strata. The leader is placed at the core, and each subsequent stratum is marked by decreasing degrees of commitment and radicality; the further removed it is from the centre, the less extremist, the more "realist" each stratum appears to the previous strata, and vice versa. Such a structure, according to Arendt, allows the totalitarian system to be shielded from potential threats posed by the factuality of the real world. Lyotard suggests that this onion-like shielding structure likens totalitarianism to an apparatus designed to block excitations: "Hypothetically, politics could change reality; totalitarian politics could change it totally: when the onion, a system of complete (two-way) filtering of the real, with the aim of transforming reality into ideology or culture."[36] At this point, Lyotard departs from Arendt's model and analysis to propose a Freudian reading of the totalitarian system. Lyotard suggests that what requires filtering is not the factuality of reality but the excitations – the anxiety – it produces.

But what, within the so-called "real world," could cause an anxiety so great that it could lead to the extermination of millions? To Lyotard, an external description of the mechanisms of the totalitarian system is insufficient, as is merely describing them in energetic terms as an apparatus of repression or filtering. He aims to locate the *source* of the anxiety he has identified. And to him, facts (or groups of people) are not anxiety-producing in themselves; they only produce anxiety and activate mechanisms of repression insofar as they awaken something foreclosed at the system's core. Here, Lyotard turns away from the libidinal economic framework to em-

---

34   Jean-François Lyotard, "Survivor: Arendt," trans. Robert Harvey and Kiff Bamford, in *Readings in Infancy*, eds. Robert Harvey and Kiff Bamford (London: Bloomsbury, 2023), 39–60.

35   Hannah Arendt, *Between Past and Future: Eight Exercises in Political Thought* (NY: Penguin Books, 1993), 99–100.

36   Lyotard, "Survivor," 53.

brace a thinking of *Nachträglichkeit* (belatedness) and originary repression, which had become prevalent in his works after *The Differend*. This framework allows him to think the persistence, within the psychic apparatus yet unbeknownst to it, of an unconscious affect, a Thing (*das Ding*, in the Lacanian sense), bound to elude consciousness. Establishing a parallel between the structures of Western thought and the psychic apparatus, Lyotard postulates an unconscious affect at the core of Western thought that escapes the grasp of consciousness; an immanent terror that is not identified as such, forever irrepresentable, immemorial.[37] And he concludes that "for such a powerful instrument of foreclosure, of forgetting, as totalitarianism to be fabricated, the Thing must appear extremely threatening.... That is where the origin of totalitarianism is to be found."[38]

Lyotard also concludes by suggesting that this source of the spirit of totalitarianism did not run dry with the defeat of historic totalitarian regimes. Indeed, he identifies ways in which the spirit of totalitarianism survives today, two of which I will now briefly outline. First, Arendt shows that totalitarian systems do not maintain their power via professional criminals but from a well-organised mass of conscientious employees. To Lyotard, these "philistines" are "ordinary folk" for whom busyness is a diversion (in a Pascalian sense) from any consciousness of nothingness, or of an ontological debt.[39] And, of course, Lyotard suggests that this was just as true for the 1930s as it was at the end of the 20th century. In both eras, the mind's forces are *put to use* and exclusively geared towards a so-called *active life* – indeed, towards business and entertainment. Second, in *The Origins of Totalitarianism* (1951), Arendt argues that terror is the realisation of laws of movement, whose aim is neither the wellbeing of humans in general nor the interest of one person in particular, but the fabrication of humankind. With totalitarianism, Nature or History are no longer sources of authority stabilising people's actions. Instead, they are regarded as movements, supra-human forces called upon to justify that terror is mobilised to realise their law, and that groups of people be eliminated to allow for fabricating humankind. All energies are mobilised towards that goal. Lyotard claims that the contemporary system no longer requires lives to be exterminated for all energies to

---

37   Lyotard outlines this analogy between the unconscious affect haunting the psychic apparatus and the "immanent terror" most precisely in *Heidegger and "the Jews,"* trans. Andreas Michel and Mark Roberts, (Minneapolis: Minnesota UP, 1990). See in particular sections 5 to 7, 15–23. For an account of Lyotard's thinking on affect, see Claire Nouvet, "The Inarticulate Affect. Lyotard and Psychoanalytic Testimony," in *Minima Memoria. Essays in the Wake of Jean-François Lyotard*, ed. Claire Nouvet, Kent Still, and Zrinka Stahuljak (Stanford: Stanford UP, 2007), 106–122. See also Claire Nouvet, "For 'Emma,'" in *Traversals of Affect: On Jean-François Lyotard*, ed. Julie Gaillard, Claire Nouvet, and Mark Stoholski (London: Bloomsbury, 2016), 37–54.

38   Lyotard, "Survivor," 53–4.

39   Lyotard, "Survivor," 54.

be mobilised towards its goal. Development is a law of movement that maximises the effect described by Arendt of a total mobilisation of all energies against entropy, according to a criterion of performativity.[40] As such, human beings are valued as productive energies, while as legal, moral, or singular persons, they are superfluous.

However, following Ernst Jünger, Lyotard argues that the democratic system and the adjustment of the law towards elevating living standards are much more powerful strategies for mobilisation than the totalitarian tools of the 1930s because they are much more acceptable to ordinary people. Propaganda is replaced by the soft rhetorics of seemingly pluralistic media. Interfaces are multiplied, no longer according to the structure of an onion, but now in networks. Delays between stimuli and responses are reduced to a level where they become imperceptible – everything happens "in real time." In the contemporary system, space and time are saturated – a saturation that, Lyotard suggests, is precisely designed to fend off excitations and repress anything that would diminish the system's efficiency:

> Massificaiton and survival, mobilization and saturation, and foreclosure are obtained more efficiently by an organization through communicational networks than by totalitarian politics. I know how brutal this diagnosis is. I very well that development is indeed a development with regard to a traditional society. I am aware of the advantages of democracy.[41]

Of course, Lyotard's analysis does not amount to naively equating the system of contemporary development with historic totalitarian regimes. In demonstrating certain analogies in their structures as well as similitudes in their function concerning this immanent, terrifying source, Lyotard suggests that one of their key differences lies in the fact that development does not – at least not for Western populations at the end of the 20th century – rely on terror to realise the law of its movement. But this does not mean it structurally excludes terror; it simply means that development as a law of movement does not need to resort to terror as long as democratic life provides for the most efficient mobilisation of energies.

As we have seen through this series of texts, the libidinal economic framework does not disappear entirely from Lyotard's writings after he allegedly abandons it in favour of a pragmatic framework. While the presence and import of Freud's economic model clearly remains marginal across Lyotard's works after *The Differend*, it is nevertheless an essential reference when describing the mechanisms of the capitalist system, combined with the energetic models inherited from evolutionary biology and thermodynamics. Should Lyotard's diagnosis of the capitalist system's ir-

40   Lyotard, "Survivor," 56.
41   Lyotard, "Survivor," 58.

reversibility – that is, his loss of faith in the possibility of a global revolution – be discarded among the discourses on "the end of history" and situated in the context of the collapse of the Soviet block and late 20th-century globalisation? On the contrary, his diagnosis – which precludes a global revolutionary perspective, but not local movements of resistance – anticipated developments 21st-century neoliberalism and the corollary surge of anxiety and revivification of terror that the world faces today.

In lieu of a conclusion, let me finish with an image. A bright yellow stream gushes into the avenue, interrupting a black stream of consumers and onlookers. A bright yellow crowd occupies a periurban roundabout, blocking the productive flows of individuals and goods irrigating the system. Yet, if we consider the irruption of the Yellow Vests movement as an event in Lyotard's sense – in the sense of a flood of energies such that the regulating system does not manage to process or bind them – then this event is "quantitative," and not "qualitative." Sociologically, the heterogeneous Yellow Vests movement comprises precarious or proletarianised workers from the lower middle classes with no prior activist experience.[42] They belong to a group that used to take pride in working hard and making do, but for whom capitalism no longer bears a promise of material comfort and upward mobility. They now demand that their lives be considered more than merely energies to feed the system. In a country where mechanisation and 40 years of deindustrialisation have led to a chronic unemployment rate of ten per cent, in a system where humans are not primarily regarded as citizens endowed with rights but as resources to be managed to generate growth, their revolt states that the system is no longer tolerable to the humans that compose it. Initially, the Yellow Vests movement did not involve a demand for a revolution of the system but a demand that the promises of social justice, equality, and dignity (associated with the imaginary of the French Revolution) be upheld, and for reforms that would allow the workers' inclusion in democratic life and socioeconomic prosperity.[43] This movement only confirms Lyotard's observation that social struggles at the turn of the 21st century are no longer struggles to acquire more rights. They are struggles to defend rights already acquired – or to demand that the equality of rights be transformed into real equality. And this makes all the more worrisome the violent repression that the protesters' demands have met.

Outlining the "political economy of forces" and the challenges that would arise with globalisation in the 21st century, Lyotard noted that it would be necessary to reorganise the set-ups designed to channel forces in the system to integrate the vast amounts of energies from the former Soviet regime and the rest of the world. At the

---

42   For a detailed description of the sociological profile of the Yellow Vests, see Laurent Jean-pierre, *In Girum. Les leçons politiques des ronds-points* (Paris: La Découverte, 2019), 73–89.

43   Symbols of the French Revolution have been massively reactivated by participants of this movement.

end of his 1993 preface to the third re-edition of *Des dispositifs pulsionnels*, he asked, "Who can say that such a challenge will be overcome, and how? Will it be possible to avoid new massacres? Won't the principle of international law soon appear inappropriate for 'good' management of flows?"[44] Obviously, the tens of thousands of people dying at the gates of Europe, the walls built throughout the West, and the number of people maimed or killed in the repression of democratic movements in France and elsewhere, 25 years after Lyotard's text was written, provide a negative answer. The system perfectly accommodates right-wing populist movements, nationalist rationales, and authoritative regimes. Their racism, walls, and borders contribute to reinforcing the system's efficiency; they afford eliminating surplus flows of humans whose energies are no longer useful to the system. On the contrary, when the discontent caused by the inhuman mechanisms of the system is expressed as a demand for respect for human rights and democracy, then these demands are repressed – they endanger the system, as democracy no longer contributes to increasing the efficiency of the system but, rather, tends to slow it down.

Lyotard's theory shows that the inhumanity of neoliberal governance is not an unfortunate side effect of its rule of performativity. The system is a powerful machine precisely designed to foreclose any event that would escape its grasp and control, anything that cannot be integrated to enhance its efficiency. It is designed to repress the immemorial, immanent, constitutive terror at the core of humans and humanity. Until the end of Lyotard's career, Freud's economic framework remained a useful tool to describe how this "forgetting" is organised. However, most of Lyotard's conceptual effort would focus on bearing witness to the Thing that escapes any memory and phrasing. And this act of bearing witness, a crucial, yet minuscule act of political resistance, is no longer a matter of energy or desire.

References

Arendt, Hannah. *Between Past and Future: Eight Exercises in Political Thought*. NY: Penguin Books, 1993.

Jeanpierre, Laurent. *In Girum. Les leçons politiques des ronds-points*. Paris: La Découverte, 2019.

Lyotard, Jean-François. *Driftworks*. Edited by Richard McKeon. Los Angeles: Semiotext(e), 1984.

———. *The Postmodern Condition: A Report on Knowledge*. Translated by Geoff Bennington and Brian Massumi. Minneapolis: University of Minnesota Press, 1984.

———. *Peregrinations: Law, Form, Event*. NY: Columbia UP, 1988.

---

44   Lyotard, "Avis de Déluge," 13.

———. *Heidegger and "the Jews."* Translated by Andreas Michel and Mark Roberts. Minneapolis: University of Minnesota Press, 1990.

———. "March 23." In *Political Writings*, translated and edited by Bill Readings with Kevin Paul Geiman, 60–67. London: University College London, 1993.

———. "Avis de Déluge." In *Des dispositifs pulsionnels*, 9–15. Paris: Galilée, 1994.

———. "A Postmodern Fable." In *Postmodern Fables*, translated by Georges Van Den Abbeele, 83–101. Minneapolis: University of Minnesota Press, 1997.

———. "Emma: Between Philosophy and Psychoanalysis." Translated by M. Sanders with R. Brons and N. Martin. In *Lyotard: Philosophy, Politics and the Sublime*, edited by Hugh Silverman, 23–45. NY: Routledge, 2002.

———. "The Affect-Phrase (From a Supplement to The Differend)." Translated by Keith Crome. In *The Lyotard Reader and Guide*, edited by Keith Crome and James William, 104–110. Edinburgh: Edinburgh UP, 2006.

———. "Survivor." In *Readings in Infancy*, translated and edited by Robert Harvey and Kiff Bamford, 39–60. London: Bloomsbury, 2023.

Nouvet, Claire. "The Inarticulate Affect. Lyotard and Psychoanalytic Testimony." In *Minima Memoria. Essays in the Wake of Jean-François Lyotard*, edited by Claire Nouvet, Kent Still, and Zrinka Stahuljak, 106–122. Stanford: Stanford UP, 2007.

———. "For 'Emma.'" In *Traversals of Affect: On Jean-François Lyotard*, edited by Julie Gaillard, Claire Nouvet, and Mark Stoholski, 37–54. London: Bloomsbury, 2016.

Ritvo, Lucille B. *Darwin's Influence on Freud: A Tale of Two Sciences*. New Haven: Yale UP, 1990.

Schweber, Silvan S. "Darwin and the Political Economists: Divergence of Character." *Journal of the History of Biology* 13, no. 2 (1980): 195–289. https://doi.org/10.1007/BF00125744

Tran The, Jessica, Pierre Magistretti, and François Ansermet. "The Epistemological Foundations of Freud's Energetics Model." *Frontiers in Psychology* 9 (October 2018). https://doi.org/10.3389/fpsyg.2018.01861

Tran The, Jessica, Jean-Philippe Ansermet, Pierre Ansermet, Pierre Magistretti, and François Ansermet. "From the Principle of Inertia to the Death Drive: The Influence of the Second Law of Thermodynamics on the Freudian Theory of the Psychical Apparatus." *Frontiers in Psychology* 11 (February 2020). https://doi.org/10.3389/fpsyg.2020.00325

Negative Solidarity: The Affective Economy in Neoliberalism's Decline

Jason Read

Spinoza's question of political thought, "why do the masses fight for their servitude as if it was salvation," has taken on an unanticipated economic and social relevance since the post-2008 economic recession. With that question now displaced from its 17th-century context of taxes and bread, wars of glory, and despots, it is possible to see a struggle for servitude in how the masses clamour for more jobs, more austerity, and further persecuting the disadvantaged in the name of fiscal discipline. In a post on the blog *Splintering Bone Ashes*, Alex Williams has dubbed this particular struggle for servitude "negative solidarity." Williams defined it as "an aggressively enraged sense of injustice, committed to the idea that, because I must endure increasingly austere working conditions (wage freezes, loss of benefits, declining pension funds, erasure of job security and increasing precarity) then everyone else must too."[1]

We can point to multiple instances of negative solidarity, and with them, a changing trajectory of both imagination and affect as its meaning (i.e., its objects and narratives) shift. There is the iconic figure of the "welfare queen," and with her, the entire racialised demonisation of benefit programs for the unemployed and impoverished. There is also the migrant figure, likewise chastised for dependency and laziness on the one hand and sometimes for "stealing jobs" on the other. More recently, negative solidarity has been aimed at the public services worker – the teacher or government employee who continues to benefit, albeit ever so slightly, from union protection and collective bargaining. Such workers are seen as failing to engage in the necessary discipline and suffering of work. That "negative solidarity" can take on so many different figures – mostly pure fantasies disconnected from actual conditions – suggests that, at its core, it articulates an imagination and a particular structure of feeling. It is not so much a reflection of actual conditions and real relations as of a particular way of representing or perceiving those conditions. Articulating and elaborating a definition of negative solidarity entails a necessary

---

1   Alex Williams, "Negative Solidarity and Post-Fordism," *Splintering Bone Ashes* (blog), January 31, 2010, https://splinteringboneashes.blogspot.com/2010/01/negative-solidarity-and-post-fordist.html.

detour through affective economy. The affective economy is understood in two senses: first, that the economy (i.e., the relations of production and distribution) circulates and produces affects, sensibilities and desires, as much as goods and services, and second, that these affects are a necessary element of producing and reproducing the very conditions of work.

Affective economy: A definition

According to Gilles Deleuze and Félix Guattari, Spinoza did not just pose the question of negative solidarity (of why people fight for their servitude as if it was salvation) but also offered the basis of an answer. To grasp how, as Deleuze and Guattari put it, "desire of the most disadvantaged creature will invest with all its strength, irrespective of any economic understanding or lack of it, the capitalist social field as a whole,"[2] it is necessary to think of desire's immanence to the economy. Desire must be posited as part of the infrastructure, without passing through the mediations of ideology, the family, or the state. Deleuze and Guattari's provocation exceeds their articulation in *Anti-Oedipus* to become a general problem of contemporary Marxist thought: there is a general turn towards understanding subjectivity to be not only directly produced by the economy (i.e., without passing through superstructural mediations), but also reproducing the economy as well (i.e., to be a necessary condition of social reproduction).[3] This insight is found in Deleuze and Guattari's work and Althusser's re-examination of ideology and reproduction. It is also apparent in neo-Spinozists such as Frédéric Lordon and Yves Citton. The causes of this conceptual change, no doubt complex and numerous, have as much to do with the changing nature of capitalism itself as with the history of worker and student struggle. As capital requires more intensive, cooperative, and relational work, it needs a subject that is not just docile and compliant, showing up for work each day, but also actively desires to be put to work. They must fully identify with their work. Spinoza's identity of bodies and ideas makes it possible to grasp an economy increasingly predicated on the identity of economy and subjectivity.

---

2   Gilles Deleuze and Félix Guattari, *Anti-Oedipus: Capitalism and Schizophrenia*, trans. Robert Hurley, Mark Seem, and Helen R. Lane (Minneapolis: University of Minnesota, 1983), 229.

3   "Instead of adding a theory of the 'superstructure' to the existing theory of the structure, he [Althusser] aims at transforming the concept of the structure itself by showing that its process of 'production' and 'reproduction' *originarily* depends on unconscious ideological conditions. As a consequence a social formation is no longer representable in dualistic terms – a thesis that logically should lead us to abandon the image of the 'superstructure.' Another concept of historical complexity must be elaborated, with opposite sociological, anthropological, and ontological prerequisites": Etienne Balibar, "The Non-Contemporaneity of Althusser," in *The Althusserian Legacy*, ed. E. Ann Kaplan and Michael Sprinker (NY: Verso, 1993), 8.

How does Spinoza, a philosopher from the 17th century, make it possible to grasp this rather recent transformation? First, there is Spinoza's definition of subjectivity, of the human essence, as defined by desire. As Spinoza writes, "desire is the very essence of man insofar as his essence is conceived as determined to any action from any given affection of itself."[4] As much as Spinoza's definition posits a universal essence, it does so in a way both singular (we all have different desires depending on our particular constitution) and relational (our constitutions are the effects of our encounters and relations with others). Put differently, desire is transindividual. Desires are necessarily different and unique, determined by the affections; everyone desires according to their unique history. As Spinoza argues, we do not desire something because it is good. Instead, "we judge something to be good because we strive for it, will it, want it, and desire it."[5] Desire is fundamentally intransitive, lacking a specific telos, object, or orientation. The history of relations determines desire's object and orientations. Everyone strives to increase their joy, their capacity to act and think, but how this joy is defined is partly determined by the history of past encounters. I desire those things that seem to me to be the cause of past joys, even if I am often ignorant of the true causes of my desires or the effects of my attachments.

Everyone equally strives, but not all striving is equal. Spinoza's "conatus," or striving, is always caught between two determinations: (i) the history of encounters that assigns an individual specific objects and desires without adequately grasping their relations, and (ii) the possibility of a life oriented from an adequate comprehension of its conditions and an increase of its joy. These two different determinations are manifested in different senses of joy. One is determined by the encounters and relations that one is subject to, while the other is determined by one's capacities. This ethical division between the passive and active life animates Spinoza's thought. It is, as André Tosel argues, an ethical materialism – a materialism oriented by the division and difference of modes of individuation, considered primarily in terms of their individual, biographical relations. This materialist ethics takes as its terrain of inquiry affects, desire, and imagination as constitutive of subjectivity.[6]

Frédéric Lordon argues that Spinoza's mode of subjection can be expanded beyond the ethical distinction of modes of life to the history of the production and reproduction of subjectivity under capitalism. Doing so entails expanding the encounters that shape one's desires from the biographical to the structural. Spinoza provides an opening of this transition from the ethical to the social when he writes

---

4   Benedict de Spinoza, *Ethics* (1677), in *A Spinoza Reader: The Ethics and Other Works*, trans. and ed. Edwin Curley (NY: Princeton UP, 1994), EIIIDI.

5   Spinoza, *Ethics*, EIIIP9S.

6   André Tosel, *Du Matérialisme de Spinoza* (Paris: Éditions Kimé, 1994), 18.

that "money occupies the mind of the multitude more than anything else."[7] Money is the universal equivalent of desire not just because of past positive experiences in one's biography but also an institutional history – we live in a market society where money is the condition of any desire. Lordon can then map the coordinates of desire's institution onto two axes. The first axis is the division between production and consumption, the two separate spheres of activity in capitalist society. Production and consumption relate to wage labour and the commodity form, the two structural conditions of capitalism. Production and consumption also form the basis of different organisations of desire, joy and sadness. The second axis, drawn from Spinoza, is that of joy or sadness understood as an increase or decrease in one's power and potential.

Using Lordon's coordinates, it is possible to chart desire's history under capital. The first phase corresponds to the initial formation of capitalism, what Marx called formal subsumption. The primary institutional basis for capitalism at this stage is the absence of any alternative to wage labour, destroying the commons or any sustenance economy. Activity, the necessary activity that sustains life, is organised and oriented according to wage labour. To paraphrase Hobbes, who captured the affective composition of primitive accumulation better than Spinoza, "fear" is the "passion to be reckoned with" at this stage of capital.[8] Fear, in this sense, is the idea of future hardship or sadness. Fear is a motive, a driving force orienting the striving, the conatus, but an unstable one. People compelled by fear will work, but only as much as needed to stave off punishment or losing their job. Those who do not work do not eat, and the fear of starvation or homelessness keeps them working. Fear is not only a limited incentive but also a fundamentally unstable one. It can drive one to revolt almost as much as it can compel one to obey. Lordon then maps a second stage that roughly corresponds to Fordism and the rise of consumer society. The institutional effect of Fordism is to destroy the pleasures and pride of concrete labour – the pleasures of a particular skill – in favour of a general shift of desire away from labour towards consumption. Ford's "five-dollar day" establishes an affective economy, exchanging sadness and frustration at work for the pleasures of the newly emergent consumer society.

The final, or at least most recent, change in this affective economy reorients pleasure towards work. However, it is no longer the pleasure of a particular skill or a result but the pleasure of employment itself. It is a desire that is, as much as possible, modelled on abstract labour. The modern subject of capitalism is described by terms stripped of reference to any particular task or activity and instead refer to employability as a general ideal. The modern individual is a professional entrepreneur of him or herself. Formal subsumption, Fordism, neoliberalism – these constitute the

---

7   Spinoza, *Ethics*, EIVAPPXXVIII.
8   Thomas Hobbes, *Leviathan* (1651; reis., Indianapolis: Hackett, 1994), 177.

rough schema of the history of desire under capitalism, of the conatus. It is a history that moves from the negative affects to joyful, from fear to joy, and from consumption to production. A transition that is less a liberation, freedom from fear and wants, than a subjection. It culminates in the modern ideal to find one's realisation, one's passion, in the structure and activity of work itself. The new mantra is "do what you love, and you will never have to work a day in your life." However, in practice, this is less about revaluing a trade, or the pleasures of specific concrete labour, than finding a passion for constantly mobilising one's potential. "Professional" no longer refers to a set of skills or knowledge but a particular subjective comportment of engaged detachment. It is a history in which the gap between the capitalist's interest and the worker's striving shrinks to become barely perceptible. A world of motivated self-starters, or what Lordon calls "joyous automobiles."[9]

Negative solidarity

With the provisional structure of affective economy outlined here, it is possible to map out a subsequent stage beyond Lordon's sketch of neoliberalism, something coming after the affective economy of neoliberal motivation. In *Coming Up Short: Working-Class Adulthood in an Age of Uncertainty*, Jennifer Silva lays out some directions of the affective economy in what could be called late-neoliberalism. Silva examines what happens to lives in the United States during the post-2008 recession. These are the lives of primarily working-class people caught up in debt, with dwindling job prospects, and often living with their parents. They have been denied the promised life of careers, families, and homes of their own – they are mourning the slow decline of the Fordist dream. What Silva finds striking is the lack of any anger or political mobilisation on the part of those left out of the American dream. Being left out of the dream of a steady and linear career does not entirely exclude one from the mythology, from the ideal of work and discipline. As she describes her general findings:

> At its core, this emerging working-class adult self is characterised by low expectations of work, wariness toward romantic commitment, widespread distrust of social institutions, profound isolation from others, and an overriding focus on their emotions and psychic health. Rather than turn to politics to address the obstacles standing in the way of a secure adult life, the majority of the men and women I interview crafted deeply *personal* coming of age stories, grounding their adult identities in recovering from their painful pasts – whether addiction, childhood

---

9   Frédéric Lordon, *Willing Slaves of Capital: Spinoza and Marx on Desire*, trans. Gabriel Ash (2010; reis., NY: Verso, 2014), 53.

abuse, family trauma, or abandonment and forging an emancipated, transformed and adult self.[10]

To describe this shift along the lines outlined by Lordon, we can see a new affective orientation, one sustained neither by consumption (which is too limited, reduced to basic necessities to capture desire), or even production (as work becomes stripped of not only any joys but any fantasy of mobility and accumulation). The failures of consumption or wage labour to offer any joys do not lead to their rejection or a critical attitude to capitalism. What emerges instead is an ideal of work as discipline; self-transformation becomes the source of validation. Personal worth is found not through what one can buy, or even what one can sell of oneself, but in the sense of self-transformation or responsibility for one's condition. In other words, responsibility matters, not the results or outcome.

The focus on self-responsibility, of taking responsibility for overcoming all of one's hardships and traumas, entails a massive distrust of any collective or institutional solution and a corresponding suspicion of those who engage in them. Pride in taking responsibility for one's fate is an attempt to construct a joy, a positive condition, out of a negative sad affect. It attempts to make the difficulty of changing or altering one's condition into a source of pride or joy. Spinoza argues that the mind tends to dwell on things that increase its joy and power.[11] Lordon argues that this effect is not an innate tendency towards affirmation or liberation; rather, it explains how people can put up with the most limited possibilities for joy and power. It is less a line of flight than what keeps us confined in whatever situation we find ourselves. The tendency to affirm joy leads individuals to dwell on those tiny pleasures of the workday, the small talk and casual Fridays, or in this case, the satisfaction and sense of responsibility that stems from relying only on oneself. As the possibility of aspiring for more, even systemic change, is increasingly reduced, the tiny pleasures of daily life are elevated into objects of desire. Lordon describes this double-edged movement as follows:

> symbolic violence consists then properly speaking in the production of a double imaginary, the imaginary fulfilment, which makes the humble joys assigned to the dominated appear sufficient, and the imaginary of powerless, which convinces them to renounce any greater ones to which they might aspire.[12]

---

10   Jennifer M. Silva, *Coming Up Short: Working-Class Adulthood in an Age of Uncertainty* (NY: Oxford, 2013), 11.

11   Spinoza, *Ethics*, EIIIP54.

12   Lordon, *Willing Slaves of Capital*, 110. Note that the translation has been slightly modified here.

We can find a similar affective composition of working conditions and attitudes to-wards work in David Graeber's *Bullshit Jobs*. While Graeber spends much of the book documenting and detailing the prevailing alienation of the pointlessness of a bull-shit job, he also explains why bullshit jobs do not produce universal disdain and even rebellion. As Graeber writes, "workers … gain feelings of dignity and self-worth *be-cause* they hate their jobs."[13] Graeber's formulation inverts the classic definition of alienation in which negative affects, loss of self, purpose, and activity lead to a crit-ical relation to work. Instead, it is because one finds work to be painful, demeaning or difficult that one stays attached. Work finds its justification in and through its difficulty. This becomes, in part, an attachment to that demeaning, difficult or tax-ing dimension as a point of pride. It inverts the basic Spinozist principle that one endeavours to imagine things that increase one's joy and capacity; more precisely, it attempts to imagine one's suffering and incapacity to transform it as a point of pride, converting it to pleasure. Such a transformation of sadness into joy, passivity into activity, has as its necessary condition the sense of being completely overpow-ered and overwhelmed by one's conditions.

This sense of being incapable of changing one's conditions can be real or imag-ined. As Spinoza argues, the imagination of being powerless is the same as being actually powerless because "whatever man imagines he cannot do, he necessarily imagines; and he is so disposed by this imagination that he really cannot do what he imagines he cannot do."[14] Such an imagination has genuine effects not only on how one conducts their life but on how one imagines the conduct of others. As Graeber argues, those who take pride in their work because it is difficult are angry at those who do not work *and* those whose work is not sufficiently difficult or demanding. In recent years in United States politics, teachers and teachers' unions have been held as particular targets of contempt for their job protections, as a unionised workforce; the supposed ease of their job, shorter working days, and summers off; and the fact that their job is perceived to be rewarding. This was summed up in the attempt to identify teachers and other public service workers with the "welfare queen."[15] Oth-ers' joy, real or imagined, becomes the source of resentment. The pride taken in one's work is inseparable from the anger and jealousy one has towards others, or towards what one imagines as their imagined life of pleasure or ease.

If the fulfilment comes from the small pleasures of the workday, or work itself seen as a source of pride, then the imaginary powerlessness comes not just from the contemporary labour situation, which is increasingly subject to the rules of capital

---

13   David Graeber, *Bullshit Jobs: A Theory* (London: Allen Lane, 2018), 242.

14   Spinoza, *Ethics*, EIIIDEFXXVIII.

15   Daniel Martinez Hosang and Joseph E. Lowndes, *Producers, Parasites, Patriots: Race and the New Right-Wing Politics of Precarity* (Minneapolis: Minnesota, 2019), 19.

and profitability, but the overall sense of reduced possibility and resources that per-meate social life. This increased sense of austerity comes from declining wages and a dwindling tax base. As Monica Potts describes the attitudes in Arkansas in a *New York Times* profile:

> There's a prevailing sense of scarcity – it's easy for people who have lived much of their lives in a place where $25 an hour seems like a high salary to believe there just isn't enough money to go around. The government, here and elsewhere, just can't afford to help anyone, people told me. The attitude extends to national issues, like immigration. Where I see needless cruelty, my neighbours see necessary reality.[16]

In this prevailing sense of austerity, an individual's difficulty in paying their bills, their increased debt, is projected outward into a world in which scarcity is the rule and generosity, even equity or justice, is a kind of luxury. It does not matter that this scarcity is artificial, produced in a context of ever-increasing wealth for the wealth-iest one per cent who pocket the proceeds of declining wages and massive tax cuts. What matters is the increasing perception, the image, of limited resources and pos-sibilities. This imaginary of limitation and powerlessness is internalised as a valori-sation of one's toughness, hardness, and discipline. These become the only joys left.

It is possible to understand such a subject as the rugged individual posited against society, which is how it is often presented. The claim of being an individual, free from collective influence or belonging, is as important as being responsible. Such claims cannot be taken at face value. The prevalence of the same attitudes and ideas, the claim from so many disparate and different people to be "an individual" would seem to negate in its enunciation what is being articulated. Such an individ-uation is transindividual even if, in this case, the transindividuation takes on the paradoxical status of refusing any collective relation.

This suggests a "negative individuality" as a necessary corollary of negative soli-darity. This individuality is not only negative in refusing any collective belonging but, ultimately, in its constitution as individual as well. The very conditions that under-mine collective belonging, the persistent sense of precarity and inability to construct a coherent trajectory, also undermine the possibility of individuation, of construct-ing an individual life or identity.[17] The destruction of individuation through labour is augmented by the rise of consumer society – which effectively promises a world of "freedom, equality, and Bentham" – that has turned out to be a world of manufac-

16   Monica Potts, "In the Land of Self Defeat," *The New York Times*, October 4, 2019, https://www.nytimes.com/2019/10/04/opinion/sunday/trump-arkansas.html.

17   Robert Castel, *La montée des incertitudes: Travail, protections, statut de l'individu* (Paris: Éditions du Seuil, 2009), 443.

tured desires and digital surveillance.[18] The negative solidarity that manifests itself as a kind of free-floating anger and frustration has, as its corollary (and condition), individuals tossed and turned by the conflicts of affects and imagination without an ability to even orient individual thought or act.

The sketch of a post-neoliberal subject is a highly ambivalent one. Its ambivalence stems from the ambivalence of the affects, the tendency for every positive affect – joy, hope, love – to be shadowed by its opposite and risk becoming it. In this case, joys and pleasures are not only inseparable from pains and tribulations but a kind of transformation or revalorisation of them. The pride of work is a transformation of pain into pleasure, difficulty into responsibility. It also reveals the connection between striving and the imagination. The attachments to responsibility to a sense of worth found in work are strategies for coping with declining prospects for improved material conditions, for the pleasures of consumer society. They are remnants, often images of bygone conditions and decaying dreams. What we increasingly see in austerity is the oldest myths and legends of capital and capitalist accumulation revived against its current material reality. A moral veneer to the capitalist relation is provided by this revival, not in violent expropriation of the commons but in the narrative of so-called primitive accumulation – the story of the frugal capitalist and lazy worker. As Marx writes:

> This primitive accumulation plays approximately the same role in political economy as original sin does in theology. Adam bit the apple, and thereupon sin fell on the human race. Its origin is supposed to be explained when it is told as an anecdote about the past. Long, long ago there were two sorts of people; one the diligent, intelligent, and above all frugal elite; the other lazy rascals, spending their substance, and more, in riotous living. The legend of theological original sin tells us certainly how man came to be condemned to eat his bread by the sweat of his brow; but the history of economic original sin reveals to us that there are people to whom this is by no means essential. Never mind! Thus it came to pass that the former sort accumulated wealth, and the latter sort finally had nothing to sell except their own skins.[19]

Primitive accumulation persists, not as a myth about the origins of capital but as a lingering morality play about the present. Work, especially work understood as *real* (i.e., coded as productivist, masculine, and often white), is understood to be the source of at least symbolic value, even as its market value declines. As the Bible says, "those who do not work should not eat" – not because their work is necessary for the

---

18   Bernard Stiegler, *Acting Out*, trans. David Barison, Daniel Ross, and Patrick Crogan (Stanford: Stanford UP), 48.

19   Karl Marx, *Capital: A Critique of Political Economy, Volume I*, trans. Ben Fowkes (1867; reis., NY: Penguin, 1977), 873.

community's survival but because it is necessary to make them worthy.[20] Moreover, those who do not sufficiently fit the productivist ideal (teachers, caregivers, bureaucrats) are seen as not really working. Alternatively, to use the parlance of our times, they do not have a "real job."[21] They are suspect as well. The narrative at the heart of primitive accumulation was always defined by temporal displacement; it was an idealised version of the present, the hard worker who saves enough to become a capitalist, projected onto the past, onto capital's origins. Now it is projected into the future, the moral ideal of hard work outlasts its material necessity. As the biological necessity of work retreats into historical memory, and many jobs are far from being necessary in the sense of survival, work continues to be the basis of a moral distinction, separating the good from the bad. What connects the past and the present, the fantasy of survival and the morality of work, is an increasing sense of scarcity and the virtues of difficulty. The story about the moral value of work is all that remains as working time is increased and work itself is subject to the logics of casualization and precarity.

Spinoza's understanding of the constitution of ideas, of the mind as a spiritual automaton, is as important for grasping the contemporary sense of work as his understanding of desire's organisation. It is as much a matter of inadequate ideas as it is the reorganisation of desire. Just as our desire is oriented by our encounters and affects our mind, our thinking is a sort of spiritual automaton shaped by its encounters and relations. As Spinoza argues, so-called universal notions, such as "man" or "dog," often stem more from confusion than comprehension. They are inadequate ideas, unable to grasp or comprehend their genesis. They are particular ideas and impressions passed off as universal ideas. As Spinoza describes this process:

> It should be noted that these notions are not formed by all in the same way, but vary from one to another, in accordance with what the body has more often been affected by, and what the mind imagines or recollects more easily. For example, those who have more often regarded men's stature with wonder will understand by the word *man* an animal of erect stature. But those who have been accustomed to consider something else, will form another common image of men – for example, that man is an animal capable of laughter, or a featherless biped or a rational animal.
>
> And similarly concerning the others – each will form universal images of things according to the disposition of his body. Hence it is not surprising that so many controversies have arisen among the philosophers who have wished to explain natural things by mere images of things.[22]

20   Max Horkheimer, *Dawn and Decline: Notes 1926–1931 and 1950–1960*, trans. Michael Shaw (NY: Seabury Press, 1978), 83.

21   Hosang and Lowndes, *Producers, Parasites, Patriots*, 25.

22   Spinoza, *Ethics*, EIIP40Schol.

Similarly, we could argue that work, labour, and productivity are said in many senses. When it comes to work, there is the general physical notion of energy expended in displacement and transformation; the economic sense, of activity, any activity, done for a wage; the more diffuse sense in which any activity defined by effort and difficulty is dubbed work, such as homework or housework; and, finally, a moral idea of discipline and value attached to the last two meanings. These different meanings of "work" traverse physics, anthropology, economics, and ethics, shifting from natural necessity to specific social relations. The different senses do not only, as the passage from Spinoza indicates, stem from different encounters and relations, in which everyone would have their own personal and idiosyncratic definition, but there is, in every society, an attempt to impose and standardise one definition, imposing its particular sense over all others.

The dominant sense is a motley collection of everything ever believed, made up of remnants of puritan struggle, Fordist promises, and contemporary anxiety. Its anachronisms are tailored to the current conjuncture in which more is demanded of employees and less is offered in exchange. The dominant sense of work is a conjunction of the ethical and the anthropological to support the economic. As Moishe Postone writes, "this apparently transhistorical necessity – that the individual's labour is the necessary means to their (or their family's) consumption – serves as the basis for a fundamental legitimating ideology of the capitalist social formation as a whole, throughout its various cases."[23] The socioeconomic necessity of working to procure commodities is given the veneer of an anthropological or biological necessity for survival. It is this necessity that becomes the basis of its moralisation.

There is a dominant sense of work, a dominant meaning, as much as there is a dominant affective constitution of labour. Negative solidarity can be understood as a particular affective composition oriented around work. In the first instance, this composition is made up of a joy, a joy rescued from sadness and powerlessness. Work is seen as a point of pride precisely because it produces sad affects. Or, if work is unavailable or sporadic, there is still the pride in a kind of discipline and independence. This joy, or this particular transvaluation of sadness into joy, is coupled with a kind of anger or indignation at those perceived not to work hard enough, are not engaged in real work, or who rely on political power or corruption (these things are more or less synonymous) to keep their jobs. This affect, this anger, aimed at everyone from the unemployed who benefit from the last remnants of social protection to those public employees who still have union protections, must be seen as both an exclusion and an inclusion. Of course, the fantasy of the welfare queen far exceeds the reality of existing programs for the unemployed, which have been cut to a bare minimum and increasingly tied to requirements for work. Despite this, there

---

23   Moishe Postone, *Time, Labour, and Social Domination: A Reinterpretation of Marx's Critical Theory* (Cambridge: Cambridge University, 1996), 161.

is still a popular bumper sticker in the United States defining this particular kind of indignation: "Keep Working: Millions on Welfare Depend on You." The person affixing such a bumper sticker is not just angry at the person supposedly living off of their labour, but as it addresses, or interpellates, its imagined audience, it draws them together in shared indignation. There is a sense of a "we," a collectivity of "real" workers, "real Americans," an imagined universality, albeit a weak one, defined by both work as an ethical norm and basis of community. This norm only exists in its violation, in the sense of indignation at those who do not work. This is what puts the solidarity in negative solidarity. There is a unity, a community, albeit loosely defined in and through their shared engagement in work, in productive work. Work that is defined through both its physical difficulty, or at least the stoic fortitude it takes to endure it; its economic centrality, or perceived economic centrality; and ethic of individual commitment, rather than collective protections. The solidarity is negative in that it eschews any collectivity (unions are seen as the deviation rather than the expression of this collectivity precisely because they undermine the shared commitment to work that defines it) and in the way it functions as a strategy. Negative solidarity can only see any improvement, collective bargaining, protection of employment, and so on as not only partial, and thus somehow corrupt, but also as deviating from the fundamental ethical basis of work itself, which demands individual strength and fortitude. As much as negative solidarity is aimed at others, at those who are perceived not to work, seeking to discipline those who rely on state spending or those protected by union agreements, it ultimately further attenuates class struggle, obscuring actual divisions with imagined ones. It is anti-solidarity presented as imagined solidarity. The attachment to work and independence ultimately undermines its status in the world, as individual workers are left to fend for themselves.[24]

Affective economy/mythic economy

From this provisional sketch of the present, it is possible to not only bring affective economy into the present, thereby theorising a fourth period or late-neoliberalism, but also to refine and expand an understanding of affective economy. Turning back to Lordon's conception, we can see two connected limitations. First, Lordon's schema of three periods makes the fundamental error of any periodisation of history, presenting history as the displacement and transformation of self-contained epochs understood as entirely different relations to work. Against this division between different periods and times, it is possible to argue for an incomplete and partial overlap. Workers driven by fear of losing their wages were not displaced by Fordist

---

24   Hosang and Lowndes, *Producers, Parasites, Patriots*, 56.

dreams of consumption, just as working to consume has not been displaced by the neoliberal fantasy of being an entrepreneur driven by one's passionate investment in their work. These different organisations of desire coexist. They coexist not just in the same world distributed across a global economy that combines sweatshops, modern factories, and technology entrepreneurs, often within the same company or producing the same commodity, but also in the same city. These ultimately coexist, if we consider them in terms of their primarily affective dimension, in the same individual.

Lordon's emphasis on a particular affect and a particular affective orientation – love or fear – aimed towards the activity or the wage, risks overlooking one of Spinoza's central insights about affects: their ambivalence. Spinoza argues that the human body is "composed of a great many individuals of different natures," and that, when it comes to the objects of desire, "one and the same object can be the cause of many and contrary affects."[25] This complexity gives rise to the vacillation of the affects. A similar ambivalence traverses the wage relation. Sometimes one works just to pay the bills, and the fear of not being able to do so is what drives one to work, and at other times one is motivated by the possibilities of consumption, all of this is topped off, as it were, by the desire to do the work that one loves. These different affective orientations do not (only) define three separate epochs in the history of capital. They identify different affective orientations distributed not only across the same globe, nation, or city – but also across the same individual during the working day.

This brings us to the second limitation. In failing to see the heterogeneity of the affective composition of the present, Lordon fails to recognise that any unity of the present moment, its ability to hold together in the image of capitalist society, consumer society, or neoliberal gig economy, is as much an effect of the assemblage and organisation of ideas and the imagination as it is the organisation of affects and the striving of bodies. There is a dominant idea, or image of work, of its reality, value and effects, that organises work's disparate experiences and conditions. Or, more to the point, desires are structured as much by myths and ideals as they are by their material conditions. Our desire, the conatus, is oriented as much by our imagination as by the material conditions that structure labour and consumption. Spinoza writes, "both insofar as the mind has clear and distinct ideas, and insofar as it has confused ideas, it strives, for an indefinite duration, to persevere in its being and it is conscious of this striving it has."[26] Spinoza's formulation is broad, even ambivalent. The mind strives to preserve itself but does so according to its understanding or misunderstanding of what will preserve itself at a given moment. All acting, all thinking, is strategic, as Laurent Bove argues, motivated by an attempt to affirm and maximise

---

25   Spinoza, *Ethics*, EIIIP17Schol.
26   Spinoza, EIIIP9.

its power. However, strategies differ according to different understandings or imaginations of the given situation.[27] Spinoza writes, "the mind as far as it can, strives to imagine those things that increase or aid the body's power of acting."[28] Spinoza stresses the indeterminate nature of this striving; those with inadequate ideas and adequate ideas equally strive. Just as striving orients the imagination, compelling us to imagine those things that aid or capacity to act, the imagination conditions and limits striving, determining our sense of what is possible or desirable. Sometimes what we imagine to be the condition of increasing power, adding or augmenting our power of acting, is our subjection. Desire and imagination, body and mind, are subject to the same causal relations and conditions that make up history. Just as the striving of our body is constrained and captured by the wage relation and the commodity form that channels our desires, our mind is constrained and captured by the images and narratives of the culture industry.

Work is not just the basis of our economy but our ideology. Narratives of self-transformation through work inundate us. The labour relation cannot be separated from the narratives we use to make sense of it and orient ourselves, from the Horatio Alger myths to modern-day Silicon Valley gurus extolling us to find our true passion and calling in work.[29] Work is a short-circuit between the classes, not just in that it is the linchpin of the relation of exploitation of labour-power that links the two. As labour-power, it is what the capitalist class needs from the working class; and what the worker must necessarily sell to the capitalist. At the level of material conditions, this exchange links and divides the two classes; what the capitalist treats as just another commodity and cost of production is the very life and existence of the worker. At the level of representation, or myth, work does not so much divide the classes, placing them on two sides of the conflict, but unites them in the image of a common project and a universal condition. Work is not just the universal fate of humanity in the sense of the aforementioned saying, "whoever does not work shouldn't eat," but is the general condition for social belonging. To work is to be worthwhile; it is the precondition of self-respect and ethical belonging.[30] The modern capitalist increasingly presents themself as a worker and insists that they work as much as their workers, if not more so. As Étienne Balibar writes, "the capitalist is defined as a worker, as an 'entrepreneur'; the worker, as the bearer of a capacity, of a 'human cap-

---

27   Laurent Bove, *La stratégie du Conatus: Affirmation et résistance chez Spinoza* (Paris: Vrin, 1996), 15.

28   Spinoza, *Ethics*, EIIIP12.

29   Yves Citton, *Mythocratie: Storytelling et Imaginaire de Gauche* (Paris: Éditions Amsterdam, 2010), 27.

30   Kathi Weeks, *The Problem With Work: Feminism, Marxism, Antiwork Politics, and Postwork Imaginaries* (Durham: Duke UP, 2012), 62.

ital."[31] Or, to put this into contemporary parlance, capitalists are "job creators." The image of work does not divide capitalists from workers but unites them in a shared enterprise – a shared necessity made possible by the good graces of the capitalist.

Negative solidarity can thus be understood as both a particular organisation of affects, of joy and anger – pride in work and indignation at those who do not work – as well as a particular image of work, one that stresses the anthropological and moral necessity of work – everyone must work – while equally filtering this universality through the particular image of work – of work understood as "productive," something arduous enough to count as "real work." As much as real work is identified by its difficulty, its joylessness, and lack of protections, these elements are not enough to completely identify it. The image of real work, of productivism, cannot be separated from how this image is informed by and shaped by gender, race and nationality. Even within spheres of production, the "working class" is often identified with industries such as coal mining (predominantly white and rural) rather than textile production, electronics, and meat processing (much more urban and diverse).[32]

Therefore, to offer something of a conclusion: every affective composition, every organisation of desire, joys, and sadness, is also an imaginary composition, an organisation of ideas and images. They are but two different ways of viewing the same thing. Any attempt to grasp the economy or society solely through affects or the imagination is necessarily incomplete. However, when it comes to political practice, there are strategic reasons for favouring the imagination or the affects, or confronting the image of work. Negative solidarity, like every affective composition, is an articulation of both desire and imagination, and like all such articulations, it is finite and capable of being unravelled or rearticulated. There is nothing necessary about the connection between a moralising ideal of work and pride in one's hardship, as intractable they may appear. Understanding the affective and mythic dimension of the reproduction of the present is the first step in transforming it.

References

Balibar, Étienne "The Non-Contemporaneity of Althusser." In *The Althusserian Legacy*, edited by E. Ann Kaplan and Michael Sprinker, X–X. NY: Verso, 1993.

Balibar, Étienne. *Masses, Classes, Ideas: Studies on Politics and Philosophy Before and After Marx*. Translated by James Swenson. NY: Routledge, 1994.

Bove, Laurent. *La stratégie du Conatus: Affirmation et résistance chez Spinoza*. Paris: Vrin, 1996.

---

31   Etienne Balibar, *Masses, Classes, Ideas: Studies on Politics and Philosophy Before and After Marx*, trans. James Swenson (NY: Routledge, 1994), 52.

32   Hosang and Lowndes, *Producers, Parasites, Patriots*, 43.

Castel, Robert. *La montée des incertitudes: Travail, protections, statut de l'individu*. Paris: Éditions du Seuil, 2009.

Citton, Yves. *Mythocratie: Storytelling et Imaginaire de Gauche*. Paris: Éditions Amsterdam, 2010.

Deleuze, Gillles, and Félix Guattari. *Anti-Oedipus: Capitalism and Schizophrenia*. Translated by Robert Hurley, Mark Seem, and Helen R. Lane. Minneapolis: University of Minnesota, 1983.

Graeber, David. *Bullshit Jobs: A Theory*. London: Allen Lane, 2018.

Hobbes, Thomas. *Leviathan*. Indianapolis: Hackett, 1994. First published 1651.

Horkheimer, Max. *Dawn and Decline: Notes 1926–1931 and 1950–1960*. Translated by Michael Shaw. NY: Seabury Press, 1978.

Hosang, Daniel Martinez, and Joseph E. Lowndes. *Producers, Parasites, Patriots: Race and the New Right-Wing Politics of Precarity*. Minneapolis: Minnesota, 2019.

Lordon, Frédéric. *Willing Slaves of Capital: Spinoza and Marx on Desire*. Translated by Gabriel Ash. NY: Verso, 2014. First published 2010 by La fabrique éditions.

Marx, Karl. *Capital: A Critique of Political Economy, Volume I*. Translated by Ben Fowkes. NY: Penguin, 1977. First published 1867 by Verlag von Otto Meisner.

Postone, Moishe. *Time, Labour, and Social Domination: A Reinterpretation of Marx's Critical Theory*. Cambridge: Cambridge University, 1996.

Potts, Monica. "In the Land of Self Defeat." *The New York Times*, October 4, 2019. https://www.nytimes.com/2019/10/04/opinion/sunday/trump-arkansas.html.

Silva, Jennifer M. *Coming Up Short: Working-Class Adulthood in an Age of Uncertainty*. NY: Oxford, 2013.

de Spinoza, Benedict. *Ethics*. In *A Spinoza Reader: The Ethics and Other Works*, translated and edited by Edwin Curley. Princeton: Princeton UP, 1994. Original published 1677.

Stiegler, Bernard. *Acting Out*. Translated by David Barison, Daniel Ross, and Patrick Crogan. Stanford: Stanford University, 2009.

Tosel, André. *Du Matérialisme de Spinoza*. Paris: Éditions Kimé, 1994.

Weeks, Kathi. *The Problem With Work: Feminism, Marxism, Antiwork Politics, and Postwork Imaginaries*. Durham: Duke UP, 2012.

Williams, Alex. "Negative Solidarity and Post-Fordism." *Splintering Bone Ashes* (blog). January 31, 2010. https://splinteringboneashes.blogspot.com/2010/01/negative-solidarity-and-post-fordist.html.

The Antisociality of Capitalism (Some Preliminary Reflections)

Samo Tomšič

Marx, Freud, and the antisocial

Marx and Freud's work and methods have been repeatedly declared outdated, unscientific, or restricted only to the geographical, historical, and ideological context in which they emerged. In Marx's case, the 19th-century industrial revolution, the critical confrontation with early economic liberalism, and classical political economy. In Freud's case, the crisis of bourgeois family and patriarchy in early 20th-century Europe. Although they certainly remained embedded in the spirit of their time, and to an extent, reproduced certain social prejudices, Marx and Freud succeeded in developing methods and a set of fundamental concepts that allowed them to glimpse behind the "phenomenological veil," questioning how economic, social, and subjective reality appears to the sensuous and intellectual apparatus of the conscious human observer. It is this displacement that, in both critical and clinical contexts, produced a "surplus," which reaches beyond their historical circumstances and, most importantly, reaffirms both thinkers' ongoing actuality, precisely in the moment of intensified social crises. In such critical times, Marx and Freud's work thus demonstrates its irreducibility to their narrow historical frameworks, as well as to some kind of "cultural heritage" of theory. Through an encounter with the crisis-ridden developments in the present, their oeuvre reinvents its emancipatory potentials, while at the same time demonstrating that both continue to cause a certain malaise – the Freudian *Unbehagen* – since they repeatedly confront us with a troublesome aspect of our social reality that one would preferably remove from the picture, ignore and, indeed, repress – namely, the inherent aggressiveness, hostility, and cruelty of the capitalist mode of production.[1]

---

1   Already, a superficial glimpse at their work shows that crisis is indeed a significant common object of inquiry in Marx and Freud. Or perhaps more generally, what interests them above all is the fragile and unstable nature of social bonds, as well as their destructive effects on the human subject and on society as a whole.

That Marx is again taken seriously in times of economic crisis should hardly come as a surprise. In the economic field, a crisis comes in train with the vacillation of opinions, beliefs, fantasies, and prejudices that hold the economic field together (both the discipline dealing with economic processes, or what orthodox Marxists would call the "science of value," and the societal processes of extraction, production, circulation, consumption, and financialisaton). When Marx entitled his mature project "critique of political economy," he indicated that the object of his inquiry is nothing other than the blind spot – the *bévue*, the overlooked, to use a pointed term by Louis Althusser[2] – of political economy. This overlooked concerns both the source of surplus-value (specifically, the necessary link between the exploitation of labour and extraction of profit) and the impurity of economic knowledge, the fact that this knowledge is always already traversed by something that indeed deserves to be called superstition. The latter certainly comprises the well-known operation of commodity fetishism, which envisages value as a substantial quality of commodities rather than an exploitative social relation but also, and more importantly, the false conviction that (pre)accumulated wealth is a source of social virtues and actions – in other words, that economic value stands in direct continuity with ethical or moral value and is therefore inherently capable of (re)producing sociality. Contrary to the political-economic belief in the inherent rationality of economic subjects, the calculability of their "private" interests, the assumed self-regulating and self-corrective character of the markets, and the presumably inherent tendency of the rich (capitalists, monopolies, and corporations) to reinvest their wealth and profits for the benefit of society, Marx most rigorously demonstrated that the violence, aggressiveness, and crisis-character of capitalism are not to be taken as a deviation from some normative capitalist sociality, corrupted by individual, state or corporate greed. On the contrary, they are a logical consequence of capitalism's organisation of production around surplus-value. Capitalism is an organised disequilibrium, accompanied by continuous systemic violence and obsession with the constant increase of value, or what later in history was baptised "economic growth." Behind this innocent-sounding master-signifier, Marx allows us to envisage a force that is, at best, indifferent and, at worst, hostile towards human existence as a social being and eventually against life as such.

Following Marx's "speculative" developments, surplus-value is associated with a specific force of economic abstractions (value and capital) that is overtly hostile to sociality and for which he uses the term "drive" (*Trieb*).[3] Characteristic of this economic drive is the striving for uninterrupted self-valorisation of value, its detachment from

---

2   Louis Althusser, "Du 'Capital' à la philosophie de Marx," in *Lire le Capital*, edited by Louis Althusser et al. (Paris: Quadrige/PUF, 1996), 11–12.

3   The antisocial character of the drive of capital is explicitly addressed in Karl Marx, *Capital, Vol. 1* (1867; reis., London: Penguin, 1990), 230–231, 254–255, 324.

every dimension that could be described as social. Instead of (surplus-)value being reinvested to improve the conditions of social life, all human activities must enforce the self-valorisation of value and contribute to its continuous extraction. In the logic of capital, Marx thus detects an active indifference of economic processes and mechanisms to the reproduction of life. The only life that matters is the life of economic abstractions. Capital is, therefore, inherently antisocial in the sense that, by actively striving to destroy living bodies, cut social ties, and destabilise environmental systems, it ultimately undermines both the ontological (planetary), the epistemological (knowledge), and the political (labour) conditions of sociality.

Even though it could hardly appear more foreign to this economic framework, Freud's work developed in a strikingly similar direction. It increasingly confronted systemic instability, aggressiveness, and violence, as well as an underlying cultural indifference towards human suffering – a cultural cruelty, inscribed in the individual mental apparatus in the guise of the superego. Despite their speculative and sometimes overtly myth-forging character (think of the figure of the obscene primal father), Freud's mature cultural writings unambiguously address the key issue of countercultural tendencies within culture, tendencies that Freud, too, brought together in the notion of the drive (*Trieb*). This was hardly done in an uncomplicated manner, since Freud proposed several names to pinpoint this problematic, antisocial dimension of the drive – the controversial death drive, and the somewhat less prominent, yet no less crucial, drive of aggressiveness. They are two manifestations of the same violent force that Freud quite explicitly associates with cultural institutions, such as religion and morality, but also with social economy. It is worth recalling that the death drive stands for violence directed inwards, onto the human psyche (the classical Freudian example being moral and sexual masochism), whereas the drive of aggressiveness stands for externalised violence, the ultimate manifestation of which is war, Freud's main object of inquiry, but which also comprises the various forms of economic violence, including colonial and environmental.[4] For Freud, the drive, too, is associated with a surplus-object called *Lustgewinn*, yield in pleasure, a notion that Lacan eventually translated as surplus-enjoyment, in explicit reference to the economic category of surplus-value. Does this imply that enjoyment is inherently antisocial? Neither Freud nor Lacan indicated this conclusion, whether explicitly or implicitly, but their critical concerns certainly suggest that the capitalist mode of enjoyment plays a crucial role in the overall increase of antisocial tendencies within society. And further, the Lacanian homology between surplus-value

---

4   For the most recent systematic account of the intricacies of Freud's mature *Trieblehre* (doctrine of drives), see Judith Butler, *The Force of Non-Violence* (London: Verso, 2020), 151–183; Étienne Balibar, "Dying One's Own Death. Freud With Rilke," *Angelaki. Journal of the Theoretical Humanities* 27, no. 1 (2022). See also Jacqueline Rose, *Why War? Psychoanalysis, Politics, and the Return to Melanie Klein* (Oxford: Blackwell, 1993), 15–40.

and surplus-enjoyment ultimately suggests that the former can and perhaps even should be understood as a sort of systemic enjoyment.

Marx's *Capital* and Freud's extensive engagement with the cultural condition, such as in *Civilization and Its Discontents*, thus intersect at the point of a homologous surplus-object, as well as in indicating a strikingly similar diagnostic, according to which we live in a system that could be described as *organised antisociality*, actively dismantling the bonds that hold society and subjectivity together to extract from them an equally antisocial surplus (surplus-value, surplus-enjoyment).[5] In sharp contrast to the political-economic assumption of the inherent sociality of the markets – or even of a society of markets – Marx draws attention to capitalism's antisocial character by describing the capitalist organisation of production as "production for the sake of production" or "overproduction"; recognising the self-sufficient drive of accumulation and self-valorisation as capital's ultimate tendency; and introducing the notion of surplus-population, which comprises the thesis that capitalism progressively transforms humanity into a redundant form of life.[6]

Our present crisis – the increase in sexist and racist violence, the emergence of "surveillance capitalism," the climate emergency, the challenges to scientific authority due to the proliferation of conspiracy theories, fake news, etc. – is, at its core, a crisis of the social, or rather, a crisis of the concept of society, which was certainly enforced by the decades of neoliberalism – recall Margaret Thatcher's statement, "there is no such thing as society" – but which nevertheless extends back to the very historical origins of capitalism. Marx and Freud's contributions to the critique of capitalist antisociality remain crucial because they address the issue both on a historical and structural level. In recent decades, it became increasingly fashionable to diagnose the end of neoliberalism, the controversial epoch in which the "withering away of the social" intensified due to the failure and self-discrediting of 20th-century communism, followed by the breakdown of the universalist agenda in emancipatory politics. The neoliberal worldview promoted a most problematic, indeed an-

---

5   This dismantling is quite overtly expressed in the modern scientific and economic ideal, the mastery of nature, whose aggressive overtone can be hardly overlooked. We find this ideal formulated in René Descartes, albeit with more ambiguity regarding the goal of this scientific and economic mastery. Needless to add, from the viewpoint of critique of political economy and of psychoanalysis, and against the modern striving for cultural mastery of nature, the human subject falls on the side of the dominated.

6   While Marx's account of economic tendencies overtly suggests that capitalism comprises an increase in antisociality, Freud assumed a more general, and some may add, excessively pessimistic position, according to which culture as such begins to appear antisocial. Still, Freud recognises the dimension of cultural work (*Kulturarbeit*), which comprises ongoing subjective and intersubjective attempts to economise the tension between the forces that bind and the forces that unbind the social, Eros and the drive of destruction. Freud understood psychoanalysis as a component of this cultural work.

tisocial, idea of freedom, understood first and foremost as freedom of the economic sphere from every socioeconomic constraint.[7] The state may have been the first neoliberal target here, and one could add that the "withering away of the social" took the appearance of what Friedrich Engels, in another context, called the "withering away of the state."[8] Still, the neoliberal economists have been "consistently inconsistent" in their stance towards the state, on the one hand denouncing the social welfare state as authoritarian and demanding it is replaced by a "slim state," while on the other hand, they pushed for an authoritarian state, which would not shy away from rigorously implementing the most aggressive neoliberal deregulatory policies and thus become a major force in the neoliberal "dismantling of society."[9] Today's socioeconomic condition not only continues the process of the social's withering away but also accomplishes the neoliberal program of placing corporations and hi-tech companies in the function of the state. If, in the decades of neoliberalism, the corporation served as a model for the state, then today's developments show that the distinction between the two becomes blurred and the corporation imposes itself as the form of state to come (e.g., Mark Zuckerberg's ambitions with the Metaverse). Although this course of things may appear as the end of neoliberalism, it still contains the full actualisation of its antisocial and authoritarian programmatic.

Ressentimental economy

The most superficial expression of antisociality in the economic sphere is the relation of competition, which is imposed as the paradigm of social bond in the capitalist organisation of social being. Since Nietzsche, this relation is associated with a specific antisocial affect, *ressentiment*, which again resonates well with Freud problematising the increase of aggressiveness in the modern cultural condition. At the same time, this affective state leads to the very core of the capitalist striving for an antisocial "social bond" (however paradoxical this expression may seem), since it pin-

---

7   This neoliberal strategy translated into conceiving "freedom of speech" in terms of freedom to exercise verbal violence, to spread lies and misinformation, hence freedom from every accountability for words and actions.

8   Engels uses the verb *absterben*, which, in its organic connotation, means "to die off" or "to atrophy." That neoliberal capitalism brought about its own version of the withering away of the state has been argued by various commentators, including Alain Badiou and Slavoj Žižek.

9   Wendy Brown, *In the Ruins of Neoliberalism. The Rise of Antidemocratic Politics in the West* (NY: Columbia UP, 2019). That capitalism is a system of organised antisociality was honestly formulated in Thatcher's notorious remark cited above. She concludes this slogan with something that we may call "capitalist naturalism" or capitalist self-naturalisation, for Thatcher insists that if there is no such thing as society, all that truly exists are individuals and their families.

points the tension that gradually disintegrates society through the ongoing pitting of diverse social groups against each other. *Ressentiment* thus functions as an affect through which difference is effectively invested with toxicity. However, contrary to Nietzsche's perspective, the affect in question is not simply a "pathological" or "psychological" reaction to inequality, injury, and injustice. From a more structural point of view, *ressentiment* is a material-corporeal manifestation of economic relations of competition, expressing the compulsive working of these relations in individuals and social groups. Since *ressentiment* enforces the toxification of difference, it marks social being with mutual hostility. If social being bears the signification of "being-with" and eventually of "being in common," then *ressentiment* signals the antisocial subversion of social being into "being-against," a mode of being, which matches the capitalist striving for total "privatisation" of the social and of the common, or more generally, a striving to expropriate political subjects of their bodies, their lives, and ultimately of every framework that would provide them with (material and immaterial) conditions for the reproduction of life. Marx wittily brought this problematic systemic tendency to the point when he indicated that, in capitalism, political universals are subverted by economic particulars:

> The sphere of circulation or commodity exchange, within whose boundaries the sale and purchase of labour-power goes on, is in fact a very Eden of the innate rights of man. It is the exclusive realm of Freedom, Equality, Property and Bentham. Freedom, because both buyer and seller of a commodity, let us say of labour-power, are determined only by their own free will. They contract as free persons, who are equal before the law. Their contract is the final result in which their joint will finds a common legal expression. Equality, because each enters into relation with the other, as with a simple owner of commodities, and they exchange equivalent for equivalent. Property, because each disposes only of what is his own. And Bentham, because each looks only to his own advantage. The only force bringing them together, and putting them into relation with each other, is the selfishness, the gain and the private interest of each. Each pays heed to himself only, and no one worries about the others. And precisely for that reason, either in accordance with the pre-established harmony of things, or under the auspices of an omniscient providence, they all work together to their mutual advantage, for the common weal, and in the common interest.[10]

Freedom and equality, these master-signifiers of the French Revolution, are distorted by property and Bentham, whereby the latter appears here as the peak of the utilitarian ethical-political doctrine, which explained all human actions through the

---

10   Marx, *Capital*, 280.

assumption that every individual strives to maximise pleasure and diminish pain.[11] Utilitarianism further exemplifies its normative and therefore idealising take on human subjectivity in its assumption that everyone acts in accordance with their private interest. By following this line of reasoning, Bentham remained faithful to the work of Adam Smith that Marx's quote explicitly evokes ("the only force bringing them together, and putting them into relation with each other, is the selfishness, the gain and the private interest of each").

The relation between economy and sociality is indeed a major issue for classical political economy, and Adam Smith's attempt to tackle the problematic is probably the most "symptomatic." In *Theory of Moral Sentiments*, his major treatise on moral philosophy, Smith aimed at demonstrating that human passions are organised around mutual sympathy and thus governed by an inherent equilibrium. His theory of affective sympathy rests on the notion of a neutral observer that everyone assumes both in relation to themselves and others. *The Wealth of Nations*, Smith's subsequent and significantly more influential work in political economy, seems to make an important displacement by focusing on self-love and self-interest, an affective state and tendency in the subject, which at first glance seems to contradict sympathy and instead enforce antipathy, mutual exclusion, and competitiveness. However, here too, Smith repeats his conviction in the capacity of individual self-centeredness to enter in relation with other self-interested individuals, for instance, in the following famous lines:

> It is not from the benevolence of the butcher, the brewer, or the baker, that we expect our dinner, but from their regard to their own interest. We address ourselves, not to their humanity but to their self-love, and never talk to them of our own necessities but of their advantages.[12]

Here, then, Smith reformulates his earlier assumption of affective sympathy in terms of mutual economic seduction, which postulates the exact unproblematic relationality and symmetry (*quid pro quo*) that Marx denounces as mere appearance, masking the fact that behind the free and equal economic exchange are compulsion and inequality. After all, we are talking about the encounter between the possessor

---

11   Bentham thus described *utility* as "that property in any object, whereby it tends to produce benefit, advantage, pleasure, good, or happiness … [or] to prevent the happening of mischief, pain, evil, or unhappiness to the party whose interest is considered": Jeremy Bentham, *The Principles of Morals and Legislation* (NY: Prometheus Books, 1988), 2.

12   Adam Smith, *The Wealth of Nations* (London: Penguin, 1986), 119. See also Todd McGowan, *Capitalism and Desire. The Psychic Cost of Free Markets* (NY: Columbia UP, 2016), 55–56. McGowan extensively engages with the so-called "Adam Smith Problem" resulting from the incompatibilities between *Theory of Moral Sentiments* and *The Wealth of Nations*; see, again, McGowan, *Capitalism and Desire*, 128–132.

of the means of production and the possessor of nothing but their labour-power, hence the dispossessed. For Smith, however, one can advance one's own benefits by accentuating the other's advantages, and thus both sides can claim just participation in profit. And to repeat, it is mutual seduction that simultaneously affirms and tames the economic relation of competition, which drives the market dynamic, and the economic inequalities, which evidently cannot be removed from the relations of exchange.

On a more speculative level, however, the neutral or impartial spectator finds its reworked and more abstract expression in the notorious "invisible hand." It is this abstract force that organises the affective and social life of self-interested individuals in a social rather than antisocial manner, thus allowing for a higher moral and socioeconomic order to emerge. It is quite significant that Smith more frequently uses the notion of Providence, which he uses synonymously to the invisible hand, but, due to its theological connotations, the expression nevertheless represents an epistemological scandal for what would be a rigorous economic science. Unsurprisingly, the "invisible hand" enjoyed popularity among liberal and neoliberal economists, while its theological flipside was actively repressed. Providence, then, in the last instance, directs the individual's actions in a way that their "ruthless" pursuit of private interest quasi-unintentionally fosters and promotes the good of society. One could almost say that Providence "positively" conspires against any rigorous pursuit of private interest, sabotaging the latter from within. Quite tellingly, in *Theory of Moral Sentiments*, the invisible hand appears where Smith raises the question of what motivates the rich towards a just distribution of wealth:

> The rich only select from the heap what is most precious and agreeable. They consume little more than the poor, and in spite of their natural selfishness and rapacity, though they mean only their own conveniency, though the sole end which they propose from the labours of all the thousands whom they employ, be the gratification of their own vain and insatiable desires, they divide with the poor the produce of all their improvements. They are led by an invisible hand to make nearly the same distribution of the necessaries of life, which would have been made, had the earth been divided into equal portions among all its inhabitants, and thus without intending it, without knowing it, advance the interest of the society, and afford means to the multiplication of the species.[13]

This hypothesis continues to echo in the neoliberal discourse on "trickle-down economics" and in the neoliberal economic myth that the tax cuts for the rich ("job creators") will quasi-automatically stimulate investments, which will, sooner or later,

---

13   Adam Smith, *Theory of Moral Sentiments* (London: Penguin, 2009), 215.

benefit all society's members.[14] According to this line of reasoning, one could think that the rich are social against their will, almost compulsively – they cannot help it. However, this is not Smith's actual point, since, for him, sociality emerges spontaneously from the competitive interplay of multiple interests. There is no trace of compulsive action in this emergence, no negativity, that would split, alienate, or antagonise the rich, and the invisible hand or Providence stands for the benevolent "unconscious" synchronisation of private interests. From this point of view, self-interested competition in the free market ideally does not foster *ressentiment*, but on the contrary, it generates a harmony of higher order.[15]

However, *ressentiment*'s proliferation in the social and economic sphere seriously challenges the Smithian homeostatic conception of the capitalist market and social bonds. The increase of *ressentiment* signals the perpetuation of injustice and suffering, enforced by the very same relations of competition that make Providence's "natural habitat." What is more, and as Nietzsche's critique of *ressentiment* taught us, *ressentiment* is not simply an affective expression of injustice but a misplacement of suffering's cause, providing the subject with a substitute satisfaction. In other words, *ressentiment* succeeds in fusing social injustice and subjective enjoyment. As is often the case, given his rigorous philology, Nietzsche grounds his point in etymology: *ressentiment* comes from the Latin *re-sentire* (re-feel), where the link between affect and repetition is crucial. The main achievement of repetition is the internalisation of an external injury, which slowly but surely uncouples the affect from the actual injury. Here, we can also make a move away from Nietzsche, for *ressentiment* is not necessarily about memory and the impotency to forget, as Nietzsche occasionally insisted, but about forgetting the actual cause of suffering, or to put it with Marx, about mystifying structural causes of personal and social misery.

Once injustice is uncoupled from its actual cause, it can become part of a libidinal economy, in which *ressentiment* signals extracting enjoyment from suffering. *Ressentiment* thus, to repeat, offers the subject an "other satisfaction" (Lacan) and signals that an exploitative libidinal economy has been organised on the background of suffering's obscured structural causes. The flipside – and therefore the hidden truth – of *ressentiment* is *Lustgewinn*, pleasure as a surplus-product, resulting from enduring suffering and injustice.[16] This means also that we need to recognise in *ressentiment*

---

14   One could ironically repeat here, which "society"? Liz Truss, the short-serving British prime minister of September to October 2022, quite shamelessly insisted that her political priority would not be diminishing inequalities but enforcing economic growth (statements published in *The Guardian*, September 4, 2022), reconfirming that the Conservatives still foster disbelief in society's existence.

15   In the economic terrain, the formation of monopolies goes against this assumption of harmony, something of which Smith was undoubtedly aware. See Smith, *Wealth*, 222–223.

16   Of course, this "*ressentimental* libidinal economy" requires a scapegoat, in which the subjects of *ressentiment* falsely recognise the cause of their suffering.

a modality of what Freud, in his discussion of the analysand's resistance to psycho-analysis, calls "escape into illness" (*Flucht in die Krankheit*) and "profit from illness" (*Krankheitsgewinn*), which, thanks to the "oblivion" (repression), prevents the subject from working through their suffering's structural causes. Both clinical phenomena, for Freud, exemplify and radicalise unconscious resistance, which means that they stand for the resilience of the problematic structure in which the subject is embed-ded. In *ressentiment*, we can thus observe a systemic affect, at the juncture of subjec-tive and structural, which stands for material expression of systemic resistance in the subject, preventing them from loosening and eventually transforming the prob-lematic antisocial economy.[17]

Ressentiment is not simply an affective state, present in every unjust social sys-tem, but the key systemic affect of capitalism, reflecting the fact that the subject of capitalism is always already caught in the position of impotency. To repeat, a major problem with *ressentiment* is that it actively mystifies the actual causes of social misery, thus blurring the view of structural relations of exploitation, and feeding false aetiologies of suffering. Looking back at the history of philosophical confrontations with the explosion of *ressentiment* in modernity, Michael Ure dis-tinguishes three forms of *ressentiment*: moral, socio-political, and ontological.[18] Even though the socio-political resentment is relational – directed towards others (reaction to their unjust attitude towards us, or indifference) – it continuously runs the risk of repeating the errors of ontological resentment, which rests on a problematic substantialisation or essentialisation of one's own suffering and or-ganises an entire worldview around this operation. The interaction between moral and socio-political *ressentiment*, on the one hand, and ontological, on the other, contains a specific loop, which explains the primacy of ontological *ressentiment* and, at the same time, its derivation from the socio-political framework. The primacy of ontological *ressentiment* is retroactively constituted: derived from an unjust socio-political situation, such as economic inequality, *ressentiment* is postulated as an existential affect, which transcends the historical circumstances and imposes an affective or emotional filter, through which an individual or a social group "contem-plates" reality.[19] In any case, the efficacy of *ressentiment* lies in its capacity to provide

---

17   According to Freud, something similar happens in melancholia, where the actual loss has been forgotten, and the subject is consumed or taken hostage by the lost object. Neverthe-less, unconscious repetition forms a mode of remembering and affect a corporeal manifesta-tion of this repetition. See Sigmund Freud, "Trauer und Melancholie," in *Studienausgabe*, vol. 3 (Frankfurt am Main: Fischer Verlag, 2000).

18   Michael Ure, "Resentment/Ressentiment," *Constellations* 22, no. 4 (2015). In my discussion of ressentiment, I rely on Ure's systematic historical and theoretical developments.

19   This is also how *ressentiment* becomes organised in a libidinal economy, for instance, when prohibition of enjoyment turns into a distinct source of surplus-enjoyment. For Lacan (*Le Séminaire, livre XVI, D'un Autre à l'autre* [Paris: Éditions du Seuil, 2006] and *Autres écrits* [Paris:

an efficient substitute satisfaction from that which the subject of *ressentiment* is (presumably) deprived. This substitute satisfaction is overtly marked by aggressiveness, which is directed both inwards and outwards, against the inner and the outer world, against the subject and the social bond, thus amounting to nihilism's expansion and intensification, as Nietzsche already correctly diagnosed. One could therefore repeat Lacan's occasional remark on jealousy and say that *ressentiment* is always the wrong affective reaction to injustice and deprivation, since it projects and hence misplaces their cause into the other, the neighbour.

This is where Smith's homeostatic theory of moral and economic sentiments encounters its limit. Smith assumes a harmony, which testifies to the possibility that the subjects identify with each other through their sentiments, or that they put themselves in the other's shoes, thus becoming de facto alienated from their self-interest. The affective life is thus supposedly characterised by a common pathos, shared suffering, even if this share is indirect, such as in the case of the rich, who could not be further away from the existential threats of poverty, racism, war, and other forms of violence. Being affected through the pain and the injustice experienced by others always already implies that they become objects of thought. In *ressentiment*, however, a community is formed by enforcing shared hostility, indeed an antisocial sociality, in which affective bonds are conditioned by the continuous fabrication of scapegoats, personifying and therefore mystifying the causes of existential, economic, and social misery. This implies that the field of affects must be in perpetual disequilibrium and empathic bonds are continuously dismantled. We can remark in passing that the assumption of affective empathy must not be mistaken for social bond rooted in solidarity. While empathy assumes that affective life of distinct political subjects can reach the point of equilibrium (understood as a social relation without tension and contradiction), solidarity implies the exact opposite. Because there is no such thing as affective sympathy, solidarity must be enforced as an affective response to the toxic capitalist nexus of competition and *ressentiment*. Further, whereas economic liberalism presupposes a non-alienated subjectivity, anchored in private interest (individuality), solidarity demonstrates that the human subject is constitutively alienated and decentred – indeed, a "political animal," whereby political means as much as relational. The subject is constitutively related, to others and to itself.

Liberalism can only postulate a social character of capitalism on the condition that it assumes a metaphysical foundation of sociality – a figure of the "Other of

---

Éditions du Seuil, 2001], 435), renouncing enjoyment was the main social imperative of capitalism. For a longer discussion of the link between renunciation of enjoyment and *ressentiment*, see Samo Tomšič, "The Politics of Resentment and Its Pitfalls," in *Populism and the People in Contemporary Critical Thought*, ed. Alexander Stagnell, David Payne, and Gustav Strandberg (London: Bloomsbury, 2023).

the Other," to put it with Lacan. This is where the economic superstition inaugu-
rated by Adam Smith and enforced by the neoliberal antisocial revolution comes in.
The belief that the market's invisible hand will regulate economic greed and lead to
just redistribution of wealth exemplifies this redoubling in the Other. The Market already stands for the economic conception of the big Other, the register of economic
relations. Smith did not bother mystifying the religious roots of modern economic
science; however, his notion of Providence and of the invisible hand mark a heterogeneity in the market dynamic and disequilibrium, since they operate as an ordering and stabilising principle in the chaotic field of competition and *ressentiment*. Only
when the market is supplemented with the hypothesis of Providence can it become a
"normative order," capable of self-regulation and endowed with rational behaviour.
Providence unveils Smith's belief in the existence of an economic Law, purified of
every excess, obscenity, and violence. Perversion of economic laws is then always external and comes about when the economic sphere is subjected exclusively to private
interests, or when private interest overrides the public interest, such as in the case
of monopoly formation. In the end, Smith did intuit that monopolies necessarily
enter competition with the state and impose themselves as an alternative figure of
sovereignty.

Next to the moral, the socio-political, and the ontological, *ressentiment* requires
a structural reading, since it stands for an affect that plays the key role in sustaining the reproduction of capitalist relations and mechanisms of exploitation. Max
Scheler[20] indicated such a structural reading, explicitly associating *ressentiment* with
the logic of competition and the processes of valorisation (specifically with Marx's
account of the circulation money-commodity-money).[21] In doing so, Scheler drew
attention to systemic toxicity and rejected Nietzsche's speculations on the link between *ressentiment* and Judeo-Christian tradition. In Scheler's reading, *ressentiment*
is a thoroughly modern affective state, resulting from the break brought about by the
progressive expansion of capitalist relations of production into all spheres of social
and subjective existence. At the core of this break lies the discrepancy between political universalism (freedom and equality) and economic universalism (commodification and valorisation) that Marx equally addresses in his discussion of the political-
economic foursome (freedom, equality, property, and Bentham). In Nietzsche's scenario, in turn, *ressentiment* comes in the guise of radical envy, the subjects of *ressentiment* falsely believing that the other deprives them of their enjoyment, happiness,

20   Max Scheler, *Das Ressentiment im Aufbau der Moralen* (Frankfurt am Main, Vittorio Kloster-
      mann, 2004), 14–15.
21   Scheler's insight into the economic function of ressentiment has been recently re-accentu-
      ated and linked with our contemporary surveillance capitalism by Joseph Vogl, *Capital and
      Ressentiment: A Short Theory of the Present*, translated by Neil Solomon (Cambridge: Polity,
      2023).

and life without lack (hence without negativity). Understood in this way, *ressentiment* necessarily economises the interplay between lack and surplus, an asymmetry we encounter at the core of the capitalist drive of accumulation and self-valorisation. The drive of capital, as Marx insisted, stands for the insatiable demand for surplus-value, but this implies that it is internally marked by a persistent lack of value. Due to this endless conditioning of lack and surplus, which makes it strive for ever more value, one could say that the logic of capital, too, comes down to radical envy and ha-tred – in short, that capital is *ressentiment*al. Perhaps nothing reflects this systemic *ressentiment* better than the economic prejudice that poverty is a sign of laziness, a prejudice masking the constant systemic push for radical expropriation.

Neoliberalism elevated this economic prejudice to unprecedented heights. The Austrian-born economist and a key spiritual father of neoliberalism, Friedrich Hayek, is known for founding his economic doctrine on a strong combination of market and morals, which, just as in Smith's case, are assumed to evolve sponta-neously. Yet, the neoliberal spontaneism importantly modifies the Smithian order. While in Smith, Providence still functioned as a force, which presumably moti-vates the rich to social action, and morality thus underpins the economic sphere, neoliberalism inverted the framing. Now, it is no longer the regulatory invisible hand that conducts the economic subject's actions but individual and systemic greed. In Smith, Providence thus played the function of an ontological and ethical guarantee of the common interest, a kind of inherent goodness of the market. There is no such thing in the neoliberal reworking of classical economic liberalism, even though the Smithian notion of invisible hand continued to re-emerge in the economic debates that marked the 1990s and 2000s, albeit as a signifier with hardly any ideological efficacy remaining. With the neoliberal social engineering, from the United States via the United Kingdom to Chile, the benevolent invisible hand was replaced by a most visible fist, which aims at dismantling the social and, conse-quently, comes paired with an overt hatred of sociality. Social justice is henceforth understood as compulsive constraint, whereas greed is declared good, and without the assumption of Providence, the market spontaneity finally loses its phantasmatic grounding, revealing itself as what it always already was, a dangerous superstition, which functions as a key mystification of crisis-ridden and antisocial character of capitalism.

At the core of this neoliberal displacement from Smith's assumption of a regu-lating "Other of the Other" that guarantees the emergence of sociality out of the free market to the greedy Other of neoliberal antisociality is the conviction that society functions to constrain continuous economic growth, this presumably paradigmatic expression of the market freedom. Freedom indeed played the key role in the ne-oliberal unleashing of capital's antisocial tendencies, pursuing the ideal of "absolute freedom," disentangled from other political universals, such as equality and solidar-ity. In the prominent motto of the French Revolution, freedom still forms a "Borromean knot" with these two universals, which play the double role of constraints and conditions of freedom. However, as Marx suggested, economic liberalism already pursued a foreclosure of solidarity and replaced it with "property and Bentham," where the economic universality (economic value) and particularity (private interest) turn equality into mere semblance and uncouple freedom from every political subjectivity, instead delegating it to the market. Marx's enumeration of political categories of economic liberalism explains why a social bond grounded on this ideological *quadrivium* necessarily comes paired with *ressentiment*, which reflects the predominance of aggressive impulses in constructing social relations and interactions. In contrast to this underlying social hostility, articulating freedom and equality through solidarity proposes a possible translation of what Freud continuously understood with Eros, the force that forms unions, links, and relations. On the level of solidarity, we find difference affirmed, while in *ressentiment* difference can only be met with animosity. That makes *ressentiment* perfectly compatible with "fraternal bonds," which may at first glance appear grounded on solidarity between the members of a fraternity, an exclusive, rather than inclusive solidarity, which nevertheless follows the logic of competition. A fraternity can hold together only under the condition that imaginary figures of menacing others are continuously fabricated, but, as Nietzsche already emphasised, once a subject or a group is organised through *ressentiment*, the latter is always directed both outwards and inwards – not only towards these presumably threatening others, but also towards members of my own group and ultimately towards myself. This tendency is directly linked with the understanding of absolute freedom qua freedom from constraints, which suggests that the other's freedom always deprives me of my own freedom, and further, that the very existence of difference is an absolute threat to my own being.

In her recent *In the Ruins of Neoliberalism*, Wendy Brown addressed the intimate link between the enforcement of absolute freedom and the increase of systemic aggressiveness by breaking the main achievements of neoliberalism down to three imperatives, which are very much compatible with the Freudo-Lacanian critique of systemic enjoyment: "society must be dismantled," "politics must be dethroned," and "the personal must be extended."[22] The first imperative overtly questions Foucault's reading of liberalism and neoliberalism, according to which the imperative of modern organisation of social life (as determined in the Foucauldian concept of biopolitics) comes down to "society must be defended."[23] Instead, we are dealing with a fundamental denial of social being's primacy over individual being. The second imperative implies that the realm of politics is to be entirely subverted and hijacked by

---

22   See, again, Brown, particularly on *ressentiment* (*In the Ruins*, 165–169), where the argument turns to Marcuse.
23   Michel Foucault, *Society Must be Defended: Lectures at the Collège de France, 1975–1976* (London: Penguin Classics, 2020).

the economic sphere, extending relations of competition, economic deregulation, and the imperative of useless surplus-production to all spheres of social and sub-jective existence. With this move, the state is "slimmed down" to the sole function of safeguarding the antisocial subversion of political life. Finally, while Brown's for-mulation of the third achievement suggests that the private or the personal operates as a foreclosure of the common, collective, or public, we must hear in the "private" precisely what Marx addresses under the structural drive of capital, rather than a simple predominance of personal egoism over the public interest (the latter issue already troubled Adam Smith, who, in contrast to Marx, remained restricted to the "psychological" sphere or appearance of the "personal"). The privatisation of poli-tics indeed manifests as expropriating human beings of sociality as such, and en-throning capital as the subject of politics.[24] By accomplishing the subversion of the relation between the political and the economic, the neoliberal orthodoxy not only demands that the economic be exempted from collective management, transforma-tion, revision, or control, but the economic doxa also insists that only by unleashing the antisocial tendencies of the socioeconomic system and of affective life can we guarantee "continuous economic growth" (which is in its essence growth for the sake of growth, and therefore uncoupled from every social value or usefulness). The self-valorisation of capital finally becomes the sole "legitimate" activity in the socioeco-nomic sphere.[25]

From Bentham to Sade

Marx's comment on the entanglement of political universals with economic par-ticulars still targets the equilibrium paradigm of 19th-century economic liberalism and its theory of political passions. Even though the name "Bentham" covers basic antisocial phenomena such as private interest and self-love, it still comprises the

---

24   Namely, the "automatic subject" that Marx (*Capital*, 255) situates on the level of fictitious (fi-nancial) capital.

25   The tendency to enthrone capital as the sole subject of politics is accompanied by another troublesome aspect of the capitalist enforcement of antisociality, which can here be merely indicated – namely, the production of social abjects that Marx addressed through the con-cept of surplus-population. With that population being excluded from the capitalist rela-tions of production, it becomes the ultimate social personification of the destiny of politi-cal subjectivity under capitalism and of the fact that the withering away of the social also implies a withering away of humanity. As Clyde W. Barrow (*The Dangerous Class. The Con-cept of the Lumpenproletariat* [Ann Arbor: The University of Michigan Press, 2020]) recently ar-gued, by speaking of surplus-population, Marx's mature work directly confronts an underly-ing dystopian dimension of capitalism, intuiting that the globalisation of capitalist relations of production amounts to a progressive lumpenproletarisation of humanity, which poses "in-surmountable obstacles to a theory of revolutionary agency" (14).

naïve yet regulative hypothesis that the dynamic of economic relations can form a stable system and is, therefore, inherently capable of sociality. Marx's entire work tirelessly demonstrates that the truth of "freedom, equality, property and Bentham" is compulsion (of economic relations, which govern our social and subjective life), inequality (following from the asymmetry between capital and labour), and expropriation (reflected, among others, in the act of economic exchange, where the selling of labour-power ultimately implies being expropriated of one's body and life). Now, which proper name could best reflect this nexus between compulsion, inequality, and exploitation, as well as their embedding in surplus-production? Lacan's work offers an implicit answer to this question: Marquis de Sade.

Sade's work revolves around a feature that Lacan somewhat enigmatically calls the "right to enjoyment." According to the established readings, this right uncovers the repressed truth of Kant's foundation of morality on the categorical imperative, a peculiar form of "moral masochism," which results directly from the idea that the realm of morality must be exempted from every "pathological" (personal, individual, or psychological) motivation. However, Sade's literature, and specifically the link between enjoyment and violence (hence, again, expropriation) that Sade continuously places in the foreground, allows us to shed critical light on utilitarianism as well. We merely need to recall the "ethical maxim" that Lacan formulates for the Sadean claim for the right of enjoyment: "'I have the right to enjoy your body,' anyone can say to me, 'and I will exercise this right without any limit to the capriciousness of the exactions I may wish to satiate with your body.'"[26] The way this maxim is formulated, it directly implies the link between enjoyment and expropriation, a radical asymmetry, which suggests that, ultimately, the condition of pursuing my right to enjoy most rigorously implies destroying the other. This point resonates particularly well with Lacan's subsequent remarks on the limits of utilitarianism:

> A word here to shed light on the relationship between law (*droit*) and enjoyment. "Usufruct" – that's a legal notion, isn't it? – brings together in one word ... the difference between utility and enjoyment. ... "Usufruct" means that you can enjoy your means, but must not waste them. When you have the usufruct of an inheritance, you can enjoy the inheritance as long as you don't use up too much of it. That is clearly the essence of law – to divide up, distribute, or reattribute everything that counts as enjoyment.
>
> What is enjoyment? Here it amounts to no more than a negative instance. Enjoyment is what serves for nothing.

---

26   Jacques Lacan, *Écrits* (NY: Norton, 2007), 648.

I am pointing here to the reservation implied by the field of the right-to-enjoyment. Right (*droit*) is not duty. Nothing forces anyone to enjoy except the superego. The superego is the imperative of enjoyment – *Enjoy!*[27]

In the utilitarian, or more broadly, legal framing of the right to enjoyment, it is still possible to postulate a link between enjoyment and happiness, which is certainly at the core of Bentham's political philosophy. Here, one could indeed say that enjoyment is assumed to serve something, in the first place, avoiding pain and pursuing happiness.[28] But, as Lacan points out, right and duty are not the same, and in this precise discrepancy lies the difference between Bentham and Sade: between the right of enjoyment and the imperative of enjoyment, between enjoyment that serves for something and enjoyment for the sake of enjoyment, or enjoyment that becomes its own purpose. This is also the difference between economic liberalism and neoliberalism (or libertarian capitalism): while liberalism still believes that capitalist economic relations can organise life so that it will enforce happiness for most of society's members, neoliberalism ultimately only cares for systemic happiness, and hence for the satisfaction of the capital's drive of self-valorisation. Surplus-value thus contains the negative instance that Lacan determines in the shift from Bentham to Sade, from the right to the imperative of enjoyment. The latter may be addressed to the subject, but what is there implied is that enjoyment always belongs to the Other, and the subject is always expropriated, both of their capacity and of their right to enjoy (or, in the words of Judith Butler, to live a liveable life). To put it differently, the imperative of enjoyment is an impossible right of enjoyment, impossible because it is detached from every subject and belongs to "Nobody" (i.e., no body), or, more specifically, to the free and deregulated Market. Ultimately, only the Market possesses the right to enjoy, while the economic subjects are obliged to enjoy – precisely the enjoyment that is the market's right. This implies, however, that they must renounce every pretence to enjoyment that does not match the demand for surplus-value. The (Sadean) absolutisation of the right of enjoyment prohibits all other articulations and organisations of enjoyment, thus making of enjoyment something that serves for nothing, and this means also turning enjoyment into a key element for enforcing capitalist antisociality.

Lacan then remarks that there is one important limit to enjoyment, which needs to be taken into consideration:

---

27   Jacques Lacan, *Seminar, Book XX, Encore* (NY: Norton, 1999), 3. Translation modified.
28   This is certainly one of Bentham's core illusions, that both psychoanalysis and the critique of political economy decisively drop; happiness is not to be included among the core categories of politics.

> As is emphasized admirably by the kind of Kantian that Sade was, one can only enjoy a part of the Other's body, for the simple reason that one has never seen a body completely wrap itself around the Other's body, to the point of surrounding and phagocytizing it. That is why we must confine ourselves to simply giving it a little squeeze, like that, taking a forearm or anything else – ouch![29]

No one ever saw a body devour another (or two bodies devouring each other); this could be one possible translation of the Lacanian slogan "there is no sexual relation." But the problem with capitalism is, again, that it successfully imposed economic competition as a paradigm of "social" relation, in which bodies do not necessarily surround and phagocytise each other (this is the ultimate Sadean fantasy), but they are nevertheless turned against each other, while being immersed in and, indeed, "phagocytised" by the economic Other (again, the market). Enjoyment here ultimately comes down to the imperative of work – not the work that would serve to safeguard or improve the conditions of individual and social life but work for the sake of work (value-producing work), which responds to the systemic "right to enjoy" and in which the capitalist Other indeed "phagocytises" the subject. Hence, the Freudian link between enjoyment and death again points to the problem of capitalist antisociality and the organisation of aggressiveness into an economic system, striving for continuous extraction of surplus-value through violent and painful "little squeezes."

How, then, should one react to this sinister dimension of capitalism? What is certain is that political resignation and pessimism inevitably lead to another type of affective conformism that is no less problematic than that of *ressentiment*, namely, melancholic resignation. In the end, what unites *ressentiment* and melancholia, despite all their differences, is that they perpetuate the production of surplus-enjoyment. To repeat Freud's valuable point, in distinction from mourning, where a loss is confronted and worked through, in melancholia the loss itself is lost, and the affective state begins extracting a libidinal profit from the state of loss itself (and precisely in this respect the loss can be declared lost or pushed into oblivion). This also explains why neither *ressentiment* nor melancholia cannot amount to a rigorous systemic critique, although they continuously create the appearance of militant criticism (such as in populism, when it comes to *ressentiment*, or in the melancholic positioning of critique such as in Adorno or Benjamin).[30]

Contrary to these affective vicissitudes of the critical faculty, the history of emancipatory movements draws a significant part of its affective motivation from the bonds of solidarity, which refuse to accept the destructive tendencies of the

---

29   Lacan, *Encore*, 23.

30   On Adorno and Benjamin, see Enzo Traverso, *Left-Wing Melancholia. Marxism, History, and Memory* (NY: Columbia UP, 2016).

capitalist mode of production as an overwhelming, pseudo-ontological necessity beyond our influence or control. Here, political subjectivity remains composed of symptomatic bodies, which certainly testify to the ongoing systemic violence and toxicity, but at the same time, continue to resist social dissolution. Marx's sole example of such a symptomatic body was that of the industrial proletariat, a figure of the revolting body, to which others have been added throughout the history of struggles for social emancipation and transformation: the female body and the colonial body, but also the aged and sick body, etc. This is not to say that the historical and lived experiences of systemic violence, to which these corpore-alities and subjectivities (not to say identities) continue to be subjected, must be compared, since such a stance re-embeds them in the (neo)liberal framework of political competition. What these corporealities do have in common, however, is the fact that their subjects are all, by possibility or reality, redundant in the eyes of the system. From a structural point of view, this redundancy is, in the last instance, the imposed fate of every subject of capitalism. The suffering bodies and figures of damaged life are social symptoms in the strong sense of the word, not only signs of capitalist antisociality running amok, but also expressions of a persevering desire for an emancipatory society. That is why resisting the framework of competition, in which liberalism strives to embed diverse emancipatory struggles, and its affective expressions (*ressentiment*) remains a key – and, at first glance, impossible – task of organising political subjectivity in these catastrophic times.

References

Althusser, Louis. "Du 'Capital' à la philosophie de Marx." In *Lire le Capital*, edited by Louis Althusser, Étienne Balibar, Roger Establet, Pierre Macherey, and Jacques Rancière, 3–79. Paris: Quadrige/PUF, 1996.

Balibar, Étienne. "Dying One's Own Death. Freud With Rilke." *Angelaki. Journal of the Theoretical Humanities* 27, no. 1 (2022): 128–139. https://doi.org/10.1080/0969725X.2022.2019479

Barrow, Clyde W. *The Dangerous Class. The Concept of the Lumpenproletariat*. Ann Arbor: The University of Michigan Press, 2020.

Bentham, Jeremy. *The Principles of Morals and Legislation*. NY: Prometheus Books, 1988.

Brown, Wendy. *In the Ruins of Neoliberalism. The Rise of Antidemocratic Politics in the West*. NY: Columbia UP, 2019.

Butler, Judith. *The Force of Non-Violence*. London: Verso, 2020.

Foucault, Michel. *Society Must be Defended: Lectures at the Collège de France, 1975–1976*. London: Penguin Classics, 2020.

Freud, Sigmund. "Trauer und Melancholie." In *Studienausgabe*, vol. 3, 197–212. Frankfurt am Main: Fischer Verlag, 2000.

Lacan, Jacques. *Seminar, Book XX, Encore*. NY: Norton, 1999.

———. *Autres écrits*. Paris: Éditions du Seuil, 2001.

———. *Le Séminaire, livre XVI, D'un Autre à l'autre*. Paris: Éditions du Seuil, 2006.

———. *Écrits*. NY: Norton, 2007.

Marx, Karl. *Capital, Vol. 1*. London: Penguin, 1990. First published 1867.

McGowan, Todd. *Capitalism and Desire. The Psychic Cost of Free Markets*. NY: Columbia UP, 2016.

Rose, Jacqueline. *Why War? Psychoanalysis, Politics, and the Return to Melanie Klein*. Oxford: Blackwell, 1993.

Scheler, Max. *Das Ressentiment im Aufbau der Moralen*. Frankfurt am Main, Vittorio Klostermann, 2004.

Smith, Adam. *The Wealth of Nations*. London: Penguin, 1986.

———. *Theory of Moral Sentiments*. London: Penguin, 2009.

Tomšič, Samo. "The Politics of Resentment and Its Pitfalls." In *Populism and the People in Contemporary Critical Thought*, edited by Alexander Stagnell, David Payne, and Gustav Strandberg. London: Bloomsbury, 2023.

Traverso, Enzo. *Left-Wing Melancholia. Marxism, History, and Memory*. NY: Columbia UP, 2016.

Ure, Michael. "Resentment/*Ressentiment*." *Constellations* 22, no. 4 (2015): 599–613. https://doi.org/10.1111/1467-8675.12098

Vogl, Joseph. *Capital and Ressentiment: A Short Theory of the Present*, translated by Neil Solomon. Cambridge: Polity, 2023.

Becoming a Master of an Island Again: On the Desire to be Bodiless

Adriana Zaharijević

Bodies and fantasies

This text is about contemporary bodies and accompanying fantasies about bodilessness.[1] My main claim is that the paradoxical longing for bodilessness has its twin face in neoliberal and authoritarian regimes of rationality – in the desire to be in complete phantasmal possession of oneself and thus invulnerable to the endless reconfigurations of the world, and in the desire to return to the phantasmal times when society was ordained as an aggregate of self-contained, self-actualising individuals. Both fantasies have been invested in creating the paradigmatic figures of our time – the neoliberal *homo economicus* and the white masculine master of his property and affairs. I wager that both regimes build on the fiction of an independent, sovereign, self-sufficient, and self-actualising being – that is, an individual. The supposition I begin with is that the notion of the individual is misleading because it acts as a paradigm of a featureless anyone, both in economic and political terms. I will instead claim that the individual is neither anyone nor everyman, a bodiless abstraction, but a very concrete abstraction of a certain kind of body, which rests upon numerous erasures of vulnerability and inter/dependence.

To counter the misleading notion of the individual as universally applicable, and to show how neoliberal and authoritarian fantasies converge, I propose we once again read Robinson Crusoe, the mariner of York, as the true representative of the modern individual. Interchanging two fictions, that is, Robinson for an individual, reveals inherent limitations of the latter, exposing, in addition, how the desire to be bodiless goes hand in hand with the desire to place and possess bodies as material or symbolic properties, which are, for various reasons, denied the capacity to be self-actualising, indivisible, and independent.

---

1   This chapter was completed with the support of the Ministry of Education, Science and Technological Development of the Republic of Serbia, according to the Agreement on the realisation and financing of scientific research. An earlier version was published in *Redescriptions: Political Thought, Conceptual History and Feminist Theory* 23, no. 2 (2020): 107–119.

Robinson Crusoe is a curious character: everyone, wherever we come from, remembers something, however vaguely, about this wretched mariner; everyone knows bits of the tedious story of a shrewd but lonesome, pious, and industrious man who happened to have spent quite a long time on an island. Many of us were taught in school that this book was a paradigm of an adventure novel. But the narrative structure of adventure, especially in its abridged forms (those that clip early colonial, capitalist ventures that tell us why Robinson ended up in the Caribbean, and what rewards he encountered once he left his "Paradise gained"[2]), easily transforms into a survival instruction manual. As Virginia Woolf claimed, he is a model of a "naturally cautious, apprehensive, conventional, and solidly matter-of-fact intelligence," a creature easily freed from socially moulded desires, turning them into well-calculated needs.[3] For this reason, already in the 19th century, Robinson often acted as a blueprint of an emerging economic man, and he regularly appeared as part of the fiction of what is in political philosophy figured as the state of nature. Robinson Crusoe is the one who lives without others, without infrastructures and institutions – his independence is absolute. His isolation from society, important for the economists, and his disposition to create society from null, important for the political philosophers, gave this adventure novel quite an unexpected afterlife.

Fiction: The mariner of York

Arguing for non-violence, a "fiction" which many of their interlocutors proclaim utterly unrealistic, Judith Butler would also begin one of their more recent analyses with this all-too-powerful and quite widely accepted fiction. "Some representatives of the history of liberal political thought," says Butler,

> would have us believe that we emerge into this social and political world from a state of nature. And in that state of nature, we are already, for some reason, individuals, and we are in conflict with one another. We are not given to understand *how we became individuated*, nor are we told precisely why conflict is the first of our passionate relations rather than dependency or attachment.[4]

Butler's fictional self-sufficient creature, set to use violence to foreground his independence represented by his possessions, has also been identified with Robinson

---

2   Mary L. Bellhouse, "On Understanding Rousseau's Praise of Robinson Crusoe," *Canadian Journal of Social and Political Theory/Revue canadienne de theorie politique et sociale* 6, no. 3 (1982).

3   Virginia Woolf, "Defoe," in *The Common Reader*, Ebook (London: The Hogarth Press, 1925), n.p., https://gutenberg.net.au/ebooks03/0300031h.html#C08.

4   Judith Butler, "Interpretare la non violenza," *Aut Aut* 384 (2019): 12.

Crusoe, although just in passing. Why do we find Robinson Crusoe, as a useful fiction, in so many places? Following Peter Hulme, who observed in his *Colonial Encounters* that "the island episode of Robinson Crusoe ... provides a simplifying crucible in which complexities can be reduced to their essential components," I want first to see what this fiction provided us with, to then see how it frames our economic and political fantasies today.[5]

The Life and Strange Adventures of Robinson Crusoe of York, Mariner, to use the book's original title, is still regularly figured as an adventure novel. However, the adventures – of an unruly youth who disobeys his father's vows, a seafarer and an investor, an early plantation owner and slave-trader – are quickly passed over to transform themselves into a survival instruction manual (and the manual it was: at the time Robinson's fate was a real possibility, not only for privateers and pirates but also for the settler-colonialists, indentured labourers, and convicts sent to faraway lands). Unlike "the real Robinson," castaway Alexander Selkirk, who spent four years and four dreadful months on a remote Pacific island, Robinson survives – entirely on his own – for 26 long years. Indeed, the tale of the mariner-colonialist is an account of arduous survival – notably free of illnesses, infirmities, and insanity; no dread, phantoms, or deliriums ever haunt him.[6] Soon enough, Robinson describes his situation thus:

> I looked now upon the world as a thing remote, which I had nothing to do with, no expectations from, and indeed no desires about [although he did desire tobacco, turnip, beans and ink] ... I was removed from all the wickedness of the world; I had neither the lusts of flesh, the lusts of the eye, nor the pride of life.[7]

What Robinson needs is circumscribed and wisely adapted. It never turns into a delirious caricature of the civilisation from which he has been temporarily banished,

---

5   Peter Hulme, *Colonial Encounters. Europe and the Native Caribbean 1492–1797* (London: Methuen, 1986), 186.

6   So much so that one wonders how this sudden erasure of society makes almost no imprint on his mind. Turnier's 1960s version of Robinson Crusoe resounds much more with our contemporary understanding of what it means to be so thoroughly left on one's own – after his first failed attempt to escape the desolate place, Turnier's Robinson "degenerates rapidly into a state of animality, discovering oblivion in the stagnant waters and noxious vapours of a pig's wallowing-hole," becoming overcome by dread and phantoms. His later delirious reconstruction of the island *as if* it were populated by more than one person is somewhat less delirious than the fully placid acceptance of life as it is in the original Crusoe. Anthony Purdy, "From Defoe's 'Crusoe' to Tournier's 'Vendredi': The Metamorphosis of a Myth," *Canadian Review of Comparative Literature* 11, no. 2 (1984): 225–226.

7   Daniel Defoe, *Robinson Crusoe*, Ebook (1719; reis., Planet eBook, n.d.), 164–165, https://www.planetebook.com/robinson-crusoe/. Further citations in text.

such as the one we encounter in the 1960s retelling of the story by Michel Tournier in his *Friday, or the Other Island*.

What frees Robinson from society is one deeply social activity: labour. On a lonely island, there is never idleness. Robinson always works – and keeps accounts of that work. This jack-of-all-trades was compelled to learn and relearn all kinds of drudgeries women and men of lower stature must have known and done in the preindustrial era. Labour is central to the adventure (one is compelled to say that labour is the adventure itself): even in complete solitude, one can be driven by continual prospering. Crusoe shows us that although the pleasures are scarce and there are no others to share them with or to protect them from, acquisition and expansion remain utterly meaningful. But in the Lockean vein, labour is necessarily linked to property. It is almost as if, for the island to become a possession, the conquest must come with toil. Locke famously claimed that property comes about by the exertion of labour upon natural resources – when a man "takes something from the state that nature has provided and left it in, he mixes his labour with it, thus joining to it something that is his own; and in that way he makes it his property"[8] – while James Mill proposed that the necessity of labour for obtaining the means of subsistence, as well as the means of the greatest part of our pleasures, is the law of nature attended with the greatest number of consequences.[9]

Thus, instead of degenerating into a delirious state confronted with woeful endless solitude, Robinson is overpowered with joy by the sight of the land "so fresh, so green, so flourishing, everything being in a constant verdure of flourish of spring that it looked like a planted garden." He surveys it "with a secret kind of pleasure," with a keen awareness "that this was all my own; that I was king and lord of all this country indefensibly, and had a right of possession" (128). His is a gaze of an invulnerable self-sufficient settler who, by mixing his labour with the lush nature, becomes its lonely but rightful proprietor. For that reason, in the words of James Joyce, Robinson Crusoe is the true symbol of the British conquest – in the early 18th century, only "a prophecy of empire," which a century later turned into a myth promoting popular colonialism.[10]

And we are compelled to agree with Joyce here. Robinson is not the natural man in the state of nature. He found himself in this tropical garden of Eden as a planter who had left his Brazilian colony on a slave-hunting mission. Although the isle is a perfect *terra nullius*, an ideal virgin land – also a perfect setting for a natural estate figure – the one who surveys and domesticates this land does so not as the one who belongs to nature. Neither does he do that as a "civilised" man who observes God's

---

8   John Locke, *Two Treatises of Government* (1689; reis., London: Rivington, 1824), 5, 27.

9   James Mill, *Government* (London: J. Innes, 1825), 9.

10   Quoted in Richard Phillips, *Mapping Men and Empire: A Geography of Adventure* (London: Routledge, 1997), 33–34.

grace and providence in nature, accepting that he is no more than a meagre part of some graceful scheme. Robinson is a plain but god-like schemer, thoroughly shaped by the civilisation he helped to create. For him,

> the island solitude is an exceptional occasion ... for strenuous efforts at self-help. Inspired with this belief, Crusoe observes nature, not with the eyes of a pantheist primitive, but with the calculating gaze of a colonial capitalist; wherever he looks he sees acres that cry out for improvement, and as he settles down to the task he glows, not with noble savagery, but purposive possession.[11]

In that sense, Robinson's state of nature is not a Hobbesian wolfish dystopia, Lockean naturalised domesticity, or Rousseau's haven of noble savages; it is instead a small colony that – peopled or not – serves as a model of primitive accumulation.[12]

In both Locke's and early utilitarian understanding, where there is labour and possession, there is always also a need for a government. In this vein, from the moment he embraced his fate, Robinson lived as a self-proclaimed sovereign. He first defines himself as a wistful king ruling over "his little family," composed of a parrot, goats, one dog, and two cats – an absolute monarch over his "servants," whom he could "hang, draw, give Liberty, and take it away" (191). In an imaginary kingly fashion, and there being no other to dispute or rebel against "his sovereignty or command" (165), he treats the land and all it bestows as an emperor.[13] Possession and dominion are here inextricably related: being a lonely emperor who possessed – or thought he had the right to possess – everything extended to people who would inadvertently set foot on the island. Robinson provides us with an axiom that property holding involves the right to subordinate, which is part and parcel of a colonialist version of the state of nature figure. After some hundred pages of loneliness, his animal kingdom becomes upgraded with several men, and Robinson exclaims:

> *My island* was now peopled, and I thought myself very *rich in subjects*; and it was a *merry reflection*, which I frequently made, *how like a king I looked*. First of all, the whole country was my own property, so that I had an *undoubted right of dominion*. Secondly, my people were *perfectly subjected* – I was absolutely lord and lawgiver – they all owed their lives to me, and were ready to lay down their lives, if there had been occasion for it, for me (emphasis added; 310).

11   Ian Watt, "*Robinson Crusoe* as a Myth," *Essays in Criticism* 1, no. 2 (1951): 100.
12   Stephen Hymer, "Robinson Crusoe and the Secret of Primitive Accumulation," *Monthly Review* 63, no. 4 (2011): 19.
13   Ian A. Bell, "King Crusoe: Locke's Political Theory in Robinson Crusoe," *English Studies* 69, no. 1 (1988).

Thus, the perfect subjection of *his* people comes only from his good will not to kill them, like the beasts and the birds he undoubtedly possessed, but to "place them" like a patron, father and benefactor.

Although the last long quotation reveals certain cheerfulness, since Crusoe finally found some company after two and a half decades, one needs to be wary of such a supposition. He is, on the whole, a model of a self-sufficient man who could and did survive on his own, free of redundant affects. What he feels is similar to what he needs, and all is gratified through tedious, repetitive, limitedly inventive work, producing a sense of continual, unhindered prospering. But there is still one affect that stands out in Robinson's story – fear. As Stephen Hymer observed, Robinson's "isolation was accompanied not so much by loneliness as by fear. The first thing he did when he arrived on his beautiful Caribbean paradise was to build himself a fortress."[14] There is, of course, a semblance of the Lockean absolute lord of his person and possessions, who, although wildly free, always remains fearful for what he is a proprietor of – his life, liberty, and estates. Fear was also the prime motivator for a Hobbesian individual in his version of the state of nature, where there was no property, no dominion, no mine and thine distinct, nothing apart from the right to war against all others.[15]

In the case of Robinson, years pass before any other to appear in sight. And, unlike Hobbesian and Lockean fictional predecessors who presumably had only sticks and stones to defend what was supposed to be their own, the fearful Robinson is well equipped with non-natural tools (to help him fortify a stronghold, to build walls and fences manically) and with arms which he knows how to use. He reserves for himself the right to war against all others, although no others are anywhere to be seen (after seeing a haunting footprint in the sand, he opts for even more seclusion and isolation, and if he leaves his fortress, he does so armed with a gun, two pistols, and a cutlass). Thus, his independence, or sovereignty, hinges on his intense *social* fear, which translates into subordination or annihilation of others.

The others are a source of fear, possible migrants besieging Crusoe's realm, the land of which he is, in his mind, a sovereign and rightful possessor. Moreover, these migrants belong to other races, and cannibal at that – races that could only be eradicated or subordinated, killed or tamed, never available for some different kind of communion. When Friday once mentions that his people saved 17 "white mens" from drowning, who have now been living for four years at "my nation," left alone by the savages who gave them victuals and "make brothers" instead of eating them, the most of what Robinson can think of is "the truce"; for him, brotherhood with cannibals is beyond imagination (286–287). This applies to "my new man Friday" as well.

---

14   Hymer, "Robinson Crusoe," 27.
15   Locke, *Two Treatises*, 159; Thomas Hobbes, *Leviathan* (1651; reis., Oxford: Clarendon Press, 1965), 98.

This unlikely "friendship" begins with an assumption of privilege and cultural superiority, so pervasive for the entire colonial encounter with the Americas.[16] Their relationship cannot liberate itself from its initial master–slave framework.[17]

Before Friday's falling on his knees in front of his new master, Robinson would mention companionship only twice: once when his dog died of old age after 16 years, and once when he saw a shipwreck of a European vessel, longing, admittedly for the first time in his solitary life, for the society of "but one soul saved out of this ship … that I might but have had one companion, one fellow-creature, to have spoken to me and to have conversed with" (240). That sudden need for companionship produced a warm, irresistible resolution to get himself "a servant, and, perhaps, a companion or assistant." But instead of a potentially unruly and bellicose European, the companion appears in the guise of an exquisitely white-looking man of colour, who becomes singled out by not being killed. To that, Friday famously responded:

> at length he came close to me; and then he kneeled down again, kissed the ground, and laid his head upon the ground, and taking me by the foot, set my foot upon his head; this, it seems, was in token of swearing to be my slave for ever (260–261).

This archetypal scene of colonial libidinality assumes a standing individual whose feet have been willingly put on a head of a non-individual or, at most, of an individual-to-be in some indefinite future moment. Friday was, no doubt, humanised (or individualised): he speaks English, if a Pidgin English (the first word he gets to know is "Master," which for him becomes Robinson's proper name), is clothed, does not eat other men but boiled and roast meat, works diligently, and is even christened by the high priest of the island. The "Massa," however, never let go of an unfounded fear – unfounded because, according to Robinson's account, they "lived there perfectly and completely happy" (283) – that Friday would once return to his nation, bring hundred or two of his countrymen, and make a feast upon him, forgetting "all his obligation to" him (287). Yet that is impossible, because "Friday works like a slave and loves like a child. In addition, he performs many of the housekeeping functions and duties of a wife."[18]

Let us, in the end, turn to one obvious fact: *Robinson Crusoe* is decidedly a gendered story, a story about a *man*, or perhaps about men. True, at the novel's beginning and end, one does encounter a few female figures: his unpersuasive mother, a true helpmeet of the symbolically recurrent figure of the father; and a widow, whom

---

16   Tzvetan Todorov, *The Conquest of America: The Question of the Other* (Norman: University of Oklahoma Press, 1999).

17   Hulme, *Colonial Encounters*, 205.

18   Ulla Grapard, "Robinson Crusoe: The Quintessential Economic Man?" *Feminist Economics* 1, no. 1 (1995): 46.

he entrusted with a sum of money, who will, for her care and faithfulness, earn a name of his benefactor and steward.[19] Finally, there is a wife who appears on a penultimate page of the novel, and, in a *single sentence*, she is married, bears three children, and dies – in the novel that lengthily and painstakingly describes hunting, making candles and earthen pots, milking goats, drying grapes to make raisins, etc. In addition to the general lack of affectivity which characterises this virile tale, the negligible "wife" episode also says something else about women. After his wife's death, Robinson returns to his "new colony in the island," where he finds about 20 young children, begotten by five female Caribbean prisoners (captive men were slaving, women were concubines). As a true patron and landowner, he took care of his little island society, providing it with "all necessary things, and particularly with arms, powder, shot, clothes, tools, and two workmen … a carpenter and a smith." After dividing the land (reserving to himself the property of the whole), he leaves for Brazil and, from there, sends a vessel with some more people, "and in it, *besides other supplies*, I sent seven women, being such as I found proper for service, or for wives to such as would take them." Since we may conjecture that the available women were natives of Brazil, Robinson naturally wanted his fellow Englishmen to do better, and he promises "to send them some women from England, with a good cargo of necessaries" (390–391). With the coming of English wives, we may expect, concubinage would be, to an extent at least, substituted by the proper institution of marriage.

Fiction: An individual as *homo economicus*, as *homo politicus*

It was only in the 19th century that Robinson Crusoe became a powerful fiction, far surpassing the frames of the novel and the adventure. That is, Crusoe became a model individual only in the century of an individual – the moment in history marked by the transference of sovereignty from a sovereign monarch to a sovereign individual; the moment in which the *laissez-faire* principle becomes a governing maxim of the new economic rationality; the moment when the sole owners of their interests populated the space where the free circulation of interests, in the form of goods and capital, had become possible; the moment of a profound transformation of the commonwealth during an age of reform; the moment in which the transformed politics of domesticity thoroughly shaped the individual body, the

---

19 The "widow" might be taken as a symbol of general benevolence with which almost everyone greets Crusoe, also remarked by Hulme (*Colonial Encounters*, 207, 213). There are many benevolent, plain-dealing, charitable, generous persons of integrity who helped Crusoe at various stages of his life, some of whose beneficence is cumulative, and has helped that after 29 years he returns to civilisation as a truly rich man, a model capitalist. This important relationality becomes invisible in abridged versions of the novel, and erased from imagination based on a self-made, self-actualised man of an island.

private and the public spheres, and asymmetrical positioning of the sexes.[20] Having engendered a fiction of its own – that is, the fiction of an individual – the 19th century contrived to find the name for it. That is also probably why Robinson lived through innumerable Robinsonades – hundreds of them having been published before 1900.[21]

Undoubtedly, one might wonder how the solitary survivor of a shipwreck – who would have spent three unimaginative decades in the Caribbean (constantly fortifying his abode and accumulating what he could in his basic economy) – could have become a representative of a modern individual. This, however, ceases to be the question once we dissect the figure of the sole owner of his interest, the subject of reform to whom the sovereignty has been transferred, and who had to be "let go" for the free and unimpeded circulation of interests to take place at all. On the one hand, in economic and political imagery, an individual is simply anyone and no one in particular, a bodiless figure beyond and without time and space, a "one" transferable into a state of nature, or to a lonely island almost at a whim. On the other hand – and this is key, since it is almost by definition omitted from the towering waves of political philosophy and political economy, but is what gave actual flesh to this spurious "everyman"[22] – an individual is the one who, by the standards of his own time, was considered the sovereign and perfectible owner of his interests; the one who knew them and acted in accordance with them, and was, therefore, granted the rights to represent himself, and the right to be the sole owner of his privacy. This individual, however, was not a bodiless anyone but a white, well-to-do, metropolitan man. The two figures differ, but they also merge, hiding behind the indeterminate and seemingly interchangeable qualifiers (anyone or everyman).

In terms of political imagery, Robinson frames John Stuart Mill's famous definition of an individual:

> The only part of the conduct of *any one*, for which he is amenable to society, is that which concerns others. In the part which merely concerns himself, his *independence*

---

20   Adriana Zaharijević, *Ko je pojedinac? Genealoško propitivanje ideje građanina* (Loznica: Karpos, 2014).

21   Phillips, *Mapping Men*, 35.

22   My understanding of an individual is much indebted to a methodological approach described by Duncan Bell in his *The Idea of a Greater Britain. Empire and the Future World Order 1860–1900* (Princeton: Princeton UP, 2007), 22, where he argues that the understanding of the history of political thought is an exercise in retrieval and archaeological reconstruction of the languages through which past generations conceived of the world and their relationship to it, which most of the time happens not at the level of the towering waves of economic and social theory but in the murky shallows of recondite and largely forgotten policy debates.

is, of right, *absolute*. Over himself, over his own body and mind, *the individual is sovereign* (emphasis added).[23]

If this were an apt description of Crusoe, only some sentences further in his *Essay on Liberty* would Mill inadvertently provide one for Friday as well, introducing a potent contradiction concerning the notion of "anyone":

> Despotism is a legitimate mode of government in dealing with barbarians, pro-
> vided the end be their improvement, and the means justified by actually effect-
> ing that end ... Until then, there is nothing for them but implicit obedience to an
> Akbar or a Charlemagne, if they are so fortunate as to find one.[24]

Domenico Losurdo defines this benevolent despotism for "the savage" on their right path to progress – destined to disappear in the distant, indeterminate future – as Mill's "pedagogical dictatorship," which stands side by side with his universalist sovereignty claims.[25] Mill stresses a common liberal belief that no monarch, baron, lord, or state had the right to relativise this independence, simply because it belonged to an individual – it defined what an individual was. An individual is of right independent in an absolute sense, as if no baron and no society existed – as if he were not only the sovereign and a rightful possessor of his own body and mind, but also of an entire island where only birds and beasts kept company to one such body and mind. However, if the body and mind belonged to a barbarian – say, Friday – his independence was equally of right, not absolute, because he was not an individual but an obedient servant who could only hope for a mild and fair lord, embodied here by Robinson himself. Similar inferences could be drawn for women, who were only in a very remote metaphorical sense legally rightful possessors of their bodies and minds.[26]

In terms of economic imagery, it was in the 19th century that Robinson became a figure used to foreground the relevance of capital, or labour, or choice, or exchange.[27] Notably, we do not find him in the thinking of Adam Smith. All these uses are remarkably absent in the 18th century, when middling sorts only began to take shape, and when the individual was only ambivalently on the horizon as the basic unit of

23   John Stuart Mill, *On Liberty* (1859; reis., Kitchener: Batoche Books, 2001), 13.

24   Mill, 14.

25   Domenico Losurdo, *Liberalism. A Counter-History* (London: Verso, 2011), 7.

26   Let us remind ourselves of Carole Pateman here: "women are not *incorporated* as individu-
      als but as women, which, in the original contract means as natural subordinates": *The Sexual
      Contract* (Stanford: Stanford UP, 1988), 181.

27   Matthew Watson, "Competing Models of Socially Constructed Economic Man: Differentiating
      Defoe's Crusoe from the Robinson of Neoclassical Economics," *New Political Economy* 16, no. 5
      (2011).

society. However, in the century of an individual, Robinson is used to posit the ax-iom of political economy – as the basis of the two most dominant economic strands, the neoclassical and later Austrian school – according to which

> what is true for the individual is true for society... all economic phenomena are
> accomplished in [man in isolation], and he is so to speak a *summary of society*. In
> the same way, the human race, taken as a whole, is a huge, collective and multiple
> man to whom the truths observed of individuality itself can be applied (emphasis
> added).[28]

Neoclassical Crusoe economics are founded on the premise that there are univer-sally valid economic laws; that is, archetypal cases extricable from contingent his-torical circumstances and social conditions, which Marx already referred to with derision.[29] As Fritz Söllner claims, "in a way, every man in neoclassical economics lives on an island of his own."[30]

Robinson's body and the fantasies of bodilessness

The invocation of the fictional figure of Robinson Crusoe had a single purpose: to be interchanged with another – politically and economically – crucial fiction, that of an individual, whose cruciality we rarely question, and which we also rarely take as fictional. As I have tried to briefly demonstrate, the fiction gained its centrality in the 19th century, which is also a time of the desired return today – a time of plenitude and acknowledged entitlements. Therefore, I will first claim that Robinson Crusoe presents itself as the embodiment of an independent, sovereign, self-sufficient, and self-actualising possessor, that is, the embodiment of an individual. Here I speak of embodiment on purpose, because this kind of body is a matter of desire, an almost non-existent body, a body which can be imagined away. My second claim is that the libidinal economies of our neoliberal authoritarian era have been shaped around a fantasy of the society of Robinsons, self-sufficient individuals in the double sense: as the individuals who desire to be and succeed in being possessors of islands of their own, and as the individuals endowed with the power to organise and define,

---

28   Frédéric Bastiat as quoted in David Hart, "Literature in Economics, and Economics as Litera-
      ture II: The Economics of *Robinson Crusoe* from Defoe to Rothbard by way of Bastiat," David
      Hart's Webpage, June 28, 2015, http://davidmhart.com/liberty/Papers/Bastiat/CrusoeEcono
      mics/DMH_CrusoeEconomics.html.

29   Fritz Söllner, "The Use (and Abuse) of Robinson Crusoe in Neoclassical Economics," *History of
      Political Economy* 48, no. 1 (2016): 45.

30   Söllner, 61.

restrict, and delimit the meaning of possession. The abstraction of a body, that is, vulnerability, is central to both.

The neoliberal regime of rationality posits an individual as if it is outside of society but from society, simultaneously social and alone, independent from the changing and transient realities, isolated *as if* the society's structures had not existed. Robinson provides an economic fantasy that every man lives on an island of his own, existing *as isolated*, even if he is among his fellow *homines economici*. For a successful application of this scheme, Robinsons need to be rational, selfish, prudent, and calculating beings, indivisible and detached from the environment (and, for that matter, detachable, that is "abstractable" from the comparable conditions of domination and exploitation, as much as Crusoe himself was abstracted from colonialism and slavery, embroiled in those often forgotten, or abridged, parts of the "Crusoe economics"). "When mainstream economists choose to ignore the historical and political aspects of Defoe's story in the construction of their stories, they are in effect denying the centrality of these phenomena to explanations of economic relations."[31] However, we should not forget that the wealth of this isolated individual, utterly unhampered by society, comes to him not from his kingly efforts on the island but from colonial appropriation, plantation slavery, capitalist contracts, and absentee ownership.

On the other hand, Robinson tells us what kind of individual builds a political society from nothing, and provides us with a potent image of the desired *homo politicus*. Again, we are dealing with a particular type of individual, not with – as the early 19th-century writers wanted us to believe[32] – probable everyman. Robinson is an adult white man brought up in an aspiring lower middle-class environment in England. He is thus neither a natural man of the contract theories who builds society as if he never knew what a non-natural (that is, the political) framework might look like, nor is he a sailor who, in his wanderings, embarks on the shores of a utopian island. Crusoe is an adult whose childhood we tend to erase, as much as we are invited to erase his capitalist and colonial past and future beyond the island. His absolute independence on an island had been preceded by various forms of (social) dependence in his (childhood and) youth, and is foregrounded by the fact that he finds a *terra nullius*, an island devoid of other people he can proclaim to be his own. Although

---

31   Grapard, "Robinson Crusoe," 40.

32   As Samuel Taylor Coleridge argued in his 1812 re-reading of *The Life and Strange Adventures*, Defoe's genius made this stranded individual not into some natural philosopher or a proto-biologist – even if "many delightful pages & incidents might have enriched the book" – because, in that case, "Crusoe would cease to be the Universal Representative – the person, for whom every reader could substitute *himself* – But now nothing is done, thought, or suffered (or desired) but what *every man* can imagine himself doing, thinking, (feeling) or wishing for": Samuel Taylor Coleridge, *Marginalia II*, in *The Collected Works of Samuel Taylor Coleridge*, ed. George Whalley (1812; reis., Princeton: Princeton UP, 1984, emphasis added), 165.

he would live in the wilderness, he is not wild, "barbarous" or "savage" – these terms remain in use for other creatures deemed not to have yet attained the status of an individual. His needs (like his skills and tools) remain social but circumscribed and wisely adapted. He remains a white proprietor, who provides us with the axiom that property holding involves the right to subordinate. And in his virile self-sufficiency, no delirious desires appear, or rather, none other than the desire to perceive himself a king and the lord, the invulnerable owner of himself and the island which is almost an extension of his bodiless body – a body which is never ill but forever sane, independent from any infrastructures, needing no institutional support.

And to be bodiless in this way, one needs to be a he. In the last pages of the novel, we indeed find a *femina economica*, a creature whose sole labour (but also choice, exchange, and capital) could be emotional and reproductive. In Robinsons' economic and political world, women have but one role: they give birth to men who live on islands of their own. Women have no part in contracting, fighting, rioting, or building – they appear on the scene at the very end, when all is settled to enable the growth, or rather the multiplication of individuals who become political or economic agents. What happens to women is they marry, bear children, and die – and they do as much in a single sentence. Women remain forever tied to their bodies. They *are* their bodies.

As stated at the beginning of this chapter, the longing for bodilessness has its twin face in neoliberal and authoritarian regimes of rationality. Such a longing is entwined with aspirations for a world sharply divided into Robinsons and Fridays, women and men, the colonists and the colonised, etc.; a world sharply divided into those who "are bodiless," and those bodied and vulnerable beings whose body ties them to a specific place in the hierarchy of things. In that sense, the individuals who live independently on islands of their own are full possessors not only of themselves but of all else they *place* on their island, which acts as an extension of their life, property, and estate. Also, the individuals who live independently on islands of their own are the same ones who *of right* – to confirm their absolute independence – define, restrict, subject, and kill those who are, for some reason or other, "islandless," or who dare to encroach the islands "not of their own." Demanding this right (again) – a return to the necessary and justified form of fortifying the (white and male) mastery over the island – is the true mark of our authoritarian libidinal economies. Thus, the society of Robinsons assumes both (i) the perpetuation of the economic illusion of abstract equality of all to, in a bodiless fashion, become the masters of an island, *and* (ii) the political claim to install inequality at the very heart of that illusion, as the natural part of the mastery.

This is a paradoxical motion of a contemporary individual: forward, in providing ever more signs of complete possession over oneself, and backwards, in search of entitlements, power, and privilege, supposedly phasing away in a world in which so many bodies sought and partially gained recognition in their dependent and non-self-sufficient ways. The backwards-looking fantasy of entitlement relies on a drive to accumulate more possessions and treat others as possessions. It assumes that the available number of islands would never be equally distributed (as the extensions of the possessors' body islands are, in fact, figured as indivisible). It also affirms that the number of islands should remain restricted and available only for the true masters. For that, the world needs to return to a fictional state where everyone knew their place.[33] And when, what is more, it was Robinsons who were "placing" other (bodies) as their phantasmal property on their phantasmal islands. It is precisely as the phantom-possession that Eva von Redecker terms the contemporary residual entitlement, the disposition to dominium – where for some to *have* it, others need to *be* it – others whose very "being the phantom-possession" implies embodiedness, vulnerability, and dependence, and where "having phantom-possession" secures the opposite – the fantasised bodilessness, invulnerability, and independence.[34] For some to be bodiless, other must remain bodies; for full possession to take place, others need to stay in the position of possessions, never attaining the status of possessors themselves.

The desire to be (or become) bodiless has been framed as rejecting any form of dependency and interdependency. The central tenet of a lonely island framework is an enduring struggle for survival: the individuals are self-sufficient because they are self-preserving and dependant solely on their enterprising wits and sturdy frame. The society of Robinsons is markedly asocial. Industriousness, plainness, and moderation, coupled with the lack of any complex desires – other than to possess – turn them into the ones who owe nothing to society, not only to others but to its infrastructures and institutions. Each one is a society of his own. Framed as Robinson, a human is, almost by nature, not dependent; framed thus, a human is also never hungry, cold, ill, or divisible. The human is *without* a body – since it either lives on an imaginary Caribbean island, free from illness, infirmities, and insanity; or has someone, like Friday, to take care of it when young, infirm, and old; or cannot ever get pregnant, that is, *become divisible*. The society of Robinsons wants to supersede a society organised around bodies and vulnerability, to erase its potential to make everyone equal in their vulnerability, something utterly inadmissible within the frame of an arithmetic aggregate of isolated and deserving individuals. The "society of Robinsons" is a fantasy of an asocial society of inventive bodiless entrepreneurs outside or beyond the bonds that make one vulnerable. But it is also, and

---

33   Brenna Bhandar ("Possessive Nationalism: Race, Class and the Lifeworlds of Property," *Viewpoint Magazine*, February 1, 2018) defines this contemporary fantasy of entitlement and *terra nullius* as a fantasy of a return to a simpler, secure time of plenitude, when everyone knew their place.

34   Eva von Redecker, "Ownership's Shadow: Neoauthoritarianism as Defense of Phantom Possession," *Critical Times* 3, no. 1 (2020).

at the same time, a fantasy of a deeply structured society of the invulnerable – of the perpetual colonisers who, of right, turn nature and people into property; manage and place them as their rightful possession, and treat them as a pure sum of well-calculated needs.

The desire to be bodiless, or to return to the fictional time of bodilessness, is not an innocent fantasy – it revolves around entitlements, possession, and conflict. Taking back control and making oneself or your country (your island) great again, in the times of neoliberalism, assumes a return to the time of the individual, who has a servant who puts his non-white head under one's foot as a token of swearing to be enslaved forever; having a woman who marries, bears children, and dies; having your fellow countrymen who continue to accumulate the wealth of your island, which remains the sole property, an extended body of a rightful master and possessor, who reaches out to other island-proprietors in an open exchange, which is then the name for a society.

References

Bell, Duncan. *The Idea of a Greater Britain. Empire and the Future World Order 1860–1900*. Princeton: Princeton UP, 2007.

Bell, Ian A. "King Crusoe: Locke's Political Theory in Robinson Crusoe." *English Studies* 69, no. 1 (1988): 27–36. https://doi.org/10.1080/00138388808598551

Bellhouse, Mary L. "On Understanding Rousseau's Praise of Robinson Crusoe." *Canadian Journal of Social and Political Theory/Revue canadienne de theorie politique et sociale* 6, no. 3 (1982): 120–137.

Bhandar, Brenna. "Possessive Nationalism: Race, Class and the Lifeworlds of Property." *Viewpoint Magazine*, February 1, 2018. https://www.viewpointmag.com/2018/02/01/possessive-nationalism-race-class-lifeworlds-property/.

Butler, Judith. "Interpretare la non violenza." *Aut Aut* 384 (2019): 9–32.

Coleridge, Samuel Taylor. *Marginalia II*. In *The Collected Works of Samuel Taylor Coleridge*, edited by George Whalley, 158–168. Princeton: Princeton UP, 1984. First published 1812.

Defoe, Daniel. *Robinson Crusoe*. Ebook. Planet eBook, n.d. First published 1719. https://www.planetebook.com/robinson-crusoe/.

Grapard, Ulla. "Robinson Crusoe: The Quintessential Economic Man?" *Feminist Economics* 1, no. 1 (1995): 33–52. https://doi.org/10.1080/714042213

Hart, David. "Literature in Economics, and Economics as Literature II: The Economics of *Robinson Crusoe* from Defoe to Rothbard by way of Bastiat." David Hart's Webpage. June 28, 2015. http://davidmhart.com/liberty/Papers/Bastiat/CrusoeEconomics/DMH_CrusoeEconomics.html.

Hobbes, Thomas. *Leviathan*. Oxford: Clarendon Press, 1965. First published 1651.

Hulme, Peter. *Colonial Encounters. Europe and the Native Caribbean 1492–1797*. London: Methuen, 1986.

Hymer, Stephen. "Robinson Crusoe and the Secret of Primitive Accumulation." *Monthly Review* 63, no. 4 (2011): 18–39. Reprint of 1971 article. https://doi.org/10.14452/MR-063-04-2011-08_3

Locke, John. *Two Treatises of Government*. London: Rivington, 1824. First published 1689.

Losurdo, Domenico. *Liberalism. A Counter-History*. London: Verso, 2011.

Mill, James. *Government*. London: J. Innes, 1825. https://oll.libertyfund.org/title/mill-government.

Mill, John Stuart. *On Liberty*. Kitchener: Batoche Books, 2001. First published 1859.

Novak, Maximillian. "Crusoe the King and the Political Evolution of His Island." *Studies in English Literature, 1500–1900* 2, no. 3 (1962): 337–350. https://doi.org/10.2307/449483

Pateman, Carole. *The Sexual Contract*. Stanford: Stanford UP, 1988.

Phillips, Richard. *Mapping Men and Empire: A Geography of Adventure*. London: Routledge, 1997.

Purdy, Anthony. "From Defoe's 'Crusoe' to Tournier's 'Vendredi': The Metamorphosis of a Myth." *Canadian Review of Comparative Literature* 11, no. 2 (1984): 216–235.

von Redecker, Eva. "Ownership's Shadow: Neoauthoritarianism as Defense of Phantom Possession." *Critical Times* 3, no. 1 (2020): 33–67. https://doi.org/10.1215/26410478-8189849

Söllner, Fritz. "The Use (and Abuse) of Robinson Crusoe in Neoclassical Economics." *History of Political Economy* 48, no. 1 (2016): 35–64. https://doi.org/10.1215/0018270 2-3452291

Todorov, Tzvetan. *The Conquest of America: The Question of the Other*. Norman, OK: University of Oklahoma Press, 1999.

Tournier, Michel. *Friday, or the Other Island*, London: Penguin, 1984.

Watson, Matthew. "Competing Models of Socially Constructed Economic Man: Differentiating Defoe's Crusoe from the Robinson of Neoclassical Economics." *New Political Economy* 16, no. 5 (2011): 609–626. https://doi.org/10.1080/13563467.2011.536209

Watt, Ian. "*Robinson Crusoe* as a Myth." *Essays in Criticism* 1, no. 2 (1951): 95–119. https://doi.org/10.1093/eic/I.2.95

Woolf, Virginia. "Defoe." Ebook. In *The Common Reader*. London: The Hogarth Press, 1925. https://gutenberg.net.au/ebooks03/0300031h.html#C08.

Zaharijević, Adriana. *Ko je pojedinac? Genealoško propitivanje ideje građanina*. Loznica: Karpos, 2014.

Erotics as First Philosophy: Metaphysics and/of Desire between Aristotle, Avicenna, Cavendish, and Spinoza

Luce deLire

Theories of desire are largely thought to belong to one of two camps: *negative desire* as lack on the one hand or *positive desire* as engine or productive flow on the other hand.[1] While some say that desire is always after something that is not present, others say that desire is to be understood as an active force. Theories of desire thus seem divided between push and pull, production and attraction, drive and drag, lust and lack, surplus and scarcity.

In this text, I explore the connection of theories of desire to metaphysics. I aim to demonstrate that erotics (theories of desire) and ontology (theories of Being) go hand in hand. Or, more radically: Erotics is (a kind of) first philosophy. I also want to argue that instead of opting for push or pull, positive or negative desires, we should understand desire to be constantly *deflecting* between and beyond the two positions. In this sense, I argue, we should be Cavendishians about desire.

In the second section of this chapter, I introduce the problematicity of *Being*. In short, *Being* cannot be defined as a thing among things – or at least it cannot be defined *like* other things. Traditionally, this problem is solved in two directions: "Being" can mean a set of particular things or "Being" can mean that thing, of which all particular things are affections, modification, properties, etc.

The third section argues that, curiously, an understanding of Being as a plurality seems wired to negative desire as lack on the one hand. And an understanding of Being as one seems connected to desire as a driving force on the other. As exemplary

---

1   Famous proponents of negative desire are Aristotle, Hegel, Rawls and most of contemporary analytic philosophy (more on this later). Famous proponents of positive desire are Spinoza and Deleuze. For an overview of positions, see Jule Govrin, *Begehren und Ökonomie* (Berlin: De Gruyter, 2020). Many thanks to Oliver Thot and Sebastian Moske for support and commentary on this text, and to Yitzhak Melamed and Jason Yonover for inviting me to present a version of this text to the *Spinoza and Early Modern Philosophy* online Colloquium.

cases, I discuss Aristotle, Ibn Sina,[2] Descartes and Spinoza. The fourth section asks for the underlying reason of this curious cartography. With Spinoza as a test case, I demonstrate that a monistic metaphysics does not in fact allow for negative desire simply because it does not leave space for real negativity. Spinoza's model helps us understand why the negative model remains nevertheless attractive: it fits the human experience. In the fifth section, I return to the problematicity of *Being*. I argue that the problem *is real*. I then develop a notion of reality as *deflection* along the lines of Margaret Cavendish's *Observations Upon Experimental Philosophy* (1668).[3] The problematicity that we experience while undertaking to think *Being* or existence itself as absolute infinity is just an adequate expression of the reality of existence itself – hazy, unstable, continuously changing, in constant withdrawal, erratic, transient etc. In the sixth section, I ask what the parallel *Erotics* to this metaphysics would look like. I find traces of such a theory in Baudrillard, Derrida and Spivak. Yet I argue that we should be Cavendishians about desire and take the deflective motion in thought to be isomorphic with the real motions in the body and elsewhere.

A note on terminology: I use the terms *'Being'* and *'existence'* roughly synonymously in the particular context of this paper. I nevertheless recognize that there may be reasons to opt for the one or the other (or another term altogether) in another context, especially regarding their use and etymology.

1. The problematicity of being

According to Aristotle, "[t]he hardest inquiry of all, and the one most necessary for knowledge of the truth, is whether being and unity are the substances of things."[4] Here is a way to understand why that is: definitions are often thought to hinge on

---

2   I am using the names "Avicenna" and "Ibn Sina" interchangeably, yet I will stick to "Ibn Sina" in the main text and use "Avicenna" only where the bibliography demands it. The reason for this is that "Avicenna" is the Latinised version of the Arabic "Ibn Sina." In an attempt of gentle decolonisation, I want to stick to the Arabic transliteration "Ibn Sina" so as to highlight that we are not talking about a white and Western man but rather about a Persian intellectual way before Western colonisation. In short, there was thinking before Western colonisation, and there will be thinking after and beyond it.

3   Margaret Cavendish, *Observations Upon Experimental Philosophy* (Cambridge: Cambridge UP, 2003). For the purpose of this chapter, I will focus on that last book. For more about her philosophy and its genealogy, see Deborah Boyle, *The Well-Ordered Universe – The Philosophy of Margaret Cavendish* (Oxford: Oxford UP, 2018), 70.

4   Aristotle, Metaphysics 3.4.1001a13, 1581. For quotes of Aristotle, I refer to the customary Bekker numbers. Translations are from Jonathan Barnes, ed., "Aristotle: The Complete Works. Electronic Edition," in *The Complete Works of Aristotle*, Bollingen Series LXXI 2, vol. 1, trans. W. D. Ross (Charlottesville: InteLex Corp., 1992).

specific differences that distinguish some thing from all other things.[5] Thus, a straight line is exactly the shortest connection between two sides, a triangle is exactly that geometric figure whose internal angles add up to 180°, etc. These qualities (shortest connection, internal angles add up to 180°) are the *specific differences* in question.[6]

Now, *Being* is a special thing. At first sight, it looks like the thing that encompasses or constitutes all other things. And that is exactly what opens Pandora's box: *If* there is a thing called *"Being,"* then we must define it by way of its *specific difference*. Now, a *specific difference* is that which *distinguishes* the thing defined from all other things. If there was a *specific difference* to *Being*, it would set it apart from all other things. We would then have a sequence of definitions, like: a boat, freedom, Luce, *Being*, the largest prime number etc. The problem is that in this case, *Being* is a thing among things – while it *excludes* all the other things. There is something about *Being* that is not all the other things. And yet, all things should *be*. If our definition of *Being* results in boats, freedom, Luce and prime numbers *not* being, then that defeats the purpose of the definition. This, then, is the *problem of Being*: We would want *Being* to capture everything, in some sense. But once we define *Being*, we do so by way of setting it apart from all other things in some way.[7] So then, *Being* will turn out to designate all things (because that is what we define it to do) *and not* to designate all things (because it requires a *specific difference from* all things as its defining feature). This, however, is a contradiction. What to do?

1. Accept the contradiction, exit philosophy, enter religious piety or mysticism. That path, I will not engage here.[8]
2. *Ontological Analogies*: Give up on *Being* as an overarching category: what we *mean* by *Being* is really dispersed into numerous categories. The classical form of this is Aristotelianism.[9]

---

5   Aristotle, Topics 6.6, Met. 7.12, 10.4, 10.8, 10.9; Gilles Deleuze, *Difference and Repetition*, trans. Paul Patton (1968, reis., London: Continuum, 1994), 31. Also Porphyry, *Isagoge – Texte grec et latin*, trans. Boethius, Alain de Libera, and Alain-Philippe Segonds (Paris: Librairie Philosophique J. Vrin, 1998), 24, sections 8–9.

6   In no way should a definition point to two different things – in that case, we speak of an *equivocation*. And it is a (some say: *the*) philosophical task to avoid or at least mark equivocations wherever they occur.

7   Aristotle makes arguments of this kind in Met. 7.13.1038b1–1038b14, 1639, Met. 7.14.1039a24–1039b2, 1641 and Met. 7.16.1040b16–1040b27, 1643. See also Hobbes in *De Corpore* (Thomas Hobbes, *The English Works of Thomas Hobbes*, vol. 1 [London: John Bohn, 1839], 83).

8   See, for example, Bernard of Clairvaux, "On the Love of God," in *Late Medieval Mysticism*, ed. Ray C. Petry (Louisville: Westminster John Knox Press, 2006), 62; Al'Ghazali, *The Incoherence of the Philosophers*, trans. Michael E. Marmura (Utah: Brigham Young UP, 2000), 3.

9   Another prominent contemporary form is axiomatised set theory, but I will not argue that point in this chapter.

3. *Ontological Univocity*: Give up on the existence of particular *beings* as distinct from *Being* itself as Ibn Sina and Spinoza paradigmatically do.[10]

Curiously, option (2) leads to a notion of *desire* as lack, a striving towards something not present within the desiring actor, while option (3) leads to a notion of *desire* as productivity, a striving hardwired into existence as such and expressed in this or that way. Before I say more about this and why it is that way, I want to exemplify my claim in a few examples.

Aristotle, of course, is paradigmatic. In his view, *Being* is predicated *analogously*: instead of signifying one thing, it is predicated in ten different ways or *categories*.[11] The most fundamental of these, called *substances*, occur in two ways. In a primary way, substances are neither predicated of an other nor are they *in* an other (i.e., individual things such as Ruby the horse). And in a secondary way, substances are predicated of an other, which they cannot be *in* (i.e. species such as horse in general). The other nine categories are specifications or accidents like quantity, quality, position, relation etc. Yet accidents fully depend on substances.[12] Thus, "what being is, is just the question, what is substance?"[13] And Aristotle's response is: only individual things and their species *are* – in the relevant sense of the word. This avoids the *problematicity of Being* in that these substances *can* be defined through a specific difference. A horse is a one-toed Perissodactyla, humans are rational animals etc. But *Being* is not a thing in this way.

---

10   A fourth way is this: give up on definitions based on *specific differences*. Both Hobbes (*The English Works*, 70) and Spinoza (ST, I.7.8–9, I/47, Ep. 60, IV/270/23) opt for a model of definitions that favour efficient causes over specific differences. That is to say, in their model, a definition should tell us *how a thing really comes about* and not *how it is different from all other things*. Yet Hobbes eventually opts for option (2) and Spinoza opts for option (3). Option (4), then, seems inconsequential regarding the eventual notion of *Being* favoured by an author. We are thus left with options (2) and (3).

11   One might wonder if "ontological pluralism" and "analogical Being" are two different things, because the former talks about Being as dispersed into multiple things while the latter talks about Being as predicated in multiple ways. However, I am not aware of anyone who would have an analogical yet monistic understanding of Being. Such an understanding would have to claim that "Being" is predicated of the *one thing*, Being, in multiple ways. But why, if there is only one thing, would we predicate it of itself in multiple ways? More precisely: if there is only one thing, why would that one thing predicate itself of itself in multiple ways? This does not seem to make much sense to me.

12   Aristotle, Met. 7.5.1031a1–1031a14, 1628.

13   Aristotle, Met. 7.1.1028b9, 1624.

Inversely, Ibn Sina famously claims the *univocity* of existence, meaning that "existence" or "Being" has "one meaning."[14] He argues as follows:[15] we do not actually need a separate definition of existence. More specifically, there cannot be one. That is because in every possible definition of "existence," we presuppose the term "existence" or something that exists. Other than in usual definitions, this is not an error but attests to the primordial and unified understanding of existence that we have. Though inexplicable, unified existence is nevertheless inevitable.[16] A mistake only occurs once we try to *add something* to our knowledge about existence. For existence is no such thing. It is always already fully known. We cannot possibly know it any better than it already is. Instead, the term "existence" or any possible argument for its necessity (such as the one in this paragraph) can only *indicate*, but never *add to* what we already know. The error thus lays with the Aristotelian mode of investigation, not with the univocity of existence. Yet, to Ibn Sina, just as to Aristotle, "the first thing to which [existence] belongs is quiddity [essence], which is substance."[17] But while for Aristotle, *Being* is predicated *analogically* of substance and its accidents, to Ibn Sina, existence is predicated *univocally*, such that everything *really exists in one and the same sense*.[18]

---

14   Avicenna, *Metaphysics of The Healing*, trans. Michael A. Marmura (Provo: Brigham Young UP, 2005), I.5.26 (Book I, chapter 5, line 26), 29.

15   See Avicenna, *Metaphysics of The Healing*, I.5.5, 23.

16   Note that this kind of argument returns in Ibn Sina's *Flying Man Argument*, a concise predecessor of Descartes' *Cogito*. See Jari Kaukua, *Self-Awareness in Islamic Philosophy – Avicenna and Beyond* (Cambridge: Cambridge UP, 2015), 31; Peter Adamson, *Philosophy in the Islamic World: A Very Short Introduction* (Oxford: Oxford UP, 2015), 84.

17   Avicenna, *Metaphysics of The Healing*, I.5.21, 27. See also Aristotle, Met. 7.6.1031a28–1031b21, 1628 for a parallel passage.

18   Are ontological monism and univocity about Being the same thing? I think so. (1) *Monism implies univocity*. If there is only one thing anyway, all predications are that one thing (if you think Spinoza was an exception, see Luce deLire, "Spinoza's Special Distinctions," *Journal of Philosophical Research*, Fall 2024, forthcoming.) (2) *Univocity implies monism*. To show this, assume the opposite: either many things "being" exist, or nothing exists. (2a) Assume any one sense of the word "being" (univocity) and simultaneously assume that there is no one thing "Being" (monism), but many (ontological pluralism). The predication is allegedly one, but the referents are allegedly many. It then seems undecidable what is "meant" by the univocal "being." (2b) Alternatively, assume that "being" is predicated univocally, while there is no thing "Being" at all. Then, all predications of "being" come out wrong in the same way (negative univocity) – nothing exists. Either (2a) "to be" has a murky referent, yielding essentially unintelligible statements. Or (2b) "to be" has no referent, yielding false statements. In the second case, nothing exists. In the first case, what it means to exist is constitutively unclear. Both seem unconvincing. Univocity is, hence, incompatible with ontological pluralism and ontological nihilism. Univocal monism, however, is both intelligible and allows for things to exist. Consequentially, univocity implies monism (2). And monism implies univocity (1). Univocity and monism are thus the same thing.

2. Theories of desire

Theories of desire generally answer to a particular question of movement: why do things move towards each other and act in particular ways? Why do people cross oceans to meet each other, or invest resources in order to access specific kinds of food? Are they motivated in the same way as the flower is to grow and the bullet is to kill? These are the kinds of questions that theories of desire, which I suggest calling *Erotics*, respond to.

Now, curiously, the analogical (pluralistic) and the univocal (monistic) approach to *Being* or existence map onto different theories of *desire*. Thus, Aristotle's view is that objects of desire are "the good or the apparent good,"[19] "i.e., that for the sake of which, [meaning] ... [final] causes."[20] The Christian tradition especially tends to interpret final causes to reside temporally *after* their effects.[21] If you want to go home to sleep, sleep comes *after* going home and yet it (allegedly) *causes* movement.[22] The most extensive study on Aristotle's theory of desire to date comes from Gilles Pearson, who understands Aristotelian desire more generally to consist in "*the prospect of*

---

19   Aristotle, De Anima 3.10, 433a27–28.

20   Aristotle, Met. 1.2, 982b11–982b28. See also Gilles Pearson, *Aristotle on Desire* (Cambridge: Cambridge UP, 2012), 62, 105.

21   Aristotelianisms of the past two millennia can be roughly divided into materialistic (judeo-islamic) and idealistic (christian) interpretations. This division crucially turns on materialists highlighting "a desiring intellect or thinking desire," while idealist interpretations tend to opt for a "deliberate forgetting" of the same (Dobbs-Weinstein, Idit. "Aristotle on the Natural Dwelling of the Intellect." In: *The Bloomsbury Companion to Aristotle*. Edited by Claudia Baracchi (ed.). London: Bloomsbury 2014, 298 – for more on that same debate, see: Bloch, Ernst. *Avicenna and the Aristotelian Left* (NY: Columbia UP, 2019) as well as and Dobbs-Weinstein, Idit. "Thinking Desire in Gersonides and Spinoza." In: *Women and Gender in Jewish Philosophy*. Edited by Hava Tirosh-Samuelson. Bloomington: Indiana UP 2004, 56.). Given the debate's age and the partially unclear status of the source material (most of what we have of Aristotle are his lecture notes), it seems unlikely that we can find out what the historical Aristotle might have been up to. However, I do not think this interferes with my general argument.

22   Elisabeth Anscombe, *Intention* (Ithaca: Cornell UP, 1976); Dennis Stampe, "The Authority of Desire," *The Philosophical Review* 96, no. 3 (1987); Warren Quinn, *Putting Rationality in Its Place* (Cambridge: Cambridge UP, 1993); Daniel Friedrich, "Desire, Mental Force and Desirous Experience," in *The Nature of Desire*, ed. Federico Lauria and Julien Deonna (Oxford: Oxford UP, 2017); Graham Oddie, *Value, Reality and Desire* (Oxford: Clarendon Press, 2005); Graham Oddie, "Desire and the Good: In Search of the Right Fit," in *The Nature of Desire*, ed. Federico Lauria and Julien Deonna (Oxford: Oxford UP, 2017). Although the Aristotelian theory is often deemed *evaluative* in that it generates *reasons* for action, this seems to be an unnecessary and unhelpful conceptual restriction.

objects of desire."[23] In this prospect, however, the driving force of desiring activity is the lack of the desired object. Let us call this *negative desire* – desire as movement by final causes and towards an absence.[24]

Ibn Sina, however, is a prime example of another interpretation of similar topics (and a similar canon). To him, desire is not chasing for something absent. For him, desire ensues from an actual encounter. More concretely, desire happens in a (partially corporeal) animal soul that has certain dispositions whenever an imposing stimulus triggers that disposition into action.[25] Desire is thus not a longing but an embodied form that may be set in motion once the necessary ingredients occur.[26] There is no space for absence in this picture.

Things, however, may still be *imagined* as absent and possibly longed for. In this case, the reality of the representation of an imagined thing in memory is all the reality there is. Thus, when I desire a kiss, that kiss, to Ibn Sina, is not retroactively causing me to act in some way from the future. Rather, the concrete image (as a memory or a pastiche of sensations) *actually triggers my disposition* to move. This, however, is not a genuinely negative or suspended kind of reality. Rather, "its form is represented internally."[27] The form is, in fact, present, namely as reactivated memory (be it a concrete memory or one collaged together), an image stored in the mind that is literally re-present-ed, or re-activated. That representation itself *causes* the movement experienced as desire. No retroactive or final causation is taking place. Let us call this *positive desire* – desire as oriented by efficient causes.

---

23   Pearson, *Aristotle on Desire*, 225. Pearson analyses the tripartite of Aristotelian desires: pleasure and revenge (117), the good (164), and the "goal" (165). For this chapter, a brief account is sufficient.

24   For examples in contemporary analytic philosophy, see David Pineda-Oilvia, "Defending the Motivational Theory of Desire," *Theoria: An International Journal for Theory, History and Foundations of Science* 36, no. 2 (May 2021): 244–247. The traditional proponents of this view on the continental side are Hegel and Lacan. See exemplarily Georg Wilhelm Friedrich Hegel, "Lordship and Bondage," in *Hegel's Dialectic of Desire and Recognition: Texts and Commentary*, ed. John O'Neill (Albany: SUNY Press,1996), especially 33; Edward S. Casey and J. Melvin Woody, "Hegel and Lacan: The Dialectic of Desire," in *Hegel's Dialectic of Desire and Recognition: Texts and Commentary*, ed. John O'Neill (Albany: SUNY Press, 1996), 227. See more extensively Jacques Lacan, *Desire and its Interpretation*, ed. Jacques-Alain Miller, trans. Bruce Fink (Cambridge: Cambridge UP, 2019).

25   Avicenna, "Selections on Psychology from *The Cure*, 'The Soul,'" in *Classical Arabic Philosophy – An Anthology of Sources*, ed. John McGinnis and David C. Reisman (Indianapolis: Hackett Publishing, 2007), The Soul Book I, chapter 5, section 4, 180.

26   Shams Inati, *Ibn Sina's Remarks and Admonitions: Physics and Metaphysics – An Analysis and Annotated Translation* (NY: Columbia UP, 2014), Part II, Class 3, Chapter 6, 357–358 (in the Arabic source), 97 (in Inati's English translation) (hereafter "II.3.6.357–358/97").

27   Inati, III.8., 367/98. See also Inati, II.3.30., 449–450/114–115.

Of course, Ibn Sina does believe in a strict normative hierarchy between the faculties of the mental apparatus. In fact, the "practical faculty" which moves the body based on reflecting "what is required by customary opinions,"[28] "should rule over the other faculties of the body in accordance with the judgments [of the theoretical faculty]."[29] This looks as though good minds were supposed to rule over bad desire-ridden bodies according to solid social norms, meaning according to a necessary purpose or *final causes*. Yet, to Ibn Sina, *theoretical* insight in its most immediate form, which we may call "intellectual intuitions," is neither brought about by forceful mental activity, nor is it opposed to desire. In fact, intellectual intuition relies on the "preparedness for accepting" sudden insight,[30] coupled with "the demand of the soul" (actively looking for insight),[31] although it may occur without the latter and despite differently directed desires.[32] To Ibn Sina, however, *receptivity for spontaneous recognition of the truth* and desire as an active force go hand in hand.[33] There is no final causation in play here, only efficient causal interaction between actualised things.

There is a link, then, between analogical ontology and negative desire, exemplified in Aristotle and inversely between univocal ontology and positive desire, exemplified in Ibn Sina. This link, however, may be spotted across the philosophical spectrum. Despite obvious candidates for the continuation of the Aristotelian model such as Ibn Rushd,[34] Ibn Hazm,[35] Kant,[36] Hegel,[37] Rawls,[38] and contemporary analytic philosophers,[39] we can find it even in Descartes. That should surprise us. To Descartes, allegedly the "father of modern philosophy,"[40] "the term 'substance' does

---

28   Avicenna, "Selections on Psychology," I.5.12, 183.

29   Avicenna, I.5.13, 186.

30   Inati, II.3.15, 403/106.

31   Ibn Sina, *The Cure (al-Shifā')*, edition by various scholars in 22 volumes, (Cairo, 1952–1983), 245–246, quoted in Dimitri Gutas, "Ibn Sina [Avicenna]," in *The Stanford Encyclopedia of Philosophy*, ed. Edward N. Zalta (Fall 2016 ed.).

32   Inati, II.3.11, 393/103.

33   Ibn Sina illustrates this process when he talks in his autobiography about his trouble understanding Aristotle's *Metaphysics*. See Dimitri Gutas, *Avicenna and the Aristotelian Tradition – Introduction to Reading Avicenna's Philosophical Works* (Leiden and Boston: Brill, 2014), 17–18.

34   Averroes, *The Incoherence of the Incoherence*, trans. Simon Van Den Bergh (Gibb Memorial Trust, 2008), 354.

35   Ibn Hazm, *The Ring of the Dove*, trans. A.J. Arberry (London: Luzac & Company, 1953).

36   Immanuel Kant, *Kritik der Urteilskraft* (Berlin: De Gruyter, 2009), AAV, 177, fn. For an English version, see Immanuel Kant, *Critique of Judgment*, trans. James Creed Meredith (Oxford: Oxford UP, 2007), 13, fn 1.

37   Hegel, "Lordship and Bondage," 33.

38   "The general desire for justice limits the pursuit of *other ends*" (emphasis added): John Rawls, *A Theory of Justice – Revised Edition* (Cambridge: Belknap Press, 1999), 5.

39   See Pineda-Oilvia, "Defending the Motivational Theory of Desire," fn. 18.

40   "[I]t was probably a German historian, Kuno Fischer (1824–1907), who first put Descartes forward as the father of modern philosophy": Christia Mercer, "Descartes' Debt to Teresa of Ávila,

not apply univocally ..., there is no distinctly intelligible meaning of the term which is common to God and his creatures."[41] Descartes is thus in Aristotle's camp regarding the nature of *Being* as predicated analogically. Famously, however, he sports a *mechanistic* program, reducing all causation to efficient causation (modelled on the interaction between billiard balls etc.). Accordingly, final causation should not have any role to play here. Thus, it looks as though Descartes was a counter-example to my general observation: analogical ontology combined with a positive theory of desire.

Now, in the *Passions of the Soul*, Descartes defines the *passions* as effects on the soul, "caused, maintained and strengthened by some movement of [bodily] spirits."[42] With "spirits" referring to Early Modern medical theories, Descartes' philosophy of passions is supposed to be strictly physiological or mechanistic, effectively based on things acting on each other. Yet he states that "desire" works to "acquire a good which one does not yet have, or avoid an evil that one judges may occur, but also [applies] if one wishes nothing but the conservation of a good or the absence of an evil." All of these, Descartes says, are directed towards the *"future [avenir]."*[43] He continues, "It suffices to think that the acquisition of a good or the avoidance [*fuit*] of an evil be possible to incite a desire."[44] Further, he explains sexual desire (*agrement*)[45] with the natural feeling of being one half of a whole that is defective (*défectueux*) without an other.[46] Both cases, desire in general and sexual desire in particular, operate by virtue of a motivational *lack*, be it the lacking object that is being projected into the future (desire) or the lacking other half (sexual desire). Neither of them can be characterised as efficient causes.[47] Desire necessarily oriented towards an absent future and sexuality missing an absent other half both exemplify a theory of *negative* desire

---

or Why We Should Work on Women in the History of Philosophy," *Philosophical Studies: An International Journal for Philosophy in the Analytic Tradition* 174, no. 10 (October 2017): 2540.

41   René Descartes, *Principles of Philosophy*, Part I, section 51 (AT VIIIA 24). Translations are from René Descartes, *The Philosophical Writings of Descartes*, vol. 1, trans. John Cottingham, Robert Stoothoff, and Dugald Murdoch (Cambridge: Cambridge UP, 1985), 210.

42   René Descartes, "Les Passions de l'Ame," in *Oeuvres Complètes de René Descartes*, electronic ed. (Charlottesville: InteLex Corporation, 2001), part I, section 27 (hereafter "I.27"). Translations are mine.

43   Descartes, II.57. Emphasis added.

44   Descartes, II.58.

45   See Anthony F. Beavers, "Desire and Love in Descartes's Late Philosophy," *History of Philosophy Quarterly* 6, no. 3 (July 1989): 288.

46   This theory responds to an old tradition of philosophies of the other half. See, for example, Plato, "Symposion," in *Plato – Complete Works*, ed. John M. Cooper and D. S. Hutchinson, trans. Alexander Nehamas and Paul Woodruff (Indianapolis and Cambridge: Hackett, 1997), 189e–193d; Govrin, *Begehren und Ökonomie*; Hazm, *The Ring of the Dove*; Lucrezia Marinella, *The Nobility and Excellence of Women and the Defects and Vices of Men*, ed. Anne Dunhill (Chicago and London: University of Chicago Press, 1999), 63.

47   For a related point, see Beavers, "Desire and Love in Descartes's Late Philosophy," 288.

and final causation. Descartes thus aligns with Aristotle on the conjunction between analogical ontology and negative desire after all – against his overall commitment to the reduction of all causation to efficient or mechanistic causation.

On the other side of the spectrum, Spinoza, a central engine of the European Enlightenment and Descartes' natural enemy,[48] has no problem characterising desire in purely positive terms. Spinoza in particular, not unlike Ibn Sina, is committed to the univocity of *Being*.[49] For Spinoza, there is nothing outside God,[50] defined as "absolutely infinite Being,"[51] who is also the only substance or *Being (Ens)*[52] and, therefore, everything there is.[53] Departing from his predecessors, Spinoza claims that absolutely infinite Being (*Ens*) is the cause of itself (*causa sui*).[54] This is crucial because, to Spinoza, desire is the particularised form of the self-causation of absolutely infinite being itself (aka reality, aka God) accompanied by consciousness thereof.[55] It is a genuine expression of divine auto-motion. For example, my desire to kiss you

---

48   See Jonathan Israel, *Radical Enlightenment: Philosophy and the Making of Modernity* (Oxford: Oxford UP, 2002), 22; Jonathan Israel, *Enlightenment Contested: Enlightenment, Modernity, and the Emancipation of Man 1670–1752* (Oxford: Oxford UP, 2008); Ursula Goldenbaum, "The Pantheismusstreit—Milestone or Stumbling Block in the German Reception of Spinoza?," in *Spinoza's Ethics: A Collective Commentary*, ed. Michael Hampe, Ursula Renz, and Robert Schnepf (Leiden: Brill, 2011); Ursula Goldenbaum, "Spinoza – Ein toter Hund? Nicht für Christian Wolff," *Zeitschrift für Ideengeschichte* 5, no. 1 (Spring 2011). See also Luce deLire, "'[E]very Day the Matter Seems to Get Worse, and I Don't Know What I Should Do.' – Violence, Spinozism and Digital Reality," in *Skin and Code*, ed. Daniel Neugebauer (Spector Books, 2021).

49   For the often-neglected historical trajectory of an Islamo-Judeo-Arabic materialistic "Aristotelian left" tradition, see Ernst Bloch, *Avicenna and the Aristotelian Left* (NY: Columbia UP, 2019); Idit Dobbs-Weinstein, *Spinoza's Critique of Religion and its Heirs: Marx, Benjamin, Adorno* (Cambridge: Cambridge UP, 2015), 35. See also deLire, "[E]very Day the Matter."

50   E1p15. Quotation of *Ethics* are from Pierre-François Moreau, ed. and trans., *Spinoza – Oeuvres IV – Ethica/Éthique* (Paris: Presses Universitaires de France, 2020), where a first number signifies a page in the Latin text and a second number the line on that page. "PUF 13/22–23" thus refers to page 13 in the Latin edition by Presses Universitaires de France, lines 22 and 23. They are noted by "E" (for *Ethics*), followed by the number of the chapter, and further specifications. So "E1p10s" refers to *Ethics*, chapter 1, proposition 10, scholium. "E3DA1" stands for *Ethics*, chapter 3, definition of affects number one, etc. Other texts are quoted from the Gebhardt edition and referenced by the so-called "Gebhardt numbers," referring to Carl Gebhardt, ed., *Spinoza: Opera* (originally 4 vols, Heidelberg: Carl Winter-Verlag, 1925; 2nd ed. Heidelberg: Carl Winter-Verlag, 1973). For example, "II/37/10–15" refers to the second volume of the Gebhardt edition, page 37, lines 10–15. "TIE" stands for the *Tractatus de Intellectus Emendatione*, followed by the paragraph and the Gebhardt number. "Ep." stands for "letter." If not otherwise noted, translations from Latin are mine.

51   E1d6.

52   See E1p10s, E1d6.

53   E1p14.

54   E1p7.

55   E3p6d, E3p9s, E3DA1.

is a partial manifestation of divine self-causation or auto-motion. If that motion goes unblocked, Spinoza says, I feel joy. Yet in the inverse case, whenever external interferences obstruct that particularised motion (my desire), I sense sadness. From these three (desire, joy, sadness), Spinoza composes all other affects.[56]

Regarding positive desire and univocal ontologies, Spinoza is a particular case. Here, individual desires *are nothing but* particularisations of the self-causing force of absolutely infinite *Being*.[57] For absolutely infinite being is all there is.[58] And so, the self-causation of absolutely infinite being *as a whole* and the causal effects of its particular manifestations (such as you, me, and all the butterflies in the universe) are distinguished only by virtue of a particular, partial comprehension. To Spinoza, the distinction between the self-causation of the universe and a candle that causes its wax to melt is like the distinction between the movement of an ocean and the movement of a particular wave within that ocean.[59] No distinction actually occurs. The distinction is really just a constriction of perspective.[60] While Ibn Sina did claim the univocity of existence on the one hand and the positivity of desire on the other hand, to Spinoza, these two claims are one and the same thing. There is not only but one existence or *Being*[61] but only one self-causing cause as well,[62] absolutely infinite Being and its various manifestations. Spinoza, then, extends the univocity of Being to the univocity of causation:[63] "God must be called the cause of all things in the same sense in which he is called the cause of himself."[64]

3. Where being meets desire

In the previous sections, I have sketched some paradigmatic cases (Aristotle, Ibn Sina, Descartes and Spinoza) to motivate my hypothesis that an analogical ontology aligns with negative desire and a univocal ontology aligns with positive desire. For all I know, the parallelism persists in the history of Western philosophy. But mere historical pastiche will not do. How is this connection between ontological and libidinal commitments not merely accidental? A possible answer comes from Spinoza.

---

56   E3p9s.
57   E1p25s.
58   E1p15.
59   E1p15s; PUF 15/24–27.
60   Really, the matter is a bit more complicated. See further Luce deLire, "Spinoza's Conceptual Distinctions" (forthcoming).
61   E1p14, E1p15.
62   Mogens Laerke, "Spinoza and the Cosmological Argument According to Letter 12," *British Journal for the History of Philosophy* 21, no. 1 (2013): 57–77.
63   Laerke, "Spinoza and the Cosmological Argument According to Letter 12," 57–77; E1p25.
64   E1p25s.

Besides standing firmly on the side of univocity, Spinoza also firmly opposes desire as lack. I am going to present three arguments to this end: an argument based on the univocity of *Being*, another based on the univocity of *causation*, and a third based on the nature of negativity.

3.1 The univocity of being

In the appendix to the first part of the *Ethics*, Spinoza argues as follows: "... [I]f God [aka absolutely infinite Being] acts because of an end [including negative desire], he necessarily wants [*appetit*] something which he lacks [*caret*]."[65] But because God is all there is, she cannot lack anything.[66] If she *did* lack something, she would not be all there is, as that lacking thing would exceed her. But God *is* absolutely infinite *Being*,[67] and everything is within God.[68] Therefore, there cannot be anything that is not in fact God. Consequentially, God cannot desire *negatively*. And because all particular things in Spinoza's framework are just modifications of God, they cannot desire *negatively* in a real sense either. For if they did, they would fundamentally differ from God in exactly that respect. And yet, given the univocity of *Being*, they are nothing *but* God.[69] Therefore, they must behave *like* God. And just as God cannot desire negatively, her particularisations cannot do so either.[70]

3.2 The univocity of causation

To Spinoza, the distinction between the absolutely infinite cause (God) and its partial manifestations (such as the construction site outside your bedroom window that wakes you up in the morning) is really just an effect of our partial perspective. Therefore, individual desire *just is* absolutely infinite self-causation particularised, or actualised *for* a certain spectator. And as there cannot be any reality to anything lacking within absolutely infinite *Being* (because that is all there is), the same must count for its particularisations. Yet again, because all things are really just particularisations of God and God is driven *positively* by the necessity of her own essence, any particular thing must be driven by the same cause, namely the necessity of the divine essence.[71]

---

65   E1App; PUF 37, 6–7.

66   See also E1p33s2.

67   E1d6, E1p10s, E1p14c1.

68   E1p15.

69   E1p15.

70   In fact, to Spinoza, the existence of final causes is the mother of all prejudices. And end-driven desire, I think, should not be an exception. E1App; PUF 34, 7–19.

71   E1p24c, E1p25, E2p10c.

3.3 The inexistence of negativity

Inversely, if there were real final causes for Spinoza, then there really was something that does not exist, or at least not yet – such as a future lover's kiss or tonight's sleep. Yet, to Spinoza, that is not the case: everything is always already actualised, including your future lover's kiss or the inexistence thereof. For if something was not yet actualised, God would lack it. But God cannot, by definition, lack anything.[72] Therefore, there cannot be anything in God that is not already actualised. And consequentially, there can be neither final causes nor negative desires.

Therefore, to Spinoza, negative desire cannot exist in a real sense. Not unlike in Ibn Sina's picture, however, negative desire *can* exist in an *imaginary* sense. For although all causal relations are necessarily determined, we may still *mistakenly* experience our goal as driving us. Thus, although that stone flying into a police officer's face is of course mistaken about her desire, she may still have the impression that she did really desire that line of flight. For in the absence of the full order of causes, we sometimes fill the blanks with non-existing causes, such as (and especially) final causes.[73] This imaginary desire is just an insufficient assessment of the actually determining causes at play. Yet that absence itself, in turn, serves as a full explanation for that imaginary desire: because I do not know what causes my desire, I ascribe the reason for desiring to the object of desire. For that is where I sense the action to happen. In fact, then, negative desire reifies a lack of knowledge into an ontological force.

An example: I love you. But I do not know why. I do not know that it is because you share some crucial characteristics with caregivers that traumatised me early in life. So I ascribe my love to your beauty, your sense of humour and overall perfection. When you are absent, I experience these characteristics as *lacking in my life*. In brief, I miss you. Without you, I am sad, my life is incomplete. I have thus turned a lack of knowledge into a magical force, pulling me towards you, situated in your particular characteristics – your smile, your jokes, the way you move. Consequentially, Spinoza's model enables us to explain *negative desire* as a kind of *positive desire*, namely as positive desire poorly understood.

Further, Spinoza's model helps us understand the connection between a univocal approach to ontology and positive desire: if everything is said to exist in the same way (and effectively as the same thing), then there simply is no negativity that would allow any *negative desire* in a real sense to get off the ground. Note that this claim is crucially connected to the univocity of *Being* – for *Being itself* has no space for non-being. In fact, *Being*, whatever it is, is that which is not non-being. But negative desire *relies* on non-being as its objective, as the pulling force, the location of lack. Yet

---

72   E1d6, E1p10s, E1p14c1, E2p8.
73   E1App; PUF 35.

without any possible lack, there cannot be a motivating force as the origin of desire either. So, if there is no lack in *Being* itself, *Being* cannot desire negatively. Now, if every particular is just a modification or determination of *Being* itself, then particulars cannot desire negatively either. And further, if every particular *cause* is just a modification or determination of *Being* as it causes itself, then the same must count here too: there are no negative causes within absolutely positive *Being*. In short, the univocity of *Being* and of *causation* leave no space for negativity – and thus no space for negative desire either.

Inversely, if *Being* is predicated analogically of really distinct things, then these things (may) well relate *negatively* to one another (although they may also not relate negatively to each other, depending on your other ontological commitments).[74] They may lack each other and be pulled in each other's directions. The question about the nature of desire is, therefore, deeply ontological. It is a question about the nature of reality, being or existence itself and about the position of negativity within it. Erotics as a field of study, then, *just is* metaphysics from another angle. In short, if reality is one, then negativity does not exist in a real sense. And consequentially, all desire must be *positive* desire, originating from a push and not a pull. Inversely, if reality is dispersed into really distinct things, then there is room for negativity in a real sense (although its existence is still not necessary). And consequentially, desire *can* be *negative* desire, originating from a pull and not a push.

But how come an analogical ontology has this inner tendency towards *negative* desire? How does "can" become "is"? As pointed out, the univocal picture provides an explanation for the disagreement between the two views to begin with: negative desire is positive desire poorly understood. Whenever we do not know what is going on, we fill the gap. It seems plausible to me that people would often go into Spinoza's trap: Where we do not have a good explanation at hand, we reify our own experiences into ontological truths. In other words, in the absence of knowledge, ignorance is being hailed as reality. And in fact, this seems to be a main reason for the prominence of *negative desire* as a paradigmatic philosophical stance: It just seems to be a fair description of our *experience*, which, however, is itself rendered by an incomplete understanding of the world at large and the causes that drive us in particular. Descartes is a good example; while trying to explain the force of desire, he goes so far as to betray his own mechanistic commitments.

---

74   Arguably, this might be a reason for the debate between the materialistic Aristotelian Left and the idealistic Aristotelian Right – see footnote 47 of this text.

4. The eclipse of existence

It would be nice if Spinoza had it right and the story could end here. And yet there is a problem. I want to argue that the problematicity of *Being* (see section 2) is not a mistake but a real phenomenon. In order to see this, we should try to think reality itself, *Being* or existence once more in the full sense of the term and see where and how exactly the undertaking fails.

When we try to think reality itself, absolute infinity, *Being*, we basically have two strategies: we can think it bottom up or top down, starting from particulars or starting from the most general level at our disposal. Let us then pursue both strategies and see what happens.

Particular things always exist by virtue of their context, other things, etc. But when exactly does the coffee I drink become a part of me? And how about the air I breathe, the society that shapes my personality, the historical era that provides the condition for my existence more generally? Each particular thing in a way overflows its particularity into other particulars and their surroundings, contexts, etc., respectively, *ad infinitum*. Each particular thing gives way to a more encompassing thing – me, the city, the universe, etc. We should think, then, that we would ultimately reach reality *itself*, existence *itself*, absolute infinity, *Being* or however you want to call it. And yet, upon thinking this ultimate frame of reference (however you want to call it), we must think it as *a thing* – as something particular. This may be an infinite, all-encompassing, ultimate *thing* – nature, the universe, *Being* – but a thing nevertheless. As the end point of a process of continuous dissolution, then, we reach an all-encompassing *particular thing* that entails all the other *things*. Yet this cannot be *Being* or reality itself, because obviously, train tracks, golf clubs, and natural numbers are real as well.

Let us then start top down. If we start thinking reality *itself* directly as absolute infinity etc., we may think it as a large, malleable sphere of indeterminacy or something like that. In this case, again, we think it as a sort of overarching *thing*, not as any set of particulars. Or else we may think reality itself as the set that entails all the (relevant) particulars. In this case, it will still eventually be one thing – *that set*, entailing all the (relevant) particulars. Or again, we may think reality itself simply as *all the particulars*. But then, we will miss combinations of particulars, such as the individual people that make up a political party or the particulars that make up a school of fish – and yet, the school of fish is not *just* a collection of individuals and the party is more than just its members.[75]

---

75   For an introduction to the related debate in metaphysical mereology, see Achille Varzi, "Mereology," in *The Stanford Encyclopedia of Philosophy*, ed. Edward N. Zalta (Spring 2019 ed.). For an equivalent in political philosophy, see Shlomo Avineri and Avner de-Shalit, eds., *Communitarianism and Individualism* (Oxford: Oxford UP, 1992).

Existence or reality in its absolute infinity must be each particular (you, me, po-
etry, etc.) and all the particulars together and a particular particular (the indeterminacy that encompasses them all) and yet cannot be any of these (as pointed out in
section 2 and just now). But in trying to think this through, one of these constantly
gets into the way of the other, the one gives way to another, collapses into it, claims
priority, and fails to fit the bill. The indeterminate sphere of things appears as *a particular thing*, yet cannot be just *one thing* because it entails all the things *and* all individual things – clearly, there are differences at play here. And each particular thing
(as pointed out above) seems only poorly distinguished from its surroundings, yet it
is not its surroundings … and yet all of this is supposed to be reality, existence, *Being*
in some sense.

Existence, reality, *Being* simultaneously occupies its role as indeterminate playing field, specified thing, set of things in such a way that they constantly tumble into
one another. Whenever we understand that *existence-as-a-thing* actually *means* existence in its unrestrictably absolute infinity, its specificity collapses into withdrawal
and indeterminacy. Existence loses its contour, stops being a thing and withdraws.
It remains inevitable, but only by way of an irregular artifice: existence itself as a
thing that dissolves in indeterminacy. It becomes a thing which is not a thing – a
~~thing~~. As soon as we envision its contours and consequences, existence as absolute
infinity ceases to be an explainable *thing* and becomes an inexplicable ~~thing~~. Nevertheless, though, this artifice (the ~~thing~~) is necessary in order to comprehend the absolute infinity of existence, if even in its virtuality, its constitutive absence, its withdrawal – *its eclipse*.[76] There is thus a necessary remnant of particularity hardwired
into the absolute infinity of existence or reality itself – its inevitable ~~thingness~~. And
likewise, there is a dissolving tendency in each particular thing that always refers
us to the next thing, to a more encompassing thing *ad infinitum* – hence an inner
pathway between particular things and existence, *Being*, absolute infinity or reality
as a whole. Like the moon is getting in the way of the sun, leading to a solar eclipse,
existence is getting in its own way, leading to another kind of eclipse – an *eclipse of
existence*.

Ibn Sina points out that "thing," just as "existence," is a term presupposed by
each possible explanation of it (see section 2 for more).[77] And yet, Ibn Sina says, we
do understand the term "thing," although in a properly *inexplicable* way.[78] The moment

---

76   "[E]*clipse (n.)* – c. 1300, from Old French eclipse 'eclipse, darkness' (12c.), from Latin eclipsis,
      from Greek ekleipsis 'an eclipse; an abandonment,' literally 'a failing, forsaking,' from ek-
      leipein 'to forsake a usual place, fail to appear, be eclipsed,' from ek 'out' (see ex-) + leipein 'to
      leave' (from PIE root *leikw- 'to leave').": "Eclipse," in Douglas Harper, *Online Etymology Dictio-
      nary*.
77   Avicenna, *Metaphysics of The Healing*, 5.1.19–26, 22.
78   Some might claim that Spinoza would disagree with this because to him, everything al-
      legedly must be explainable (see Michael Della Rocca, "A Rationalist Manifesto: Spinoza and

of eclipse between thing and existence that I described in the previous paragraph, I claim, is the location of Ibn Sina's "inexplicable" knowledge: The terms "thing" and "existence" (etc.) continuously give way to one another and thus presuppose one another. An explanation of "existence" (etc.) will refer us to things. An explanation of "thing" will refer us to existence etc. Yet the comprehensibility of the explanation shows that something is known here, although in a way that cannot be explained other than by itself.[79] And the robustness of the experience of this eclipse (it re-occurs, no matter how we try to cut the issue) in an attempt to explain existence (etc.) indicates that something real is going on.

What are we to do with this? Gladly, Margaret Cavendish can help us out. She is not only the most prolific woman philosopher of the 17th century but also one of the most underrated philosophers of the Early Modern period and beyond. Cavendish writes:

> [B]ut this I find, that there is no objection but one may find an answer to it; and as soon as I have made an answer to one objection, another offers itself again, which shows not only that nature's actions are infinite, but that they are poised and balanced, so that they cannot run into extremes … for, as nature and her parts and actions are infinite, so may also endless objections be raised.[80]

To Cavendish, continuous misalignment with one's own thoughts is neither an accident, nor does it attest to the flawedness of an argument. Cavendish claims that the continuous process of statements and their objections given a particular argument is a genuine expression of an ongoing real process. The problematicity of Being as pointed out in section 2 and just now is a paradigmatic case for a process like this: we continuously waver between Being/existence/reality as a thing, a ~~thing~~, an indeterminate surface, a particular class of things and all the things. In a Cavendishian way, then, the problematicity that we experience while undertaking to comprehend existence or reality is just an adequate expression of the reality of existence itself –

---

the Principle of Sufficient Reason," *Philosophical Topics* 31, no. 1/2 (2003): 76; Michael Della Rocca, "Rationalism, Idealism, Monism, and Beyond," in *Spinoza and German Idealism*, ed. Eckhart Förster and Yitzhak Melamed (Cambridge: Cambridge UP, 2012)). But I disagree. In fact, Spinoza's substance, aka God, is conceivable *through itself* (E1d3). It cannot, therefore, be explained by something else. Either you get it or you do not (while Spinoza arguably thinks that 'not getting' substance is impossible, see E2p46). Now, insofar as substance or God in this sense is equivalent to what in my argument occurs as reality, existence, *Being* etc., I take it that Ibn Sina and Spinoza actually agree about the epistemological status of basic notions such as existence. They are self-explanatory but *inexplicable* regarding other, less general notions. There are, of course, false ways of understanding such notions, as Spinoza points out (see E2p40s1; PUF 76/28–78/24). But that does not change the general assessment.

79   This self-explanatory version would be the Spinoza track to the same effect. See E1d3, E2p47.
80   Cavendish, *Observations Upon Experimental Philosophy*, 13. See also 26.

hazy, unstable, continuously changing, in constant withdrawal, erratic, transient, etc. This process, however, is *robust* in that it never dissolves in one direction completely. We never reach absolute indeterminacy (which would dissolve individual consciousness). We can never think of particular things *without* their correlations and embeddedness. We do not actually have access to *all the things* etc. These states (indeterminacy, an infinite sequence of things etc.) always only occur as *deflections from* some other such state etc. to infinity. I call this process *deflection* as a displacement of the idealistic claim that philosophy should be built on a process of *reflection*.[81] Existence continuously *deflects* from itself and into itself – from particularity to indeterminacy and back and elsewhere etc. The haziness of existence, I claim, is real. But how is this more than just a hypothesis?

To Cavendish, there is no difference between the deflection in thought (between arguments) and the deflection in nature. In fact, she says, they are one and the same thing. I want to offer two arguments in support of this claim.

1) The most general thing we can observe on all levels of thought and intellectual life is in fact deflection: Human culture at large is marked by continuous disagreement, questioning, revisiting and adjustment. Particular discourses show that same pattern, organised around particular questions, issues and terminologies (which are, however, themselves time and again subject to such disagreement and re-evaluation). And even in a particular mind, that same drama unfolds continuously, as Cavendish astutely observes and performatively demonstrates.[82] In fact, many religious practices, philosophies and even the empirical sciences are dedicated to *calm* or *transquilise* that continuous process of deflection.[83] The fact that terms such as "progress," "happiness," "enlightenment," or "blessedness" are often understood as victories over such continuous deflections shows just how powerful existential deflection really is – it constantly sneaks back in, must always be kept at bay, must eternally be managed and has functioned as such throughout the ages. Against many

---

81   This is close to Spivak's *"Entstellung*, or displacement as grounding in the emergence of significance": Gayatri Chakravorty Spivak, *A Critique of Postcolonial Reason* (Cambridge: Harvard UP, 1999), 219.

82   See Cavendish, *Observations Upon Experimental Philosophy*, 1–13.

83   See entries "Erleuchtung" and "Erlösung" in: Joachim Ritter, Karlfried Gründer, Gottfried Gabriel (eds.), *Historisches Wörterbuch der Philosophie*, Volumes 1 – 13 (Basel: Schwabe Verlag 1971 – 2007), digital version without page numbers. See also Pasnau, Robert, "Divine Illumination," *The Stanford Encyclopedia of Philosophy* (Spring 2020 Edition), Edward N. Zalta (ed.). There are many examples of notions that serve this purpose in more or less secularized versions. For examples, see: Clairvaux, "On the Love of God," 56; Spinoza; E4App4, E5p33s; but also Kant's notion of "disinterested pleasure" (Immanuel Kant, *Critique of the Power of Judgment* (*Kritik der Urteilskraft*), translation by Paul Guyer and Eric Matthews, Cambridge: Cambridge UP 2000, 90–96 and 42–50) or Schopenhauer's "tranquillity," in: Arthur Schopenhauer, *The World as Will and Representation*, vol. I, Judith Norman, Alistair Welchman, and Christopher Janaway (eds.), Cambridge: Cambridge UP, 2011 [translation from the 3rd edition], 220.

statements to the opposite, the deflection never stops: political discourse is ever changing, philosophy itself may be viewed as the science of existential deflection in thought, and even empirical sciences are prone to periodic revision, readjustment or revolutions.[84] If there is anything, then, that we can attest to with overwhelming evidence, it is that *deflection is real*, that the continuous give-and-take between claims and objections is inevitable. And as such, I claim, it is a genuine expression of nature as it is.

2) Now, take the opposite claim: assume that nature, other than thought, was not continuously deflecting. Assume that in nature, everything was finally hardwired in some solid form, whatever it be – the laws of nature, the smallest particles or something like that. Then, human reasoning would be said to escape nature more generally, that the constant deflection we are subjected to was peculiar to thought, or maybe even to the human mind. Instead of manifesting nature, human reasoning would then manifest a para-natural realm in its own right. And yet, in some sense, thought exists within nature *and as nature*. Thought, then, is natural and simultaneously it is not natural. This looks like a contradiction.

But maybe, to save the argument, we could say that thought is super-natural in some respect, say in its deflective tendency. Thought, then, would exist entirely in and through nature – aiming at non-intellectual objects and be hardwired into the brain. But yet, it would itself be super-natural in its deflective tendency. In making this move, however, the argument itself *performs a deflection* – it moves away from its original stance of thought as something super-natural towards a more easily defensible stance: that only the deflective tendency in thought is super-natural. And in that deflection from the original stance *against* the ubiquity of deflection, the argument falls for a *performative contradiction*; by attempting to resist the claim (of ubiquitous deflection) it actually does exactly what the claim supposes it would – deflect from its original stance. Yet this was exactly Cavendish's original claim – that there is no claim without an objection, and no objection without a defence etc., ad infinitum. Existential deflection is thus not simply correct. Rather, it demonstrates itself in its own debatability, as every possible objection about it recites its internal logic. Existential deflection is not simply true. Rather it is *inevitable* in that the claim keeps reappearing, cannot be fended off *and simultaneously* governs the debate about itself. Every critical debate about existential deflection is effectively an expression of

---

84   See paradigmatically Banu Subramaniam, *Ghost Stories for Darwin: The Science of Variation and the Politics of Diversity* (Champaign: University of Illinois Press, 2014); Thomas Kuhn, *The Structure of Scientific Revolutions* (Chicago: University of Chicago Press, 1962); Ludwig Fleck, *Entstehung und Entwicklung einer wissenschaftlichen Tatsache. Einführung in die Lehre vom Denkstil und Denkkollektiv* (Frankfurt am Main: Suhrkamp, 1980); Paul Feyerabend, *Against Method* (London: Verso, 2010).

existential deflection. That is why I agree with Cavendish about the isomorphism between deflection in thought and deflection in nature more generally.

Consequentially, there is no "real distinction,"[85] no "rigorous difference"[86] between reality as indeterminate playing field on the one hand and any particular or even all the particulars on the other hand. These are not things independent from one another, neither epistemologically nor ontologically – they can neither exist nor be conceived independently from one another. Further, particulars are not just properties of existence itself and neither is existence just the host or substance of its affections. They are *intimately connected* in a sense that I will elaborate on in the following section.[87] Let us call the difference between reality or existence as absolute infinity on the one hand and its particulars on the other hand an *intimate difference*, neither real nor rigorous, nor just an affection, a property, an accident or modification (and certainly no illusion).

The analogy approach and the univocity approach to reality, existence, *Being*, however, are snapshots of this intimacy between absolute infinity and its manifestations as it were. The struggle between the univocity approach and the analogy approach to existence can be understood to be hardwired into existence itself. It is a genuine expression of the *eclipse of existence*. Existence is such that it cannot but particularise into *things* and simultaneously dissolve into infinite indeterminacy. Whenever we think the one, the other is looming around the corner, ready for deflection. Existence sometimes looks like a set of particular things and sometimes looks like an absolutely infinite plane of reality itself etc. Yet the one approach continuously deflects into the other. In this sense, ontological univocity and ontological analogy both are genuine dimensions of this eclipse, focusing on different dimensions of it.

---

85   For more on distinctions in Descartes, see Melamed, *Spinoza and German Idealism*, 92. Spinoza discusses "the threefold distinction of things: Real, Modal, of Reason" (*CM* II.V., I/257–258; also E1p15s; PUF 16/10–11). For more on the connection between the middle ages and the early modern period regarding distinctions, see Tad Schmaltz, *The Metaphysics of the Material World: Suarez, Descartes, Spinoza* (Oxford: Oxford UP, 2019), 103. See also deLire, "Spinoza's Special Distinctions."

86   Jacques Derrida, *Life Death*, trans. Pascale-Anne Brault and Michael Naas (Chicago: The University of Chicago Press, 2020), 37.

87   For preliminary studies, see deLire, "Spinoza's Special Distinctions."

5. Seduction as erotic deflection

Positive desire is often called a kind of *production*.[88] *Negative* desire may accordingly be called a kind of *attraction*, from Latin *attrahere* ("to draw, to pull"). Here, the lack motivates the action by pulling it towards the lacking thing. In this section, I will argue for desire as *seduction*. Desire itself is *deflecting* from one state into the other.[89] In other words, we should be Cavendishians about desire.

Jule Govrin has recently demonstrated that both *negative* and *positive* approaches towards desire continuously collapse into each other.[90] Is there thus room for a third theory or a third kind of desire in line with the eclipse of existence outlined in the previous section? Are there theories of desire as deflection beyond production and attraction, beyond positive and negative, beyond push and pull?

We can indeed find explications of such a theory of desire in some philosophies of the 20th century. With Jean Baudrillard, we may call it *desire as seduction*, especially if taken, with Sylvia Plant, "literally."[91] Seduction, in this sense, is the process of accumulation and "disaccumulation,"[92] continuous expression of reversibility,[93] contraction, and dissolution – *libidinal deflection* in the terminology developed in the previous section.[94] What I called *"eclipse"* above, to Baudrillard, is a "void" "at the very heart of power."[95] Seduction thus encompasses both production and attraction, push and pull, in that it describes their *deflection* into one another.[96]

---

88   Most famously in Gilles Deleuze and Félix Guattari, *Anti-Oedipus – Capitalism and Schizophrenia*, trans. Robert Hurley, Mark Seem, and Helen R. Lane (Minneapolis: University of Minnesota Press, 1983), 3.

89   That is also why *both* approaches have significant explanatory power. They are, as it were, in themselves infinite, may function as ultimate explanatory models for the set of phenomena under inquiry.

90   See Govrin's case studies of Plato, Hegel, Klossowski, de Lauretis, and others in Govrin, *Begehren und Ökonomie*.

91   Sadie Plant, "Baudrillard's Women – The Eve of Seduction," in *Forget Baudrillard?*, ed. Chris Royek and Bryan S. Turner (London: Routledge, 1993), 105.

92   Jean Baudrillard, *Forget Foucault*, trans. Nicole Dufresne (Los Angeles: Semiotext(e), 2007), 54. See also Plant, "Baudrillard's Women," 89, 96.

93   Baudrillard, *Forget Foucault*," 53. See also Jean Baudrillard, *Seduction*, trans. Brian Singer (Montreal: New World Perspectives, 1990), 10.

94   Note that although interesting especially regarding "the trans-sexuality of seduction which the entire organization of sex tends to reject" (Baudrillard, *Seduction*, 7–8), I want to point out that Baudrillard's theory has an inherently sexist angle and is at times conceptually murky. Although a great resource, it would need a serious reworking. For an on point feminist critique of Baudrillard, see exemplarily Plant, "Baudrillard's Women," 97, 103–105.

95   Baudrillard, *Forget Foucault*, 54.

96   Baudrillard, 54. For a general critique of Baudrillard's *Seduction*, see Douglas Kellner, "Jean Baudrillard," *The Stanford Encyclopedia of Philosophy*, ed. Edward N. Zalta (Winter 2020 ed.).

A similar model may be found in some of Jacques Derrida's works. He expresses it as the *dynamis* between philosopher and philosophy,[97] the seductive force of *differance*,[98] or simply as the origin of pleasure. Other than Baudrillard, however, Derrida insists on a certain difference as the driving force of desire as seduction: "*Mimesis* brings pleasure only if it allows us to see in action what is nevertheless not given in action itself, but only in its very similar double, its *mimeme*."[99]

His point is that the seductive force of representation emerges from the difference *within* a represented thing between its reality and its intelligibility. In fact, the proximate distance that we have to represented things is the location of pleasure. What would otherwise incite horror, discomfort, or disgust may cause pleasure and excitement in its representational form – an image, a hyperrealistic simulation, an anecdote, etc. The great success of movies and computer games on war, crime, catastrophes, and mystical creatures attests to this point. And yet the condition of this pleasure is exactly the intelligibility itself of the terrifying, disgusting or discomforting thing. It is the fact that we can watch a family drama unfold without being involved, see wolves take out a village without being immediately threatened, that enables pleasure and enjoyment of movies, games, and storytelling. And yet representation does not befall the represented thing from the outside like a demonic force.[100] Rather, representability lives in the heart of each thing. Without intelligibility, representation (good or bad, true or false) would be impossible. This difference between the reality and the representation of the thing *within the thing* is an example of that *intimate difference* that we touched on earlier regarding the difference between reality or existence as absolute infinity and its manifestation in particular things. It is a difference *within the thing* that allows the thing to be what it anyway is. In this case, the *intimate difference* occurs between the real and the intelligible (as real).[101]

---

97   Jacques Derrida, *Otobiographies – The Teaching of Nietzsche and the Politics of the Proper Name*, trans. Avital Ronell (NY: Schocken Books, 1985), 5. See also Derrida, *Life Death*, 26.

98   Jacques Derrida, "Plato's Pharmacy," in *Disseminations*, trans. Barbara Johnson (London: The Athlone Press, 1981), 70.

99   Jacques Derrida, "White Mythology: Metaphor in the Text of Philosophy," *New Literary History* 6, no. 1 (1974): 5–74, 39. For related passages, see exemplarily Derrida, "Plato's Pharmacy," 40, fn 35; Jacques Derrida, "Parergon," in *The Truth in Painting*, trans. Geoffrey Bennington and Ian McLeod (Chicago: University of Chicago Press, 1987), 39.

100   Except that, according to Derrida, this is the ur-demonic force. See Derrida, "Plato's Pharmacy," 117; Jacques Derrida, "Cogito and History of Madness," in *Writing and Difference*, trans. Alan Bass (London: Routledge, 1978), 68.

101   That is why to Spinoza, desire is the *consciousness* of the striving for perseverance in existence *both* in the body *and* in the mind: it is awareness of the *intimate difference* of that striving with itself.

Now, as Spivak points out, desire as deflection (or *seduction*) must always relate to *its material conditions*.[102] "What is marked [by the deflection] is the site of desire."[103] In other words, what is visible through the solar eclipse is a trace of the sun as it is blocked by the moon. And what occurs as the trace of desire as deflection or seduction is its material underpinning. That is why sexual relations never occur outside their gendered, racialised, and otherwise politically charged conditions. If anything, desire as seduction is a particular deflection from those conditions. As pointed out earlier, a certain distance aestheticises horror into shuddering enjoyment. And likewise, a certain distance turns political differences into libidinal attractions. Sexual desire, then, is another flavour of that intimate difference within each thing, embedded within a set of cultural norms and material practices.

And yet what both Baudrillard and Derrida lose out of sight is the question of *movement*.[104] As pointed out above, for Aristotle, Ibn Sina, Spinoza, etc., *desire* is an answer to a particular problem: Why do things move? Are we just stuck in linguistic determination without movement? Neither Baudrillard nor Derrida seem to have good answers to this question.[105]

What would Cavendish say? Cavendish understands that once motion has left the philosophical system, we cannot put it back in. This has in fact been a problem in Aristotelianism and still is one to Descartes, which is why both Aristotle and Descartes require a first mover to set nature in motion in the first place. Cavendish, however, turns the problem of motion from its head to its feet by positing self-motion as the general principle of nature itself: "[T]here is but one ground or principle of all ... variety, which is self-motion, or self-moving matter."[106] To her, nature itself is infinite "in her actions, ... parts ... and has no set bounds or limits."[107] Nature is also eternally self-moving in itself, while particular things are patterns of motion *within* that overall auto-motion of infinite nature itself.[108]

But motion of what? This is in fact Cavendish's clou: "[M]otion is material; for figure, motion and matter are but one thing."[109] In fact, motion and matter are dis-

102   Gayatri Chakravorty Spivak, "Scattered Speculations on the Question of Value," *Diacritics* 15, no. 4 (Winter, 1985): 73–93.
103   Spivak, *A Critique of Postcolonial Reason*, 207.
104   Is this because they go into the trap of idealism and tacitly understand desire, seduction etc. as the *internal* movement of the soul?
105   Derrida comes closest to this question, as far as I know, in his notes on the spacing of time and the temporalisation of space regarding *différance*. See, for example, Jacques Derrida, "Différance," in *Margins of Philosophy*, trans. Alan Bass (Sussex: The Harvester Press, 1982), 9; Derrida, "Cogito and History of Madness," 74.
106   Cavendish, *Observations Upon Experimental Philosophy*, 70.
107   Cavendish, 199.
108   See also Boyle, *The Well-Ordered Universe*, 70.
109   Cavendish, *Observations Upon Experimental Philosophy*, 73.

tinguished as body and place are.[110] According to Descartes, whenever a body moves, the space it occupies moves with it. And even when a space is supposedly empty, it in fact still harbours something – just not the thing we would expect to be there.[111] Thus, when a city is empty, it is empty *of people*, but the buildings, the streets, etc. are still there.

Analogously, Cavendish argues, *motion is always motion of matter*. It is always *something* that is moving. And consequentially, "if motion should be transferred or added to some other body, matter must be added or transferred."[112] For if there is no motion without matter, what then is being transmitted when motion is transmitted, if not matter? And yet, when a billiard ball hits another, no material part of the one ball suddenly becomes a part of the other ball. Consequentially, Cavendish concludes, material things essentially *move themselves* and interact in a way that adjusts to the auto-motion of other things.[113] And inversely, *matter is always in motion*. For each particular thing, to Cavendish, is a certain pattern of motion. "[P]articular natures are nothing else but a change of corporeal figurative motions, which make this diversity of figures."[114] And because nature itself is entirely material, particular things must be material as well, distinguished only by their differing patterns of motion.[115]

Motion, then, is motion *of matter* and matter is always already *in motion*. Matter and motion are thus linked in a peculiar way; in fact, "motion and matter are but one thing."[116]

And yet there seems to be *some* distinction. It want to suggest that we read this as another instance of that *intimate difference* constitutive of a thing. Cavendish herself does not specify why we should distinguish matter and motion in the first place if they are allegedly "one thing."[117] I, however, want to suggest the following.

A thing only moves with respect to something else that functions as its reference point.[118] *Regarding other things*, then, a thing is a pattern of motion. But if we abstract from its embeddedness in a context, then a thing is just a particular formation of matter, its own thingness. Understood in this way, there is no real, no rigor-

---

110   Cavendish, 48.

111   Descartes, *The Philosophical Writings of Descartes*, II.10, AT VIIIA 45.

112   Cavendish, *Observations Upon Experimental Philosophy*, 200; Descartes, *The Philosophical Writings of Descartes*, 74.

113   This is also the foundation of her epistemology; see Boyle, *The Well-Ordered Universe*, 77. For Cavendish's materialistic feminist politics, see Lisa Walters, "Redefining Gender in Cavendish's Theory of Matter," in *Margaret Cavendish – Gender, Science and Politics* (Cambridge: Cambridge UP, 2014).

114   Cavendish, *Observations Upon Experimental Philosophy*, 197. See also 191.

115   Cavendish, 205–206.

116   Cavendish, 73.

117   Cavendish, 73.

118   See also Cavendish, 27.

ous distinction between motion and matter. But neither can the difference between matter and motion in this sense be described in terms of modifications, affections or properties. For *all a particular thing is*, regarding another thing, is its pattern of motion. And *all a particular thing is*, abstracting from other things, is its matter. Yet the intelligibility as a pattern of motion is hardwired into each particular thing. Nothing prevents being perceptible to other things. Likewise, infinite nature itself cannot *not* manifest in its particulars. The intelligibility as motion of Cavendishian things is thus not an accident or a modification of that thing – it is the thing. The same counts as its existence-as-a-thing in abstraction from other things. This, then, is another instance of that *intimate difference* constitutive of existence, *Being* or (as Cavendish calls it) *infinite nature* as deflection. A difference within the thing (hence intimate), constitutive of its thingness, but not rigorous: deflection of the thing *into its own intelligibility*, hence its existence for others.

Although Cavendish does not talk about desire explicitly in this context, we can now reconstruct a Cavendishian theory of desire. In the terminology of the previous section, to Cavendish, motion, in fact, *is* a determined section of the deflection of *Being* itself. Some particular desire then is another manifestation of that same deflecting movement, a pattern of motion or deflection. Every particular thing is defined by its desire, by its pattern of motion. We *sense* this desire mostly when it is being blocked or suspended – longing for a lover, craving food, hoping for a better world. Yet the moving force experienced in these occasions is just what determines us most fundamentally. Consequentially, seduction in general is the infinite deflecting movement of nature itself. And each individual desire is a particularisation of this infinite seduction of nature. In this sense, I think we should be Cavendishians about desire.

6. Summary and conclusion

In this text, I have argued that there is a parallelism between ontologies and erotics, between theories about existence, *Being*, reality, infinite nature (etc.) on the one hand and desire on the other hand. I argued that univocal ontologies go along with theories of desire as production and analogical ontologies (tendentially) go along with theories of desire as attraction. I have further demonstrated that the division into analogical and univocal ontologies is not exhaustive. With Ibn Sina and Cavendish, I claimed that the problematicity of *Being*, its apparent ungraspability, is not a mistake of reason but an expression of reality itself. I then argued for a theory of desire as *seduction* along the lines of the parallelism between ontologies and erotics. Both desire and existence are caught in continuous *deflection*. This theory of desire conveniently encompasses both the erotics of production and erotics as attraction: attraction deflects into production and vice versa. This explains why they (attraction/production) exist, why they are convincing and why they are nevertheless insufficient: attraction and production are states, phases or manifestations of the overall deflection of desire. I take it, then, that deflective ontology and the erotics of seduction are all the more compelling. In brief, let us become Cavendishians.

References

Adamson, Peter. *Philosophy in the Islamic World: A Very Short Introduction*. Oxford: Oxford UP, 2015.

Al'Ghazali. *The Incoherence of the Philosophers*. Translated by Michael E. Marmura. Utah: Brigham Young UP, 2000.

Anscombe, Elisabeth. *Intention*. Ithaca: Cornell UP, 1976.

Aristotle, *The Complete Works of Aristotle*. Bollingen Series LXXI 2. Vol. 1. Edited by Jonathan Barnes. Translated by W. D. Ross. Charlottesville: InteLex Corporation, 1992.

Averroes. *The Incoherence of the Incoherence*. Translated by Simon Van Den Bergh. London: Gibb Memorial Trust, 2008.

Avicenna, "Selections on Psychology from *The Cure*, 'The Soul.'" In *Classical Arabic Philosophy: An Anthology of Sources*, edited by John McGinnis and David C. Reisman, 175–208. Indianapolis: Hackett Publishing, 2007.

———. *Metaphysics of The Healing*. Translated by Michael A. Marmura. Provo: Brigham Young UP, 2005.

Avineri, Shlomo, and Avner de-Shalit, eds. *Communitarianism and Individualism*. Oxford: Oxford UP, 1992.

Baudrillard, Jean. *Forget Foucault*. Translated by Nicole Dufresne. Los Angeles: Semiotext(e), 2007.

———. *Seduction*. Translated by Brian Singer. Montreal: New World Perspectives, 1990.

Beavers, Anthony F. "Desire and Love in Descartes's Late Philosophy." *History of Philosophy Quarterly* 6, no. 3 (July 1989): 279–294.

Bernard of Clairvaux. "On the Love of God." In *Late Medieval Mysticism*, edited by Ray C. Petry, 54–65. Louisville: Westminster John Knox Press, 2006.

Bloch, Ernst. *Avicenna and the Aristotelian Left*. NY: Columbia UP, 2019.

Boyle, Deborah. *The Well-Ordered Universe: The Philosophy of Margaret Cavendish*. Oxford: Oxford UP, 2018.

Casey, Edward S., and J. Melvin Woody. "Hegel and Lacan: The Dialectic of Desire." In *Hegel's Dialectic of Desire and Recognition: Texts and Commentary*, edited by John O'Neill, 223–232. Albany: SUNY Press, 1996.

Cavendish, Margaret. *Observations Upon Experimental Philosophy*. Cambridge: Cambridge UP, 2003.

Deleuze, Gilles, and Félix Guattari. *Anti-Oedipus: Capitalism and Schizophrenia*. Translated by Robert Hurley, Mark Seem, and Helen R. Lane. Minneapolis: University of Minnesota Press, 1983.

Deleuze, Gilles. *Difference and Repetition*. Translated by Paul Patton. London: Continuum, 1994.

deLire, Luce. "'[E]very Day the Matter Seems to Get Worse, and I Don't Know What I Should Do.' – Violence, Spinozism and Digital Reality." In *Skin and Code*, edited by Daniel Neugebauer, 23–49. Spector Books, 2021.

———. "Spinoza's Conceptual Distinctions." *Journal for Philosophical Research*, Forthcoming.

———. "Spinoza's Special Distinction." Forthcoming.

———. *No Limits, No Regrets – Spinoza's Metaphysics of Infinity*. Forthcoming.

Della Rocca, Michael. "A Rationalist Manifesto: Spinoza and the Principle of Sufficient Reason." *Philosophical Topics* 31, no. 1/2 (2003): 75–93. https://doi.org/10.58 40/philtopics2003311/215

———. "Rationalism, Idealism, Monism, and Beyond." In *Spinoza and German Idealism*, edited by Eckhart Förster and Yitzhak Melamed, 7–26. Cambridge: Cambridge UP, 2012.

Derrida, Jacques. "Cogito and History of Madness." In *Writing and Difference*, translated by Alan Bass, 36–76. London: Routledge, 1978.

———. "Différance." In *Margins of Philosophy*, translated by Alan Bass, 1–28. Sussex: The Harvester Press, 1982.

———. "Parergon." In *The Truth in Painting*, translated by Geoffrey Bennington and Ian McLeod, 151–198. Chicago: University of Chicago Press, 1987.

———. "Plato's Pharmacy." In *Disseminations*, translated by Barbara Johnson, 61–172. London: The Athlone Press, 1981.

———. "White Mythology: Metaphor in the Text of Philosophy." *New Literary History* 6, no. 1 (1974): 5–74. https://doi.org/10.2307/468341

———. *Life Death*. Translated by Pascale-Anne Brault and Michael Naas. Chicago: The University of Chicago Press, 2020.

———. *Otobiographies – The Teaching of Nietzsche and the Politics of the Proper Name*. Translated by Avital Ronell. NY: Schocken Books, 1985.

Descartes, René. "Les Passions de l'Ame." In *Oeuvres Complètes de René Descartes*. Electronic ed. Charlottesville: InteLex Corporation, 2001.

———. *The Philosophical Writings of Descartes*. Vol. 1. Translated by John Cottingham, Robert Stoothoff, and Dugald Murdoch. Cambridge: Cambridge UP, 1985.

Dobbs-Weinstein, Idit. "Aristotle on the Natural Dwelling of the Intellect." In *The Bloomsbury Companion to Aristotle*, edited by Claudia Baracchi, 297–310. London: Bloomsbury, 2014.

———. "Thinking Desire in Gersonides and Spinoza." In: *Women and Gender in Jewish Philosophy*. Edited by Hava Tirosh-Samuelson. Bloomington: Indiana UP 2004, 51–75.

———. *Spinoza's Critique of Religion and its Heirs: Marx, Benjamin, Adorno*. Cambridge: Cambridge UP, 2015.

Feyerabend, Paul. *Against Method*. London: Verso, 2010.

Fleck, Ludwig. *Entstehung und Entwicklung einer wissenschaftlichen Tatsache. Einführung in die Lehre vom Denkstil und Denkkollektiv*. Frankfurt am Main: Suhrkamp, 1980.

Friedrich, Daniel. "Desire, Mental Force and Desirous Experience." In *The Nature of Desire*, edited by Federico Lauria and Julien Deonna, 57–76. Oxford: Oxford UP, 2017.

Gebhardt, Carl ed. *Spinoza: Opera*. Originally 4 vols, Heidelberg: Carl Winter-Verlag, 1925. 2nd ed. Heidelberg: Carl Winter-Verlag, 1973.

Goldenbaum, Ursula. "The Pantheismusstreit—Milestone or Stumbling Block in the German Reception of Spinoza?" In *Spinoza's Ethics: A Collective Commentary*, edited by Michael Hampe, Ursula Renz, and Robert Schnepf, 325–351. Leiden: Brill, 2011.

———. "Spinoza – Ein toter Hund? Nicht für Christian Wolff." *Zeitschrift für Ideengeschichte* 5, no. 1 (Spring 2011): 29–41. https://doi.org/10.17104/1863-8937-2011-1-29

Govrin, Jule. *Begehren und Ökonomie*. Berlin: de Gruyter, 2020.

Gutas, Dimitri. "Ibn Sina [Avicenna]." In *The Stanford Encyclopedia of Philosophy*, edited by Edward N. Zalta. Fall 2016 ed. https://plato.stanford.edu/archives/fall2016/entries/ibn-sina/.

———. *Avicenna and the Aristotelian Tradition: Introduction to Reading Avicenna's Philosophical Works*. Leiden and Boston: Brill, 2014.

Harper, Douglas. *Online Etymology Dictionary*. Last accessed May 11, 2021. https://www.etymonline.com/word/Eclipse.

Hazm, Ibn. *The Ring of the Dove*. Translated by A. J. Arberry. London: Luzac & Company, 1953.

Hegel, Georg Wilhelm Friedrich. "Lordship and Bondage." *In Hegel's Dialectic of Desire and Recognition: Texts and Commentary*, edited by John O'Neill, 29–36. Albany: SUNY Press, 1996.

Hobbes, Thomas. *The English Works of Thomas Hobbes*. Vol. 1. London: John Bohn, 1839.

Inati, Shams. *Ibn Sina's Remarks and Admonitions: Physics and Metaphysics – An Analysis and Annotated Translation*. NY: Columbia UP, 2014.

Israel, Jonathan. *Enlightenment Contested: Enlightenment, Modernity, and the Emancipation of Man 1670–1752*. Oxford: Oxford UP, 2008.

———. *Radical Enlightenment: Philosophy and the Making of Modernity*. Oxford: Oxford UP, 2002.

Kant, Immanuel. *Critique of Judgment*. Translated by James Creed Meredith. Oxford: Oxford UP, 2007.

———. *Kritik der Urteilskraft*. Berlin: de Gruyter, 2009.

———. *Critique of the Power of Judgment* (*Kritik der Urteilskraft*). Translated by Paul Guyer and Eric Matthews, Cambridge: Cambridge UP 2000.

Kaukua, Jari. *Self-Awareness in Islamic Philosophy – Avicenna and Beyond*. Cambridge: Cambridge UP, 2015.

Kellner, Douglas. "Jean Baudrillard." In *The Stanford Encyclopedia of Philosophy*, edited by Edward N. Zalta. Winter 2020 ed. https://plato.stanford.edu/entries/baudri llard/#PataMetaTriuObje.

Kuhn, Thomas. *The Structure of Scientific Revolutions*. Chicago: University of Chicago Press, 1962.

Lacan, Jacques. *Desire and its Interpretation*. Edited by Jacques-Alain Miller. Translated by Bruce Fink. Cambridge: Cambridge UP, 2019.

Laerke, Mogens. "Spinoza and the Cosmological Argument According to Letter 12." *British Journal for the History of Philosophy* 21, no. 1 (2013): 57–77. https://doi.org/10 .1080/09608788.2012.696052

Marinella, Lucrezia. *The Nobility and Excellence of Women and the Defects and Vices of Men*. Edited by Anne Dunhill. Chicago: University of Chicago Press, 1999.

Mercer, Christia. "Descartes' Debt to Teresa of Ávila, or Why We Should Work on Women in the History of Philosophy." *Philosophical Studies: An International Journal for Philosophy in the Analytic Tradition* 174, no. 10 (October 2017): 2539–2555. https: //doi.org/10.1007/s11098-016-0737-9

Moreau, Pierre-François, ed. and trans. *Spinoza – Oeuvres IV – Ethica/Éthique*. Paris: Presses Universitaires de France, 2020.

Oddie, Graham. "Desire and the Good: In Search of the Right Fit." In *The Nature of Desire*, edited by Federico Lauria and Julien Deonna, 29–56. Oxford: Oxford UP, 2017.

———. *Value, Reality and Desire*. Oxford: Clarendon Press, 2005.

Pearson, Gilles. *Aristotle on Desire*. Cambridge: Cambridge UP, 2012.

Pineda-Oilvia, David. "Defending the Motivational Theory of Desire." *Theoria: An International Journal for Theory, History and Foundations of Science* 36, no. 2 (May 2021): 243–260. https://doi.org/10.1387/theoria.21489

Plant, Sadie. "Baudrillard's Women – The Eve of Seduction." In *Forget Baudrillard?*, edited by Chris Royek and Bryan S. Turner, 88–106. London: Routledge, 1993.

Plato. "Symposium." In *Plato: Complete Works*, edited by John M. Cooper and D. S. Hutchinson, translated by Alexander Nehamas and Paul Woodruff, 457–505. Indianapolis: Hackett, 1997.

Porphyry. *Isagoge – Texte grec et latin*. Translated by Boethius, Alain de Libera, and Alain-Philippe Segonds. Paris: Librarie Philosophique J. Vrin, 1998.

Quinn, Warren. *Putting Rationality in Its Place*. Cambridge: Cambridge UP, 1993.

Rawls, John. *A Theory of Justice: Revised Edition*. Cambridge: Belknap Press, 1999.

Ritter, Joachim, Karlfried Gründer, and Gabriel Gottfried, eds. *Historisches Wörterbuch der Philosophie*. Vols. 1–13. Basel: Schwabe Verlag, 1971–2007.

Schmaltz, Tad. *The Metaphysics of the Material World: Suarez, Descartes, Spinoza*. Oxford: Oxford UP, 2019.

Schopenhauer, Arthur. *The World as Will and Representation*, vol. I. Edited by Judith Norman, Alistair Welchman, and Christopher Janaway. Cambridge: Cambridge UP, 2011.

Spivak, Gayatri Chakravorty. "Scattered Speculations on the Question of Value." *Diacritics* 15, no. 4 (Winter, 1985): 73–93. https://doi.org/10.2307/464935

———. *A Critique of Postcolonial Reason*. Cambridge: Harvard UP, 1999.

Stampe, Dennis. "The Authority of Desire." *The Philosophical Review* 96, no. 3 (1987): 335–381. https://doi.org/10.2307/2185225

Subramaniam, Banu. *Ghost Stories for Darwin: The Science of Variation and the Politics of Diversity*. Champaign: University of Illinois Press, 2014.

Varzi, Achille. "Mereology." In *The Stanford Encyclopedia of Philosophy*, edited by Edward N. Zalta. Spring 2019 ed. https://plato.stanford.edu/archives/spr2019/entries/mereology/#AtoOthOpt.

Walters, Lisa. "Redefining Gender in Cavendish's Theory of Matter." In *Margaret Cavendish – Gender, Science and Politics*, 37–99. Cambridge: Cambridge UP, 2014.

The Unconscious Freedom of Our Libidinal Economy, or, Existentialism After Freud

Todd McGowan

The unconscious wrench

The libido does not strike anyone as the realm of freedom. We experience libidinal drives as if they drive us, not as if we freely choose them. The male inability to control erection functions as a synecdoche for the absence of libidinal freedom. Just as men cannot have an erection on demand (or get rid of it), no one can will themselves to sexual desire.[1] Our sexual desires strike us as if an alien took over our conscious will and directed it regardless of our wishes. This constraint that accompanies the libido renders it an unlikely site for constituting the subject's freedom. The libidinal economy functions more determinatively than the material economy, which itself constrains what is possible through its laws of exchange. And yet it is my claim that freedom is inextricable from unconscious sexuality – that the libidinal economy is actually the realm of freedom. As subjects, we are unconsciously free. The constraint in the unconscious is freeing because it pulls the subject out of its social context and gives it breathing space from the external constraints of this situation.[2] Libidinal economy frees subjectivity from its social determinations.

Even though Freud discovers the unconscious, associating it with freedom cuts against his own conception. Freud is, unapologetically, a psychic determinist. His most extensive discussion of psychic determinism occurs in the *Psychopathology of Everyday Life*. Here, he identifies this determinism with the unconscious while re-

---

1   For Saint Augustine, male lack of control over erection is the indication of original sin. Although Augustine has no conception of freedom, he does theorise lust in terms of an absence of control.

2   Alain Badiou suggests an opposition between situation and event. The situation, for Badiou, is the realm of unfreedom, the normal existence in which one follows social determinations. The event marks the point of disruption of the everyday, the point at which freedom explodes on the situation. Thus, fidelity to the event is the only possible freedom in Badiou's theoretical universe.

serving freedom for conscious acts. Freud insists that the unconscious is the realm of necessity, not freedom. He writes:

> it is not necessary to dispute the right to the feeling of conviction of having a free will. If the distinction between conscious and unconscious motivation is taken into account, our feeling of conviction informs us that conscious motivation does not extend to all our motor decisions.... But what is thus left free by the one side re-ceives its motivation from the other side, from the unconscious; and in this way determination in the psychical sphere is still carried out without any gap.[3]

As Freud sees it, the unconscious determines our acts to such an extent that it leaves no gap in which freedom might emerge. Our conscious will may be free, but our unconscious desire is the realm of unrelenting psychic determinism. The doctrine of the unconscious seems to put all pretensions of human freedom to bed. Or at least that is how Freud understands his doctrine.[4]

It is significant that in his discussion of psychic determinism, Freud discusses freedom in a traditional way, in terms of free will. He sees the conscious belief in free will as compatible with unconscious psychic determinism. Such a belief, according to Freud, simply misses the role that the unconscious plays in structuring how peo-ple act. Freedom is necessarily conscious in Freud's conception because it is associ-ated with the capacity to will – the deliberation that results in a thoughtful decision – not with our forms of libidinal satisfaction. He never fully considers the possibil-ity that the unconscious libidinal economy might itself be the site of freedom, that freedom is the product of our unconscious desire rather than our conscious will.

The closest that Freud comes to this position is his theory of an original choice of neurosis. Through this conception, Freud moves towards an association of the unconscious with freedom that he never develops. In *An Autobiographical Study*, he writes, "the localisation of the point of fixation is what determines the *choice of neu-rosis*, that is, the form in which the subsequent illness makes its appearance."[5] At this point, it seems as if the subject's freedom resides in its unconscious reaction to its

---

3   Sigmund Freud, *Psychopathology of Everyday Life*, trans. Alan Tyson, in *The Standard Edition of the Complete Psychological Works of Sigmund Freud*, vol. 6, ed. James Strachey (1901; reis., London: Hogarth Press, 1960), 254.

4   This is not simply Freud's idiosyncratic take on his own discovery. Many proponents of free-dom challenge the idea of an unconscious because they are wary of the damage that this agency would do to the cause of freedom. For instance, despite devoting considerable atten-tion to Freud's discoveries (and writing a screenplay about his life), Jean-Paul Sartre rejects the unconscious in order to preserve human freedom. For Sartre, once one concedes that the unconscious exists, the cause of freedom is gone for good.

5   Sigmund Freud, *An Autobiographical Study*, trans. James Strachey, in *The Standard Edition of the Complete Psychological Works of Sigmund Freud*, vol. 20, ed. James Strachey (1927; reis., London: Hogarth Press, 1959), 36.

situation. The phrase "choice of neurosis" suggests a measure of freedom. Through this choice, the subject determines itself rather than accepting what has been imposed on it.

But when he conceives of the psychoanalytic intervention, Freud retreats from this association of the unconscious with freedom. Psychoanalytic treatment becomes, for him, a process of granting the patient some purchase on its unconscious desire. In place of being ruled by unconscious determinism, Freud proposes relating to this determinism through conscious choice. He goes so far as to associate freedom with the conscious ego in opposition to unconscious desire. In this way, Freud turns to a standard definition of freedom that views our unconscious libidinal economy as a problem of determinism that freedom must overcome.

This position receives its clearest articulation in *The Ego and the Id*. Here, the justification for psychoanalytic treatment is the conscious freedom it grants to the ego relative to the subject's unconscious desire. In a footnote to that work, Freud states, "analysis does not set out to make pathological reactions impossible; but to give the patient's ego *freedom* to decide one way or the other."[6] Far from identifying freedom with the original unconscious choice of neurosis, he identifies freedom with the operations of the conscious ego. Here, freedom is, once again, free will.

Freud's identification of freedom with free will represents his turn away from the radicality of his insight into the disruptiveness of the unconscious. It represents his lingering investment in a liberal conception of freedom that actually founders on the psychoanalytic discovery of the unconscious. This is a point where Freud is not Freudian enough. The existence of the unconscious reveals that a psychic determinism drives the decisions of the conscious will. But it also introduces a structure into the psyche that puts it at odds with the social determinants that would shape it. The unconscious is the site of the subject's singular revolt against what the social order would make of it.[7]

---

6   Sigmund Freud, *The Ego and the Id*, trans. James Strachey, in *The Standard Edition of the Complete Psychological Works of Sigmund Freud*, vol. 19, ed. James Strachey (1923; reis., London: Hogarth Press, 1961), 50.

7   This is a point that Joan Copjec insists on in *Read My Desire*. According to Copjec, we are never just the product of a social law but also a reaction against it. This reaction emanates from the unconscious. Copjec writes, "The subject is not only judged by and subjected to social laws, it also judges them by subjecting them to intellectual scrutiny; in other words, the subject directs a question, '*Che vuoi?* What do you want from me?' to every social, as well as scientific, law" (*Read My Desire: Lacan Against the Historicists* (Cambridge: MIT Press, 1994), 28). This question directed towards the social order about desire is fundamentally an unconscious one, a question marking the defiance of the unconscious relative to the imperatives it encounters.

Everyone, except Victor of Aveyron, is born into a social context.[8] This context makes coercive demands on the subject that attempt to generate conformity to the norms of the social order. But the subject does not straightforwardly adopt the demands the social order places on it. Instead, it relates to these demands unconsciously. The unconscious marks the point at which the subject does not just accede to what society wants. It is a hiccup in the process of social determination.

The unconscious is not the place of reflection. Its automatic form is incompatible with a process of deliberation in which one weighs competing possibilities and ultimately chooses one. This image of careful consideration between different possibilities is not the form of freedom that the unconscious harbours. Instead, it provides a freedom that the subject most often experiences as a compulsion. As the unconscious impels one in a specific direction, one feels powerless against this push. But this drive is an expression of freedom because it follows its logic regardless of external pressures and without the support of any authority figure. Our unconscious responses show no fealty to the powers that be. Instead, the unconscious articulates the subject's singular response to its existential situation. The experience of unconscious freedom feels like necessity, but this feeling of necessity indicates how the unconscious defies any authority that would determine it.

Identifying freedom with the unconscious requires challenging the prevailing conception of freedom in capitalist society. Capitalism's imperatives rely on a liberal conception of freedom for ideological support, a support that a liberal philosophical tradition has been eager to provide.[9] The liberal conception of freedom – freedom as a free will that consciously chooses among various options – fulfils the exigencies of capitalist society. Liberal freedom is ultimately the freedom to choose what one will buy and sell. Its blindness to the capitalist economy's role in determining this buying and selling is integral to its appeal. In contrast, the lack of attention to unconscious freedom, even from Freud himself, is the result of its fundamental incompatibility with capitalist society. The freedom of the unconscious puts a wrench in the functioning of this society. Our libidinal economy prevents the capitalist economy from running without a hitch. This is because libidinal economy drives us to act against our self-interest.

---

8   Victor of Aveyron lived outside of the social order until the age of 12, when French villagers discovered him. As a result of this early absence of a social context, he never learned to speak or communicate effectively with humans, despite years of instruction.

9   The philosophical tradition of liberal freedom remains vibrant to this day, but its original thinker is John Locke, who locates liberal freedom to do whatever one wants in nature. In the *Second Treatise on Government*, he writes, "The *Natural Liberty* of Man is to be free from any Superior Power on Earth, and not to be under the Will or Legislative Authority of Man, but to have only the Law of Nature for his Rule." John Locke, *Two Treatises of Government* (1690; reis., Cambridge: Cambridge UP, 1988), 283. Locke clearly sees freedom as the lack of external constraint on the individual.

The self-interested liberal

The central tenet of the liberal conception of freedom is that individuals must be left alone to pursue their interest. This form of freedom is consonant with capitalist society, in which individual self-interest trumps concerns about the collective. From Jean-Jacques Rousseau to John Stuart Mill to Milton Freidman, defenders of liberal freedom insist on this idea as the bedrock of a free society. As Mill puts it in *On Liberty*, "the only freedom which deserves the name, is that of pursuing our own good in our own way, so long as we do not attempt to deprive others of theirs, or impede their efforts to obtain it. Each is the proper guardian of his own health, whether bodily, *or* mental and spiritual."[10] In this view, freedom is inextricable from pursuing one's own interests. The liberal conception of freedom emphasises free will. The conscious will is free to decide the individual's path without external constraint.

But the liberal conception of freedom never stops to consider where my conception of my interest comes from. It assumes the identity of my self-interest with my subjectivity, as if a subject's self-interest derives immediately from the essence of that subjectivity. In other words, for the liberal, my interest is genuinely my own. This assumption does not hold up under closer examination.

As long as the subject pursues its interests, it accepts the interests that come from social authority. What's in my interest is what the social order deems worthwhile, not what challenges the dictates of this order. If we think about any form of self-interest, this quickly becomes evident. My desire for a high-paying job, a fancy car, a luxury house, or a gold watch originates in what the social order depicts as valuable. By pursuing what I value, I pursue what I have been made to value.

This is why narcissism is never a radical position but always a conformist one. My interest is never initially my own but that of the Other or social authority. This social authority determines where I direct my freedom, which is why liberal freedom is always directed towards bettering my position within the social order rather than defying its imperatives. It aims at what others value, not what others disdain. Pursuing self-interest is always pursuing social success, which is why it is inextricable from conformism.

---

10   John Stuart Mill, *On Liberty*, in *Utilitarianism and On Liberty* (1859; reis., Malden: Blackwell, 2003), 97. As Milton Freidman puts it, "The heart of the liberal philosophy is a belief in the dignity of the individual, in his freedom to make the most of his capacities and opportunities according to his own lights, subject only to the proviso that he does not interfere with the freedom of other individuals to do the same. This implies a belief in the equality of men in one sense; in their inequality in another" (*Capitalism and Freedom* (1962; reis., Chicago: University of Chicago Press, 2002), 195). Although Friedman is much more concerned with defending capitalism than Mill, he nonetheless asserts a very similar conception of freedom, which suggests the link between liberal freedom and the capitalist economy.

Liberalism assumes that subjects find satisfaction by advancing themselves within society. According to this logic, the more status one attains in society, the more satisfaction one has. Liberal freedom manifests itself in social triumphs, such as earning a great deal of money, finding an attractive spouse, or obtaining a respected job. In each case, freedom allows the subject to succeed. Liberal freedom leads to avoiding or overcoming failure by pursuing one's self-interest. Liberal freedom assumes that the subject is driven to succeed.

The liberal assumption is that those with the most material success have access to the most freedom. The wealthy can fly to Fiji at a moment's notice, purchase a new jacuzzi for their second home, or travel to space with Elon Musk. Most of us have pecuniary restrictions on what we can do; the materially successful do not. They enjoy a freedom about which we can only dream. However, this conception of freedom fails to consider the libidinal economy of the wealthy. Our libidinal economy does not satisfy itself through triumphs such as buying a mansion but through obstacles and failures, which is precisely what great wealth enables one to avoid.

Liberal freedom is also the freedom to fail. If there were no failures, the freedom to succeed would have no significance.[11] But failure represents a setback that the self-interested person tries to avoid. Failure stems from the limits on freedom, marking a point where freedom cannot fully determine the course of subjectivity. Even though it does not always realise it, liberal freedom exists only insofar as it strives for success.

One's successes are not the source of satisfaction within the psychic libidinal economy. This is what is most counterintuitive about this economy. The pleasure of success is fleeting compared to the satisfaction of the obstacle and the struggle it inaugurates. In this sense, the psychic economy runs contrary to the capitalist economy, just as it runs contrary to the liberal conception of freedom. The libidinal economy runs on the subject's failures, not its successes. These failures are paradoxically also the sites of the subject's freedom. We are only free at the moments when our unconscious acts subvert our conscious will.

I am free only when I choose against my own interest, when I pursue a direction that defies my own self-interest. In other words, freedom exists at the antipode of the liberal conception. This is because my interest is always the product of external

---

11   The apostles of liberal freedom all insist on the importance of allowing people to make poor choices and to fail. The freedom to fail is the necessary correlate of the freedom to succeed, which is the liberal doctrine. As Milton Friedman puts it, "Those of us who believe in freedom must believe also in the freedom of individuals to make their own mistakes. If a man knowingly prefers to live for today, to use his resources for current enjoyment, deliberately choosing a penurious old age, by what right do we prevent him from doing so?" (*Capitalism and Freedom*, 188). Failures provide the incentive that help to drive everyone else in the direction of success, which is why someone such as Friedman cannot avoid discussing this apparent downside of liberal freedom.

forces that erect it as an illusion that guides my conscious actions, but that fades whenever I approach it too closely. For instance, if I identify my own interest with obtaining a million-dollar salary, it is clear, first of all, that this image of self-interest is not my own. It comes from the capitalist society in which I exist. I have merely taken over the idea of self-interest that this society broadcasts everywhere nonstop. It is thus pathological, in the sense that it derives from an external agency.[12] This apparent self-interest is not my own.

But this is only the beginning of the problem with the liberal conception of freedom to follow one's self-interest. The liberal freedom to follow one's self-interest leads inevitability to disappointment. It founders on its own moments of success. When I finally obtain the salary I want, I will not find the happiness I expect. Instead, I will imagine happiness in earning two million dollars per year or maybe no longer having to work. Whatever image I construct of my self-interest will always suffer from this deficit: the attempt to realise it will expose it as an illusion that will necessitate constructing another image.

Without self-interest as a genuine possibility, the liberal conception of freedom falls apart. The absence of interest as motivation gives the subject nothing to pursue. The liberal subject is cast adrift without any mooring. Mill makes this dependence explicit in *On Liberty*, but every thinker evoking liberal freedom must rely on it. Once we strip self-interest away, our conception of freedom must look beyond the liberal horizon.

Immanuel Kant was the first genuinely to break with the liberal conception of freedom. For Kant, freedom does not consist in advancing one's own interest or procuring one's own self-interest but in precisely the opposite direction. One attests to the actuality of freedom only through suspending one's interest to follow the moral law. The law's fundamental restriction of interest plays a necessary role in the constitution of freedom. Without self-limitation through giving itself the moral law, the subject would never emerge as free. As Kant sees it, there is no freedom without radical self-restriction.

Kant complicates the straightforward liberal conception of freedom by introducing the detour of the law's restriction. He understands that my own self-interest is actually foreign to me, the result of an imposition by an external logic that prioritises it. The law asserts my freedom by stripping away the priority of this intruder and thereby enabling me to grant priority to the law that is in me but functions as an internal constraint on my will or inclination. As Kant puts it in *Critique of Practical Reason*, "freedom, the causality of which is determinable only through the law,

---

12   Immanuel Kant defines the pathological as those considerations that arise from external circumstances and serve to block the subject's ethical activity. For Kant, even perfectly normal attitudes such as filial devotion or patriotism could have a pathological function insofar as they do not emerge out of the subject's own self-relating.

consists just in this: that it restricts all inclinations, and consequently the esteem of the person himself, to the condition of compliance with its pure law."[13] Although the law restricts, this restriction frees the subject from its dependence on the illusion of self-interest or the compulsion of external determinants.

But because Kant has no theory of the unconscious, he cannot grasp the full radicality of his insight. He identifies the moral law with freedom, but he ultimately aligns free adherence to the moral law with the subject's ultimate interest. In the last instance, the defiance of one's own interest leads back to a greater self-interest, when God rewards the subject for its moral choices. Kant cannot do without this incentive for morality. Without it, freedom would lead to unhappiness, and we would have no incentive to pursue it. In this way, Kant's inability to theorise the unconscious – or, to say it differently, his inability to fully accept the reality of satisfaction in unhappiness – causes him to retreat from freedom back to self-interest. Kant gives ground to liberalism when he imagines happiness as a reward for the moral subject's free choices.

Driven to tears

It would require Freud to add the next crucial turn of the screw to Kant's formulation of the relationship between the subject and its own interest. With his discovery of the death drive in 1920, Freud conceives of a subject that finds satisfaction in its failures rather than its successes.[14] But Freud hints at it well before 1920. This conception of satisfaction in the libidinal economy is present in Freud's initial theory of the unconscious in *Studies on Hysteria* in 1895. From the moment he first theorises it, the unconscious, like the Kantian moral law, undermines the subject's self-interest to provide satisfaction for the subject. For Freud, to say that the subject has an unconscious is to say that it is not a purely self-interested entity. The unconscious is how the subject derails itself.

Although he has no intention to build on Kant's legacy, Freud does precisely that when he conceives of the unconscious as the foundational psychic agency, especially as he theorises it in his later years after discovering the death drive. The unconscious acts against the subject's interest. It satisfies itself through its subversion of the subject's conscious self-interest. Its satisfaction transcends all mean egoism. Although it is not solely an ethical agency, the unconscious never leaves the subject free to act

---

13   Immanuel Kant, *Critique of Practical Reason, in Practical Philosophy*, trans. and ed. Mary J. Gregor (1788; reis., NY: Cambridge UP, 1996), 203.

14   Freud first articulates the idea of the death drive in *Beyond the Pleasure Principle* in 1920 and then attempts to delve into its implications for the rest of his life. But he never reaches an understanding of it that he himself finds totally satisfying.

purely in self-interest. Its grounding principle is the satisfaction that derives from failure, not success.

When the unconscious manifests itself, it often spells trouble for the social prospects of the subject. Unconscious desire undermines conscious wishes. On the most basic level, an unconscious slip can reveal a desire at odds with what one consciously hopes to accomplish. Say I try to advance my interest by complimenting my boss for the sake of a promotion. But instead of stating, "I really liked your presentation in the meeting," I say, "I really liked your ejaculation in the meeting." Rather than obtaining the promotion I hoped for, I may be sent to sexual harassment training or fired. The slip has the effect of subverting what I wish would happen.

But the slip, the manifestation of the unconscious, not what I consciously wish for, expresses my freedom. While the slip undermines my prospects for employment, it simultaneously asserts the distance that separates me from the social imperatives that swirl around me. The slip expresses my defiance of what my social context would make of me, my refusal to simply obey. By engaging in the slip, I affirm the singularity of my subjectivity. The slip indicates my inability to be exactly what the social order would make of me.

Fortunately, not every expression of unconscious freedom leaves me facing sexual harassment charges or unemployed. But freedom does always have the effect of damaging me in some way. There is no freedom outside of self-destruction.[15] In the self-destructive act, I cut into my social position and undermine what the social order has made of me. The free act does not give the subject something additional but takes something away. It occurs at odds with the subject's self-interest, which the subject puts up as a barrier to its freedom.

Libidinal economy works against self-interest. It produces the satisfaction that sustains the subject through the continual sacrifice of the subject's own interest. In the psychic economy, this is the only function that self-interest has. I do not pursue it; I sacrifice it to satisfy myself. This satisfaction frees us from our dependence on the lure of self-interest by exposing its nullity. Only by sacrificing my own interests can I recognise their illusory status that compels us as long as we pursue them.

Freedom is identical to the subject's satisfaction. When the unconscious manifests itself against self-interest, it asserts the subject's freedom. This assertion satisfies the subject by recapitulating the loss that founds subjectivity. The subject emerges through a loss that gives it something to desire. Without this loss, the

---

15   No film has depicted the connection between freedom and self-destruction like David Fincher's *Fight Club* (1999). When watching the film, it is almost impossible to believe that it survived the rigid censorship of Hollywood system, which attempts to bring the disruptions of the unconscious back into an ideological narrative. For an unequalled discussion of the film's radicality, see Anna Kornbluh, *Marxist Film Theory and Fight Club* (NY: Bloomsbury, 2019).

subject is nothing at all, which is why it can find satisfaction only by losing, never by attaining its object. There is no original object to obtain or to desire: subjectivity loses its object into existence and gives itself something to desire by sacrificing. Through failure, the subject actualises the structuring loss that defines it and constitutes an absent object to enjoy. Failure is the only way we have available to us to give ourselves something to enjoy. The pleasure of success, in contrast, is always fleeting. This is why sports champions always talk about the possibilities for the next year immediately after winning this year's championship. Winning leaves one bereft of an object to enjoy, so one must conjure it by recalling what one does not have.

The problem is that the structure of consciousness is absolutely opposed to the subject's form of satisfaction. No one can consciously pursue failure without transforming failure into success. This is what Blaise Pascal is getting at when he claims that "all men seek to be happy. This is without exception, whatever different means they use. They all strive toward this end…. The will never takes the slightest step except toward this object. This is the motive of every action of every man, even of those who go hang themselves."[16] Pascal is undoubtedly correct when we think purely about conscious will: we strive to realise our self-interest and achieve happiness. But the subject is not just a conscious being. Because Pascal could never read Freud, he could not take stock of the existence of an unconscious that aims at undermining happiness rather than promoting it.

Even when we recognise the existence of the unconscious, we cannot consciously pursue loss in the way the unconscious does. By hanging myself, to cite Pascal's example, I consciously aim at realising my self-interest and relieving myself of the pain of existing. No matter how extreme the act, including suicide, I cannot consciously accede to the aims of the unconscious. I can never consciously take up my unconscious freedom. The unconscious acts freely prior to the intrusion of consciousness, which always lags. Because consciousness pursues self-interest, my conscious will can never be free in the way the unconscious is.

If we are unconsciously free, then freedom is radically opposed to free will. Free will is determined. Freedom appears not through deliberation and decision but in our actions that express the unconscious. We do not consciously guide these actions. Instead, we experience our unconscious acts as compulsions. We experience our freedom only as an inability to do otherwise. When acting unconsciously, we act against our conscious will. Through the unconscious, I assert my freedom from both external constraint and the constraint of my self-interest, which is nothing but an illusion that I have taken over from external forces.

---

16   Blaise Pascal, *Pensées*, trans. and ed. Roger Ariew (1670; reis., Indianapolis: Hackett, 2005), 181.

The most that consciousness can do in the face of our unconscious freedom is to acknowledge its priority and identify the unconscious act as an expression of the subject's desire. It must try to catch up with a freedom that always remains ahead. Most of the time, we disavow our free acts as missteps that we endeavour to correct through subsequent repair efforts. For instance, we tell our lover that we did not mean to call them by the name of our ex-lover. Nevertheless, the misstep is the fundamental form of freedom because freedom is located in the unconscious rather than in our conscious control. The only part that consciousness has to play in freedom is accepting our unconscious acts as the manifestation of freedom.

Insofar as everyone has an unconscious, everyone is free. But psychoanalysis's psychic and political lesson is that one must reconcile oneself to one's freedom. My free acts occur before I have consciousness of them. They appear to me as aberrations that threaten to detour my secure existence. Consciousness can never catch up to these free acts and articulate them. It always comes after my freedom. But I must look at these threats that the unconscious poses to my security as the form that my freedom takes and reconcile myself to its fundamental disruptiveness. The unconscious leads the way for the subject by exploding the illusion of the good that guides its conscious activity.

Free capitulation

Not every irruption of the unconscious affirms the subject's break from its social determinants. That is, the unconscious is not inherently a radical agency in the psyche. The unconscious is not inherently Robespierre or Lenin. This would seem to complicate the link between the unconscious and freedom. However, if we examine our unconscious forms of obedience, it becomes clear that even these manifestations of the unconscious bespeak the subject's freedom insofar as they do not just directly follow the social situation out of which they emerge.

There are moments when our unconscious aligns with our society's superegoic injunctions. The superego is social authority internalised, the psychic agency responsible for social authority's power over the subject. Although most people have a conscious sense of morality, the superego is primarily unconscious, which is why it is such a demanding psychic force. While we may become consciously aware of its injunctions, their source remains unconscious. When we heed the injunctions of the superego, following the unconscious is a form of obedience to the social order, a mode of conformity. The role of the unconscious in the superego indicates that the unconscious is not simply an agency of defiance, not simply a site of psychic radicality. It does not only disrupt our insertion into the social order but can facilitate it when it harbours superegoic imperatives.

When subjects capitulate to superegoic imperatives, they do more than just obey. They take their obedience further than is socially necessary. They take their obedience to the point where they derive enjoyment from their capitulation. The enjoyment that the superego produces is the enjoyment of excessive obedience, an obedience that goes beyond what any authority demands of us.[17]

External authorities require only a certain degree of capitulation – one must wear a suit to work, say, or own a smartphone – and then do not make any additional demand after one obeys to this extent. These authorities leave people free after they capitulate enough – for instance, no external pressure compels one to purchase ten phones for oneself. The superego is much more exigent. The more one gives in to it, the more that it demands one gives.

Freud notices this unrelenting force of the superego as an unsurmountable difficulty when one tries to quench its thirst for obedience. As he theorises the superego in *Civilisation and Its Discontents*,

> the more virtuous a man is, the more severe and distrustful is its [the superego's] behaviour, so that ultimately it is precisely those people who have carried saintliness furthest who reproach themselves with the worst sinfulness. This means that virtue forfeits some part of its promised reward; the docile and continent ego does not enjoy the trust of its mentor, and strives in vain, it would seem, to acquire it.[18]

The superego places the subject in a no-win situation. One can never obey enough to appease its exigency. It does not just demand capitulation but always demands even more capitulation.

The unrelenting nature of the superego derives from its relationship to the death drive. Superegoic imperatives use the subject's self-destructiveness as a disciplining mechanism. The superego transforms the self-destructiveness of the drive into a force that serves the social authority. Under the compulsion of the superego, the subject enjoys its excessive obedience. The subject punishes itself for its failures while getting off on this punishment, like the medieval monk flagellating himself for his transgressions – or someone today upbraiding herself for spending too much time unproductively watching videos rather than studying or working. Here, the subject's self-laceration, which otherwise works against social authority, operates in service of this authority thanks to the superego. When the unconscious expresses itself in

---

17   Jacques Lacan identifies the imperative of the superego with the command to enjoy. Although it is an agency of restriction that appears moralising, the superego drives the subject to enjoy itself.

18   Sigmund Freud, *Civilisation and Its Discontents*, trans. James Strachey, in *The Standard Edition of the Complete Psychological Works of Sigmund Freud*, vol. 21, ed. James Strachey (1930; reis., London: Hogarth, 1961), 125–126.

the superego, it seems to function as a site of capitulation rather than defiance, of unfreedom rather than freedom.

But even our unconscious adherence to the superego marks a moment of freedom. When unconsciously following the superego's imperatives, we do obey the social demand through these actions. Nonetheless, enthralled by the superego, my capitulation to the social authority is never simply capitulation. When I follow the superegoic injunction, I transform what the social order demands of me into my own form of enjoyment, as much as when I defy this authority unconsciously. The superego misinterprets external social authority in the same way that my desire misinterprets the desire of the Other. This is why I am responsible for my superegoic capitulation, even though the superego is the internalisation of social authority. Although the superego is an agency of conformity and ethical turpitude, it nonetheless is a site of freedom when it manifests itself unconsciously, which is almost the only form the superego takes. Following the dictates of the superego represents a free capitulation. Its link to the unconscious is its link to freedom.

The limits of finitude

The thinker most committed to freedom in the twentieth century contends that any conception of freedom depends on rejecting the unconscious. Jean-Paul Sartre devotes his primary philosophical work to an insistence on human freedom. As Sartre sees it, our freedom has its basis in the orientation that we give to our entire existence. If we have an unconscious, then this orientation ceases to be free and becomes the result of a force outside our control. Positing the unconscious imperils freedom because it eliminates responsibility.

This is not to say that Sartre is utterly hostile to psychoanalysis. Towards the end of *Being and Nothingness*, he proposes his own version of it, "existential psychoanalysis." The problem with this coinage is that existential psychoanalysis strips away the most radical (and essential) piece of psychoanalytic thought – the unconscious. Sartre has to rid subjectivity of the unconscious to preserve freedom due to his conception of the unconscious as alien to subjectivity.

When he discusses Freud in *Being and Nothingness*, Sartre clarifies that the unconscious, as he understands it, is not part of the I or subjectivity. He writes, "by the distinction between the 'id' and the 'ego,' Freud has cut the psychic whole into two. I am the ego but I am not the id. I hold no privileged position in relation to my unconscious psyche. I am my own psychic phenomena in so far as I establish them in their conscious reality."[19] What bothers Sartre about Freud's conception of

---

19   Jean-Paul Sartre, *Being and Nothingness*, trans. Hazel E. Barnes (1943; reis., NY: Washington Square Press, 1956), 50.

the unconscious is that it marks a point at which the subject is not itself, a point at which the subject is not responsible for itself – and thus not free. For Sartre, understanding our libidinal economy in terms of the unconscious implies ceding control of subjectivity to an alien force and abandoning the possibility of the subject's self-determination.

The problem of freedom appears to doom once and for all the idea of a marriage between psychoanalysis and existentialism. The former appears as a philosophy of psychic determinism in contrast to the latter's insistence on freedom. But these two theories have much to offer each other. Existentialism reveals to psychoanalysis that its interventions must concern the subject's freedom, while psychoanalysis shows existentialism that it must locate freedom within the unconscious rather than confining it to consciousness. In this sense, each theory moves the other past a fundamental stumbling block. Existentialism pushes psychoanalysis past its psychic determinism, and psychoanalysis demonstrates that existentialism cannot confine its conception of freedom to conscious decisions.

Instead of conceiving the psychoanalytic critique of the consciously free subject as a refutation of existentialism, we can see it as a way of reformulating existentialism that takes the priority away from consciousness and moves it to the unconscious – creating an existentialism based on the libidinal economy. Existentialism that gives priority to the unconscious appears to betray the fundamental tenet of existentialism – my free decision. But the essential problem with existentialism lies in its focus on consciousness. This focus prevents it from taking stock of not only unconscious desire but also the power of ideology to determine conscious decisions.[20] When we turn to the unconscious as the paradoxical site of freedom, the response to the problem of ideology becomes much clearer and a more defensible conception of freedom emerges.

The split between consciousness and the unconscious as a starting point entails a divide between focusing on the finitude of the subject and its infinitude. The notion of our inherent finitude unites existentialist thinkers even when they disagree on what constitutes it. For instance, finitude marks a critical disagreement between

---

20   In his critique of Sartrean existentialism, Herbert Marcuse contends that the philosophy of freedom becomes an ideology itself when it completely obliterates material determinants in the way that Sartre does. Marcuse states, "If philosophy, by virtue of its existential-ontological concepts of man or freedom, is capable of demonstrating that the persecuted Jew and the victim of the executioner are and remain absolutely free and masters of a self-responsible choice, then these philosophical concepts have declined to the level of a mere ideology, an ideology which offers itself as a most handy justification for the persecutors and executioner" ("Existentialism: Remarks on Jean-Paul Sartre's L'Être et le Néant," Philosophy and Phenomenological Research 8, no. 3 (1948): 322). Existentialism becomes an ideological justification for Marcuse because its conception of freedom writes the material forces of capitalist society out of the picture. Sartrean freedom becomes just a reinvention of liberal freedom.

Martin Heidegger and Sartre. Heidegger theorises finitude in terms of our being towards death: we are finite entities since death limits our possibilities. In contrast with Heidegger, Sartre views death as absolutely alien to subjectivity. He links finitude to freedom. Finitude, for Sartre, is integral to and even follows from our freedom.

I am initially free because I do not have an infinite number of choices. Were I an infinite being, I would be unable to choose and be condemned to unfreedom. My finite situation both limits my freedom and, at the same time, enables my freedom. For Sartre, a freedom without limits is no freedom at all. But then, when I choose, I introduce a limit into my being and produce my finitude. Since there is no escape from choice – I am condemned to freedom – there is no escape from finitude. We are finite because we are lacking beings. Our freedom occurs not through overcoming our lack but through identifying with it. We are free only insofar as we lack. If we were complete, we would cease to be free.

This is another point at which existentialism and psychoanalysis appear to come together perfectly. Sartre's insistence on the lacking subject seems to parallel Lacan's. It is even tempting to claim that Lacan simply plagiarises the lacking subject from Sartre, in whose intellectual shadow he emerges as a theorist. But Sartre's alignment of lack with finitude marks an essential point of divergence. For psychoanalysis, we are lacking beings not because we are finite beings but because we are infinite. This is the point at which psychoanalysis follows the lead of German Idealism rather than phenomenology and points towards a wholly different version of existentialism – an existentialism that takes the unconscious as its point of departure.

We are infinite beings because our desire transcends every empirical object and continues without regard for the passing of time. Our lack is the emblem of desire transcending its object, not of it coming up short. As beings of desire, rather than beings of instinctual need, we find ourselves moved by a force that does not obey the restrictions of the finite world. The infinitude of subjectivity does not respect death as an endpoint.

Of course, psychoanalysis must avow that the subject dies, that it is finite in the sense that Heidegger privileges. Death remains an unsurpassable trauma that annihilates all the subject's freedom. But death traumatises the subject not because the subject is finite but because the subject is infinite. This is a crucial point of distinction. If subjects were nothing but finite beings, their death would be the unremarkable indication of this finitude. But no subject approaches death in this way. We approach it instead as something that we project ourselves beyond, which is why its trauma so impacts us. Our capacity for transcending death and attaching ourselves to a desire that aims beyond the finite world represents the subject's infinitude. This infinitude makes death unbearable for the subject.

The distinction between conceiving the subject as finite or infinite has important implications for how we think of the subject's freedom. A free finite subject always has possibilities that it cannot realise because they lie beyond the limitations of its finitude. The finite situation determines the limits of freedom, even though these limits are fundamentally enabling. Without the situation, without a limitation of freedom, there would be no freedom. But at the same time, the finite subject experiences these barriers to its freedom as injustices.

I live in an area where the only employment opportunities are mining cobalt under horrific conditions or joining a paramilitary group. At the same time, I see other choices like investment banking and corporate law that are utterly closed off to me. My finitude expresses itself through what is not possible for me. The finite subject constantly encounters barriers that make evident its finitude and that make this finitude any everyday reality. These barriers manifest themselves in the form of others (who have the possibilities denied to me) or the Other (the authority that polices the border that keeps me in my situation).

The inherent tendency of the finite subject is to view these others (and especially the Other) as illegitimate barriers to its own potentiality for action. Even though Sartre tells me that my freedom's restrictions are constitutive, I experience these restrictions as unjust. The right of the Other constantly intrudes on the subject and highlights the subject's limit. The prison bars of finitude appear in the form of the Other, causing the subject to lash out at the Other with aggression. While Sartre recognises the necessity of the barrier to freedom that others represent, he nonetheless theorises aggression as one of the fundamental relations to others that result from this barrier

For the infinite subject, the Other has a vastly different role. Lack, here, is not simply impoverishment or limitation but also a possibility. The subject does not run up against the Other's limitation but constantly goes beyond it. It experiences the failure of desire not through the figure of the Other but in the act of desiring itself. If the finite subject tends to be paranoid about the Other, the infinite subject views the Other not just as a limitation but also as a condition of possibility for subjectivity's project.

Sartre contends that the initial presence of others and their projects limit my freedom. My project must emerge against the background of these others that alienate me from myself. He does admit that the limitation of others and the situation they create are necessary. There is, for him, no freedom outside of the situation that limits it. Nevertheless, at the same time, he theorises this limit as exterior to my freedom. It is an external barrier rather than an internal (or internalised) enabling limit. He fails to see that the presence of the Other within me is the starting point of all freedom.

This mistaking of the external barrier for the internal limit stems from the blind spot that haunts Sartre's philosophy and all derivatives of existentialism from the beginning. The third party is the fundamental absence in existentialism (and phe-nomenology, its parent). The encounter that the existentialist imagines is an en-counter with the other, an encounter that initially occurs without a mediating third. However, the mediating third does not come along after the fact. It is what enables any encounter between subject and other.

Third first

In *Being and Nothingness*, Sartre indicts psychoanalysis for always looking at the sub-ject from the standpoint of the Other (which is necessary to make the unconscious visible). It seems impossible to preserve the idea of the existential project while granting the existence of unconscious desire. But I contend that understanding the existential project as unconscious offers a way to offset some of the more damning critiques of existentialism and formulate an existentialism that grapples with the influence of the Other. Rather than starting with the isolated subject as Sartre does, we can recognise how the mediation of the Other is there from the start. We discover our existential project not through self-reflection but in encounters with otherness when the unconscious manifests itself. The unconscious nature of our existential project forces us to take the Other as the starting point of our existential project.

The main thrust of psychoanalysis, following in the wake of German Idealism, is that the third party is not only in force for every one of the subject's encounters but also that subjectivity emerges through the third party's mediation. The third party – what Kant calls the "transcendental categories," or what Hegel calls "*Geist*," or what Lacan calls the "big Other" – provides the primary point of reference through which the subject takes up its own relation to the world. Freud did not simply identify the third party with the unconscious, as if our unconscious were the direct representa-tive of the Other implanted in the psyche. Instead, our engagement with the third party produces an unconscious irreducible to either the third party (the Other) or the conscious subject.

The existential priority of the third party eliminates the subject as a philosophi-cal starting point, as it is for all existentialist thinkers, including Martin Heidegger (despite his rejection of the term for what he calls *Dasein*). There is not an initial im-mediate relation to the world that the subject subsequently loses when it encounters the mediating influence of the third party.[21] Instead, the third party plays a forma-tive role in the emergence of the free subject. The subject must relate to itself and

---

21   From the opposite corner of the philosophical universe, this is also the position of Ludwig
      Wittgenstein. Wittgenstein stakes out a similar claim when he insists that there is no private
      language. This is Wittgenstein's way of saying that the third party comes first, that our private
      feelings find their model in public utterances.

its needs through a mediating third party, which is why its needs transform into unconscious desires.

Desire, or the fundamental project of the subject, is not the result of the subject's original choice that occurs against the background of a series of others and their projects. I do not determine my project through conscious choice. The presence of others does not serve simply to limit my possibilities. Instead, my project is, first and foremost, an act of unconscious interpretation.

The subject arrives at its desire by interpreting the desire of the third party or Other. The Other or social authority does not simply imprint its ideology on me. Instead, I relate to the promulgation of this ideology through how I interpret the ideological injunction.[22] I emerge as a desiring being by an interpretation consonant with how I begin to desire. This alienation of my own desire is absolutely primary. I have no desire outside of an alienated desire of the Other. I have no project that is mine before the project that comes from the Other, a project that I attempt to discover through my interpretive act.

But the central role that the Other plays in my desire's emergence does not eliminate the subject's freedom. Instead, it changes where we locate freedom. My freedom is not found in the act of originating the desire or the project. It is not that I am "free" because I can invent my project out of whole cloth and then work on pursuing its realisation.

My freedom is found, rather, in the act of unconscious interpretation of the Other's desire, an act that occurs in the libidinal economy. Through interpreting the Other's desire, I arrive at my own. Unconscious interpretation is the free act that separates me from the Other. Its freedom consists in its incapacity to be literal. I cannot take what the Other tells me literally because the terms through which the Other signifies its desire are not transparent, even to itself. The opacity of the Other's demand addressed to me activates my unconscious in response. It renders my interpretation of this demand – that is, my desire – free.

No matter how carefully I hew to the Other's project as the Other describes it, I always misunderstand it because the Other does not understand itself. It is impossible for me to simply adopt the Other's desire or project through the act of interpreting it. There is no such thing as perfect obedience, despite conscious efforts. When I interpret, I distort the Other's desire into my own. I am the misreading of what the

---

22   The problem with Louis Althusser's famous conception of ideological interpellation is that he imagines it working even when it fails. I misrecognise myself as the subject of an ideological hail that is not necessarily intended for me, and this misrecognition constitutes me as an ideologically interpellated subject. Given the structure of the unconscious, however, it would be more correct to say that the ideological hail fails even when it succeeds. My recognition of an ideological hail always skews my relationship to the Other, no matter how much I consciously want to capitulate, because I have an unconscious.

Other desires. My failure to correctly interpret the Other's project is how I assert my freedom.

I get my own freedom right insofar as I get the Other's desire wrong. But this freedom is always ahead of my conscious subjectivity. I must look for it in what escapes my conscious control. When I act as if under compulsion but without following external dictates, I gain a privileged insight into how my freedom looks. Freedom is never deliberative but always takes me by surprise. I am free at the moments when I cannot act otherwise.

Destroying freedom

When he conceives of the unconscious, Freud does not believe he is developing a theory of freedom. On the contrary, he contends that a strict necessity governs the structure of the libidinal economy. He calculates how the psyche functions based on the necessity that governs it, which is one reason why he believes that one day we might discover physiological explanations to replace psychoanalytic ones. But Freud never took stock of how the logic of the unconscious shatters the image of self-interest for every subject. Once we understand how the unconscious satisfies itself through the destruction of our own interest – which Freud began to theorise in *Beyond the Pleasure Principle* in 1920 – discovering its association with freedom becomes the next logical step. Freud could not take this step because the only conception of freedom that he had available to him was the liberal one, a freedom that conceptualises freedom in terms of the conscious will. Freud was not a careful reader of Kant and did not read Hegel at all. The result is that he could not identify the subject's annihilation of its own self-interest with the subject's ultimate assertion of freedom.

No social order can privilege genuine freedom for its adherents. To do so would strip away their attachment to the order and pave the way for a constant threat of the order's overthrow. The liberal capitalist order seems to fly in the face of this logic because it thrives on freedom and could not function without a free market that enables producers and consumers to choose the commodities they will produce and consume. The paradoxical conclusion is that capitalism relies on freedom, but freedom embodies the annihilation of any ruling social link. The solution to this riddle lies in exploring the nature of freedom: the freedom that would break from the ruling order is distinct from the freedom of choice that sustains the capitalist system. In fact, capitalist freedom of choice depends on abandoning unconscious freedom, which is the form of genuine freedom and the only possible basis for a political rupture. The oxymoron of unconscious freedom serves as the engine for a political break insofar as it involves a refusal of the givens that determine our situation. Unconscious freedom expresses a libidinal economy that runs counter to political economy, a freedom of desire rather than conscious will. This sort of freedom cannot be directly conscious and can only become so after the fact. One can identify uncon-scious freedom only in the form of the event that compels one to act.

The liberal conception of freedom has dominated thinking for so long because it works hand in hand with the illusion that we are self-interested beings. It also aligns with our common sense. It seems completely logical that we are free when we consciously decide to pursue the end that we deem would advance our interests. Pre-serving this image of freedom has the effect of preserving self-interest as obtainable and worthy of pursuit. Deprived of self-interest, liberal freedom evaporates as well. Freud's discovery of the unconscious points towards a radically different conception of freedom after self-interest proves unsustainable. Unconscious freedom not only survives the death of self-interest but thrives via its sacrifice.

References

Copjec, Joan. *Read My Desire: Lacan Against the Historicists.* Cambridge: MIT Press, 1994.

Friedman, Milton. *Capitalism and Freedom.* Chicago: University of Chicago Press, 2002. First published 1962 by University of Chicago Press.

Freud, Sigmund. *Psychopathology of Everyday Life.* Translated by Alan Tyson. In *The Standard Edition of the Complete Psychological Works of Sigmund Freud.* Vol. 6. Edited by James Strachey. London: Hogarth Press, 1960. First published 1901.

———. *The Ego and the Id.* Translated by James Strachey. In *The Standard Edition of the Complete Psychological Works of Sigmund Freud.* Vol. 19. Edited by James Strachey. London: Hogarth Press, 1961. First published 1923.

———. *An Autobiographical Study.* Translated by James Strachey. In *The Standard Edition of the Complete Psychological Works of Sigmund Freud.* Vol. 20. Edited by James Strachey. London: Hogarth Press, 1959. First published 1927.

———. *Civilisation and Its Discontents.* Translated by James Strachey. In *The Standard Edition of the Complete Psychological Works of Sigmund Freud.* Vol. 21. Edited by James Strachey. London: Hogarth, 1961. First published 1930.

Kant, Immanuel. *Critique of Practical Reason.* In *Practical Philosophy*, translated and edited by Mary J. Gregor, 133–272. Cambridge: Cambridge UP, 1996. First pub-lished 1788.

Kornbluh, Anna. *Marxist Film Theory and Fight Club.* NY: Bloomsbury, 2019.

Locke, John. *Two Treatises of Government.* Cambridge: Cambridge UP, 1988. First pub-lished 1690 by Awnsham Churchill.

Marcuse, Herbert. "Existentialism: Remarks on Jean-Paul Sartre's *L'Être et le Néant*." *Philosophy and Phenomenological Research* 8, no. 3 (1948): 309–336. https://doi.org/10.2307/2103207

Mill, John Stuart Mill. *On Liberty*. In *Utilitarianism and On Liberty*, edited by Mary Warnock, 88–180. Malden: Blackwell Publishing, 2003. First published 1859.

Pascal, Blaise. *Pensées*. Translated and edited by Roger Ariew. Indianapolis: Hackett, 2005. First published 1670.

Sartre, Jean-Paul. *Being and Nothingness*. Translated by Hazel E. Barnes. NY: Washington Square Press, 1956. First published 1943 by Éditions Gallimard.

What is the Libidinal Economy of Antiblackness?

Christopher Chamberlin

Afropessimism offers a critique, not a theory of libidinal economy. By reconstructing that critique here, I hope to show how afropessimism's understanding of antiblackness is derived from a theory of history that is itself constructed through a critique of libidinal economy. That theory of history tessellates around a specific concern – both critical and political – over the *absence* of black revolution.

From the outset, we should be clear that the critique I intend to detail takes as its object a classical, early 19th-century understanding of economy (one veneered with scientific bona fides by the promulgation and lateral application of the laws of the conservation of energy from the field of physics) as a closed system, one presumably governed by the logics of harmony and equilibrium, organised by a metaphysics of equivalence and intrinsic value, and operating according to the general principle of conservation (of meaning or productive forces).[1] A bad, long-running common sense bequeaths this worldview, one on which afropessimism trains its crosshairs, and that necessarily imagines the human as an essentially pleasure-seeking or utility-maximising animal. This rationalist notion of subjectivity, which even 20th-century economic psychology and behavioural economics complicated on their own terms, still infiltrates theories of racialisation of all stripes. What I have in mind are those critical projects that, in one way or another, presuppose that white supremacy derives its so-called irrational vitality – its political legitimacy as well as its affective profitability – from the pleasure it provides (or pain it spares) its benefactors: whether we have in mind the notion of a "public and psychological wage"[2] it extracts from racial superordination, the enjoyment it stages from its accompanying spectacles of black suffering, or the fear and anxiety that antiblackness simultaneously produces and defrays. If this conceptualisation of the psychological utility of racism does not, in the end, seem very "irrational" at all, that is because it ascribes to antiblackness an essential economism of desire. While not in the immediate monetary ("material") interests of its benefactors, antiblackness is still

---

1 David Bennett, *The Currency of Desire: Libidinal Economy, Psychoanalysis, and Sexual Revolution* (London: Lawrence & Wishart, 2016).

2 W. E. B. Du Bois, *Black Reconstruction* (NY: Harcourt, Brace and Company, 1935), 700.

conceived as libidinally ("sexually") rational or politically interested. This will not do, if for no other reason than that such a notion of white supremacy renaturalises political economy's proposition that "greed" is essential to human psychology into some basic harmony of narcissistic interests.

As if surplus libido could be in the interest of a sovereign self! As if the drive could be sublimated without loss!

In the end, such a notion of libidinal economy only recycles a psychological truism adopted by every classical political economist that Marx critiqued, all of whom posit the individual ego as a "rent-seeking" agent in the pursuit of utility or happiness or certain moral sentiments; one who, because they are somehow transparent to themselves, because they are not alienated (or unconscious) in any significant sense, begin and end by making free choices in free markets – whether commercial or sexual or both. We could find Freud's early metapsychological precept on the economism of the unconscious guilty of the same sin, insofar as he, too, initially treats desire as the design of a scrupulous accountant: in wishes or jokes, Freud suggested, "a gain in pleasure corresponds to the saving of psychical expenditure."[3] So here I am only restating the obvious: the critique of political economy is already a critique of libidinal economy. And that is because those critiques revolve around a shared object: the subject, the economically minded ego, or what Sylvia Wynter names the "bio-economic subject."[4] Afropessimism, in turn, involves a critique of the economies disputed by both Marxism and psychoanalysis: it solders a disjunctive unity between these dual (and frequently duelling) traditions of critical theory by rebaptising their methods and concepts through the historical-structural instance of racial slavery.

If there is no economistic subject as just described, that is consequent to the fact that *there is no (libidinal or political) economy* in this traditional sense. In rooting its critical concerns in the problematic inexistence of economy, afropessimism shares a vertex with, and a fair share of the ambitions of, a project on the "primary question of economy" proposed by Georges Bataille.[5] It is in his work that this classical conception meets its ruination, where we find an emphasis on nonreproductive expenditure and destruction over investment and conservation, where we see the dynamics of waste and extravagance elevated over use and growth into touchstones of the

3   Sigmund Freud, "Jokes and their Relation to the Unconscious," in *The Standard Edition of the Complete Psychological Works of Sigmund Freud*, trans. James Strachey (1905; reis., London: Hogarth Press, 1960), 114.

4   Sylvia Wynter, "Unsettling the Coloniality of Being/Power/Truth/Freedom: Towards the Human, After Man, Its Overrepresentation—An Argument," *CR: The New Centennial Review* 3, no. 3 (Fall 2003): 318.

5   Georges Bataille, *The Accursed Share: An Essay on General Economy*, trans. Robert Hurley (NY: Zone Books, 1988), 10.

limits of economisation, and where these dynamics cover an area of concern dealing with matter and human energy as such. Such a project, contended Bataille, "may hold the key to all problems posed by every discipline concerned with the movement of energy on the earth."[6]

If afropessimism is consubstantial with a project of general economy at this scale – and this is one of my implicit arguments – it is a grave mistake to date its birth to a simple shift in attention from the rational interests that racial domination serves (the economic utility of slavery and its afterlives) to the irrational wishes it satisfies (the erotic complexes that motivate and reward those institutions). Not that the body of afropessimist writing is always free of passages that could suggest such an inversion, but a better interpretation is possible, which we can start to reconstruct from the beginning.

Frank B. Wilderson III, in his early 2003 article "Gramsci's Black Marx," deems a supplemental inquiry into the libidinal economy of slavery as the red thread of afropessimism's (at the time still-unnamed) intellectual canon.

> It's important to bear in mind that for [Saidiya] Hartman, [Walter] Johnson, [Orlando] Patterson, and [Hortense] Spillers the libidinal economy of slavery is more fundamental to its institutionality than is the political economy. In other words, the constituent element of slavery involves desire and the accumulation of black bodies and the fact that they existed as things "becoming *being for* the captor." The fact that black slaves laboured is a historical variable, seemingly constant, but not a constituent element.[7]

The ensemble of "direct relations of force" that comprise the libidinal economy are strictly incompatible with the field of power executed through the wage relation, just as they are inassimilable to the gendering matrix installed via the reproductive labour (domestic and sexual) extracted through and beyond the wage relation. But the latter – the forces and relations of political economy that gender the sexual division of labour – are also only instituted through an interdiction and organisation of the violence of libidinal economy. Power (i.e., the political) mediates terror (i.e., the libidinal) and erects itself upon it, confirming Jean-François Lyotard's guiding axiom that every political economy is libidinal.[8] Put another way, libidinal economy is the structural antagonism within, or the impossibility and immanent ruin of, every

---

6   Bataille, *Accursed*, 10.

7   Frank B. Wilderson III, "Gramsci's Black Marx: Whither the Slave in Civil Society?" *Social Identities: Journal for the Study of Race, Nation and Culture* 9, no. 2 (2003): 239, n 4. Internal quotation is from Hortense J. Spillers, "Mama's Baby, Papa's Maybe: An American Grammar Book." *Diacritics* 17, no. 2 (1987), 67.

8   Jean-François Lyotard, *Libidinal Economy*, trans. Iain Hamilton Grant (Bloomington: Indiana UP, 1993), 108–122.

political economy. So already here, in the earliest hours of afropessimism's intervention, a quilting between the political and libidinal economy is clearly visible. The impossibility of economy as such – the fact that no system of power *relations* can cohere into a *body* of power – manifests through the libidinal economy's subversion of the political economy.

For Wilderson, the libidinal economy ultimately produces and manages access to black death, the latter a notion that historicises what Lyotard elsewhere calls an intensity or pulsion – an intrinsically useless force, something non-exchangeable, "inevaluable and unaccountable."[9] It refers to the force of libidinal investment that exceeds any act of economisation (it is impossible to invest or capitalise intensities fully) and remains inassimilable, as the waste by-product of every procedure of governmentality. Freud called this force "the death drive," a notion reworked more recently by Willy Apollon and the Québec school of psychoanalysis as the "unbound" drive that surges forth through the effraction of the living being by the advent of the faculty of speech unoriented by (and inassimilable to) adaptation or biological survival,[10] unleashing thereby an "energy that is diverted from the organism in the creation elicited by [a] representation that is outside of perception."[11] On the other end of the spectrum, to radically dispose of such an intensity, to enact a total divestment of drive energy, is equivalent to what Jacques Derrida calls an "expenditure without reserve," an "irreversible usage of energy ... that apparently interrupts every economy."[12] Such an act of total discharge, as with the "pure" drive itself, is unserviceable to any dispensation of sovereignty, just as it impedes the procedures of conservation and equivalence that subtend value production. The drive's useless force and its total expenditure are inimical to investment; and both of these liminal states of the drive – being but two faces of the same coin – are dissimulated everywhere by the organisation, territorialisation, and investment of libido in relations of power. It is only by capitalising the drive, by instantiating those relations through the cathexis of social objects, in a process that can nevertheless never be fully consummated, that intensities are organised into various dispositifs of libidinal enjoyment – what we can call *modes of jouissance*. We will return to this notion and specify its contribution to formulating the problematic of the absence of black revolution at the end of this chapter.

Let me first warn the reader, then, about two misprisions that tend to shroud the whole topic of the libidinal economy of antiblackness. First, it would be folly to speak of any intrinsic coincidence between the aim and object of antiblackness, to assign

---

9   Lyotard, *Libidinal Economy*, xvi.

10   Willy Apollon, "The Limit: A Fundamental Question for the Subject in the Human Experience," *Konturen* 3 (2010): 107.

11   Willy Apollon, "The Subject of the Quest," trans. Daniel Wilson, *Penumbr(a)* 2 (2022): 4.

12   Jacques Derrida, *Margins of Philosophy*, trans. Alan Bass (Brighton: Harvester Press, 1982), 19.

it an instinct for self-preservation, whether that be maintaining white supremacy, reproducing symbolic power, or even accumulating (surplus-value or bodies). Antiblackness is rather the uninterrupted uprooting of itself, an ontological crisis, one that – and this boggles the political imagination – cannot be sustained without opposing itself, without a binding of its energies and a blocking (or territorialisation) of its intensities, the latter being the necessary and adequate conditions under which various *formations* of antiblackness can emerge – imaginary and symbolic formations that rely on, but always remain distinct from, the *real of antiblackness*. What Frantz Fanon called negrophobia, although perhaps one of antiblackness' historically privileged forms – comprising a structure of relations that grounds an aggressive mass psychology – occurs only on the condition that the real of antiblackness is drained into a common identification against a black imago.[13] But negrophobia is not essential to antiblackness; the latter can theoretically exist without the former. The real of antiblackness rather subverts economisation of any sort and, with it, capital itself, which maintains its grip on the material conditions of life – vesting the political economy with its miraculous powers of adaptation – through this unceasing internal subversion.

We are led to an equally dead end if we insist on any straightforward distinction between the "rational" interests and the "irrational" exuberances of antiblackness, and precisely because the political and the libidinal are dimensions of the same process, always part of the same antagonistic cocktail, just as Bataille notes that "real life, composed of all sorts of expenditures, knows nothing of purely productive expenditure … [and] nothing of purely unproductive expenditure."[14] The point is that the "psychic" and the "material," the flow of capital and the metonymy of desire – even if separating them out is provisionally useful as a heuristic device – are only ever found compressed in the same inorganic economy.

Against separating the psychic and the material, we might instead open a more useful distinction between the immaterial structure of slavery and the historical-material conditions from which it arises but to which it is irreducible. For the Marxist critic Alberto Toscano, the critique of political economy, at its core, involves a "*critique of ideologies of materiality*" (emphasis in original)[15] that applies equally to materialist ideologies of slavery. Only by distinguishing between slavery's material conditions (its social forms, juridical institutions, and the bodies they materialise) and its structure (antiblackness as such) can one explain its formal determination of the biopolitical crises of black life today: "the skewed life chances, limited access

13   David Marriott, "Bonding Over Phobia," in *The Psychoanalysis of Race*, ed. Christopher Lane (NY: Columbia UP, 1998), 428.

14   Bataille, *Accursed Share*, 12.

15   Alberto Toscano, "Materialism Without Matter: Abstraction, Absence and Social Form," *Textual Practice* 28, no. 7 (2014): 1225.

to health and education, premature death, incarceration, and impoverishment."[16] Here, a certain internal dialectic links the material (concrete) and immaterial (abstract) dimensions of antiblackness. The intangible forms that inhere in exchanging, accumulating, and destroying black bodies, which are embedded in the social practices of racial domination, from chattel bondage to the murder of black people, both of which can be considered variants of a more general reproductive oppression of black women,[17] evacuate the body of its historicity and abstract from it a signifier – blackness – that transcends the material basis of its fecundation and takes on a symbolic life of its own. This new distinction – again, between what Saidiya Hartman calls a *formal* or symbolic "racial calculus and political arithmetic" and the *material* conditions of the "afterlife of slavery," which *may or may not* be positively correlated to it[18] – is roughly divided, in afropessimism, between its intertwined critiques of economy: the political economy encompassing the historical and material formations of antiblackness, and the libidinal economy indexing their constant displacement, the impossible unity between antiblackness' form and content, and the intrinsic volatility, the inhibition of its own aim, that guarantees that *antiblackness does not stop materialising itself.*

"Slavery and freedom do not refer to material well-being."[19] For James Oakes – whose close attention to the negative juridical status of the slave, bearing as it does such an "uncanny resemblance"[20] to Frantz Fanon's calibration of blackness as a defect in ontology, justifies including him as a fellow traveller of afropessimism – slavery's governance, unlike the symbolic instruments employed to organise the social space of political freedom, has a peculiar legal and symbolic status. Never directly governed or juridically defined, racial slavery in the southern United States rested on an indeterminate negation of society. "Where the law in general establishes the rules by which men and women organise their social, personal, and political relations, the law of slavery merely declares those laws irrelevant to the slaves themselves."[21] The law of slavery integrates – without incorporating – slavery *into* society based on its foreclosure *from* society. The slave (and slavery) is therefore not a status that can be differentiated – quantitatively or qualitatively – from the status of

16   Saidiya Hartman, *Lose Your Mother: A Journey Along the Atlantic Slave Route* (NY: Farrar, Straus and Giroux, 2007), 6.

17   Dani McClain, "The Murder of Black Youth is a Reproductive Justice Issue," *The Nation*, August 13, 2014, https://www.thenation.com/article/archive/murder-black-youth-reproductive-justice-issue/.

18   Hartman, *Lose Your Mother*, 6.

19   James Oakes, *Slavery and Freedom: An Interpretation of the Old South* (NY: Norton, 1998), xvi.

20   Jared Sexton, "Don't Call it a Comeback: Racial Slavery is Not Yet Abolished," *openDemocracy*, June 17, 2015, https://www.opendemocracy.net/en/beyond-trafficking-and-slavery/dont-call-it-comeback-racial-slavery-is-not-yet-abolished/.

21   Oakes, *Slavery and Freedom*, 56.

freedom (and its free subject). The slave is the absence around which slavery society materialises. Post-slavery society, in turn, constitutes itself on a certain Hegelian negation of the negation of society, or around the valorisation of the slave's constitutive absence. The critique of libidinal economy reckons with the fact that, like the economy or the sexual relation, *antiblack society does not exist*.

It should be clear by now that the libidinal economy is not somehow more important than the political economy, but that its critique clocks the effects of the absence of any "outside" to the relations of power. The critique of libidinal economy describes capital in its inorganic totality, in its hegemonising relation to its own outside. It is a theoretical procedure for determining the consequences of the fact that there is no "sacred" space beyond political economy. It thus provides a critical position from which to recognise that all conceptualisations of a point of reference beyond it, all hope in the existence of an instance of lack or excess that would undo capital, are illusions native to any (critique of) political economy that does not account for the libidinal. Indeed, there is perhaps no more consistent point across the history of the critique of libidinal economy than this one, from Lyotard's rebuffing of an anthropological romance about a body or primitive society outside the economising logic of capitalist social formations ("*there is as much libidinal intensity in capitalist exchange as in the alleged 'symbolic' exchange*" [emphasis in the original][22]) to Samo Tomšič's axiom that it is not exploitation that alienates the worker under capitalism, but that capitalism derives its tenacious grip on life and limb by exploiting the subject's fundamental alienation by the structure of the signifier ("capitalism exploits the 'ontological weakness' of human beings"[23]) – and finally, to Wilderson's contention that racial blackness has no ontological plenitude before or beyond the "metaphysical holocaust" of transatlantic slavery.[24] There is nothing in human nature, nothing outside the Western episteme, nothing before or after the advent of racial slavery that is not already fundamentally alienated by the structure of the symbolic, which means that the current conjuncture – slavery and capital in their identity and difference – procures its powers over the subject precisely by exploiting the lack at the core of the human experience and harnessing the libidinal energy unleashed by the collision between body and speech. *Therein* lies its aneconomic efficiency, antiblackness' perverse intransigence, its defective success.

When Étienne Balibar writes that the "real universality" of global markets is achieved by constructing abstract relations of equivalence – not equality – across all

---

22   Lyotard, *Libidinal Economy*, 109.

23   Samo Tomšič, *The Labour of Enjoyment: Towards a Critique of Libidinal Economy* (Berlin: August Verlag, 2019), 54.

24   Frank B. Wilderson III, *Red, White & Black: Cinema and the Structure of U.S. Antagonisms* (Durham: Duke UP, 2010), 38.

things,[25] he does not imply that history is at its end or that capital is complete. On the contrary, post-slavery capital is built on including or valuing its constitutive alterity, what we have called the slave or the "inevaluable" real of antiblackness, which demands renewing our attention on the exclusions and incommensurabilities that emerge *within* the social. The political economy – including the global market and the penetration of its rationality into the crevices of private life – is both realised and detotalised through its infiltration of, and dispossession by, the field of surplus jouissance. *Capitalist power is universalised by including its own subversion within itself; and racial blackness is the talisman of the inclusion of the slave as negation of value, meaning, and pleasure.* As such, the libidinal economy, representing both the inner negation and driving force of power relations and value production, results in a twofold figure, an "extimacy" of economies, where the irruption of libidinal intensities – the very subversion of political economy – is captured, capitalised, and integrated into the global process of equivalence and valorisation. Such a twofold figure of economy that accounts for the productive and destructive aspects of antiblackness is a consistent feature in the last decades of black cultural theory: whether in the dialectic between the violent expenditure of blackness and its dissimulation in the transactions of racial value,[26] the complex between the general (meaning-destroying) and restrictive (meaning-making) economies of white supremacy,[27] to the topology between the symbolic economy of the body and the real of the flesh,[28] and through to the asymmetrical reciprocity between the coherence and incoherence of psychic life.[29] The latter – psychic incoherence – is the heading under which Wilderson now indexes the problematic of libidinal economy first fully explored in his *Red, White & Black*.

Since it is not a substantive thing, the *libidinised* political economy of antiblackness (or what we could also call the *politicised* libidinal economy) must instead be defined by the logic of its processes. Freud called the displacement and condensation of libido the "primary process" of the unconscious. For Wilderson, the abstract processes of the political economy of antiblackness – again, the *fungibility*, *accumulation*, and *destruction* of black bodies – are the primary process of the libidinal economy of antiblackness. A psychic mode of enjoyment corresponds to each of these primary processes: *fungibility* is conditioned by the alienability of blackness as a sig-

25   Étienne Balibar, "On Universalism: In Debate with Alain Badiou," *transversal texts*, June 2007, https://transversal.at/transversal/0607/balibar/en.

26   Lindon Barrett, *Blackness and Value: Seeing Double* (Cambridge: Cambridge UP, 1999), 11–54.

27   Jared Sexton, *Amalgamation Schemes: Antiblackness and the Critique of Multiracialism* (Minneapolis: University of Minnesota Press, 2008), 27–29.

28   Hortense J. Spillers, "Mama's Baby, Papa's Maybe: An American Grammar Book," *Diacritics* 17, no. 2 (Summer 1987): 67–68.

29   Frank B. Wilderson III, *Afropessimism* (NY: Liverlight Publishing Co., 2020), 250.

nificr,[30] engendering a limitless variety of meanings endowable with a pleasure of sense (*jouis-sens* or "enjoyment-in-sense"); *accumulation*, on the other hand, is a mode of jouissance structured on the modality of inhibition, or the intensifying postponement of gratification (the surplus-enjoyment found in thriftiness or anal-retentive characters, for instance); *destruction* involves an extravagant expenditure, the discharge of libidinal tension through aggression, the transgression of the law, or the destruction of normative ideals (as found in the premodern potlatch or gratuitous antiblack police violence now); and all three modes of enjoyment are saturated in the jouissance of compulsion, in the structure of failure and the repetition of the same. Each mode of jouissance, none of which can be described as simply or only pleasurable, therefore produces different subjective modalities, different ways of libidinally capitalising on (and subjectively relating to) antiblack subjection. A certain fantasy frames each of these modes of enjoyment too, just as they mirror various patterns of historical experience (mass incarceration, police killings, the "donning" of blackness in music, style, and sex, and so on). But antiblackness is *not* any *one* of these logical processes; rather, the libidinal economy consists of the mechanisms through which black death – the real of antiblackness – is deintensified, regulated, and invested in various subjective and collective modes of enjoyment.

Perhaps the most frequently cited of afropessimism's definitions of libidinal economy is found in Wilderson's first theoretical monograph:

> Jared Sexton describes libidinal economy as "the economy, or distribution and arrangement, of desire and identification (their condensation and displacement), and the complex relationship between sexuality and the unconscious." Needless to say, libidinal economy functions variously across scales and is as "objective" as political economy. It is linked not only to forms of attraction, affection, and alliance, but also to aggression, destruction, and the violence of lethal consumption. Sexton emphasises that it is "the whole structure of psychic and emotional life," something more than, but inclusive of or traversed by, what Antonio Gramsci and other Marxists call a "structure of feeling"; it is "a dispensation of energies, concerns, points of attention, anxieties, pleasures, appetites, revulsions, and phobias capable of both great mobility and tenacious fixation."[31]

What is presented in template form here is the force of the libidinal (sexuality and the unconscious) and its simultaneous negation by economisation, and we should therefore carefully separate out what are identified here as its economic processes – distribution and arrangement, condensation and displacement, all the forces that

---

30   Christopher Chamberlin, "The Transmission of Slavery," *European Journal of Psychoanalysis* (April 2021), https://www.journal-psychoanalysis.eu/articles/the-transmission-of-slavery-c-chamberlin/.

31   Wilderson, *Red, White & Black*, 7.

contribute to the great mobility of affective investments – from the libidinal economy as such, which cannot cohere *as* an economy precisely because its interminable flux is proof of its inability to equilibrate itself as a system. Libidinal economy cannot escape what is always and everywhere improper to economy: its object, the drive. The libidinal is economised whenever its movement is fixed (cathected or invested) in "concerns, points of attention, anxieties, pleasures, appetites, revulsions, and phobias." The implacability of antiblackness does not reside in some insurmountable, invariable element but in its regular, inexhaustible processes, through which it constantly transforms in the attempt to totalise or objectify itself. *Antiblackness is impossible*, and that is why it does not stop realising its own terror.

What we have here is the only structural "law" of antiblackness, which is that change – driven by the incommensurability between the drive and its object, between antiblackness and economy as such – is its only constant. Antiblackness, like the Lacanian real, is that which always returns to the same place. What then displaces this incommensurability and prevents the aim and object of antiblackness from settling into any single form? How do the modes of jouissance that "successfully" attach the subject to the formations of racialisation and instruments of domination fail? On this question of historical change, afropessimism no doubt endorses a heavily de-romanticised version of the Marxist premise that a universal antagonism is the engine of history: antiblackness is transformed through structural crises, which come to a head when political agencies at various scales realise the internal contradiction between the libidinal relations of terror (metonymically, the slave) and the political relations of power (metonymically, the human). Such a theory of resistance as the engine of dialectical history is, of course, not Marxism's or afropessimism's alone but rooted deeply in the Black Radical Tradition, as exemplified in W. E. B. Du Bois' contention that the most successful general strike in the history of the United States – slaves' *en masse* abandoning plantation work – served as the tipping point of the Civil War and catalysed the crisis of the colour line in the following century.[32]

But the hypothetical enclosure of the libidinal by the political – slavery's negative assimilation into the structure of capital – is not consummated without a remainder; capital, as we have already highlighted, constantly subverts itself *because* it incorporates the unexchangeable and incommunicable real of antiblackness that resists its economic procedures. If the internecine conflict between the political and the libidinal results in what Lyotard calls the constant "dissimulation of intensities into values and values into intensities,"[33] could we not similarly describe post-slavery capital as the interminable dissimulation of antiblackness into value and values into antiblackness? If so, that means, on the one hand, that the antagonism between

32   Du Bois, *Black Reconstruction*, 55–83.
33   Lyotard, *Libidinal Economy*, 110.

capital and slavery is internal to capital; and on the other, that the subject of political economy, the proletariat, and the subject of libidinal economy, the slave, are neither separate nor identical entities but the *same non-whole subject determined by a binary internal structure*.

With that we are returned to the opening question on the theory of the subject of economy, and to a rather vexing conclusion: the particular historical structure of post-slavery capital is defined by its relation to a *universal subject*. Not a subject of political representation, not one that shares a common sociological extraction, inhabits the same cultural milieu, or shares the same history, but one alienated by the universal structure of the signifier and that is subject to the same extra-cognitive laws of discourse. This is a highly specific notion of the subject, one reduced by Claude Lévi-Strauss to what he calls the "human symbolic function," but one also surprisingly reaffirmed in the Civil Rights Era clinic. In the 1960s, the psychoanalytic psychiatrists William Grier and Price Cobbs – who should also be read as afropessimists *avant la lettre* – analysed how their African American patients psychically lived the abstract materiality of racial domination. As summarised in their explosive manifesto, *Black Rage* (1968), the considerable extensions of psychoanalysis that their clinical work required only reinforced a notion of the universal structure of the symbolic. This results in their theoretically and ethically principled *refusal* to racialise the subject at the level of the unconscious:

> There is nothing reported in the literature or in the experience of any clinician known to the authors that suggests that black people *function* differently psychologically from anyone else. Black men's mental functioning is governed by the same *rules* as that of any other group of men. Psychological principles understood first in the study of white men are true no matter what the man's color (emphasis in original).[34]

Libidinally, each subject is the indeterminate effect of the symbolic laws that structure and articulate antiblackness. Fungibility, accumulation, and destruction of black bodies determine every subject, including black subjects (even if they relate to these formations in ways as specific as their collective and individual singularity); not only that, but these libidinal dispositifs, and the particular ways they capture the free drives to attach subjects to their social position, are limited in their scope and variety to those that historically predominate in the libidinal economy of antiblackness. Finally, this means that social antagonism – personified in the intractable combat between "human" and "slave" – is the engine of history in the truest, ambivalent sense: antagonism is not only the source of structural transformations (whenever the drive escapes economisation and wherever the subaltern

---

34   William H. Grier and Price M. Cobbs, *Black Rage* (NY: Bantam Books, 1968), 154.

revolts) but also its limit (when and where the drive is bound to the social order and subjection is capitalised).

Long before, Frederick Douglass had already posited a denaturalised notion of the subject as the basis for a theory of history structured by the dialectic between slavery and freedom: "The limits of tyrants are prescribed by the endurance of those whom they oppress."[35] This notion of "endurance" – of slaves' ambivalent attachment to their social and political position – resonates with the psychoanalytic premise that the desire of the human subject is rooted neither in nature nor in culture but in the unconscious; that the subject of this denaturalised desire does not even organically incline toward life, having no naturally precluded capacity to adapt – or rather mal-adapt – to their material conditions. Death, that is, is also no limit to desire. For Douglass, this variable power to accommodate or refuse subjection determined the limit of slavery *and* its condition of possibility. Where oppression could and would be borne, racial tyranny would continue unabated; when it becomes unbearable, tyranny enters a crisis, and the possibility of its transformation through a political act arises. The endurance or *drive* of antiblackness is thus strictly correlated to the inherent nonproductivity of desire and the limitless perversity of libidinal en-joyment. And an unflinching reckoning with the slave's "resilience" as the principal determinant of the structural resilience of antiblackness is a theme carried across the afropessimist critique of libidinal economy, where the subject – the slave's *relation to* their structural position, beyond the structural position itself – consistently comes into view as the decisive factor of antiblackness' aneconomic efficiency.

To give you a sense of the consistency with which this theoretical and political concern arises in afropessimism's texts, I will only provide a few points of reference that meditate on the relation between an *underdetermined universal subject* and the *overdetermined structure of antiblackness*, through which a critique of the economism of libidinal enjoyment swims into focus.

Saidiya Hartman first unambiguously located enjoyment as the axis of racial relations under slavery: not only the white subject's enjoyment, as found in aboli-tionists' pleasurable identification with the pain and suffering of slaves, but more importantly, black subjects' enjoyment. The "instrumental recreations of plantation management" stabilised routine violence by eliciting the libidinal expenditures of the subjected; plantation dances and other forced amusements amounted to a "use of the body as an instrument against the self"[36] that pitches the subject's *jouissance* against their social, political, and organic life.

---

35   Frederick Douglass, "West India Emancipation Speech," *University of Rochester Frederick Douglass Project*, originally presented August 3, 1857, https://rbscp.lib.rochester.edu/4398.

36   Saidiya Hartman, *Scenes of Subjection: Terror, Slavery, and Self-Making in Nineteenth-Century America* (NY: Oxford UP, 1997), 22.

James Oakes elsewhere catalogues how southern plantation owners responded to the resistance of slaves (from sabotage to open rebellion) through "patterns of accommodation." By winning informal rules that limited violence and interference in their lives, slaves secured conditions that reduced overt conflict between oppressor and oppressed and thus paradoxically made domination sustainable. "[T]he fact that so many masters learned not to interfere too deeply in the private lives of slaves is testimony to the implicit compromise that masters and slaves had to respect if the system was to function at all."[37]

Grier and Cobbs similarly analyse the prevalence of a "black rage" that afflicted their patients to inquire precisely into the paradoxical *rarity* of revolt against the Jim Crow system, into the mechanisms that bind the intensities of suffering instead of discharging them in rebellion. "The question we must ask is: What held the slave rebellion in check for so long?"[38] Their conclusion? That a matrifocal source of inhibition, reinforced through routine violence, converts black rage into a masochistic grief. Their question was undoubtedly shared by Frantz Fanon, whose political and clinical practice consistently concerned itself with how and why the internalisation of aggression arises as the default response by the colonised, a project condensed in a question that David Marriott shorthands in the following way: "Why do people disavow what could truly liberate them?"[39]

Could the lesson of the critique of libidinal economy concern precisely the subject's masochistic investment in their own domination – and power's inverse interest in the enjoyment of its subjects? Could elaborating the link between the subject of desire and the social and historical economisation of enjoyment indicate how a violence otherwise unserviceable to management and control, without a value proposition, nevertheless "works" simultaneously for and against its subscribers? This project's scandal – and so the scandal of afropessimism – would be this: it analyses domination on the level at which it is libidinally invested by the defeated who *enjoy their living death – up to and including their extermination*. To get at its radically impersonal character we could even say: *it, antiblackness, enjoys*. And to remove any final ambiguity entailed by the English word "enjoy," we should more plainly state that *subjection is jouissance*, including for those whose so-called rational interests would most benefit from that subjection's demise. Unless we confuse enjoyment with consent, and mistake freedom for the lifting of repression, this simple point justifies nothing and remains psychoanalytically uncontroversial.

I want to conclude by collating two incendiary passages from the history of the critique of libidinal economy. The first, "the most exorbitant claim in all of Lyotard's

37   Oakes, *Slavery and Freedom*, 147.
38   Grier and Cobbs, *Black Rage*, 59.
39   David Marriott, *Whither Fanon? Studies in the Blackness of Being* (Stanford: Stanford UP, 2018), 41.

outrageous book,"[40] dares to expound on the perverse relationship between capital (and thus labour) and the proletariat:

> the English unemployed did not become workers to survive, they – hang on tight and spit on me – enjoyed [ils ont joui de] the hysterical, masochistic, whatever exhaustion it was of *hanging* on in the mines, in the foundries, in the factories, in hell, they enjoyed it, enjoyed the mad destruction of their organic body which was indeed imposed upon them, they enjoyed the decomposition of their personal identity, the identity that the peasant tradition had constructed for them, enjoyed the dissolution of their families and villages, and enjoyed the new monstrous *anonymity* of the suburbs and the pubs in the morning and evening.[41]

The proletariat is here alienated thrice over: first by the signifier that (through its imposition of an imaginary body) alienates the subject from their desire; then from their surplus-value; and finally *through their own enjoyment*, or by how the technologies of modern life and extraction (the second level of alienation) fantasmatically suture the absence that grounds the subject in symbolic exchange (the first level of alienation). It is not that the subject throws themselves into the machinery of work out of a misguided attachment to survival over liberation, much less out of a cowardly refusal to risk their life in a dialectical overcoming of the master, but that they are seduced by the destruction of the alienating corporeal and symbolic schemas imposed on them. The dissolution of the imaginary ("organic" or "peasant") body makes alienation and exploitation – even death – enjoyable. For Lyotard, several dispositifs characterise the relationship between the proletariat and the capitalist libidinal economy: the jouissance of anonymity, the jouissance of repetition, the jouissance of self-destruction, and so on.

Now let us turn to a passage from Wilderson, which can be found in various modified forms throughout his writings, and which works through the problematic of an *ahistorical – yet historically imposed – unconscious*:

> The Human need to be liberated *in* the world is not the same as the Black need to be liberated *from* the world; which is why even their most radical cognitive maps draw borders between the living and the dead. *Finally, if we push [David] Marriott's findings to the wall, it becomes clear that eradication of the generative mechanisms of Black suffering is also not in the interests of Black revolutionaries.* For how can we disimbricate Black juridical and political desire from the Black psyche's desire to destroy the Black imago, a desire which constitutes the psyche? In short, bonding with Whites and non-Blacks over phobic reactions to the Black imago provides

40   Eleanor Kaufman, "The Desire Called Mao: Badiou and the Legacy of Libidinal Economy," *Postmodern Culture* 18, no. 1 (September 2007).

41   Lyotard, *Libidinal Economy*, 111.

the Black psyche with the only semblance of psychic integration it Is likely to have: the need to destroy a Black imago and love a White ideal. "In these circumstances, having a 'white' unconscious may be the only way to connect with – or even contain – the overwhelming and irreparable sense of loss. The intruding fantasy offers the medium to connect with the lost internal object, the ego, but there is also no 'outside' to this 'real fantasy' and the effects of intrusion are irreparable" (Marriott, "Bonding over Phobia," 426) (emphasis in original).[42]

The "overwhelming and irreparable" real of antiblackness is sutured through what, in the above, is described as an unconscious desire (to "destroy the Black imago") and an economic interest (in constituting "the psyche") that together foreclose a political need (to be "liberated from the world").

Wilderson is clear that psychic integration is only ever an ideological semblance. The coherence of identity, the wholeness of the body, is denied by the structure of the signifier that constitutes the subject in its cleavage from a radically alien drive that permanently displaces its foundation. Where a "White unconscious" constitutes the shared symbolic heritage, antiblack hostility becomes the *exclusive* mechanism for constituting the semblance of psychic integration, while the drive it radically alienates, the intensity that remains structurally inassimilable to the body and disjunctive to the self, is consequently racialised through a "Black imago" that represents (or gives an image to) the unrepresentable real of antiblackness. This consequently introduces the desire for the destruction of (and disidentification from) the Black imago as the only ideological route to the overcoming of castration, the disalienation of the subject, and the recovery of a fantasmatic organic body. But this *neurotic* pursuit of psychic integration through a mutual phobic hostility to the Black imago is only one subjective strategy for containing and enjoying the overwhelming real of antiblackness.

There is also a second subjective strategy: the perverse enjoyment gained in the fetishistic circumvention of the symbolic that aims to destroy every semblance of psychic integration. This is the jouissance that accompanies, precisely, the decomposition of the body and the deconstruction of personal identity. Yet the perverse enjoyment of the destruction of one's own ego, identity, and body is only a semblance of disalienation that is as imaginary as the neurotic pursuit of psychic integration constructed through the negrophobic complex of unconscious identifications and disidentifications. And that is because the former – the jouissance of dissolution or the abject pleasure in the "shattering of the subject"[43] – organises the real

---

42   Frank B. Wilderson III, "The Vengeance of Vertigo: Aphasia and Abjection in the Political Trials of Black Insurgents," *InTensions* 5 (Fall/Winter 2011): 33–34.

43   Benjamin Noys, "Shattering the Subject: Georges Bataille and the Limits of Therapy," *European Journal of Psychotherapy and Counselling* 7, no. 3 (2005): 128–131.

of antiblackness *not* through the repression of castration (i.e., the denial of the structure of the signifier) but through the *libidinal capitalisation* of the subject's alienation from blackness. If the neurotic quest for embodiment and coherent identity *represses* the structure of castration, then the perverse quest for the enjoyment of castration equally disavows the structural impossibility of a "beyond" of castration, betraying a tenacious attachment to psychic coherence of a second order.

If we recall that for Wilderson, Human and Black subjects are equally, if asymmetrically, subjected to the libidinal economy and its alienation of blackness (i.e., fungibility, accumulation, destruction), then "the ability to take pleasure in abjection" that Darieck Scott describes as a method of "racialisation through sexual humiliation,"[44] as with the moral masochism Fanon tracks throughout *Black Skin, White Masks* – which he finds in white subjects who, wracked by guilt of their own antiblack aggression, objectify themselves to an aggressive black other in the staging of an imaginary self-punishment – are mechanisms in which the self-destructive enjoyment of castration itself disavows castration. The point here is that *black subjects, too, enjoy the mad destruction of an organic body imposed upon them, relishing in the decomposition of their personal identity.*

And which "organic" body has been imposed here if it is not quite the same peasant body that enters Lyotard's historical purview? Because the racial structure of primary identification retroactively superimposes whiteness onto a universal corporeal schema that precludes the existence of a black body on the imaginary level, as I have argued elsewhere,[45] it is only possible to assume one body: a white one (or a non-black body). We are, therefore, brought to this paradoxical conclusion. *For all subjects – regardless of their racial identity – it is the destruction of the historically imposed white body that is enjoyed. The dissolution of whiteness is thus as essential a component of the libidinal structure of antiblackness as the phobic hostility to blackness.*

An axiom of the critique of libidinal economy of antiblackness: social death does not exist except through its libidinal capitalisation. And its investment, by those who materially and erotically benefit from it, as much as by those who are undone by bearing the brunt of its gratuitous violence, makes its force available for the constitution of the modern subject.

---

44   Darieck Scott, *Extravagant Abjection: Blackness, Power, and Sexuality in the African American Literary Imagination* (NY: NYU Press, 2010), 169.

45   Christopher Chamberlin, "Affective Ankylosis and the Body in Fanon and Capécia," *Studies in Gender and Sexuality* 19, no. 2 (2018): 125.

References

Apollon, Willy. "The Limit: A Fundamental Question for the Subject in the Human Experience." *Konturen* 3 (2010): 103–118. https://doi.org/10.5399/uo/konturen.3.1 .1391

———. "The Subject of the Quest." Translated by Daniel Wilson. *Penumbr(a)* 2 (2022): 1–14.

Balibar, Étienne. "On Universalism: In Debate With Alain Badiou." *transversal texts*, June 2007. https://transversal.at/transversal/0607/balibar/en.

Barrett, Lindon. *Blackness and Value: Seeing Double*. Cambridge: Cambridge UP, 1999.

Bataille, Georges. *The Accursed Share: An Essay on General Economy*. Translated by Robert Hurley. NY: Zone Books, 1988.

Bennett, David. *The Currency of Desire: Libidinal Economy, Psychoanalysis, and Sexual Revolution*. London: Lawrence & Wishart, 2016.

Chamberlin, Christopher. "Affective Ankylosis and the Body in Fanon and Capécia." *Studies in Gender and Sexuality* 19, no. 2 (2018): 120–132. https://doi.org/10.1080/1 5240657.2018.1456018

———. "The Transmission of Slavery." *European Journal of Psychoanalysis* (April 2021). https://www.journal-psychoanalysis.eu/articles/the-transmission-of-sl avery-c-chamberlin/.

Derrida, Jacques. *Margins of Philosophy*. Translated by Alan Bass. Brighton, UK: Harvester Press, 1982.

Douglass, Frederick. "West India Emancipation Speech." *University of Rochester Frederick Douglass Project*, originally presented August 3, 1857. https://rbscp.lib.roche ster.edu/4398.

Du Bois, W. E. B. *Black Reconstruction*. NY: Harcourt, Brace and Company, 1935.

Freud, Sigmund. "Jokes and their Relation to the Unconscious." In *The Standard Edition of the Complete Psychological Works of Sigmund Freud*, 32–48. Translated by James Strachey. London: Hogarth Press, 1960. First published 1905 by Hogarth Press.

Grier, William H., and Price M. Cobbs. *Black Rage*. NY: Bantam Books, 1968.

Hartman, Saidiya. *Scenes of Subjection: Terror, Slavery, and Self-Making in Nineteenth-Century America*. NY: Oxford UP, 1997.

———. *Lose Your Mother: A Journey Along the Atlantic Slave Route*. NY: Farrar, Straus and Giroux, 2007.

Kaufman, Eleanor. "The Desire Called Mao: Badiou and the Legacy of Libidinal Economy." *Postmodern Culture* 18, no. 1 (September 2007). https://doi.org/10.1353/pmc .0.0008.

Lyotard, Jean-François. *Libidinal Economy*. Translated by Iain Hamilton Grant. Bloomington: Indiana UP, 1993.

Marriott, David. "Bonding Over Phobia." In *The Psychoanalysis of Race*, edited by Christopher Lane, 417–430. NY: Columbia UP, 1998.

Marriott, David. *Whither Fanon? Studies in the Blackness of Being.* Stanford: Stanford UP, 2018.

McClain, Dani. "The Murder of Black Youth is a Reproductive Justice Issue." *The Nation*, August 13, 2014, https://www.thenation.com/article/archive/murder-black -youth-reproductive-justice-issue/.

Noys, Benjamin. "Shattering the Subject: Georges Bataille and the Limits of Therapy." *European Journal of Psychotherapy and Counselling* 7, no. 3 (2005): 125–136. htt ps://doi.org/10.1080/13642530500219665

Oakes, James. *Slavery and Freedom: An Interpretation of the Old South.* NY: Norton, 1998.

Scott, Darieck. *Extravagant Abjection: Blackness, Power, and Sexuality in the African American Literary Imagination.* NY: NYU Press, 2010.

Sexton, Jared. *Amalgamation Schemes: Antiblackness and the Critique of Multiracialism.* Minneapolis: University of Minnesota Press, 2008.

———. "Don't Call it a Comeback: Racial Slavery is Not Yet Abolished." *openDemocracy*, June 17, 2015. https://www.opendemocracy.net/en/beyond-trafficking-an d-slavery/dont-call-it-comeback-racial-slavery-is-not-yet-abolished/.

Spillers, Hortense J. "Mama's Baby, Papa's Maybe: An American Grammar Book." *Diacritics* 17, no. 2 (Summer 1987): 64–81. https://doi.org/10.2307/464747

Tomšič, Samo. *The Labour of Enjoyment: Towards a Critique of Libidinal Economy.* Berlin: August Verlag, 2019.

Toscano, Alberto. "Materialism Without Matter: Abstraction, Absence and Social Form." *Textual Practice* 28, no. 7 (2014): 1221–1240. https://doi.org/10.1080/0950 236X.2014.965901

Wilderson, Frank B., III. "Gramsci's Black Marx: Whither the Slave in Civil Society?" *Social Identities: Journal for the Study of Race, Nation and Culture* 9, no. 2 (2003): 225–240. https://doi.org/10.1080/1350463032000101579

———. *Red, White & Black: Cinema and the Structure of U.S. Antagonisms.* Durham: Duke UP, 2010.

———. "The Vengeance of Vertigo: Aphasia and Abjection in the Political Trials of Black Insurgents," *InTensions* 5 (Fall/Winter 2011): 1–41. https://doi.org/10.25071 /1913-5874/37360

Wilderson, Frank B., III. *Afropessimism.* NY: Liverlight Publishing Co., 2020.

Wynter, Sylvia. "Unsettling the Coloniality of Being/Power/Truth/Freedom: Towards the Human, After Man, Its Overrepresentation – An Argument." *CR: The New Centennial Review* 3, no. 3 (Fall 2003): 257–337. https://doi.org/10.1353/ncr.2004.0015

A Jouissance Beyond Capitalism: Lacan, the Feminist Critique, and the Libidinal Economy of Capitalism

Vladimir Safatle

> Whether something actually exists or not, this is of little importance.
> It can perfectly well exist in the full sense of the term, even if it doesn't really exist.
> – Jacques Lacan[1]

"Jouissance is the substance of everything we speak about in psychoanalysis,"[2] Lacan said. This statement highlighted the structuring role of the concept of jouissance within Lacan's thought and clinic. However, it appears relatively late. We can even say that the term "jouissance," one of the most important concepts within Lacanian metapsychology and praxis, will have to wait for *The Ethics of Psychoanalysis* (*Seminar 7*) to be systematically presented. Its (re)appearance responds to a displacement, increasingly visible in Lacanian thought, towards thematising the clinical use of dynamics linked to the dimension of the Real – that is, dynamics that are not an object of symbolisation, verbalisation and remembrance within the clinic.

But let us note a significant bibliographical fact. After its presentation in *Seminar 7*, the concept of jouissance will return to be the central object of analysis, mainly in *From An Other to the other* (*Seminar 16*), *The Other Side of Psychoanalysis* (*Seminar 17*), and *Encore* (*Seminar 20*). There is a significant fact in this distribution. The thematisation of jouissance returns to Lacan's central concerns immediately after the events of May 1968, since *Seminar 16* begins at the end of 1968. It is evident, in this context, how Lacan makes jouissance a fundamental concept within psychoanalytically oriented so-

---

1 Jacques Lacan, *The Seminar of Jacques Lacan. Book II: The Ego in Freud's Theory and in the Technique of Psychoanalysis*, trans. Sylvana Tomaselli (Cambridge: Cambridge UP, 1988), 229. Translation altered. Most translations from French in this chapter are mine. Future references are to the original French.

2 Jacques Lacan, *Le Séminaire. Livre XVI: D'un Autre à l'autre* (Paris: Seuil, 2006), 45. For a comprehensive analysis of the concept of jouissance in Lacan, see Christian Dunker, *O cálculo neurótico do gozo* (São Paulo: Escuta, 1998).

cial critique: reprising jouissance is, in a sense, his response to what occurred in May 1968. Lacan reads capitalism not via political economy but a libidinal economy constructed through certain significant homologies with Marxist critique. This means that capitalism and its forms of subjection will be described from the impacts they produce in the field of desire. But it is not a matter of recovering the theme, so dear to authors such as Reich and Marcuse, of capitalism as an economic system producing modes of existence based on repression and conformation to disciplinary patterns of conduct. In fact, in Lacan's eyes, capitalism is a system of jouissance's "spoliation"[3] – of plunder, of integrating jouissance into the logic of mercantile production. Understanding such dynamics of spoliation would be a fundamental condition for effectively transformative political struggles.

Lacan could make such a statement because he knew capitalism was abandoning its repressive hegemonic matrix in favour of a form of subjection by continuous incitement. Strengthening the discourse of autonomous individual decisions tends to create social bonds linked to the discourse that "everyone has the right to his form of jouissance" (or even "everyone *must* find his form of jouissance"[4]), which will eventually be realised in the pluralist liberation of the multiplicity of possible forms of sexuality in our liberal democracies. In this way, the *incitement of jouissance* has become the true driving force of the libidinal economy of consumer society. This represents a challenge to social criticism, for if the concept of jouissance ultimately fills two distinct functions (it will establish the critique *and* normal modes of functioning of capitalist societies), every revolt must deal with the subjective structures of libidinal investment in the prevailing social order.

The possibilities of transformative social action are thus linked to the advent of a jouissance capable of opening the experience beyond the social inscription of desire within the symbolic structure. But to do so, it will be necessary to understand the extent of this jouissance inscribed in the modalities of social reproduction and fundamental to preserving capitalism. Lacan will call it "phallic jouissance." This is the Lacanian way of discussing the patriarchal matrix of capitalism: the dependence between its socialisation regimes and perpetuating a form of desire proper to a libidinal organisation thought from within a masculine horizon, with its regimes of homogeneity, phantasm, and identification. To discuss jouissance within capitalism means discussing how desire is socialised via a fundamental reference to a masculine mode of libido, hence the horizon for both masculine and feminine positions.

---

3   Jacques Lacan, *Le Séminaire. Livre XVII: L'envers de la psychanalyse* (Paris: Seuil, 1991), 92.

4   The superego in Lacan does not function exactlyw as an apparatus of internal repression but as a distressing incitement to jouissance. Hence, he reminds us that the true imperative of the superego in contemporary times is "Enjoy!" – jouissance transformed into an obligation. Jacques Lacan, *Le Séminaire. Livre XX: Encore* (Paris: Seuil, 1975), 10.

In this sense, if Lacan says, in one of his best-known propositions, that "Woman does not exist," it is because there is not exactly a gender "binarism" in our societies. There is, in fact, something much more brutal, namely, a gender "monism." Only man exists; only the masculine mode of libido organisation defines the integrity of the field of social inscription of jouissance within our societies. But this non-existence suggested by Lacan is not a mere limit to experience.[5] Modifying the libidinal economy of capitalism will be connected to assuming something understood as impossible and non-existent in our social situation – namely, a non-phallic form of jouissance. There is a dialectic here that critical thinking will need to know how to handle.

Taking this into account, we can approach jouissance by showing how it is a fundamental political concept. It allows an understanding of the dynamics of capitalism's integration and opens the space for thematising the subjective processes of rupture with such forms of integration. Its origin, which cannot escape us, is not found in Freudian texts, although Lacan strives to make Freudian incidences of the term "*Genuss*" indications of a concept. But if we want to find the true reference to the Lacanian use of the concept of jouissance, we should look to Georges Bataille.[6] So let us begin by remembering the context in which Bataille develops his concept. Even the obvious differences between Lacan and Bataille regarding jouissance require recomposing the initial space of problems understood by Bataille.

Bataille and the critique of labour society

Bataille uses the concept of jouissance as the fundamental axis of a social critique based on the capitalist society of labour. That is, in his hands, the concept will be, from the beginning, linked to a specific social theory in which the critique of capitalism is inserted in a broader horizon regarding the advent of labour as a fundamental mode of human activity. Let us remember, for example, statements such as:

Labour requires conduct in which the calculation of effort, related to productive efficiency, is constant. It demands rational behaviour, where the tumultuous move-

---

5   It could not be otherwise for someone who says, "From one instant to the next, because the unconscious exists, you are carrying out the demonstration by which inexistence is grounded as what is preliminary to what is necessary. ... Inexistence is not nothingness" (Jacques Lacan, *Le Séminaire. Livre XIX: ...ou pire* [Paris: Seuil, 2011], 52).

6   Lacan's examples of jouissance, such as potlatch and Sade (Lacan, *Le Séminaire. Livre VII: L'éthique de la psychanalyse* [Paris: Seuil], 1986), or Saint Teresa of Avila (Lacan, *Le Séminaire. Livre XX: Encore* [Paris: Seuil], 1973), come directly from Bataille. On the relation between Bataille and Lacan, see Carolyn Dean, *The Self and Its Pleasures: Bataille, Lacan and the History of the Decentered Subject* (Ithaca: Cornell UP, 1992).

ments unleashed at feasts and usually in games are frowned upon. If we could not restrain these movements, we could not work, but labour introduces the very reason to restrain them.[7]

In this passage, we see Bataille insisting upon a model of calculation, measurement and quantification derived from the logic of labour and foreign to the "unproductivity" of these modes of social relationship like parties and games, in which the experience of jouissance is lodged. Such a model is inseparable from the notion of "utility," as well as from a time in which activities are measured to calculate efforts and investments, with regard to "productive efficiency," with its refusal of waste as the supreme horizon of the morality of our actions. There is a capacity for control based on the possibility of predicting results proper to labour as a mode of appropriation of my strength and objects – control embodied in the primacy of utility. About the notion of "utility," Bataille writes:

> Theoretically, utility has pleasure as its goal – but only in a moderate form, for violent pleasure is regarded as *pathological* – and is limited, on the one hand, to the acquisition (practically production) and conservation of goods and, on the other hand, to the reproduction and conservation of human lives … On the whole, any general judgment about social activity implies the principle that every particular effort must be reducible, to be valid, to the fundamental needs of production and conservation.[8]

Utility appears not only as a description of the rationality proper to the capitalist socioeconomic system but crucially as the fundamental principle of the moral subjects proper to such a system. The rational subjects within capitalism are those who organise their actions with a view to self-preservation, the conservation of their goods, the economic calculation of their efforts, and enjoying moderate forms of pleasure, that is, forms of pleasure that do not place us outside our domain. They are rational because they always submit their affectivity to reflection on utility and measure.

Against this labour society, Bataille wants to appeal to everything excessive, everything capable of mobilising a jouissance that is not confused with maximising pleasure and displeasure and, above all, every social action that appears unproductive. Every society is crossed by the need for experiences of excess, expenditure, and destruction that, from the point of view of the economic demands of production and maximisation, are simply irrational. This leads Bataille to affirm that the utilitarianism of capitalist society – its logic linked to constituting agents maximising their interests – could only be broken by the circulation of jouissance and its fundamental

---

7   Georges Bataille, "L'érotisme," in *Œvres complètes X* (Paris: Gallimard, 1987), 44.

8   Georges Bataille, "La notion de dépense," in *Œuvres complètes I* (Paris: Gallimard, 1987), 303.

manifestations – eroticism and the sacred – as if jouissance were the foundation of the social criticism of capitalism. Having the same idea in mind, Lacan says, "jouissance is that which serves no purpose,"[9] that which has no "utility." Or, even that "the pleasure principle is this barrier to jouissance, and nothing else."[10]

Eating fresh brains

How could such concept of jouissance operate within the analytic clinic? Refusing the defence of a naturalistic liberation of desire, rejecting even the possibility of a self-care that would lead to affirming the "man of pleasure" (as argued by Foucault),[11] Lacan brings jouissance to the clinic. His clinic should lead the subjects to relate with a jouissance that crosses them and takes them out of the domain of the self, without submitting them to the domain of some fabricated lost naturalness of impulses and passions.

In this sense, Lacan increasingly insists that human experience is not a field of behaviours guided only by ordering images (Imaginary), by socio-symbolic structures (Symbolic) that aim to guarantee and secure identities, but also by a disruptive force whose correct name is Real. Here. The Real is not to be understood as a horizon of concrete experiences accessible to immediate consciousness. The Real is not linked to a problem of objectively describing states of affairs. It concerns a *field of experiences* that cannot be adequately symbolised or colonised by ideal images of strong social circulation. This explains why the Real is always described negatively and dismissively, as if it were a matter of showing that there are things that only offer themselves to the subject in the form of negations. Hence propositions like "The Real is the impossible." The Real indicates an experience of exteriority concerning the processes of material reproduction of life. It preserves its negativity as a way of preventing experiences of difference from being crushed by the possible determinations of the present.

If we ask ourselves how such a perspective works clinically, we have a prime example through Lacan's commentary on one of Ernst Kris' clinical cases.[12] This is a clinical vignette presented by Kris about a young scientist unable to publish his research. Such impossibility is derived from a compulsion, which he believes he has, to plagiarise. Thus, we find a patient who organises his subjective position based on the

9   Lacan, *Le Séminaire. Livre XX*, 10.
10   Lacan, *Le Séminaire. Livre XVI*, 277.
11   On the relations between Lacan and Foucault, see Nadia Bou Ali and Rohit Goel, eds., *Lacan Against Foucault: Subjectivity, Sex and Politics* (London: Bloomsbury, 2018).
12   Jacques Lacan, *Écrits* (Paris: Seuil, 1966), 393–398, 598–602. The case is in Ernst Kris, "Ego Psychology and Interpretation in Psychoanalytic Therapy," *The Psychoanalytic Quarterly* 20, no. 1 (1951).

proposition, "I cannot publish what I write, because deep down I am a plagiarist." It resonates with his behaviour, in his youth, of petty theft of books and candy. It also brings into play a mode of intersubjective relation by comparison that refers back to his relations with his father and his grandfather, a "great father" (*grandfather*), a renowned scientist, who achieved the success that his father could not.

One day, the patient comes to the analytic session claiming to have found a book that contains the ideas of texts he had written, even though he had not published them. Kris intervenes by asking to read the book, concluding that there is nothing of what the patient fears. On the contrary, Kris says, the patient was projecting onto the other ideas that he would like to have. Kris thus intervenes at the level of "reality appreciation," trying to get the patient to accept that "we always deal with other people's ideas, it's a question of knowing how to deal with them." When presenting his interpretation, Kris hears the following response from the patient: "Always when my analysis session ends, just before lunch, I like to walk down a street where I find a restaurant that offers one of my favourite dishes: fresh brains."

Lacan will say that such a response exposes the failure of Kris' intervention. For even if Kris' analysis were not incorrect, the desire to "eat fresh brains" remains to be analysed. It matters little whether he is a plagiarist, but a confusing mix of a desire for authorship and plagiarism seems structuring and insurmountable. This leads us to insist that a primordial and raw oral jouissance (expressed in the desire to eat fresh brains or, again, in an Oedipal dream of a battle with the father in which books were weapons and conquered books were swallowed during combat) appears to block an essential dimension of linguistically structured recognition – namely, the dimension of "publication," of becoming public, of assuming for the Other the form of one's ideas. For such an oral relation has something that cannot be inscribed in a recognised form, something deeply fusional, something of a confused field in which distinctions of identity no longer hold. This jouissance breaks the possibility of the subject "having a name," "being in a place that is his own." The I "wants to know nothing" about it because such jouissance has been expelled as radically beyond the limits of the pleasure principle.

Therefore, the only possible form of recognition appears through "a totally incomprehensible act of the subject."[13] An *acting out* that he repeats, as if translating into imaginary form what he should be able to apprehend in symbolic form. But the patient's "no," in saying, "I can't publish, I am not someone who can publish his ideas," is inverted by the analyst into a statement like "you can publish; our ideas always come from others." This means a blockage in the more careful listening to this "no." It was not possible to hear how such a denial was more brutal because it called for developing an experience with language in which the confusion of deeply oral relations could find a form. This was impossible within a language marked by the

---

13   Lacan, *Écrits*, 398.

individualised boundaries of one who feels, at every moment, unduly entering the domain of another, being unmasked as a plagiarist. The analysis should, therefore, lead the subject to reconstitute his mode of existence based on this jouissance, even at the price of not knowing who he is and what the "limits," what "determinations," clearly define his presence in the world.[14] For this jouissance is a form affirming de-centring and dispossession. It is the collapse of the subject's illusions of identity and the libidinal basis for openness to what does not bear his image.

How to enjoy capitalism

However, the critical function of the concept of jouissance will become more com-plex as Lacan tries to provide a theory of the libidinal structure of capitalism.[15] La-can will understand that capitalism could never be a mode of existence based on the simple renunciation of jouissance. In fact, no mode of social existence builds its dy-namics of adhesion through simple repression. Capitalism is based on what Lacan calls the spoliation of jouissance – in the inscription of its excess and lack of measure within the dynamics of social reproduction.

We must speak of "spoliation" because it is not a simple negation. Jouissance be-comes what the dynamics of Capital's self-valorisation seeks to produce, as if the libidinal axis of the subject's adherence to capitalism passed through the belief that the jouissance that drives us could be realised within the dynamics immanent to Capital; as if the logic of this dynamic of production were the immanent expression of "our nature." That is, as if our desire naturally sought capitalism, its form of pro-duction, and its existence.

Let us underline this point to better understand the kind of contribution psy-choanalysis can make to the critique of capitalism. It will not explain its historical formation, the transformation of the social forms of production, nor will it seek to "psychologise" the political struggles against its social structures of subjection. There is not and cannot be a "psychoanalysis of the social," as if we could treat social life as a field of symptoms, even if social life produces symptoms. It is important to say this to remember that social struggles are not symptoms, with their logic of a ciphered

---

14   This cannot be otherwise for someone who so strongly links "impossible" and "real" as a clini-cal horizon, as we see when Lacan defines the unconscious as "a metaphorical term to desig-nate the knowledge that only sustains itself by presenting itself as impossible so that, from this, it is confirmed as real (understand, real discourse)" (Jacques Lacan, *Autres écrits*, [Paris: Seuil, 2001], 425).

15   On such a libidinal theory of capitalism, see Samo Tomšič, *The Capitalist Unconscious: Marx and Lacan* (London: Verso, 2015); Cláudio Oliveira, "Capitalismo e gozo: Marx e Lacan," *Tempo Social* 11, no. 22 (2004).

message directed to an Other. They are social struggles, with their immanent force of dismissal of authority and realisation of demands for justice.

However, psychoanalysis will be able to accurately expose the "rhetoric" of Capital, its strategies for justifying the demands of production and labour from an alleged rooting of economics in our psychology. For economics is the continuation of psychology by other means. It is part of the rhetorical strategies of adhering to capitalism to define the form of production of wealth and goods as expressing the satisfaction of interests and the maximisation of pleasure, to define the imperatives of competition and enterprise as an expression of naturalised traits of human behaviour. Our social servitude is founded on naturalising a certain psychology that serves as the basis of the reigning economy. The psychoanalytic critique of capitalism is embedded in decomposing such a psychological foundation of the economy. It reminds us how capitalism colonises our jouissance, and our only alternative is to withdraw this jouissance out of the mode of production that colonises it.

Let us note, for example, a precise and fundamental point of Lacanian libidinal economy, namely, the way Lacan will read the Marxist proposition that the entire rationality of the productive process in capitalism is subjected to the extraction of surplus-value, whether in its absolute or relative form. The fact that the horizon of labour is organised not from the production of use-values rooted in our alleged systems of needs, but from the exponential valorisation of value itself, express a certain form of social determination of our desire.

Lacan's greatest influence on this point is the critique of *homo œconomicus* made by Louis Althusser in his "The Object of Capital" (part four of *Reading Capital*). In this classic text, Althusser recalls how Marx seeks to describe a mutation in the very concept of value, separating it from the current notions of profit and income. We know the importance, for Marx, of labour's capacity to create value. This value, however, is not based on a normative anthropology in which value itself would find its foundation as an immediate expression of a system of needs it can satisfy.[16] As if the "need" of the human subject defined, by itself, the very nature of economic activity and was confirmed by it.

Althusser insists that the concept of surplus-value breaks this underlying and "happy" anthropology, since behind the economy we will no longer find the naturalness of the subject of needs in search of the best satisfaction. We will find an "automatic" dynamic of self-valorisation of value, of the transformation of Capital itself

---

16   "Classical economics can only think economic facts as belonging to the homogeneous space of their positivity and measurability, under the condition of a 'naive' anthropology that founds, in the economic subjects and their needs, all the acts by which economic objects are produced, distributed, received and consumed": Louis Althusser, ed., *Lire Le Capital* (Paris: PUF, 1996), 368.

into the true subject of the economic process. We will not find the subject's expression through labour but the production of the subject through the dynamics of value production itself. As Marx wrote, "production thus not only creates an object for the subject, but also a subject for the object."[17]

Lacan tries to define what would be the libidinal basis of such a form of subjection, of the subject's production by the object of Capital. This is because the political reflection made by psychoanalysis has never been content to explain processes of social subjection by coercion and direct violence, although it has never denied their existence. The political problem that psychoanalysis inherits from modern political philosophy is: how do subjects desire their own servitude? Lacan's answer is: capitalism has changed our form of jouissance, by producing a mutation in the rationality of economic production.[18] Capitalism subjected jouissance to the rhythm of indifference towards sensible objects, of the interchangeability of what has its mode of existence in a generic axiomatic, of the self-referential process that has an end in itself, whose only purpose is its quantitative measure. Thus, it made us desire just like workers submitted to Capital as an automatic subject.

Let us better understand this point. Capitalism imposes on all spheres of social reproduction of life ideals of behaviour based on rationalising actions from a dynamic of maximising performances and intensities. Actions that aim at the pure maximisation of performances must be organised in a manner homologous to economic activities based on extracting surplus-value and, consequently, on circular self-valorisation of Capital. This rationality proper to a society organised on circulating what has no other function than to valorise itself needs to socialise desire, leading it to be caused by the *pure measure of intensification*, by the pure push to amplification that establishes the objects of desire in an incessant and surplus circuit called "*plus-de-jouir*" by Lacan. Thus, it is possible to state, with Dardot and Laval, that "'accountable' subjectivation and 'financial' subjectivation ultimately define a subjectivation as an excess of the self over the self or even the indefinite surpassing of the self."[19]

Since it is, however, an accounting logic, at no time should the excess call into question the internal normativity of the capitalist process of accumulation and performance. For this is a quantitative excess that is not transformed into qualitative change. On the contrary, every excess is financially codifiable; it confirms the previously defined code. As Hegel would say about other phenomena, this excess is the

---

17   Karl Marx, *Grundrisse* (London: Penguin, 1993), 92.

18   This is the meaning of statements such as, "Our starting point can only be to question the ideology of pleasure through what renders everything that sustained it a little out of date. It is convenient to place ourselves at the level of the means of production, insofar as, for us, these are what condition the practice of this pleasure" (Lacan, *Le Séminaire. Livre XVI*, 112).

19   Pierre Dardot and Christian Laval, *La nouvelle ordre du monde* (Paris: la découverte, 2013), 437.

mark of a bad infinity, because it does not pass to the true infinity of what changes its own form of determination from itself, of what is infinite because it realises itself paradoxically producing the negation of itself; a negation that, when integrated, procedurally modifies the structure of the previously presupposed totality. Rather, it is the bad infinity of what is always haunted by a never-embodied beyond, a beyond whose only function is to mark reality with the seal of inadequacy, of the bitter taste of the "not yet."[20] The analysis of capitalism has always needed a theory of the two infinities. Thus, when Lacan says that capitalism is driven by a "*plus-de-jouir*," surplus-enjoyment, one must listen to what this term effectively says: this jouissance is a progression to infinity that is never actualised and that, for this reason, must mark every object consumed with the "consumption" of the object, that is, with the seal of its annulment, its erasure, its indifference. The "*plus-de-jouir*" is, at bottom, a "*pas-encore-jouir*," or not-yet enjoyed.

So, there is a turn of the screw in this theory of the libidinal economy of capitalism. It is in propositions like, "The *plus-de-jouir* is a function of renouncing jouissance under the effect of discourse."[21] That is, this jouissance codified by the capitalist process of production is sympathetic to a certain "renunciation" of jouissance.[22] Here, the theme of the renunciation of jouissance produced by submission to the alienated time of labour returns (a Bataillean theme par excellence that reminds us how the time of jouissance and the time of labour cannot be confused).[23] For jouissance to become *plus-de-jouir*, the homologue of surplus-value, it must lose its capacity to be the force that dispossesses me and reconfigures me through reference to what is qualitatively different from me. Lacan speaks, in this context, of "renouncing jouissance under the effect of discourse," because discourse produces a loss through the inscription of the subject in the signifier, inscription in an ordered symbolic universe. Subjection to the signifier could not be done without a loss of jouissance coming from partial drives, those drives that do not know reference to an "I."

---

20   "*La plus-value, c'est la cause du désir dont une économie fait son principe: celui de la production extensive, donc insatiable, du manque-à-jouir*": Lacan, *Autres écrits*, 435. Roughly translated: "Surplus-value is the cause of the desire that an economy makes its principle: that of extensive, and therefore insatiable, production, of lack-in-enjoying." This logic can produce, in turn, a subjectivity marked by the experience of debt, of continuous indebtedness. See, in this regard, Jorge Aleman, *Razón fronterisa y sujeto del inconciente: conversaciones con Eugenio Trías* (Barcelona: NED Ediciones, 2020).

21   Lacan, *Le Séminaire. Livre XVI*, 19. Or again, "*le plus-de-jouir est autre chose que la jouissance. Le plus-de-jouir est ce qui prénd, non pas à la jouissance, mais à la perte de jouissance*": Lacan, *Le Séminaire. Livre XVI*, 116. Roughly translated: "The plus-de-jouir is something other than jouissance. The plus-de-jouir is what leads, not to enjoyment, but to the loss of enjoyment."

22   Which explains why he cannot sustain himself without suffering: "How each one suffers in his relation to jouissance, while he only inserts himself into that jouissance through the *plus-de-jouir*, that is the symptom" (Lacan, *Le Séminaire. Livre XVI*, 41).

23   "Labour implies the renunciation of jouissance": Lacan, *Le Séminaire. Livre XVI*, 39.

The inherent patriarchy of Capital

With this problematic in mind, we can better understand the unique Lacanian way of associating capitalism and patriarchy. In Lacan, patriarchy is not simply a form of male domination based on the binary division of gender. Since there is no subjection without some form of satisfaction, patriarchy is a form of jouissance that implicates all subjects, regardless of their gender orientation. In this sense, capitalism needs patriarchy because of desire's power to produce other forms of social relations. Capitalism needs the primacy of its phallic jouissance to subject everyone's plastic desire to a form of fixity; it needs patriarchy to domesticate subjects under a political and phantasmatic form of domination.

At first glance, it may seem, however, that Lacan understands this patriarchal order as insurmountable. After all, he will say in several contexts that the phallus "is the fundamental signifier through which the subject's desire can make itself recognised as such, whether in the case of a man or a woman."[24] This demonstrates how the phallus can *construct a Universal* capable of unifying the singular experiences of desire.[25] There were several criticisms of this Lacanian phallic "monism," mainly from sectors of feminism.[26] Let us remember, for example, how Nancy Fraser synthesises this criticism, following Dorothy Leland's critique of Lacanian determinism, when she notes:

> Phallocentrism, woman's disadvantaged place in the symbolic order, the encoding of cultural authority as masculine, the impossibility of describing a nonphallic sexuality – in short, any number of historically contingent trappings of male dominance – now appear as invariable features of the human condition.[27]

In this sense, psychoanalysis appears as a technology to preserve the heteronormative and binary structure that serves as a basis for colonising bodies through normalising the positions of men and women. In Lacan's case, we would have a system

24   Jacques Lacan, *Le Séminaire. Livre V: Les formations de l'inconscient* (Paris: Seuil, 2005), 273.
25   A point well developed by Monique David-Ménard, *Les constructions de l'universel* (Paris: PUF, 2001).
26   One of the foundations of this criticism was provided by Derrida, when he insisted that the Lacanian primacy of the phallus meant "there is only one libido, therefore no difference, and even less an opposition within libido between the feminine and the masculine, indeed, it is masculine by nature" (Jacques Derrida, *La carte postale* [Paris: Flammarion, 1985], 528).
27   Nancy Fraser, *Fortunes of Feminism: From State-Managed Capitalism to Neoliberal Crisis* (London: Verso, 2013), 146. We can find similar critiques in Rosi Braidotti, *The Posthuman* (Cambridge: Polity Press, 2013) and Luce Irigaray, *Speculum: de l'autre femme* (Paris: Minuit, 1972).

of differences that would not escape sexual binarism and the patriarchal genealogy of the name.[28]

But let us note initially how there is something singular in this "for all" produced by recognising desire through the phallus. For the phallus is, at the same time, the signifier *par excellence* of desire[29] and the signifier that *embodies the lack proper to castration*: "the signifier of the point where the signifier lacks/fails."[30] We are facing a contradiction, unless we admit the existence of something like a *castration desire* or the necessary sustaining of a radical inadequacy between desire and empirical objects.[31] For this reason, authors like Judith Butler will accuse Lacan of a politically suspect "religious idealisation of the 'lack,' humility and limitation before the Law."[32] For Lacan would insist that the only possible form of desire's recognition would pass through its symbolic inscription, hence via a signifier that embodies the failure to name desire; something akin to a negative theology disguised as a clinic of psychic suffering with paralysing political consequences; just as it would paralyse the position of someone who sustains an order that they know to be inadequate, but without being able to overcome it; it would be the most astute and perverse form of conservation of a law that should have been abandoned long ago.

Indeed, Lacan argues for the phallus as a general process of socialising desire because he wants to insist on the generality of castration. That is, the phallus is not a generalised norm but a generalised inadequacy. If castration were not a generic process that extends to everyone, then we would have to admit that social life preserves some people from the violence of its modes of determination and limitation. That is, we would have to accept that there are subjects who would preserve an immanent relation to jouissance, subjects who would enter the social order without being marked by alienation's violence. This would be, perhaps, the worst of all the fantasies of compensation to social violence: the fantasy that there is some point at which this social order allows subjects not to subject themselves. In other words, to generalise castration is to affirm that no existence is preserved from alienation, even those that,

---

28   As charged in Paul B. Preciado, *Can the Monster Speak? A Report to an Academy of Psychoanalysts*, trans. Frank Wynne (London: Fitzcarraldo Editions, 2021). See also Tania Rivera, "Subversões Da Lógica Fálica – Freud, Lacan, Preciado" ["Subversions of Phallic Logic: Freud, Lacan, Preciado"], Psicanalistas peala Democracia, December 24, 2019, https://psicanalisedemocracia.com.br/2019/12/subversoes-da-logica-falica-freud-lacan-preciado-por-tania-rivera/.

29   "It is not simply sign and signifier, but presence of desire. *It is the real presence*": Jacques Lacan, *Le Séminaire. Livre VIII: Le transfert* (Paris: Seuil, 1998), 294. A presence that transforms the phallus into "the signifier of power, the sceptre and also that thanks to which virility can be assumed": Lacan, *Le Séminaire. Livre V*, 274.

30   Lacan, *Le Séminaire. Livre VIII*, 277.

31   Since the phallus is only "a general symbol of this margin that always separates me from my desire": Lacan, *Le Séminaire. Livre V*, 243.

32   Judith Butler, *Gender Trouble* (NY: Routledge, 1999), 72.

in our current societies, are placed as non-binary, as monstrous (cp. Preciado, *Can the Monster Speak?*). No existence can speak in the name of a present difference amid the society of capitalist (patriarchal) violence still in force. This will only be a form of imposture.

However, there are at least two distinct types of effects resulting from this passage through castration: one produces the regimes of existence, the other makes room for the experience of the non-existent. The first case leads us to phallic jouissance, the other leads us to discussions about feminine jouissance. These two effects – it is always worth remembering this – take place *in the same bodies*. Human bodies are crossed by these two effects. There is no human body subjected to the forms of phallic jouissance without producing inadequacies. One reason for the extreme violence of those who struggle to recognise themselves within the logic of phallic jouissance is that they do not know what to do with another experience of jouissance that haunts them. Once again, there is no binarism in Lacan. There is monism, but there is no position without a presupposition that negates it. Therefore, there is no position that is not unstable and open to becoming.

In this sense, Lacan's insistence in speaking about the irreducibility of sexual difference does not simply express its dependence on a heteronormative mode of existence. This would mean confusing oppositional-representational difference with self-referential difference, which only happens in antidialectical positions. Sexual difference, in Lacan, is the expression of an irreducible distance that separates me from myself; it expresses the mode of relation that I have regarding my own "sexuality." The difference is internal to me, not an external relation to another. That is, it is a self-referential difference, not the expression of oppositions characterised by material incompatibilities. It is not the difference between man and woman, as two specific sets of persons. And how could it be if woman is a non-existent? Sexual difference is an internal difference between existence, and what such existence denies as non-existent to exist.[33] To assert such an internal distance to oneself has a strong political and transformative rationale.

Each form of individual and consciousness is determined by the very structure that makes us exist and oppresses us. Yet Monique Wittig says about the notion of sexual difference as Lacan uses it:

> The concept of difference between the sexes ontologically constitutes women into different/others…. But for us there is no such thing as being-woman or being-man…. The concept of difference has nothing ontological about it. It is only the way that the masters interpret a historical situation of domination. The function

---

33   It could not be otherwise for someone who says, "Sexuality is precisely the domain, if I can put it that way, where no one knows what to do about what is true" (Jacques Lacan, *My Teaching* [London: Verso, 2008], 21).

of difference is to mask at every level conflicts of interest, including ideological ones.[34]

"Different" is that which is always placed in a relation of subalternity. This criticism tries to break down the naturalisation of the obligatory social relationship between "man" and "woman," taking such categories to their point of exhaustion. In fact, it is not a matter of ontologising difference, as if it were possible to leave the current historical situation to give timeless validity to that which is the fruit of precise historical-social coordinates. But it is necessary to speak of an "ontology for us" – that is, for us, such experience has an ontological irreducibility. This is said with a view to preventing us from speaking of an existence that does not yet have a figure, and should not have one. For it is not exactly difference that appears as an ontological weight here, but non-existence. Understanding the political function of such a strategy would prevent us from regressing to the situation of criticising Lacan for placing us before needs that "escape the control of consciousness and therefore the responsibility of individuals."[35] For to imagine that some effective form of political action will be produced by consciousness and individual agents is to ignore where emancipated agency can really come from. It certainly will not come from what is conformed to as the property and attribute of an individual. An ontology of the non-existent is politically necessary.

Genre trouble

Let us try to better understand Lacan's strategy. To understand what phallic jouissance is, we need to define how castration works within it. This appears initially as affirming a "for all" – its dimension of norm that determines the totality of existents is clearly assumed. But such an assumption requires a complement. Castration's implied experience of lack necessarily demands a phantasmatic complement, as if it were a lack that simply perpetuates our dependence on expecting completeness. Castration is thus reduced to a lack that is only a return to the fantasy that *someone* has not gone through the experience of castration, keeping for himself the sovereignty of the immediate identity between will and action, between wanting and doing.[36]

34　Monique Wittig, *The Straight Mind and Other Essays* (Boston: Beacon Press, 1992), 29.

35　Wittig, *The Straight Mind*, 30.

36　This is what is meant by the formula of male sexuation ($\forall x\, x\Phi$ / $x\neg\Phi\, x$), namely, "everyone goes through castration" and "there is at least one who does not go through castration." The contradiction between the two propositions is the axis of the organisation of phallic jouissance. See Lacan, *Le Séminaire. Livre XX*, 73.

The subject may try to occupy this place in a passage to the act of his perverse fantasies, or it may be occupied by an Other who will appear as uncastrated, an Other who lacks nothing and to whom the subject will devote a relation of subjection. This Other can be incarnated in another subject or the Law, the Mission, the Ideal, the Leader, the Father, the Company, the State, the Woman, etc. Thus, if it is true that "man sustains his jouissance through something that is his own anxiety,"[37] one must remember that such anxiety normally leads him to feed the phantasmatic representation of a sovereign place of exception. Under the primacy of phallic jouissance, the subject will thus always be open to superegoic investment in authoritarian figures that recover the structure of the *primal father*, whose will seems to hover above all restrictions. He will enjoy lack (with the relative depreciation of the objects that present themselves to him) and the search for completeness (with the idealisation immanent to such a search). It will be a jouissance based on the continuous play between frustration and idealisation. This desire as lack and restriction has thus, necessarily, a catastrophic return in the political field (because it is libidinally realised in the investment of authoritarian figures and institutions) and subjective (because it makes the subject depend on their own frustration).

But there is more to Lacan than phallic jouissance,[38] and it is at this point that we can understand the political nature of feminine jouissance. What feminine jouissance shows is how it is possible to start, not exactly from affirming castration as a function of a "for all" that constitutes a normative and restrictive universality, but from castration as an *impasse of existence*, as a pressure from a non-existent towards another existence.[39] This refusal to link castration to the advent of a totality shows how, in this context, "lack" functions differently, producing other effects. In the case of the feminine position, assuming the lack of desire, in fact, expresses the refusal of a false totality in the name of another totality, which Lacan calls the "universal not all." This is radically distinct from the act of acknowledging lack to sustain the phantasmatic completeness of an uncastrated Other.

Thus, if this feminine jouissance is proper to a position that "does not exist" (since the Woman does not exist), this is not simply a cult of aporia or negative theology. Non-existence should be understood here as an active process that aims to break the limits of the current modes of existence, the limits of the forms of jouissance endorsed by capitalism and its patriarchy. This non-existence is active because it seeks to produce another order. The impossibility of describing a non-phallic sexuality, to which Nancy Fraser points, is, on the contrary, a pressure that seeks to give

---

37   Lacan, *Le Séminaire*, Book X, session of March 20, 1963.
38   As we see, among many other references, in Lacan, *Le Séminaire. Livre XX*, 26.
39   Therefore, the feminine position does not have as its basic proposition $\forall x\Phi x$ but $\neg\ x\neg\Phi\ x$. That is, its foundation is the impossibility of the existence of someone who has not gone through castration.

body to the impossible. This is a strategy of dialectical negativity, not a mere passive contemplation of the impasse.

In this context, universal not-all is the expression of the possibility of a relation between what denies false totality (what is not-all) and what seeks to produce a common field (what still sustains expectations of universality). It is a way for lack to use the impasse, a way for jouissance to use the unmeasured to realise itself as an experience of infinitude.[40] And it is not an accident that, at this moment, we find Lacan recover the same examples that Bataille used to talk about eroticism and the sacred. It is enough to remember his reading on the jouissance of the ecstatic Saint Teresa of Ávila.

Some may see this as an insidious way to push the feminine into an ethereal, inapprehensible mysticism; a last colonial strategy towards the feminine by male ghosts (a rather common mix of saint and whore that would only make sense within male ghosts). But that would be to miss the central axis of Lacan's strategy – namely, to insist that power (in this case religious power) tries to colonise a jouissance that can surpass it, forcing social life to deal with what breaks its regimes of existence, hierarchy, and production. And for making this jouissance emerge, it is necessary to confront itself at its extreme point of contradiction; it is necessary that language finds its twisting point, until it is forced to say, "*If there were another*." But Lacan continues,

> there is no other than phallic jouissance – except the one concerning which woman doesn't breathe a word, perhaps because she doesn't know it, the one that makes her not-whole. It is false that there is another one, but that doesn't stop what follows from being true, namely, that it shouldn't be / could never fail to be that one.[41]

This language that says this – there is no other jouissance except the one concerning which woman does not breathe a word, except that which, if there were, would be another, and language that claims it is false that there is another one, which does not prevent us from saying that it should not be this one – is the photograph of an emergent process taking language to its twisting point; a process that refuses identification, that refuses naming and identity, collapsing the order from within,

---

40   "As soon as you deal with an infinite set, you cannot posit that the not-whole implies the existence of something produced based on negation or contradiction. You can, at a pinch, posit it as an indeterminate existence. But, as we know from the extension of mathematical logic, mathematical logic qualified as intuitionist, to posit a 'there exists,' one must also be able to construct it, that is, know how to find where that existence is": Lacan, *Le Séminaire. Livre XX*, 94.

41   Lacan, *Le Séminaire. Livre XX*, 56.

as something indescribable born out of what seemed the most familiar. This is a political strategy of producing difference that could not, under any circumstances, be
confused with restoration.

Lacan can be criticised for placing the woman in a position in which she does
not talk – breathily – about her jouissance, in which she knows nothing of her jouissance. But it would be necessary to remember that this ignorance is, for Lacan, constitutive of our general modes of alienation. The masculine position believes to speak
and finds itself at every moment in an empty speech that is nothing but the simple
repetition of the code. In this context, saying nothing is the beginning of a real transformation.

On the other hand, we could say that Lacanian psychoanalysis is indifferent to
the problem of gender performativity. It has no problem at all in assuming multiple
gender inscriptions. For its central issue lies elsewhere, namely, in the structures of
relationality (which, of course, cannot be abstracted from gender determinations).[42]
It seeks to bring bodies to assume a form of relationality in which a jouissance can
circulate that disaccustoms us from capitalism's regime of identity, accumulation,
and accounting. This form can occur in multiple regimes of relationality, even between a woman and a man.[43]

Does capitalism conclude castration?

It is at this point that perhaps Lacan's central statement becomes clearer:

> What distinguishes the capitalist discourse is this: *Verwerfung*, the rejection out-
> side all fields of the symbolic ... the rejection of what? Of castration. Any order, any
> discourse that resembles capitalism leaves out what we will simply call the things
> of love.[44]

An incorrect reading of this statement would lead us to believe that Lacan accuses
capitalism of being unaware of the impossibility of satisfying desire, its constitutive
lack, through proliferating means of incitement and pleasures, as if we were seeing

---

42 See, in this regard, Lacan, *Le Séminaire. Livre XX*, 131, in which Lacan speaks of a relation of
recognition within which the sexual relation ceases not to be inscribed.

43 Therefore, another dimension of Monique Wittig's critique of Lacan seems inadequate to us.
The accusation that Lacanian psychoanalysis naturalises the heterosexual contract – preventing any other form of categorical production beyond that horizon – fails to understand how
the analytic process must break this "contract" and how the experience of oppression it entails is by no means neglected. Only the social injunction "you-will-be-straight-or-not-be" is
to be taken in the dialectical sense described above. The not-being is not nothing.

44 Jacques Lacan, "La troisième" (unpublished manuscript).

yet another version of a moral critique of supposed capitalist *hedonism*. Capitalism would thus disregard castration because it would impose on us endless substitutive satisfactions.

We could also ask if Lacan is unaware of a phenomenon well described by Deleuze and Guattari, regarding the mode of desire's operation under capitalism. For, in this reading, capitalism would reduce desire to the register of possession and, consequently, of lack. This reduction of desire to the register of lack would make castration the experience *par excellence* of socialised desire.[45] Under capitalism, subjects would see in desire the expression of what only manifests itself as incompleteness and inadequacy. As if capitalism were a society of managed dissatisfaction. This thought leads Deleuze to state:

> It's all very well to say to us: you understand nothing, Oedipus, it's not daddy-mummy, it's the symbolic, the law, the arrival at culture, it's the effect of the signifier, it's the finitude of the subject, it has the "lack-to-be which is life." And if it's not Oedipus, it will be castration, and the supposed death drives. Psychoanalysts teach infinite resignation, they are the last priests (no, there will be others after them).[46]

That is, castration appears here as the emblem of an infinite resignation before the impossibility of jouissance and the finitude of the subject. It would impose a pragmatics of inadequacy that could only have deleterious moral and political consequences.

However, the phenomenon that Lacan has in view is another, almost inverse one. Namely, how such inadequacy is not a resignation but the path of a production. In this sense, let us remember how the problem of castration will eventually fit into discussions regarding the performance of sexual intercourse:

> the subject realises that he does not have the organ of what I would call the unique, unary, unifying jouissance. This is exactly what makes jouissance *one* in the conjunction of subjects of the opposite sex. Namely, what I insisted on last year, by highlighting the fact that there is no possible subjective realisation of the subject as element, as sexed partner in what is imagined as unification in the sexual act.[47]

Castration appears to realise the absence of what could ensure the fusional achievement of a unitary jouissance. If this unitary jouissance existed, it would ensure a

---

45   See Gilles Deleuze and Félix Guattari, *L'anti-Œdipe* (Paris: Seuil, 1971), 98.

46   Gilles Deleuze and Claire Parnet, *Dialogues II* (NY: Columbia UP, 2007), 81–82.

47   Jacques Lacan, "Le Séminaire. Livre XV: L'acte psychanalytique" (unpublished manuscript), session of January 17, 1968.

kind of univocity of being capable of allowing the subjects a conjunction that would be a return to the submission of experience to an identifying thought. There is no possible univocity, that is what castration says. Therefore, there is no possible realisation of the subject as a sexual partner in the unity of the sexual act. Here it may become clearer why Lacan said, famously, there is no sexual relationship. For it is the case that jouissance does not inhabit spaces of fusion or complementarity. No, we do not complement ourselves; we are too mutilated to want to complement ourselves, or even for the act of complementing to have any meaning. Not having a sexual relationship, realising that it does not exist, is a certain cunning. The cunning of those who say, "we are too mutilated to have the right to exist"; there is something in us that reminds us that we could be someone else, and that ends up leading us to love non-existence.

This is what led Lacan to state that castration marks "the subject being unequal to any possible subjectification of sexual reality."[48] This point is decisive. If there is an inequality between the procedures of subjectivation and the sexual, if it is not possible to subjectivise the sexual in its integrity – as we can do, for example, when we say "my sexuality," submitting the sexual to the condition of a predicative attribute of a subject – it is because the sexual is the very space in which something placed as an irreducible difference emerges. The inscription of this difference will be a fundamental political operation because it will provide the matrix for the general relations to difference within social life. As if the problem of difference in the field of the sexual would provide the basis for the multiple forms of relation to difference in other fields of social experience.

This explains why perhaps the most important proposition here is: "castration, which is the sign with which an avowal dresses itself up, the avowal that jouissance of the Other – of the body of the Other – is promoted only on the basis of infinity."[49] That is, as counterintuitive as this may seem, castration appears as a condition for realising a certain infinitude linked to jouissance. Because, in this context, castration indicates that the sexual relation, this form of relation between incarnated subjects mediated by desire and language, this relation between bodies that are also speaking bodies, that are libido and signifier articulated, cannot be realised as unity, as an affirmation of the primacy of the One, as the constitution of relations of complementarity, of symmetry. It is realised as a relation in disjunction: the only way, in Lacan's eyes, to emerge with a relation to difference is the fundamental area of the ethical and political contribution of psychoanalysis. But this is a way to open experience to the possibility of another jouissance.

In this sense, affirming that capitalism forecloses castration means to insist that, inside it, there is no space for an infinitude that does not take place under the

---

48   Lacan, "Le Séminaire. Livre XV," session of February 7, 1968.
49   Lacan, Le Séminaire. Livre XX, 13.

infinitely bad form of the *plus-de-jouir* and its maximisation of performance. This is an infinitude that reminds us that its actualisation can only take place under the condition of dissolving the modes of relation as they have so far constituted and so far allowed the material reproduction of our social life. Therefore, capitalism knows nothing about the things of love. Like eroticism in Bataille, love would not know what to do within an accounting infinity. On the other hand, the idea of foreclosure (*Verwerfung*) here appeals to a notion of expulsion from the symbolic order and return in the Real under the multiple forms of social delirium. The jouissance expelled from the symbolic order is not simply eliminated; it returns as that which seems at every moment to put such order in check from the outside, and it haunts it with all the paranoid forms of delirium (persecution, grandeur, destruction, and so on).

What Lacanian psychoanalysis shows us, then, is that the direction of treatment, the modalities of clinical intervention, are inseparable from the deepening of critique in relation to the libidinal economy of a social order that is entangled with capitalism and its forms of existence. It leads us to break our bonds with such an order in the name of a jouissance that capitalism seeks – by all means – to destroy.

References

Aleman, Jorge. *Razón fronterisa y sujeto del inconciente: conversaciones con Eugenio Trías*. Barcelona: NED Ediciones, 2020.

Althusser, Louis, ed. *Lire Le Capital*. Paris: PUF, 1996.

Bataille, Georges. "L'érotisme." In *Œvres complètes X*, Paris: Gallimard, 1987.

———. "La notion de dépense." In *Œuvres complètes I*, Paris: Gallimard, 1987.

Bou Ali, Nadia, and Rohit Goel, eds. *Lacan Against Foucault: Subjectivity, Sex and Politics*. London: Bloomsbury, 2018.

Braidotti, Rosi. *The Posthuman*. Cambridge: Polity Press, 2013.

Butler, Judith. *Gender Trouble*. NY: Routledge, 1999.

Dardot, Pierre, and Christian Laval. *La nouvelle ordre du monde*. Paris: la découverte, 2013.

David-Ménard, Monique. *Les constructions de l'universel*. Paris: PUF, 2001.

Dean, Carolyn. *The Self and Its Pleasures: Bataille, Lacan and the History of the Decentered Subject*. Ithaca: Cornell UP, 1992.

Deleuze, Gilles, and Félix Guattari. *L'anti-Œdipe*. Paris: Seuil, 1971.

Deleuze, Gilles, and Claire Parnet. *Dialogues II*. NY: Columbia UP, 2007.

Derrida, Jacques. *La carte postale*. Paris: Flammarion, 1985.

Dunker, Christian. *O cálculo neurótico do gozo*. São Paulo: Escuta, 1998.

Fraser, Nancy. *Fortunes of Feminism: From State-Managed Capitalism to Neoliberal Crisis*. London: Verso, 2013.

Irigaray, Luce. *Speculum: de l'autre femme*. Paris: Minuit, 1972.

Kris, Ernst. "Ego Psychology and Interpretation in Psychoanalytic Therapy." *The Psychoanalytic Quarterly* 20, no. 1 (1951): 15–30. https://doi.org/10.1080/21674086.195 1.11925828.

Lacan, Jacques. *Autres écrits*. Paris: Seuil, 2001.

———. *Écrits*. Paris: Seuil, 1966.

———. "La troisième." Unpublished manuscript.

———. *Le Séminaire. Livre V: Les formations de l'inconscient*. Paris: Seuil, 2005.

———. *Le Séminaire. Livre VII: L'éthique de la psychanalyse*, Paris: Seuil, 1986.

———. *Le Séminaire. Livre VIII: Le transfert*. Paris: Seuil, 1998.

———. *Le Séminaire. Livre X: L'angoisse*. Paris, Seuil, 2004.

———. *Le Séminaire. Livre XIX: ...ou pire*. Paris: Seuil, 2011.

———. "Le Séminaire. Livre XV: L'acte psychanalytique." Unpublished manuscript.

———. *Le Séminaire. Livre XVI: D'un Autre à l'autre*. Paris: Seuil, 2006.

———. *Le Séminaire. Livre XVII: L'envers de la psychanalyse*, Paris: Seuil, 1991.

———. *Le Séminaire. Livre XX: Encore*. Paris: Seuil, 1975.

———. *My Teaching*. London: Verso, 2008.

Marx, Karl. *Grundrisse*. London: Penguin, 1993.

Oliveira, Cláudio. "Capitalismo e gozo: Marx e Lacan." *Tempo Social* 11, no. 22 (2004): 9–24.

Preciado, Paul B. *Can the Monster Speak? A Report to an Academy of Psychoanalysts*. Translated by Frank Wynne. London: Fitzcarraldo Editions, 2021.

Rivera, Tania. "Subversões Da Lógica Fálica – Freud, Lacan, Preciado" ["Subversions of Phallic Logic: Freud, Lacan, Preciado"]. Psicanalistas peala Democracia. December 24, 2019. https://psicanalisedemocracia.com.br/2019/12/subversoes-da-logica-falica-freud-lacan-preciado-por-tania-rivera/.

Tomšič, Samo. *The Capitalist Unconscious: Marx and Lacan*. London: Verso, 2015.

Wittig, Monique. *The Straight Mind and Other Essays*. Boston: Beacon Press, 1992.

Karatani for Libidinal Economy: Invariance and Praxis

Daniel Tutt

The Japanese philosopher Kojin Karatani has developed a sophisticated theory of history and praxis, offering a "parallax" reading of Kant and Marx that aligns the Kantian ethical system with an immanent critique of commodity exchange as Marx develops in *Capital*. Kant's ethical reflections are not ahistorical or immaterial, as Marx and many Marxists point out. On the contrary, the universal dimension of Kant's ethics cannot be realised in just any given social arrangement; Karatani argues that for the "Kingdom of Ends" to come about, and Kant insists on a materialist modification of the commodity mode of exchange. Kant thus becomes a necessary interlocutor to Marxian praxis, and Karatani shows that even for Kant himself, the commodity exchange that dominated in Kant's own time – merchant capitalism – had to be transcended as a precondition for any enactment of Kantian ethics. These ethics are thus co-thinkable not only with Marx's critique of commodity fetishism and capitalism, but the Kantian ethical theory informs Marx's praxis, offering a utopian account of world revolution.

There remains a problem in this parallax account of Marx and Kant that neither answer – namely, the problem of human aggression and conflict, including their role in revolutionary sequences. How does human aggression find a proper outlet in a social order? What comes in the wake of a world war or a period of intensified violence? It is Freud and psychoanalysis – that is, the critique of libidinal economy – that treats these problems of human aggression and violence most adequately. Freud offers a historical logic in the dialectic between the death drive and the superego. Karatani's reading of the Freudian theory of the death drive provides a crucial corrective to Marxist praxis – specifically historical materialist praxis, which fails to provide a plausible theory for overcoming the state form without incurring excessive violence. Libidinal economy – the insights of psychoanalysis on the political and psychic economy – can provide insights into these matters, and the Freudian theory of the death drive builds on Kant's more abstract ruminations on "asocial sociability." The death drive – which posits internal aggressivity and is a theory of subjectivity not reliant on consciousness (reason) but grounded in an account of nature – and Kant's theory of man's "asocial sociability" are homologous. The psychoanalytic concept refines Kant's thought to the extent that death drive accounts for the force of freedom in history. We can only correctly understand this as a dialectic between asocial sociability and reason.

There is what I name an *invariant* principle in Karatani's theory of the Freudian death drive. It emphasises the "non-conscious" element of subjectivity in history, locating this *invariant* force within a dialectic of the Freudian death drive and superego. From this subjective dialectic, Karatani theorises a negative, revolutionising tendency in human history. It is thus fitting that Karatani refers to this impulse in history as "religion" or a force that realises and enacts a materialist "associationist" mode of social exchange relations. From the perspective of libidinal economy, we name this perspective *invariant* as there remains a minimal degree of agitation, an excess that persists despite and beyond revolutionary sequences and changes in social life. The invariant perspective locates a consistency within the social – an *asocial* dimension intrinsic to human subjectivity, per Freud's theory of the death drive.

We will discuss four ways Karatani's theory of the death drive and the dialectic with the superego contributes to the field of libidinal economy. First, Karatani's theory helps us see how a social order develops a mode of exchange wherein internal aggressions are given an outlet primarily in the sphere of the aesthetic and imagination. Although the nation-state governs this under capitalism, we speculate that a revolution of commodity exchange would precisely modify the composition of this aesthetic sphere of exchange, while retaining this sphere to mediate in-built aggressions. This can also be thought of as the mode of culture. As such, we will see how Karatani's theory of libidinal economy differs from Freud's idea that culture as a distinct sphere of social life plays a vital role in mediating aggression. Second, Karatani shows how death drive and superego account for forms of negation and collective agitation (revolution, crisis, war) that modify social affects, sensibility and potentials for mitigating collective aggressions, resentments and negative social affects, specifically within capitalist social life. In other words, the superego and death drive dialectic contains a clear affect theory. Third, by adding a theory of libidinal economy to the wider project of Karatani's transcritique – combining Kantian ethical praxis with the Marxist theory of history – this philosophy lends itself to an entirely new mode of Marxist revolutionary praxis. This critique maintains a distance from the historical and dialectical materialist traditions. Karatani sees these orientations as prone to violence and aggression due to privileging the productive sphere as the site of revolutionary praxis. We will here understand why Karatani's libidinal theory is essential for his theory of revolutionising capitalist commodity exchange. Fourth, we will show that Karatani offers a more positive rejoinder to Freud's pessimistic liberal conclusions regarding capitalism *and* to radical Marxist theories of libidinal economy, such as Jean-François Lyotard, which find no way to transcend the deadlocks of constitutive aggression and asocial affects that capitalism foments. Karatani develops an entirely new mode of exchange premised on the gift and reciprocity exchange in the domain of common civic and political life, and his insights are useful for a revolutionary politics of the commune and anticapitalist politics.

In the first part of this chapter, we examine the dialectic of death drive and superego and discuss how this model can be further theorised and applied to historical periods and revolutionary sequences. After developing a historical account of the invariant perspective of death drive and historical change, we examine Karatani's superego theory and discuss the important dialectical account of death drive and superego undergirding the invariant perspective. What of the old order is preserved in the new during a revolutionary sequence, crisis or liberatory movement? How do in-built aggressions find an outlet in each social order? Karatani, like Freud, insists that the national-cultural sphere functions as a site for expressing inner aggressions. We conclude this part by probing whether Karatani indeed has a theory of the political or ideology. We then examine Karatani's theory of libidinal economy and history concerning other Marxist thinkers that use Freudian insights. By reading Karatani with Lyotard's *Libidinal Economy*, we argue that Karatani's thought overcomes some limitations in Lyotard's theories of exchange; namely, through a positive theory of the superego as a regulator of psychic life, Karatani can isolate the superego not solely as a deterrent to revolutionary possibilities, as Lyotard insists. We then consider Norman O. Brown's theory of history in *Life Against Death: The Psychoanalytical Meaning of History* as it centres a theory of the Freudian death drive as an agency of historical change. However, unlike Karatani's invariant approach, Brown relies on a theory of libidinal economy that is ultimately mystical and thus gets caught up in a non-revolutionary account of historical change. Unlike these approaches to libidinal economy, we argue Ernst Bloch's writings on Freud, specifically his concept of the "not-yet-conscious," is a theory of subjective freedom that complements Karatani's idea of "mode D." We conclude that Bloch is a theorist of libidinal economy very much in line with Karatani's invariant perspective: he envisions a form of revolutionary subjectivity becoming unmoored from negative capture in death drive repetition.

In the second part of this chapter, we show how Karatani's praxis, known as "Associationism," is informed by his theories of libidinal economy. Associationism conceives of revolutionary tactics and strategies that weaken commodity exchange's dominance by emphasising practices such as boycotting, consumer struggles and developing alternative currencies. These tactics do not prioritise interventions in labour (as we find in historical materialist socialist strategies) but rather emphasise the sphere of circulation and exchange for revolutionary action. We show how Karatani's libidinal economic analysis informs associationism's praxis. Karatani is deeply attentive to the role of collective human aggression and aims to overcome the pitfalls of violence that plagued 20th-century socialist revolutions, from Stalinism to Maoism. We also argue that a more expansive form of associationist praxis is possible beyond the specific "New Associationist Movement" that Karatani founded in Japan. This praxis would benefit from thinking anticapitalist movements, such as the 1990s anti-WTO protests up through more recent uprisings such as Occupy Wall Street and Black Lives Matter, as "exchange struggles" and thus in line with Karatani's broader praxis. Circulation and exchange struggles negate the ubiquitous power of commodity exchange. It is through tactics such as stopping circulation, blocking port access for shipping and property damage, and even uprisings such as riots and rebellions that such struggles outside of the immediate sphere of labour are very much thinkable with Karatani's proposals. As a praxis, Karatani's emphasis on non-violence is an admirable feature of the Associationist praxis. However, several problems go unaddressed and overlooked, namely the role of ideology, the dictatorship of the proletariat, and class struggle. These shortcomings are examined and critiqued to conclude.

Part 1: Libidinal dialectic of history: Death drive and superego

Understanding modes of exchange

In *The Structure of World History*, Karatani presents four distinct modes of exchange that have governed societies throughout world history. These modes come to be intermeshed within a given order, and a dominant mode of exchange governs any particular social order. *Mode A* is what he names reciprocal exchange, and it is premised on reciprocity as the basis of social relations; it emerged in primitive tribal societies. This mode is composed of a tribal gift-giving form of exchange. The social system governing this mode tends to be "mini-systems," in which no larger federation or state sovereign governs them, but a series of semi-autonomous mini-systems relate through gift exchange. These mini-systems remain prone to hostility, conflict, and war, but gift exchange is at the heart of governing the mediation of these conflicts. *Mode B* is a form of exchange governed by a sovereign king or ruler, and this mode gives rise to the "world system" consisting of mini-empires such as the period of European feudalism. The sovereign (or king) is the principal overseer of each exchange relation, granting legitimacy to every form of exchange within the society. Mode B is thus the birth of the social contract, and Thomas Hobbes is the exemplary philosophical perspective of mode B. The social arrangement is one where exchange is under the purview of the sovereign ruler that operates on a logic of "distribution and plunder," rather than gift exchange governed by ideals of reciprocity. Where there is a share of resources in societies governed by mode B, this decision is overseen by sovereign diktat, which is again based on distribution and plunder. *Mode C* is commodity exchange, where the sovereign is no longer embodied in the Hobbesian king. Instead, it becomes money itself – namely, the accumulation of money and the exchange system that develops under the money-form. Importantly, mode C appears in precapitalist social formations when an empire reaches a sta-tus of a globalised or regionalised federation and establishes a common currency across different polities.[1] Karatani writes that mode C "acquires an objectivity that transcends human will"[2] at the heart of reification – or the pervasive encroachment of commodity exchange over every domain of social life. In social orders where this domination of mode C is present, people's consent to enter labour contracts freely and sell their labour-power is also present. This paradox of freedom – freedom is re-ducible to the freedom to sell one's labour-power – makes the very basis of the social contract in capitalist (and precapitalist social orders dominated by mode C) deper-sonalised and abstract. *Mode D*, the fourth mode, is a regulative mode that seeks a return to reciprocal forms of exchange and thus transcends the other three modes, aiming to return social relations to mode A once again. Each mode has developed distinct spheres from the communal (A), to the state (B), to the market (C), to the fourth mode (D), which functions as a regulative idea and a logic of negativity within social life, manifested in revolutions and other forms of political agitation. While the mode of exchange governed by commodity relations is dominant within capitalist social orders, the state is also present in such orders. It is governed by a different, historically prior mode of exchange based on plunder and redistribution. Despite these overlapping logics of exchange in our contemporary capital-nation-state or-der, the dominant mode C (commodity exchange) remains hegemonic over the other modes. In this case, the nation and state are subordinated to mode C's domination.

Types of mode exchange	Mode A: Community	Mode B: State	Mode C: Market	Mode D: Association
Descrip-tion	The reciprocity of the gift (or "pooling" through com-mons)	Ruling and pro-tection (also called "plunder and redistribute")	Commodity exchange (capitalist market)	Transcends other modes, with the return of mode A at a higher level of complexity

Table 1: Karatani's Modes of Exchange

---

1   Although Greece during the time of Socrates (400 BC) had no capitalist social system, the Greek mini-system had developed a form of exchange that Karatani calls "mode C" – a pre-capitalist form of commodity exchange in which the mini-system had a common currency.

2   Kojin Karatani, *The Structure of World History: From Modes of Production to Modes of Exchange*, trans. Michael K. Bourdaghs (Durham: Duke UP, 2014), 89.

Within the nexus of capital-nation-state, mode A governs the national sphere, and Karatani says this is the sphere of imagination. Nationalism emerged under capitalism in the early 1800s in tandem with the labour-power commodity's formation. In the capitalist nation-state, workers must have adequate training, education, and skills, including exposure to relations with others (e.g., a multicultural and cosmopolitan world system), so that they learn to adapt to conditions of labour in which they will work with strangers. The national sphere negates the cosmopolitan basis that capitalism relies on for a harmonious source of labour-power and becomes a site of social life where collective solidarity is organised. The nation

> emerges when, following the overthrow of the absolute sovereign by a bourgeois revolution, each individual acquires freedom and equality. But these alone are not sufficient... a sense of solidarity is also required. In the French Revolution, the slogan was "Liberty, equality, fraternity." Here liberty and equality are concepts deriving from reason, but fraternity belongs to a different order: it signifies a sentiment of solidarity linking together individuals. A nation requires this kind of sentiment. Different from the love that existed within the family or tribal community, *it is a new sentiment of solidarity that arises among people who have broken away from those earlier bonds.*[3]

The nation is the site of social life where the contradictions and limitations of human solidarity produced by capital are worked out via imagination. The national sphere is thus an outlet for the aggressions kicked up by commodifying labour-power that citizen-labourers must undergo in the market. However, if we consider this sphere of social life in a context in which mode C is not dominant – namely, where labour-power is not commodified as it is under capitalism – the national sphere does not have to be structured around national identifications and the irrationalisms, such as patriotism, that often attend to these identifications. In other words, this sphere of social life, also known as "culture," can be thought of as a sphere where human solidarity can be cultivated under the logic of reciprocity.

The paradoxical point here is that the nation's organisation already aims to resolve and restore mode A within social life but faces only a partial realisation of the higher objectives of solidarity that mode A demands. This fundamental limitation of human solidarity within capitalism is evidenced in Adam Smith's theory of the importance placed on the affects of "pity" and "compassion" in social life. Karatani argues that these two moral virtues are thought of by Smith in his early, pre-political-economic writings when he was a moral theorist under the influence of the Sentimentalist moral philosopher Francis Hutcheson. When Smith refines his theory of

---

3   Karatani, *The Structure of World History*, 212–213. Emphasis added.

capitalism in *The Wealth of Nations*, he is faced with the contradiction that a counter-vailing affect to keep solidarity in harmony – namely, sympathy for others – is not realisable in capitalism because of mode C's dominance. Smith argued that constitu-tive selfishness drives the human labourer. In his theory of the individual, Smith had to account for the centrality of mode C (commodity exchange's dominance). In so doing, the higher virtues of pity and compassion could not be realised through sym-pathy (as was his attempted solution) but remained unrealised within the limited sphere of the nation/culture. This example shows that the sphere of mode A remains a site where unmet solidarities are negotiated through imagination and aesthetic practices.

Now that we have a grasp on the interrelation of the three primary modes within capitalist social life, we turn to a discussion of mode D, a mode Karatani refers to as a "regulative" mode that comes about to negate the dominant mode and return to mode A but in a higher form. There is thus a form of teleology in Karatani's logic of the modes of exchange in that the logic of mode D realises gift exchange based on the other modes. In various places, Karatani discusses the logic of this movement of mode D as "religion,"[4] by which he means religion in a way like Kant's "religion," realised in a world republic that has abolished state and capital. In other areas, he refers to mode D as provoked by repression and the death drive in the Freudian sense of the concept.[5] Overall, as a political mode of historical change, Karatani theorises communism as "mode D," a repetitive demand to break from mode C commodity exchange and return to reciprocal exchange across each mode of exchange. In this account of history and praxis, we can take the example of the French Revolution and subsequent revolutionary periods as enactments of mode D; the French Revolution was a collective demand for a return to more fundamental arrangements of free-dom, equality, and fraternity. These collective demands were also thinkable as a li-bidinal upsurge. This logic repeats in history as a form of negation that seeks to break apart oppressive modes that dominate social relations.

The most accessible example Karatani provides of this form of reason is his account of Socrates and the form of universal equality or "Isonomia" that he placed at the centre of his teachings. Isonomia is an example of mode D because Socrates' speculative philosophy emerged in a material context of exchange relations gov-erned by a primitive mode C commodity exchange. Socrates lived during a wider unification of various polities in the Greek world, including instituting a com-

---

4   See Karatani, *The Structure of World History*, ch. 5; Kojin Karatani, *Isonomia and the Origins of Philosophy*, trans. Joseph A. Murphy (Durham: Duke UP, 2017), Appendix.

5   Karatani's main discussion of psychoanalysis as a key feature of mode D is found in Kojin Karatani, *Nation and Aesthetics: On Kant and Freud*, trans. Jonathan E. Abel, Hiroki Yoshikuni, and Darwin H. Tsen (Oxford: Oxford UP, 2017).

mon currency.[6] In Socrates' time, mode C (commodity exchange) was introduced in proto-form through precapitalist merchant confederations of mini-states. Karatani argues that Socrates' philosophy, in the primary concept of Isonomia, is a demand for a return to mode A in a higher form.

While mode D is a regulative idea of revolution that occurred before the rise of capitalism, Karatani argues that within capitalism, it was Kant who discovered mode D in his ethics, specifically with the categorical imperative. The categorical imperative is only truly possible in a society where the form of exchange goes against mode C (commodity exchange). The notion of always treating others *as ends and not as means* is impossible in a social order – for example, capitalism – in which commodity exchange is paramount. Kant's ethics were only possible in social conditions of associationism, which consists, Karatani writes, "of the return of reciprocal exchange in a higher dimension."[7] This interpretation of Kant notably differs from the Rawlsian "distributionist" mode of justice that many liberal commentators of Kant emphasise. In Karatani's reading, Kantian ethics is exchangist and not distributionist. Society must enter associationist arrangements as the primary mode of dispensing justice and establishing the categorical imperative – that is, by treating persons and future persons as ends and not as means. Thus, the categorical imperative is actualised in a mode of exchange that transcends the merchant capitalism of Kant's time and the financial capitalism of our time.

This reading of Kantian ethics enables us to read Marx and Kant in an entirely new light. The early Marx, like Kant, argued that communism would come about as the realisation of free associations, a position that he shared with Kant. More controversially, Karatani argues that the early Marx shared Proudhon's view of the state as a form of associationism, and Proudhon's non-state-centred communism is in line with Kant's cosmopolitanism premised on the state's absence. Karatani argues that after the Paris Commune of 1871, the Proudhonian anarchist anti-statist position became an unthinkable antinomy for Marx and Marx absorbed an anti-statist view into the heart of his theory because of this impasse of the question of how to destroy the state. Overall, this example shows Karatani's method of transcritique of Kant with Marx, as an undecidable theory becomes "bracketed" in Marx's thought – in this case, abolishing the state. There is an immediate benefit in this idea of bracketing an unthinkable point within Marx's thought that invites a certain de-intensification on the priority of sectarian ideological battles that inevitably arise between anarchists and Marxists. Indeed, if Kant's framework of history and ethics is deeply linked to the vision of a future in which nations and states dissolve into a federation of communes no longer reliant on a state, then this is like what Marx (and anarchists) advocate.

---

6   See Karatani, *Isonomia*, specifically the chapter "Colonization and Isonomia."

7   Karatani, *The Structure of World History*, 231.

Not only is Kant linked to the Marxist project of a stateless arrangement of social relations no longer governed by mode C (commodity exchange), Kant's theory of what fundamentally drives historical change lies in an underappreciated passage from his *Idea for a Universal History with a Cosmopolitan Purpose*. In this short text, which reads like a manifesto, Kant argues that the essence of human nature lies in what he names "unsocial sociability," or the idea that a fundamental antagonism drives communal bonds and ties. Kant writes, "man has an inclination to associate with others, because in society he feels himself to be more than man, i.e., as more than the developed form of his natural capacities."[8] If the logic of what propels human civilisation is unsocial sociability, then it is immediately clear why Freud and psychoanalysis become heirs to Kantian ethics and politics. Although vaguely construed, Kant's notion of antagonism contains a significant homology with the Freudian notion of the death drive as a central concept at the heart of thinking large-scale social arrangements.

In *Transcritique: On Kant and Marx* (2003) and *Nation and Aesthetics: On Kant and Freud* (2017), Karatani argues that the libidinal insights of Freud offer a missing analysis of aggressivity and violence. Human aggression, he suggests, manifests in any social order irrespective of its relative status of equality or mode of exchange. This is what Kant means by nature – a form of antagonism which becomes the cause of a law-governed society. To the extent there is a telos of world civilisation for Kant, it is not found in the peaceful coexistence of a reason-bound view of humankind that negotiates a peaceable social order. The emphasis on nature, or what Kant calls the "cunning of nature," in contrast to what Hegel called the "cunning of reason," emphasises nature as subject. Karatani insists that this is not mere rhetoric. Kant's idea of nature is a form of subjectivity both immanent within a social order and a logic of history evidenced in a dialectic of conscious/non-conscious forces. It is impossible to think the source of asocial sociability from a Hobbesian viewpoint based on mutual hostility with only human will and understanding. Instead, according to Kant, only something derived from hostility itself could overcome hostility, and this is what Kant refers to as nature: the dimension of human life where there is no subject of consciousness.

In bringing psychoanalysis into the transcritique of Kant and Marx, Karatani is also importantly offering a critique of representational politics. So while mode D is thought along the lines of the Kantian regulative idea – an idea that cannot be represented – the link to libidinal economy comes about in negation and revolution, which aims at a social order governed by a utopian mode of exchange. This mode is what Karatani names reciprocal gift exchange or associationism. While a primary

---

8   See Immanuel Kant, *Idea for a Universal History from a Cosmopolitan Point of View*, in *On History*, trans. Lewis White Beck (1784; reis., London: The Bobbs-Merrill Co., 1963). In the fourth thesis, the concept of "asocial sociability" is elaborated at some length.

force of mode D is non-representational, it continuously modifies existent mode A relations within the social order; mode D is thus a principle of freedom enacted in struggles. Revolution and negations of the social order do not end "unsocial sociability." Instead, the subject of nature Kant develops, and the notion of "world peace" that Kant writes about in his later work is in line with communism as a world republic no longer hampered by the state and the market as organised around commodity exchange. Further, the very movement of this change within human communities is made possible not by human reason or the moral will but by "unsocial sociability," or the "antagonism" innate in human beings.

Karatani draws our attention to the fact that, upon describing the death drive in *Beyond the Pleasure Principle* (1920), Freud confronted the historicity of World War I in the war neurotics he was treating. Through this discovery, we locate the core of Karatani's invariant perspective. We should not think of death drive as a standalone antagonism that libidinally or biologically propels collective action and revolution in history. Instead, it is a force in dialectical tension with the superego. To understand this vital relation, we must revisit the historical context in which Freud discovered the death drive. The principle of the repetition compulsion found empirical proof in the nightmares of the veterans of World War I and how their dreams unlocked a particular sadistic drive. Although Freud sought to apply the logic of the repetition of the death drive to his grandson's play with toys – the fort-da game – and traumatic neuroses more generally, it was the war neuroses as manifest in dreaming that served as the most persuasive argument for the concept. We must, Karatani exclaims, "read the death drive as an historical concept."[9]

Reading the death drive as a historical concept means that we remain attentive to the broader social context in which Freud was operating; 1920 saw the chaotic aftermath of the collapse of the German Empire, one of the last strongholds of the aristocratic order in Europe, after World War I. This period also witnessed the rise of the Bolshevik socialist revolution in Russia, adding a spirit of egalitarianism to the broader European political climate. In Berlin and the other cities across central Europe where Freud sought to grow psychoanalysis, this progressive social context led him to experiment with a more egalitarian form of the psychoanalytic clinic. This period is documented by Elizabeth Danto in her study *Freud's Free Clinics: Psychoanalysis and Social Justice 1918–1938*. Danto shows how Freud sought to expand psychoanalysis in line with the era's social-democratic and socialist-inspired values. Freud advocated lessening regulations on analyst training and lifting payment requirements for working-class analysands to receive analysis, and virtually every one of Freud's most prolific initial psychoanalyst disciples, including Wilhelm Reich, re-

---

9   Karatani, *Nation and Aesthetics*, 47.

ceived their training analysis for free.[10] However, despite this egalitarian political climate, Karatani describes the situation in the following way:

> Freud, after *Beyond the Pleasure Principle*, albeit uncomfortably, attempted to reinforce culture, or the superego. It is not external control, but the aggressive drive itself that can inhibit the aggressive drive. By this thinking, he insisted on the necessity of maintaining the Weimar regime. It should be noted, however, that it was not the war itself but the patients who repeated the war every night that compelled Freud to take a drastic turn that changed the meaning of the superego and culture. Freud speculated that individuals should be cured of neurosis, but that states did not have to be cured of neurosis, namely culture.[11]

The Weimar regime is the superego of this specific historical moment. Recognising that there remains aggression independent from the political situation – a residue of the old order in the new order – meant that the sphere of culture and nation became a significant area for releasing and managing repression, a zone governed by the superego. This insight reflects Freud's political liberalism. Freud avoids the question of a revolution in the regime of capitalist private property, fearing that such a revolution would lose grasp on managing surplus repression. Herbert Marcuse argues similarly that the cultural sphere is granted the task of making surplus repression conscious, thus enabling it to be mourned.[12]

Nevertheless, Freud's view, his *liberalism*, must be understood in relation to the theoretical dimension of the discovery of the death drive, which modified how the superego functions. After the invention of the "death drive" concept, the superego is no longer an external censor of repression from institutions and the social world. Instead, the aggressive drive inhibits from within and thus differently corresponds to the superego. Therefore, Freud argued that conscience is formed not by the severe and superior (i.e., external) other but by a renunciation of one's aggressivity – psychic energy passed into the superego and wielded on the ego. Simultaneously, he insisted that this view was compatible with his former view of the superego as a censor.[13] Both logics of the superego are at play: external censorship and inner-directed logic tied to the death drive. However, after he discovers the death drive's centrality, the primary logic of the superego is mediated by the inner-directed death drive.

However, the fact that Freud's great discovery of the death drive coincided with the collapse of the European aristocracy presents a crucial truth of this discovery: a

---

10   Elizabeth Danto, *Freud's Free Clinics: Psychoanalysis and Social Justice 1918–1938* (NY: Columbia UP, 2005), 123–127.

11   Karatani, *Nation and Aesthetics*, 48.

12   For a more elaborated example of this argument, see Herbert Marcuse, *Eros and Civilization* (NY: The Beacon Press, 1955).

13   Karatani, *Nation and Aesthetics*, 50.

social order undergoing a liberationist upsurge will still be confronted with superegoic mechanisms. Paradoxically, collapsing ego ideals and unstable censor mechanisms do not portend a collapse of the superego. On the contrary, the egalitarian social order can indeed bring about a crisis of the superego. Freud sought to develop the death drive theory to locate a specific outlet for this aggressive drive that remains lingering after the horrors of the war and the advent of a more progressive social order. Suppose the Freudian discovery of the death drive accounts for a logic by which a certain mediation of history, namely, the cunning of nature, comes about. What is the function of the superego in such a context? Is it also to be read in line with the Kantian moral law? Freud introduces the superego with an explicit "super" moral state: "from the point of view of instinctual control, of morality, it may be said of the id that it is totally non-moral, of the ego that it strives to be moral, and of the superego that it can be super moral and then become as cruel as only the Id can be."[14] Karatani embraces these two logics of the superego in a way similar to Adorno, for whom morals derive from the "objectivity of society," the external censor of existing morals and values as well as from "the repressive form of conscience to develop the form of solidarity in which the repressive one will be voided."[15]

Ètienne Balibar reveals the heart of this antinomy of the superego when he describes the superego as a mode of authority that can be made emancipatory or furthered in each social order, but which also situates the subject in a "psychic tribunal." The superego concept emerges from two terms: "over" (Über) and "compulsion" (Zwang), the latter being inseparable from the law and especially the right to punish. The superego is not equivalent to the Kantian concept of the "categorical imperative" as a structure of the unconscious; this would re-establish, in another modality, the subordination of law to morality. The superego is instead a form of simultaneous *obedience* to, and *transgression* of, the law. Balibar writes:

> No social norm would be effective, nor would the respect for norms produce the "excessive" guilt (Schuldgefühl) and the "need for punishment" (Strafbedürfnis) which Freud describes as characteristic of the "severity" or "cruelty" of the Superego, which derive from its "instinctual" nature or from the retroactive effect of the "id" at the heart of the "ego" that it represents, and that ends up instituting the absurd equivalence between obedience to the law and the transgression of the law.[16]

---

14   Sigmund Freud, *The Pelican Freud Library, Vol. 11* (London: Harmondsworth Publishing, 1984), 395.

15   Ètienne Balibar, *Citizen Subject: Foundations for Philosophical Anthropology* (NY: Fordham UP, 2017), 241.

16   Balibar, 243.

The superego operates on a double bind of adherence and transgression to the law simultaneously, and the effect of this double bind is that the subject undergoes guilt. "How could the subject (the unconscious ego) not feel guilty of failing to reconcile what is both enjoined and prohibited?"[17] The superego establishes a "tribunal" that reveals itself to be constituted at the same time by a personal instance inscribed within a genealogical succession and an impersonal instance formed by a network of institutions or apparatuses of domination and of coercion that includes the "family," which constitutes, *par excellence*, their intersection. These two modes of injunction switch places and injunctions: "The superego, it is the family!" – "The family, it is the superego!"[18]

It is crucial to notice how the superego is inscribed in a "network of institutions and apparatuses of domination and of coercion"[19] and that, even though the superego is a psychic tribunal, this is not to be understood as producing conditions of voluntary servitude for the subject. On the contrary, the superego connects the subject to the collective. However, just as the superego's psychic tribunal situates the subject in a concrete communal instantiation between the network of domination and coercion and the impersonal genealogical status, Karatani will emphasise the impersonal dimension in a significant way.

In a reading of Freud's 1928 essay on humour, Karatani argues that the superego is not to be understood solely as the agency of repression and censorship but as that which, "in humor, speaks such kindly words of comfort to the intimidated ego." We find this unique impersonal dimension of the superego in humour in contrast to jokes. Where humour functions with spontaneity and activeness (i.e., not consciously), jokes function consciously. We are presented again with the invariant dimension of the death drive appearing in the superego through humour. By stressing how autonomy derives not from outside (i.e., the father or social norms) but inside, the invariant perspective also intimates periods of collective life in which the superego is absent.

Since the superego is the harbinger of the affect of guilt when it instantiates itself on a given social order, as we developed above, Karatani draws our attention to the fact that there are prolonged periods in post-war capitalist life in the Western countries that effectively witnessed an absence of superego. Superego formations emerge at moments provoked by crisis, revolt or war; that is, a repressive communal project ushers them into existence. This means a reign of a social order without superego is governed primarily, although not exclusively, by the affect of shame. As previously mentioned, at the affective level, the instantiation of superego typically follows a period of social unrest – war, crisis, revolution – and in such moments,

---

17   Balibar, 243.
18   Balibar, 249.
19   Balibar, 249.

social orders can expect conditions of guilt to predominate. As Balibar indicates, it is necessary that the radical "feeling of guilt" engendered by absolute coercion be "repressed and perpetuated, and along with it, the paradoxical equivalence of intentions and acts, behaviours of obedience and movements of transgression."[20] What this points to is the function of guilt in the binding of superego formations over subjective life. As such, Karatani argues that the negative social affects this brings mean something significant for civic and social life. Namely, the social order must contain an *other scene* by which these negative and antisocial affects of guilt can be granted a proper outlet.

What precisely is this other scene? For Karatani, the existence of the superego requires the sphere of culture or what Enlightenment thinkers theorised as the national sphere: an imaginary sphere of social life where the sentimentality of aesthetic expressions of the citizenry is given a zone of free expression. Mode A (primitive gift exchange) governs the national sphere. In a certain sense, this means it is the most distant from the dominating mode C, which governs social relations in contemporary capitalism. Nevertheless, what Karatani draws our attention to in the very idea of the nation is that product of the contradictions and antagonisms kicked up by the modes of state and capital (B and C) and that, by extension, it is not a transcendentally necessary zone of social life. We do not know the precise composition of the nation following a revolutionary sequence that would usurp the predominance of commodity exchange. However, we can wager the need for an outlet zone to exist for in-built aggressions and repressions within any given social order. How must this other scene of culture or nation (mode A) be constructed in such a way that it serves as the other scene, and what is it other to? As we will examine later, even if a social order is governed by mode A (gift exchange) as the dominant mode of social life, there remain forms of social and political conflicts generated based on gift economies. There are distinct means of utilising gifts as the means for reparation of conflicts. We cannot say that the sphere of culture and the nation would completely wither in Karatani's theory of revolution. Karatani does not posit a distinct zone of "political" social existence; instead, in emphasising social relations in modes of exchange, these spheres of collective life govern in overlapping ways, and the notion of an ontologically separate zoning of social life is not in line with this theory.

Freud offers a liberal answer to the bigger question of how civilisation manages collective in-built aggressions and general resentments. In *Civilization and Its Discontents'* conclusion, he argues that the reign of private property itself is the best means to inhibit the aggressive drive.[21] For Freud, it appears that the very persistence of mode C and the reign of private property provides an outlet, along with culture,

---

20   Balibar, 241–254.

21   Sigmund Freud, *Civilization and Its Discontents*, trans. James Stratchey (1930; reis., NY: Norton, 2010), 148–149.

for aggression. Thus, there is a degree of resentment that a society based on private property perpetuates, which Freud seems to cast as necessary for maintaining a degree of repression. We are again reminded of Freud's ambiguous embrace of the progressive era of post-war Europe and simultaneous insistence that something of the symptom of the older order remain within the new. This position puts Freud at loggerheads with Karatani's insistence that a social order governed by commodity exchange limits freedom. At this point of contrast, the invariant principle of nature located within the core of subjectivity – what we elaborated above as mode D – or an internalising of the aggressive drive not determined by consciousness comes into focus. Karatani is utilising the Freudian apparatus differently than Freud himself did and with different political objectives. For Karatani, Freud's novel discovery is the invariant dimension that enhances the zone of freedom for human beings in ways that link that freedom as a collective, subjective form of freedom beyond repression but attuned to the persistence of aggression. In other words, for Karatani, capitalism fails to manage the constitutive problem of subjective aggression because the very resolution of the problem is only exacerbated, not granted the space for a mode of exchange wherein constitutive antagonisms can be more thoroughly worked through.

Karatani's invariant theory of libidinal economy comes into greater focus for the field of libidinal economy when we compare it not only with Freud's liberal account but also with the heterodox Marxist work by Jean-François Lyotard, *Libidinal Economy* (1974). Both Lyotard and Karatani, at first blush, have much in common: both have sought to rework Kantian philosophies of representation and critique, and both philosophers argue for rethinking collective liberation by way of the death drive. However, we immediately sense the significant difference between their ways of conceiving death drive when we look at Lyotard's work:

> We must grasp the fact that the system of capital is not the site of the occultation of an alleged use-value which would be anterior to it – this is the romanticism of alienation, Christianity – but primarily that it is in a sense more than capital, more ancient, more extended; and then that these so-called abstract signs, susceptible to provisional measurement and calculation, are in themselves libidinal.[22]

The "abstract signs" that Lyotard references in this passage are Klossowskian phantasms, or ultimately unexchangeable remainders of *jouissance*. In Pierre Klossowski's idea of the phantasm, although Plato's Republic no longer exists, there are no longer cities or government – it is only in the field of economics that the conspiracy of the

---

22   Jean Francois Lyotard, *Libidinal Economy*, trans. Ian Hamilton Grant (1974; reis., Bloomington: Indiana UP, 1993), 81–82.

pulsional social body exists.[23] Like Klossowski, Lyotard thinks exchange as a form of libidinally-charged matter, a "living currency." This radicalisation of the Freudian theory of libido makes commodity exchange a scene where what is at stake is the exchange of enjoyment itself, which calls for an entirely new form of critique. The Marxist distinction between use value and exchange value is no longer useful in this critique. Instead, the phantasms never cancel debts; that is, life and enjoyment are exchanged in commodity exchange. As such, exchange does not reference another order or a signified. Lyotard's notion of exchange is non-dualist, without reference to an outside order founded on alienation. Therefore, in his view, the demand of the masses is not on the side of any invariant principle. Instead, the closest collective demand of the masses is "long live the libidinal!" not "long live the social!"[24] Lyotard's anti-social theory posits that the objects to be traded (for *jouissance*) are incommensurable and incalculable, so any notion of gift is relegated to a Pascalian wager because the gift is beyond reason, unexchangeable. In other words, there is no alterity of *jouissance* because the sensible sign of exchange value dissimulates what Lyotard names the tensor sign, which would then have to be confused with use-value. Lyotard warns:

> He who gives without return must pay. The time of *jouissance* is bought. The time of his ravaged, jubilant, sacred body is converted into cash (and it is expensive). The payment returns him into the cycle, into death. His death is instantiated on the cosmic body.[25]

Responding to Deleuze and Guattari's variety of immanent critique, Lyotard puts forward a mode of critique left to the enemy: "be inside and forget it, that's the position of death drive." Lyotard thus offers a pessimistic and postcritical analysis of libidinal economy. For Lyotard, the superego does not need resurrection or mutation – as articulated above – because, like critique, it only deploys militarist ethics. The superego has an ethics only meant to fend off insurrection against the id. Thus, the projects of critique and psychoanalysis hollow out an interior in which they seek to re-draw the boundaries of energetics. Lyotard probes this interior space in his theories of the "libidinal band," which refers to an assemblage capable of freeing intensities from the repressive strictures of commodity exchange. But this agency does not constitute a well-developed theory of praxis. Lyotard even abandons the entire project of Marxist critique in an infamous distinction between what he shrewdly names "Young Girl Marx" and "Old Man Marx." Little Girl Marx, or the early Marx

23   Pierre Klossowski, *Living Currency*, trans. Vernon Cisney, Nicolae Morar, and Daniel W. Smith (London: Bloomsbury Academic, 2017), 91.
24   Klossowski, 66.
25   Klossowski, 184.

interested in the theory of revolution as a utopian achievement of nonalienation, represents only a phantasy of a non-alienated region, a form of praxis that only starts the project of religion all over again.[26] Old Man Marx represents a more rational model of praxis that never reaches the totality, remaining forever removed from real action, always waiting for a perfect critique to align with a revolutionary moment that inevitably misses.

Karatani's thinking of the dialectical relation between superego and death drive is a more positive rejoinder to Lyotard's pessimistic idea that capital captures every libidinal force, that every intense sign appears as a coded sign. Karatani is undoubtedly in line with a reading of Marx that does not shy away from religion. Indeed, associationism establishes a form of religion in modernity, although this is an incomplete project. Karatani thinks of a coming world republic on a socialist basis, which has removed commodity exchange as the primary mode of organisation. However, this associationism is not a search for identity, or the localisation of desire, masculinisation, becoming conscious, power, or knowledge as Lyotard would have it; it is based on an invariant impulse of freedom from the hold of commodity exchange on social life. For Lyotard, (and even for Freud, too) there is no way out of mode C. In contrast, for Karatani, there is a dialectical logic to revolutionary upsurges that point our attention and analysis towards the unsocial sociability that can be processed in common civic and political life. In Part 2 of this chapter, we turn to where we locate this domain of social life, or what we have called the other scene. From this insight, we will then apply further thinking to what it implies for political organisation and ways to overcome the dominance of mode C. And as we have developed thus far, revolutionary subjectivity will contain a remainder of unsocial sociability and superegoic forces will form around these remainders in concrete materialist ways. This is an insight for libidinal economy; subjectivity struggles to overcome social relations dominated by mode C, and this struggle points to a regulative idea, to something which cannot be achieved through reason alone, to something which Enlightenment and education cannot overcome.

Why is it helpful to think of this dialectic as aiming towards enacting reciprocal forms of social exchange and abolishing commodity exchange? The theory of the gift is at the very heart of this question, and there is sizeable anthropological literature that has accounted for the psychological dimension of primitive gift economies. In his *The Structure of World History*, Karatani is attentive to these lineages of research and knowledge. The fact that tribal and prefeudal societies had extensive and complex gift economies shows something about how gift economies contain the potential for a society not based on egoism. In his famous work *The Gift* (1925), the anthropologist Marcel Mauss assumes that gift exchange primarily involves social solidarity. In other words, we must learn something about the potential for solidarity in

26   Lyotard, *Libidinal Economy*, 107.

the modern world from gift economies. However, as an aside, it is important to note that Mauss was not a communist and was a state bureaucrat deeply suspicious of the Bolshevik refusal to pay the debts of the czar after they seized power. Mauss wanted to maintain a capitalist mode of exchange and perhaps implement the wisdom of gift economies onto that edifice. This is not the case with the communist thinker Karatani, who sees a non-representable upsurge and movement of communism in gift exchange. Marx described communism as the movement aimed towards abolishing all things.

Other psychoanalytic thinkers have turned to gift exchange in their historical analysis. Norman O. Brown discusses societies of gift exchange as if they are beyond repression. In *Life Against Death* (1959), he situates the death drive as the logic of historical time: "only repressed life is in time," and "repression and the repetition compulsion generate historical time."[27] Brown is a mystical Freudian who believed that psychoanalysis provided the necessary intellectual equipment for ushering humanity towards a mystical break from the bondage of the death drive. For Brown, breaks from the death drive usher the subject, almost messianically, into eternity, or the mode of unrepressed bodies. *Life Against Death* is a psychoanalytic theory of history searching for sensual release from repressive social conditions. Brown follows Freud's statement in *The Economic Problem in Masochism* that, "the cultural task – the life task? – of the libido, namely, is to make the destructive instinct harmless.[28] As modern civilisation is instrumentally structured in regimentation and repressive order, it cannot free *eros* or the life drive. Thus, a complete break from the constrictors of repressive society requires deploying the pleasure principle as a form of negativity. Thus, unlike the invariant perspective, Brown, like Herbert Marcuse in *Eros and Civilization*, argues that the pleasure principle precedes its domination by the reality principle, and that there is a missing pleasure principle to restore. This view informs a praxis which suggests that revolutionary struggle ought to restore a lost libidinal paradise.[29] It is important to note that there are theoretical and political differences between Marcuse and Brown, particularly about questions of liberation and death drive. In his critical review of Brown's *Life Against Death*, Marcuse rails against the mystical conception of the death drive and Brown's exaggerated stance on liberation, arguing that Brown effectively reduces the question of liberation to "transubstantiation." As Marcuse writes, "Brown's 'way out' leaves the Establishment behind – that

---

27   Norman O. Brown, *Life Against Death: The Psychoanalytical Meaning of History*, 2nd ed. (1959; reis., Middletown: Wesleyan UP, 1985), 93.

28   Sigmund Freud, *The Economic Problem in Masochism*, trans. James Stratchey (1924; reis., London: The Hogarth Press, 1961), 260.

29   See Bernard Stiegler's excellent discussion of Marcuse's *Eros and Civilization* in *The Lost Spirit of Capitalism*, trans. Daniel Ross (Cambridge: Polity Press, 2014), 44–45.

is, the way out is indeed mystical, mystification" and notes that his theory "mystifies the possibilities of liberation."[30]

Against the overly sensualist and biologically derived account of libido and pleasure principle as we find in Brown, and to an extent also in Marcuse, or the more pessimist Augustinian theory of libido we find in Klossowski and Lyotard, Karatani's invariant perspective does not situate the problem of liberation as a pure overcoming or as an impossibly rare event. Karatani's account is far more dialectical; as discussed, this is a praxis that must be centred on altering mode C commodity exchange to enact the libidinal and affective shifts we have elaborated thus far.

Karatani is not alone in the libidinal economy field, and other thinkers have developed similar proposals that combine insights of a Freudian libidinal economy with Marxist praxis. The German utopian Marxist philosopher Ernst Bloch is one such thinker to present a libidinal theory of revolution. It is very much in line with the invariant perspective. In a brief passage in *The Structure of World History*, Karatani cites a concept developed by Bloch, the "Not-Yet-Conscious," and suggests that this idea gets close to what he means by mode D, but Karatani does not further specify. In Bloch's *Principle of Hope* (1954), the Not-Yet-Conscious is raised as a specific rebuttal to the bourgeois element within psychoanalytic thought that bases the proposal of the unconscious on the "totally regressive proposition" that "the repressed is for us the model of the unconscious."[31] For Bloch, the bourgeois class basis of psychoanalysts perverted the development of its theory:

> More than ever the bourgeoisie lacks the material incentive to separate the Not-Yet-Conscious from the No-Longer-Conscious. All psychoanalysis, with repression as its central notion, sublimation as a mere subsidiary notion (for substitution, for hopeful illusions), is therefore necessarily retrospective. Admittedly, it developed in an earlier age than the present one, around the turn of the century it took part in a so-called struggle against the conventional lies of a civilized mankind. Nevertheless, psychoanalysis developed in a class which was superannuated even then, in a society without future. So Freud exaggerated the dimensions of the libido of these parasites and recognized no other onward, let alone upward drive.[32]

The Not-yet-Conscious does not emerge within a ruling class. It appears in liberatory moments and uprisings within a proletariat or "rising class." Bloch cites examples of the French Revolution, peasant rebellions during the Middle Ages, and the Bolshevik Revolution of 1917. These uprisings all shared a common relation to the

30   Herbert Marcuse, "Love Mystified: A Critique of Norman O. Brown," *Commentary Magazine*, February 1967.

31   Ernst Bloch, *Principle of Hope*, trans. Neville Plaice, Stephen Plaice, and Paul Knight (1954; reis., Cambridge: MIT Press, 1995), 137.

32   Bloch, 137.

Not-Yet-Conscious that manifested itself in the slogans and images of revolution that pointed towards nothing short of "the realm of freedom." Revolutionary movements, rising classes, and the proletariat in certain situations of the class struggle in history possess a preconscious of what is to come, thus locating "the psychological birthplace of the New."[33] Although Bloch's conception of the class dimension of the Not-Yet-Conscious romanticises the proletariat – "rarely," Bloch writes, "does this class display neurotic features"[34] – this theory ties in directly to his more expansive theory of utopia. The Not-Yet-Conscious breaks bourgeois "contemplation," or the idea that bourgeois consciousness can only truly think "What Has Become." The Not-Yet-Conscious point is reached where "hope itself, this authentic expectant emotion in the forward dream, no longer just appears as a merely self-based mental feeling, but in a conscious-known way as utopian function."[35]

What Bloch's Not-Yet-Conscious opens for the broader invariant perspective is a way of thinking about the break in consciousness that a revolutionary action brings about. The Not-Yet-Conscious identifies an element of a fundamental newness in the break, uprising or revolution; this contrasts with the Freudian model of the infamous "return of the repressed," in which something repressed determines what is to come. For Bloch, there remains an invariant element that is not destined to a bad infinity or an utterly inescapable death-driven repetition of the old in the birth of the new.

Part 2: Karatani's praxis: Associationism

To fully grasp how Karatani theorises a break from commodity exchange, we now discuss Karatani's praxis of associationism, a series of tactics and political organising strategies aimed at dissolving state and capital (mode B and mode C). Karatani critiques historical materialism and Marxist-Leninist theories of praxis by arguing that a major flaw in this wider field of theory – broadly known as historical materialism – is that its praxis led to conceptions of the state and the nation as intrinsic parts of the superstructure of society, on par with art or philosophy. These revolutionary socialist movements, including Marxist-Leninism, notionally sought a form of socialism beyond the nation-state form. However, they could not dissolve the nation or state as distinct categories of social life because both are inextricably bound up in modes of exchange. In Marxist theory, particularly historical materialism, people tend to privilege a revolutionary praxis focused on seizing the means of production of capitalist society, or what Marx called the "base" structures of capitalist so-

---

33   Bloch, 113.
34   Bloch, 128.
35   Bloch, 144.

ciety (i.e., industry, labour, and other centres of production). Karatani argues, on the contrary, that the failures of 20th-century Marxism, specifically the communist revolutions in Russia, China, and elsewhere, were due to general neglect of thinking revolution at the level of the modes of exchange. Once these 20th-century movements seized the means of production, transforming the superstructure – the wider spheres of culture and education – was the primary task. The nation and the state were predicted to wither through enlightening the people. However, as we know, these movements never adequately transformed the nation or the state – and it was in these domains that the most profound violence and upheaval occurred.

In the post-Bolshevik revolution period (1917–1940s), as in the Chinese Cultural Revolution (1966–1976), the task of the ongoing revolution or the "permanent revolution" was set on overcoming the imaginary structures of nation and state to drive towards a communist arrangement of society. This task called for enlightenment, that is, the proper education of the masses (Maoism), the cultivation of a trained vanguard (Leninism), and so on. However, this task left untouched, or did not privilege, revolutionising the modes of exchange. So the modes of exchange largely remained tethered to forms of commodity exchange and were held within the purview of capitalist modes of exchange, albeit with a planned and centralised/nationalised economy. In other words, the praxis Karatani prioritises revolutionising modes of commodity exchange to forms of reciprocal gift exchange.

In Karatani's Borromean logic, then, 20th-century revolutionary communist movements seized the state, nation, and economy, thus controlling the three spheres of revolutionary demands coming out of the French Revolution: liberty (market), fraternity (nation), and egalitarianism (state). Freedom represents the primary mode of exchange; fraternity represents the people's national unity; egalitarianism represents the state-form. However, in Karatani's critique, 20th-century Marxism falsely saw the state (egalitarianism) and national (fraternity) spheres as superstructural extensions of society and thus saw these spheres as fundamentally rooted in the base mode of production. As such, they were theorised to wither through programs of education. But thinking these categories as superstructural effects failed to adequately link the project of superstructure struggles, what we might call *representational* struggles – such as education of the masses, the promotion of revolutionary art and culture – to base struggles (or struggles of production and labour). As Karatani has argued, this occurred because they neglected the modes of exchange inherent in the state form – and exchange being the core component of the base.[36] Thus, what occurred in 20th-century socialist movements of state communism, as we know full well, was that capital ended up holding hegemony over social relations within the nation and the state – that is, commodity exchange eventually overwhelmed all three spheres. Perhaps there is no better evidence of

---

36   Karatani, *The Structure of World History*, 2.

this than contemporary Chinese communism, which has fully adapted to capitalist modes of exchange, and the degree to which the national sphere remains tied to a communist zeitgeist is mostly in mythical and cultural forms.

Karatani's critique points to the broader premise of historical materialism – that the modes of production are the primary site of revolutionary struggle – not being a thesis that bears the weight of recent history. Against this conception, Karatani argues that the state and nation should be understood as extensions of the base – namely, as extensions of dominant modes of exchange. What might a praxis that emphasises the modes of exchange over that of production look like? In answering this question, it is first important to ask whether there is effective resistance to capital at the level of the mode of production because if you take the governing hegemony of mode C seriously, you will understand that its proliferation extends to all areas of social reproductive life as well as the industrial labour process. Therefore, resistance within the circulation sphere is a preferred site to wage struggle because the subject resisting in this ubiquitous sphere holds a higher potential to resist as a free subject. They may be less encumbered, for example, by superegoic constructions that might plague a worker in a corporation or factory who must deal with bosses. Resistance to mode C at the productive level still maintains the edifice of capital valuation, and no resistance is possible if we limit ourselves to thinking resistance to mode C along the production process alone; as Marxists, it is necessary to grasp capital as a totality. Karatani observes, "if workers decide to resist capital, they should do so not from the site where this is difficult but rather from the site where they enjoy a dominant position vis à vis capital."[37] Resistance at the exchange site is the optimal form of resistance to mode C for proletarians to create a universal subject attentive to the dynamics of the superego and death drive we discussed above. Suppose Freud's fundamental insight apropos the "psychic tribunal" of the superego is indeed correct. In that case, resistance at the site of labour, where the subject is the least free, involves entanglement with the double bind of the law within the repressive sphere of labour. There is thus a reason informed by the insights of libidinal economy to focus praxis against capitalism within the sphere of circulation and consumption. In theory, resistance will involve collective action less prone to resentments, repressions, and violence. Since capital forces us to work but not buy, a consumer struggle retains a degree of autonomous freedom of the individual. It thus enables resistance to capitalism to not arbitrarily separate other struggles from working-class struggles.

Struggles against mode C taking the form of circulation struggles also offer an opportunity to create new currencies and credit systems. The primary tactic in these struggles is the boycott which has a specific advantage – it is legal. Boycotts typically take two forms: refusal to buy and sell, and for the method of the boycott to

---

37   Karatani, 290.

work, an alternative economy must exist. Tactically, this includes the boycott within consumer capitalism, but the boycott Karatani envisions takes the role of refusing to sell and to buy. To compel people in this direction, noncapitalist alternative consumer economies must be created. In a more refined level of organisation, in which forms of state power might open for proletarian takeover, there is also a central international dimension to associationist praxis. This dimension drives towards a new world system of states centred around reciprocal gift exchange, using tactics such as voluntary disarmament of weapons, free exchange of production technology, and abolishing intellectual property restrictions. What would an international alliance formed around the gift look like across nation-states? Perhaps things such as mutual disarmament plans and sharing technology across nations would function as gifts that might eventually challenge the hegemony of the real bases of capital and nation.

There are immediate challenges that the associationist praxis opens: questions of scalability – how can methods of boycott compel large swaths of the population to take on anticapitalist agitation, especially when the predominance of liberal modes of political critique leaves the deleterious effects of commodity exchange unexamined? Does there not need to be a prior consciousness-raising movement against capital at the site where people are least free, precisely in the sphere of labour? Further, perhaps most surprising in the associationist theory of praxis is how it foregoes the period in a revolutionary sequence, identified by Marx as the "dictatorship of the proletariat," or the stage in which the proletariat seizes state power directly. Perhaps the question of power seizing, and the inevitable violence that comes with it, is not theorised as a necessary sequence of revolutionary struggle due to Karatani's emphasis on modes of exchange over that of the political as a distinct or separate sphere of social life.

At the same time as these critiques of associationism are real and compelling, there are other benefits to the associationist praxis for Marxist struggles today. For example, associationism can be thought to align with existing theories of communisation and insurrectionary struggles. The movements that opened with the anti-WTO protests in the early 1990s in Seattle, known broadly as the "anti-globalisation" struggles, up to the Occupy movement and Black Lives Matter – all deploy the tactics of what Joshua Clover refers to as "circulation struggles."[38] These insurrections seek property destruction and stoppages to circulating goods and commodities and are thus aiming to halt the ease of circulation globally. While these circulation struggle tactics of revolt align with a shared goal of disrupting the dominance of mode C, it is not clear that these tactics are proactive in forging an alternative mode of exchange through communal alternatives to currency exchange, the introduction of gift economies based on reciprocity, etc.

---

38   Joshua Clover, *Riot. Strike. Riot: The New Era of Uprisings* (NY: Verso Books, 2016).

In conclusion, we find Karatani's thinking of the dialectical relation between superego and death drive offers a more positive rejoinder to liberal and even to some radical Marxist theories of libidinal economy, such as Lyotard. They find no way to transcend the deadlocks of constitutive aggression and asocial affects that capitalism foments. It is not merely the exchange of commodities in the market sphere that can overcome "unsocial sociability," an entirely new mode of exchange premised on the gift and reciprocity must be introduced in the domain of common civic and political life. These are insights for a radical politics of the commune and anticapitalist politics as much as they are insights for a more comprehensive and revolutionary theory of libidinal economy.

References

Balibar, Ètienne. *Citizen Subject: Foundations for Philosophical Anthropology*. NY: Fordham UP, 2017.

Bloch, Ernst. *Principle of Hope*. Translated by Neville Plaice, Stephen Plaice, and Paul Knight. Cambridge: MIT Press, 1995. First published 1954.

Brown, Norman O. *Life Against Death: The Psychoanalytical Meaning of History*. 2nd ed. Middletown, CT: Wesleyan UP, 1985. First published 1959.

Clover, Joshua. *Riot. Strike. Riot: The New Era of Uprisings*. NY: Verso, 2016.

Danto, Elizabeth. *Freud's Free Clinics: Psychoanalysis and Social Justice 1918–1938*. NY: Columbia UP, 2005.

Freud, Sigmund. *Civilization and Its Discontents*. Translated by James Stratchey. NY: Norton, 2010. First published 1930.

———. *The Economic Problem in Masochism*. Translated by James Stratchey. London: The Hogarth Press, 1961. First published 1924.

Freud, Sigmund. *The Pelican Freud Library, Vol. 11*. London: Harmondsworth Publishing, 1984.

Kant, Immanuel. *Idea for a Universal History from a Cosmopolitan Point of View*. In *On History*, translated and edited by Lewis White Beck, pgs. 11 – 26. London: The Bobbs-Merrill Co., 1963. First published 1784.

Karatani, Kojin. *Isonomia and the Origins of Philosophy*. Translated by Joseph A. Murphy. Durham: Duke UP, 2017.

———. *Nation and Aesthetics: On Kant and Freud*. Translated by Jonathan E. Abel, Hiroki Yoshikuni, and Darwin H. Tsen. London: Oxford UP, 2017.

———. *The Structure of World History: From Modes of Production to Modes of Exchange*. Translated by Michael K. Bourdaghs. Durham: Duke UP, 2014.

———. *Transcritique: On Kant and Marx*. Translated by Sabu Kohso. Cambridge: MIT Press, 2003.

Klossowski, Pierre. *Living Currency*. Translated by Vernon Cisney, Nicolae Morar, and Daniel W. Smith. London: Bloomsbury Academic, 2017.

Lyotard, Jean-François. *Libidinal Economy*. Translated by Ian Hamilton Grant. Bloomington: Indiana UP, 1993. First published 1974.

Marcuse, Herbert. "Love Mystified: A Critique of Norman O. Brown." *Commentary Magazine*, February 1967. https://www.commentary.org/articles/herbert-marcuse/love-mystified-a-critique-of-norman-o-brown.

———. *Eros and Civilization*. NY: The Beacon Press, 1955.

Stiegler, Bernard. *The Lost Spirit of Capitalism*. Translated by Daniel Ross. Cambridge: Polity Press, 2014.

Datamining Desire: Short-Circuits in the Libidinal Economy

Alexis Wolfe

> To be seen is the ambition of ghosts, and
> to be remembered is the ambition of the
> dead.
> — Friedrich Nietzsche[1]

When confronted with a sense of internal chaos, one makes attempts to control the external world; when external chaos rules, grasping for internal control becomes a kind of compulsion, a ritual, a refuge. Crisis feels eternal because we are governed by it. Psychoanalytic thinkers have described how unceasing crisis has become the unreality of a public managed by a form of power manifest in the total synthesis of politics and spectacle.[2] As a result, subjectivity is shaped in a well of entangled and accelerating crises that reinforce individual and collective powerlessness at every turn.

We are trapped in the echo of collapsing democracy – a crisis rooted in a more fundamental crisis at the level of the symbolic order. French psychoanalyst Jacques Lacan described the realm of language, intersubjective relations, meaning creation, and law as the symbolic order – it is here that we encounter the other, normativity, and ideological convention.[3] Since the 1980s, public institutions in the West – structures that have historically worked to varying degrees to produce and sustain social ties – have been in a state of decay. This decay has seeded a new regime of technocratic power and austerity that leaves public infrastructure and services underfunded, the welfare state in persistent deterioration, and workers precarious – their futures undermined by enormous amounts of debt. As Isabell Lorey declares,

1   Friedrich Nietzsche, *Ecce Homo, The Portable Nietzsche* (Toronto: Penguin Random House, 1977), 660.
2   Christopher Lasch, *The Culture of Narcissism* (NY: Warner Books, 1979), 147.
3   Jacques Lacan, *Écrits*, trans. Bruce Fink (NY: Norton, 2002), 83.

we are currently experiencing a "return of mass vulnerability" – navigating an accelerated and abject existence that offers no relief from itself.[4]

To compensate for this sense of acute vulnerability, subjects retreat inward, investing libido in self-objects and withdrawing from the other – the other being the realm of the not-I, "the others," those we encounter in social life. Chronic uncertainty, rapid change, and precarity produce libidinal fields based on energy conservation. In survival, we protect, safeguard, and hoard our energy.

Our condition is not unlike that of a child growing up in an alcoholic home: navigating continued uncertainty, the child is never quite sure what treatment they will receive from parental figures. They make themselves small and self-sufficient. They learn to entertain themselves and stay out of the way. They become skilled thermometers of mood shifts and, in their helplessness, withdraw from the world of the other (primarily parental caregivers in this case) to live in fantasy worlds of their creation.

Most painfully, the narcissism of young children causes them to blame themselves for the tension and chaos in their environment as they stand unable to grasp the complexity of relationships and demands that besiege their overwhelmed or distracted parents. Sensing a problem, the child lives in tension but lacks a concept of its origin. A young child lives in a one-to-one relationship with the world – everything that happens is happening because of me, for me and to me. Unsure of a tension's origin, the child makes themself the problem – they must be upset because of something I did, it must be something inherently wrong with me that causes mom to drink. At this point, it becomes far less painful to live in a realm of fantasy than in the world of others.

Steeped in the confusing and ceaseless chaos of social, environmental and political crisis, we retreat inward. Once we grow bored, overwhelmed or intolerant of the doom and gloom, we escape into fantasy – entrepreneurial fantasies, fantasies of fame, fantasies of omnipotence.

The crisis at hand is multifaceted. In what follows, we will turn to OnlyFans, pandemic life, Moshfegh and Houellebecq to witness its multiple fronts. We will try to understand how declining symbolic efficiency reduces our capacity to desire and isolates us in repetitions of the drive. We will observe how drive is instrumentalised towards capital's aims and the impression this leaves on the human spirit. From there, we will survey the psychological patterns this system rewards and sustains, to then turn our attention towards the pathway back to desire, towards object-love, towards reintegration of the symbolic.

---

4   Isabell Lorey, *State of Insecurity: Government of the Precarious* (London: Verso, 2015), 53.

New intrusions

On the external level, crises of capitalism are revealing limits of expropriation. These limits are mirrored by internal crises of psychic oversaturation and exploited drive. The machinations of techno-capitalism tend to datamine processes of desiring to gain information to support the development of technologies to exploit human energy called drive. Subjects can sense their desire predated upon, seduced, and mined for its value. All around, capital's machinations wring natural resources like water, minerals, oil, and attention for profit. This is possible only by breaching boundaries. When capital accumulation meets a limit, it surpasses it by breaching boundaries – attempting to privatise and monetise new expanses and aspects of external and internal space. To seduce participation for these new internal extractions, subjects are promised convenience and entertainment in exchange for their attention and data. This process of seducing attention and datamining desire leave the subject in a state of dissonance – feeling at once overstimulated and empty, catered to but alone. Desire is simultaneously stimulated, solicited and extinguished.

On the material plane, subjects of late capitalism are left without ground to stand on as systems of collective safeguarding have crumbled and wages have stagnated since the 1970s. This hollowing out of protective systems and precariatisation leaves large swaths of the population defenceless – accidents, illness, or unemployment swiftly disintegrate one's remnant economic security.[5] Poverty haunts and compels workers to take on increasingly precarious jobs.[6] Precarity involves a kind of endless navigation of crises – supply chains, viral infection, and social distrust. These conditions demoralise the human spirit and fray social bonds by heightening avoidance, competition and nihilism, and incentivising escapism and numbness.

I'm so tired, I've been desiring all day!

Why is desire so tired? There is an excess of signs. Franco Berardi explains that we live in conditions of semiotic inflation: "when more and more signs are buying less and less meaning."[7] Semiotic inflation constitutes an engulfing aspect of cultural capitalism that absorbs and instrumentalises our despair and, in return, offers intoxicating, fatalistic modes of forgetting.[8] This form of libidinal organisation ex-

---

5   Guy Debord, *Society of the Spectacle* (Black & Red: Oakland, 2010), 114.
6   J. Benach et al., "Precarious Employment: Understanding an Emerging Social Determinant of Health," *Annual Review of Public Health* 35, no. 1 (2014).
7   Franco Berardi, *And. Phenomenology of the End. Cognition and Sensibility in the Transition from Conjunctive to Connective Mode of Social Communication* (Helsinki: Aalto ARTS Books, 2014), 95–96.
8   Franco Berardi, *The Soul at Work* (Cambridge: MIT Press, 2009), 156.

hausts desire because it keeps the mind so busy, so full of untethered meaning – meaning without symbolic grounding. Unsupported by collective symbolic systems of meaning, the subject is compelled to swim through a sea of signs, operating as a deterritorialised "debtor-addict" subject – what Mark Fisher describes as a node of consumer power, an object of biopolitical control, and a source of attentional and libidinal energy.[9] As debtor-addict subjects, we experience the world as paradoxically boring yet exhausting, overly controlled yet chaotic.

Byung-Chul Han adds the dimension of competition to this formulation. He identifies the dominant structure of subjectivity emerging in these conditions as the achievement subject.[10] Fixated by markers of individual success, the achievement subject carves out a piece of reality for herself and holds fast to controlling it. This can look like ambition aimed at climbing the corporate ladder, growing one's "influence" online, or striving to some evolved state of perfect "wellness." The coordinates of the achievement subject's desire are highly attuned to predetermined nodes in the consumer market. This makes the charge of drive easy to exploit.

Similar to the subject whose interface with the other takes on painful qualities and opts to live instead in a world of fantasy and daydreams, the achievement subject experiences a retraction of the libido into self-objects. The achievement subject will forgo meaningful relationships with the other in favour of a narcissistic withdrawal into a fantasy of self-empowerment. She compensates for a world whose narratives of progress are failing by scripting a fantasy of progress, growth and improvement of the self.

The achievement subject is voracious in her relationship to the world – everything stands as a potential tool for self-maximisation and expression. Lacking connection to a longstanding, collective narrative, she inhabits a decentralised narrative ephemera. This subject's scale of time is condensed, warped, and narrowed – she inhabits moments, jumping from image to image, dissociating from history. For her, meaning shifts rapidly – the symbolic terrain is unstable, full of terrible history. She is driven by a pursuit of novelty.

The symbolic exists as a recording of history. It is a collection of stored memory, populated by language, ritual, and tradition. With the decline of symbolic efficiency, subjects are severed from longer time scales – detached from practices and myths that carry a sense of duration and collective meaning. Without symbolic rooting, the achievement subject is severed from meaning-production as a historical process – a captive of a dislocated present. Here, her value lies in her ability to adhere to a disposition of flexibility, nomadism, and competition, limiting her engagement with a world that is symbolically mediated.

---

9   Mark Fisher, *Capitalist Realism: Is There No Alternative?* (NY: Zero Books, 2009), 25.

10   Byung-Chul Han, *The Burnout Society* (Stanford: Stanford UP, 2015), 8.

Technocratic governance dismantles symbolic modes of relating with its promise of liberalisation – it insists with its promise to free the human from dependence on governmental control.[11] Technocracy implies we are governed not by fallible systems of human judgement but by infallible directives calculated by scientific measures. The technocratic experiment has, however, functioned to undermine the symbolic dimension implicit in human decision-making. Symbolic modes of relation require commitment, sincerity, narrative continuity, and communication that exceed the instrumental aims of everyday exchange relations.

Subjects grieve the loss of symbolic identity by taking refuge in imaginary identities – fluctuating, hybrid, transient, and virtual modes of identification.[12] Digital space integrates these new identities into its circuitry of drive and capital quite efficiently. It is at this point that the libidinal economy starts to short-circuit. Virtual space eliminates the negativity through which the symbolic field is forged by circumventing the reality of the other. In digital space, subjects attempt to individuate and connect in a realm generated without negativity, of pure information, but fail. In the excess of self-referential exploration, the subject encounters a crisis of desire.

Lack of lack and its consequences

Lacanian psychoanalysis differentiates between desire and drive. Desire can never be fulfilled; it searches endlessly for a sense of jouissance that can never be attained.[13] Lacan explains that desire is always a desire *to desire*. And yet, this is precisely what moves it – its sense of lack and its continual invitation to find new objects to desire. Alternatively, drive attains jouissance through the repetitive process of never reaching it – drive's failure is its success. It runs in a loop. The satisfaction of drive is derived from its repetition. It is in this way that drive *captures* the subject.

The movement of drive is endlessly compatible with capital's imperative of continuous growth. We are always caught in the ceaseless repetition of drive. Now we navigate digital fields designed to make a profit on every microcosmic flicker of its trace. We are confronted with a psychologically sophisticated infrastructure designed and implemented to organise and direct the flows of human energy called drive.

The fullness of digital capture – the vastness and effectiveness of personalised entertainment – tries to remove and distract from lack with the promise that lack

---

11   Fisher, *Capitalist Realism*, 28.

12   Jodi Dean, *Blog Theory: Feedback and Capture in the Circuits of the Drive* (Malden: Polity Press, 2010).

13   Dean, *Blog Theory*, 40.

can be avoided. This system threatens desire because lack, with its emptiness, exists as the creative void through which desire can emerge. Caught in the repetitions of drive, our relation to the other is reduced in its intensity, complexity and closeness. The circuitry of drive in digital space functions through attachment to self-objects. It is as though the libidinal circuitry of the achievement subject remains partially caught in Lacan's mirror stage – trapped in a space of preoccupation with one's own reflection, generating little interest in the other.

The enterprise of influence

Digital space dominates libidinal flows. In the shift from an industrial economy of manual labour to one of self-enterprise and cognitive labour, desire's object of investment becomes not simply economical but also psychological. The market smoothly absorbs desire's imaginal identifications and embraces the rapid and memetic (repetitious) qualities they confer on production.[14] Here, in the height of self-branding, the digital medium, a field of projection, invites the subject to transform herself into a project – an efficient, attractive enterprise of influence. Here, her libidinal investments follow the flows of the market, making the line that delineates her own desire from the desire of production increasingly difficult to decipher.[15]

As our desire aims more and more towards commodities, towards the self as commodity, the social-symbolic fabric loses its grasp on libidinal flows. As relationships organise around the principles of competition, we begin to divest from symbolic objects and overinvest in self-objects that support the self as an enterprise.[16]

Competition, Berardi writes, implies a "risky narcissistic stimulation" – it carries a mythos that reads, "few are chosen, one's individual initiative is the measure of your person."[17] The competitive schema reduces social reality to a stage of performative calculus, effectively flattening relationships to resemble fragmented and thin exchanges of influence. Narcissistic stimulation implies an abandonment of the other and an attitude of betrayal and indifference – it is a process that sacrifices love.[18] At its roots, a narcissistic social structure proves paranoid and deeply insecure. It operates as a libidinal system short-circuiting on its lack of resonance, its excess of positive charge. Suffering from an entanglement of existential insecurity

---

14   Berardi, *The Soul at Work*, 78.
15   Berardi, 24.
16   Berardi, 80.
17   Berardi, 99.
18   Love in the sense of Freud's mature, object-love. See Sigmund Freud, "On Narcissism," in *The Freud Reader*, ed. Peter Gay, trans. James Stratchey, (NY: Norton, 1989), 553.

and economic precarity, Berardi affirms that the principles of a competitive society reduce the collective dimension of human life to a "skeleton of fear and necessity."[19] From within this fearful vision, the achievement subject over-functions, hyper-investing in self-objects to compensate for a lack of symbolic resonance, burning out on fears of rejection and death.

These conditions initiate and demand a state of forgetfulness – they disincentivise contemplation and curiosity by sustaining an aura of hurried distraction. In delineating the West's transition from a disciplinary society to an achievement society, Byung-Chul Han describes the subject of the latter as ruthlessly turning against himself, exhausted and disgusted with having to become himself.[20] This transition involves a collective movement from a superego that instils manifold "should-nots" to a permissive superego (disguised as the absence of one), demanding innumerable "shoulds and cans" – a superego that regiments enjoyment. Han describes the shift from a "disciplinary world of hospitals, madhouses, prisons, barracks and factories" to a "society of fitness, studios, office towers, banks, airports, shopping malls, and genetic laboratories"[21] where salvation is found in the perfection of one's body and the achievements of one's mind.[22]

These systems produce different spiritual crises. Where the obedience subject of a repressive era suffers from a crisis of inauthenticity (how, in one's conformity, does the spirit assert its authentic desire?), the achievement subject suffers a crisis of engulfment (there is never enough time to do all the things I want to do). The crisis confronting the achievement subject is concocted as capital's imperative towards continuous growth seeps into the very structure of one's being. The symptoms of this crisis are well documented – burnout, depression, addiction, difficulties sustaining attention – experiences shaped by a lost relationship to the creativity of desiring-production. Capital's insistence on unceasing growth is fundamentally hostile to the nervous systems and emotional reality of living beings.

Perform and obey

Even as principles of achievement dominate late capitalism's libidinal field, elements of a more repressive obedience society still linger in the libidinal economy of the 21st century. As such, the fears and pathology of both structures play an active role for the achievement subject. Where obedience delimits and represses desire, the achievement paradigm overcodes and paralyses it. Together, these forces create

19   Berardi, *The Soul at Work*, 133.
20   Han, *The Burnout Society*, 8.
21   Han, 8.
22   Lasch, *The Culture of Narcissism*, 42.

an overwhelming need to *do* something, paired with an uncertainty about authentic action. Here, we oscillate between blindly striving and numbing out.

Christopher Lasch explains in his *Culture of Narcissism* that our transition into a permissive society supplants the parental superego with a harsh, punitive superego that, in the absence of social prohibitions, derives its psychic energy from the destructive, aggressive impulses within the id.[23] This new superego of compulsory enjoyment demands adherence to the rules of social intercourse but neglects to ground these rules in a transcendent moral code. Lasch sees this failure as encouraging self-absorption.[24] Han's demonstration of the achievement subjectivity echoes Lasch's analysis on this front – both describe a subject competing incessantly with oneself, becoming one's own judge and victim. This subject subscribes to a regime of excessive self-monitoring in the absence of objective morality.

Disciplining the nervous system

Lasch suspects that the "self" emerging in these conditions is plagued by a pervasive sense of inner emptiness.[25] He identifies the pathologies of this new self in anxiety, depression, grandiosity, and infantilism. Modern psychiatry might typify these attributes with schemas of "personality disorders," a label commonly prescribed by psychiatrists working with populations who attend addiction treatment programs. Lasch describes a swarm of lost souls navigating an increasingly hostile, complex, and unforgiving world, surviving on false pride and compensation. Rootless, groundless, disoriented, and lonely human beings are often the type who find themselves repetitively involved with substances – external objects that silence the internal noise. Addiction lies on the other side of achievement on the coin of competitive society. It is no coincidence that addictive repetitions are capital's preferred mode of accumulation. Addiction plays many roles in a competitive society – it soothes, sedates, enhances, and stimulates; it gives one an "edge" over their competitor; it compensates and distracts from a lack of meaning. For example, dependence on stimulants to attend to the demands of daily life functions as an invisible, normalised, collective practice. The use of sedatives to come down, numb, and forget is similarly accepted as an essential fixture in surviving the drudgery of late capitalism.

Ottessa Moshfegh's 2018 novel *My Year of Rest and Relaxation* gracefully denaturalises these conditions by pushing them to excess.[26] Moshfegh's unnamed 26-year-

---

23   Lasch, 40.

24   Lasch, 42.

25   Lasch, 42.

26   Ottessa Moshfegh, *My Year of Rest and Relaxation* (NY: Penguin Press, 2019).

old cosmopolitan and artistically disillusioned protagonist responds to the achievement society's demands by foreclosing the possibility of achievement altogether. Sticking to a year of psychotropic-induced sleep and delirium, punctuated by quick trips to the corner store, she embraces abjection by disavowing productive existence and contemporary expectations. In her desire for self-annihilation and sleep, this protagonist embodies the unrecognised, fantasised desire for an end to striving for many. She is "taking some time off" from existence itself.

The secret desire Moshfegh's protagonist taps into – the desire to opt-out, refuse enjoyment, refuse self-promotion, refuse achievement subjectivity – is activated by a profound sense of alienation and rebellion. Moshfegh's protagonist finds comfort in refusal, finally asserting some agency. In choosing isolation and purposelessness, she avoids inevitable failures – collapsed ideals, dreams, and goals despite great effort and hard work.[27] By disentangling herself from the achievement paradigm, Moshfegh's protagonist seeks death but also aims for recalibration. Sleeping all day and night with few breaks, she reflects, "I was finally doing something that really mattered. Sleep felt productive ... when I'd slept enough, I'd be okay. I'd be renewed, reborn."[28] This image recalls Jonathan Crary's idea that sleep exists as an "uncompromising interruption of the theft of time from us by capitalism" and thus remains a site of crisis in the global market as it cannot be colonised to produce anything of value (although sleep apps and pharmaceuticals are beginning to change that).[29]

Sleep is a rare opportunity where the achievement subject is not forced to consciously grapple with guilt. The guilt characteristic of an achievement society is not the same as existential guilt, derived from living in bad faith. Rather, this kind of guilt is an instrumentalised, neurotic form of guilt that fuels the performance principle. This neurotic form of guilt antagonises the process of desiring. Having nothing to do with symbolic law, neurotic guilt is precisely what kills desire.[30] Lacan considers guilt for the obsessional neurotic as fundamentally plagued by a crisis of desire.[31] Moshfegh's protagonist is specifically anti-achievement in that she does not see her self-imposed isolation as surrendering to the death drive or an escape from guilt; instead, it is a life-affirming project of self-preservation through hibernation – a recognition of human limitation and an attempt "to save [one's] own life."[32]

---

27   Moshfegh, *My Year*, 14.

28   Moshfegh, 51.

29   Jonathan Crary, *Late Capitalism and the Ends of Sleep* (NY: Verso, 2013), 10.

30   Jacques Lacan, *Seminar V: Formations of the Unconscious. July 2, 1958: You are the One You Hate*, trans. Cormac Gallagher (London: Karnac Books, 2002), 373.

31   Lacan, *Seminar V*.

32   Moshfegh, *My Year*, 7.

The crisis of the symbolic as a crisis of desire

While plenty has been written about individuals wishing to drop off the grid and escape the complexity of capitalist and digital life, Moshfegh's protagonist does not opt-out in search of enlightenment, symbolic restoration, or self-understanding.[33] Instead, she seeks the absolute destruction of her consciousness – a system of programmed drives and alienated aspirations. Submerged in a cocktail of benzodiazepines, tranquilisers, and hypnotics, Moshfegh's protagonist repeats watching the same few films on mute, orders excessive amounts of Chinese delivery and shops for lingerie online. In her attempts to stave off desire, its truth returns in strange symptoms: packages delivered to her door and confused voicemails responding to her winding, incoherent, emphatic voice messages. Moshfegh is clear: desire insists. Her protagonist's unsuccessful mission to erase herself resembles an attempt at symbolic death. This protagonist is not unlike Sophocles' Antigone, existing in the realm between two deaths.[34] Self-exile, disavowal of the erotic, pharmaceutical-induced sleep – Moshfegh's protagonist manufactures a system of symptoms that signal collapse at the level of the symbolic order.

The horror of deterritorialisation

The social field produced by deterritorialisation exists in a realm between two deaths. With disintegration of symbolic networks of kinship, we are exposed to the horror of living among each other without meaningful communication, social-symbolic identity or collective rites. Deterritorialisation is the process of unveiling or demystifying the aspects of existence that sustained an element of mystery or profundity in premodern and modern societies. We can think of this process as occurring in three stages – in three narcissistic injuries to human-centric ontologies. Freud himself recognised these consecutive insults to human narcissism in the Copernican revolution's decentring of the universe, Darwin's decentralisation of life in evolutionary biology, and, finally, in the decentring of thinking in his theory of the unconscious.[35]

The horror of deterritorialisation is witnessed in Michel Houellebecq's novel *Serotonin*.[36] Here, the narrator, Florent-Claude Labrouste, a depressed agricultural

---

33   For example, Tao Lin's *Leave Society* (2021) or John Krakauer's *Into the Wild* (1996).

34   Slavoj Žižek, *The Ticklish Subject: The Absent Centre of Political Ontology* (London: Verso, 1999), 170.

35   Samo Tomšič, *The Capitalist Unconscious: Marx and Lacan* (London: Verso, 2015), 86.

36   Michel Houellebecq, *Serotonin* (NY: Farrar, Straus and Giroux, 2019).

scientist, spends his days mourning the "disappearance of the Western Libido,"[37] which is at once the loss of his desire and a loss occurring in a world stripped of its erotic quality, subsisting as a "neutral surface without relief or attraction."[38] Where Moshfegh's protagonist seeks an end to the tyranny of her desire, Houellebecq's narrator struggles to accept what he senses as the ultimate defeat of eros – desire's extinction by a fundamentally demystified and de-eroticised world.

Negotiating the forces of global capitalism, Labrouste exiles himself from society and drifts from Paris to rural France, bearing witness to the eruption of class conflict and enduring the plague of loneliness that engulfs him. Placated with manufactured neurotransmitters, Labrouste personifies a libidinal economy organised by the principles of nihilism. He sees his misery conditioned in a complex world populated by simple natures and spends the novel eulogising the lost fantasy of eros. Nostalgia for a more vital moment in time is a motif common to Houellebecq's work, but in *Serotonin*, he is most explicit: the West is suffering a collapse of the erotic, and this loss is directly related to foreclosed meaning-making systems that exist outside or beyond consumer capitalism.

Desiring misery

Various thinkers have attempted to express the contemporary experience in which human beings suffer the loss of a libidinal glue to hold us together at the level of meaning and affect. In his analysis of the capitalist libidinal economy, Bernard Stiegler refers to this state as one of "symbolic misery." Symbolic misery describes the annulment of singularity and the elimination of desire – a subjection of "existence to subsistence."[39] For Stiegler, the symbolic exists as a logical and semiotic horizon that conditions a circuit of sensibility, which is the principle process in unfolding individuation.[40] We can also think of symbolic misery as a collective experience of soullessness, drawing on Berardi's understanding of the soul as a container of affective and libidinal forces that "weave together a world of attentiveness: the ability to address, care and appeal to one another."[41]

This process appears frequently in Žižek's work on the decline of symbolic efficiency or what he sometimes describes as the crisis of the big Other.[42] The decline

---

37   Houellebecq, 286.

38   Houellebecq, 304.

39   Bernard Stiegler, *Symbolic Misery, Volume 2: The Katastropē of the Sensible* (Cambridge: Polity Press, 2015), 119.

40   Stiegler, 31.

41   Berardi, *The Soul at Work*, 10.

42   Slavoj Žižek, *For They Do Not Know What They Do: Enjoyment as a Political Factor* (NY: Verso, 1991).

of symbolic efficiency is a process through which meanings from cultural memory are extracted from social systems, commodified and projected through the logic of exchange as opaque fragments of humanity's lost relationship to higher orders of metaphysical, spiritual, and social significance. At the experiential level, this appears in the loss of ritual, ceremony, and rites-of-passage. Conditions of declining symbolic efficiency heighten doubt with regard to expressions of sincerity, belief, and desire. This doubt leads to apathy, which sustains a kind of denarrativised life, like that of Houellebecq's narrator, who is exhausted with having to live a life "deprived of reasons to live and reasons to die."[43] Without external realities to cast down meaning from beyond, the subject retreats inward, perhaps seeking psychotropic relief to avoid falling into a state of complete and abject despair.

The crisis of desire constitutive of both Moshfegh and Houellebecq's protagonists is a function of a symbolic collapse occurring at a particular historical moment of ambient fatalism and withdrawal. Central to this collapse is the loss of the ability to believe. Stiegler regards the "liquidation of belief by capitalism" as a process that initiates the "liquidation of desire."[44] Beliefs operate as intimate pacts between subjects and the big Other, so that the contingency, incompleteness and incoherence of the Real can be concealed and, thus, tolerated. These pacts are undermined by scientism and scepticism and general processes of deterritorialisation.[45] Without belief, subjects get trapped in an infinite loop of drive and encounter fewer opportunities towards individuation. The call to *become* within the context of the other and the beyond can be avoided.

Lacking opportunities to individuate, we forget how to desire.[46] Unsure of how to use this muscle, we look to cultural authorities to tell us how and what to desire. To our despair, or perhaps relief, we are instructed to turn away, shut down, numb out. Indeed, Houellebecq's Labrouste laments, "civilization just dies of weariness, of self-disgust – what could social democracy offer me? Nothing of course, just the perpetuation of absence, a call to oblivion."[47]

Stiegler sees symbolic misery as the loss of "aesthetic participation."[48] He describes the loss of the producer's working knowledge (technical skills) and the consumer's deprivation of the opportunity to participate in "aesthetic occurrence" as a consequence of work's transformation by machines, starting in the 19th century.[49]

---

43   Houellebecq, *Serotonin*, 73–74.

44   Bernard Stiegler, *The Lost Spirit of Capitalism* (Malden: Polity Press, 2014), 12.

45   Slavoj Žižek, *Looking Awry: An Introduction to Jacques Lacan Through Popular Culture* (Cambridge: MIT Press, 1991), 71.

46   Lasch, *The Culture of Narcissism*, 40.

47   Houellebecq, *Serotonin*, 137.

48   Stiegler, *Symbolic Misery*, 23.

49   Stiegler, 23.

This leaves the subject excluded from circuits of sensibility and the process of individuation. Individuation, for Stiegler, is a process entailing continuous yet contingent generative expressive acts. In these acts, she (the subject) is always more than herself. This excess is the "very manifestation of her existence," in which she becomes what she is by exteriorising herself, which is also to say, exclaiming herself. As she exclaims the "sensational singularity," she participates in creating desire.[50]

This "exclamation," following lack's transformation into excess and the positing of an object of desire, is a pathway through the "circuit of affects," weaving "the motives" of psychosocial individuation. Symbolic misery blocks this process as soon as individuals have become "indifferent to the flux," nihilistic about expression's potential, inhibited, without a vision for the "sensational singularities" that persist and often without the motivation to understand why. Such misery is born of the human's relegation to that of an assistant or appendage to machines and her internalisation of an inferior or redundant position.

The model of capitalism under analysis here is akin to what Stiegler calls the aesthetico-libidinal model of capitalism – a system that consumes libidinal energy to reproduce itself in channels (for decoded flows) designed with limits and controls. This system is an effective manager of libidinal flows. We are managed through the seduction of our attention. Inhabiting this system creates the fear of becoming redundant, if not totally "burdensome" – statuses imbued with a sense of economic insecurity and existential anxiety. Houellebecq depicts the heights of such anxiety in *Serotonin* with the collision between French farmers, facing redundancy in a world of globalised free trade, and France's riot police.[51] Labrouste fixates on the suicidality of the farmers as it parallels his own. While the former represents a crisis in material and political life – industries collapsing in a hostile, deregulated market – the latter marks a spiritual collapse, a deflated reaction to social-symbolic redundancy, a nihilism symptomatic of a crisis of meaninglessness. Houellebecq connects the same process that outsources production to countries with fewer labour protections, lowering the cost of production, so is libidinal energy outsourced to technological devices to lower the intensity of affect encountered in the Real. Production's intimacy is hidden away in free-trade zones and digital networks so that we can safely experience consumption and emotion without encountering its entire truth.

---

50   Stiegler, 42.
51   Houellebecq, *Serotonin*, 217–225.

A realm between two deaths

In conditions of symbolic misery, ideals held in the past seem to disintegrate under any close examination and the project of imagining new ideals to replace them and motivate action feels overwhelming. Nostalgia feels cheap, tired, and unsatisfying, while the terror of the climate crisis compromises aspirational visions of the future. Without an object of desire (an object of libidinal investment that presupposes a future reward), there is little left to bind the particular to the universal, humans to each other or the present to future. Lasch sees the "widespread loss of confidence in the future" as generated by the fact that competitive society leaves the working class in a state of "living for the present" where a "desperate concern for personal survival, sometimes disguised as hedonism," grips the population.[52] Here, in the space between symbolic and material death, time contracts to produce a series of tedious, denarrativised, discontinuous presents.

The disruption of the COVID-19 pandemic brought parts of collective grief to consciousness. Many lost material security or toiled in "essential" jobs for poverty wages. Some others, with access to more resources, seemed to embrace self-isolation and enjoy the novelty of disruption. There was comfort in seeing one's internal fear and private chaos manifest in the external world as a shared, collective phenomenon. Suspended in crisis mode, we could now witness those around us reflecting on the lack of meaning endemic to their lifestyle and question its ultimate aims. In the first few dream-like weeks of the pandemic, we saw celebrities and social media influencers publicly confronting existential questions of aloneness, meaninglessness, and non-being. This was a moment in the haze of uncertainty, a softening of the performance principle, consumer excess, and achievement imperatives. While transiting a world-historic moment, subjects were invited to share a purely digital, fragmented, and incoherent (imaginary) form of solidarity.

Within the privileged class, the opportunity to obey government orders, practice solidarity, and perform a Social Good simply by staying home, cancelling plans, and spending time with loved ones fulfilled an inner wish. The ability to spend time with one's family, in the garden or practising hobbies was restored, granting the achievement subject an opportunity to opt-out guilt free and take a vacation from injunctions to perform, develop, succeed, etc. Still, it did not take long for the imperatives of achievement and obedience to creep back into social conscience (see, for example, Figure 1). Subjects were encouraged to use this pandemic as an "opportunity" to learn a new skill (coding, graphic design), start a side hustle (online business) or finish a project they are working on (the manuscript, the cookbook, the home renovation, etc.).

---

52   Lasch, *The Culture of Narcissism*, 129.

Jeremy Haynes
@TheJeremyHaynes

If you don't come out of this
quarantine with either:

1.) a new skill
2.) starting what you've been putting
off like a new business
3.) more knowledge

You didn't ever lack the time, you
lacked the discipline

4:38 AM · April 3, 2020

3K Retweets   **12.6K** Likes

Figure 1: Tweet by Jeremy Haynes, April 3, 2020
(https://twitter.com/TheJeremyHaynes/status/12
45767684484202496).

The people desired quarantine?

Wilhelm Reich famously understood that desire aims at its own domination. It was
with this formulation that he asserted, controversially, that the people desired fascism.[53] By extension, we can posit that, exhausted by the performance principle and
competitive society, the people desired quarantine. The months and years preceding
COVID-19's viral disruption were characterised by accelerating political and affective feedback loops – a tireless sprint towards sense-making in an increasingly complex media environment. The working class subsisted by perpetually treading water
in the infinite depths of debt, and the professional-managerial and entrepreneurial
classes contended with mechanistic and meaningless striving. Those permitted to
self-isolate found their life structured by a kind of leisurely obedience: stay home,
teach yourself how to earn an income online, self-brand, grow your influence.

   Elevation of a cosy, private, and self-focused lifestyle to the status of fulfilling
a kind of dire social obligation let the achievement subject forego all the corporeal
complexities of solidarity to discover an isolated, obedient, and performative form
of solidarity in negativity: the removal of possibility rather than its affirmation. This
total separation of public and private is, however, a privilege exclusive to cognitive

---

53   Wilhelm Reich, *Mass Psychology of Fascism* (NY: Farrar, Straus and Giroux, 1970).

258 Libidinal Economies of Crisis Times

labour – society organised around a division between those who "worked from home" and those who served the people who worked from home. Those workers deemed "essential" (from fast food workers to medical staff), and those living paycheque to paycheque or laid off, could not experience the self-congratulatory enjoyment of the former category. This class became removed from others whose very "existence became a factor of insecurity."[54]

On this level, the pandemic revealed a truth of material deprivation. Self-isolation measures exposed whether or not one's living conditions were genuinely liveable. People in cities discovered their reliance on public or private-public spaces (coffee shops, bars) to avoid spending time in small, overpriced, dilapidated housing. The decade-long housing crisis in most major cities that forces workers to accept run-down, close quarters for more than half a month's earnings came into sharp focus. You could no longer deny that, for those living in cosmopolitan environments, private, personal space is reserved for the wealthy. Realities of class – divisions of labour, distributions of space – became impossible to ignore. Further, the intrusions were not simply material. Crises of capitalism are responded to with increasingly intimate forms of colonisation. It is not only the space of one's home or car that exchanges of capital have gained access to, but now, intrusions are made into one's internal landscape – psychic space is for sale.

Monetised intimacy

As previously mentioned, capital responds to crises by breaching boundaries, extending its appropriative efforts towards capturing new resources. Seeking eternal, continuous growth, capital targets natural resources like water and air, in addition to social resources like care and attention to extract a profit. Stiegler affirms that "capturing and harnessing libidinal energy is now the basis of capitalism."[55] As public space continues to wither and private entities envelop further territory, intimate space – regions that contain one's inner experience – become sites of monetisation. This means that the loss of public space is accompanied by an additional loss of intimate, private space. For example, customised advertising tracks and influences our individual and collective patterns of free association. As a result, space – space to think, dream, and live outside a commodified schema – is difficult to come by. It must be intentionally cultivated. Personal space, both internal and external, have become sites of privilege.

Digital platforms like Uber, Airbnb and OnlyFans permit the public to enter the very fabric of one's private world. These instruments allow the space of one's vehicle,

---

54   Berardi, *The Soul at Work*, 104.
55   Stiegler, *The Lost Spirit*, 29.

home, and body to integrate seamlessly with monetisation. The economic relations between public consumers and private contractors are brokered by corporations that offer immaterial supports (i.e., platforms) for transactions involving material elements. Despite the lack of labour protections or guaranteed income, the people offering these services often defend the platforms that host them, citing the freedom these new flexible economic relationships afford. Someone working an eight-hour shift in the service industry might spend three to four hours driving people around in their vehicle for Uber or delivering food on their bicycle before retiring for the night. The flexibility of the gig economy makes exploitation much smoother. It entertains no threat of organised labour and avoids all accountability for its workers. This system allows statisticians to exclaim that unemployment has decreased based on the fact that people are working two or three jobs simultaneously. Precarious labour in the gig economy comprises most of the new jobs in the post-2008 market. This new arrangement profits greatly on the structure of the achievement subject. Reliance on income generated through these increasingly intimate services only intensifies in moments of crisis, as indicated by labour trends following the 2008 economic recession and COVID-19 pandemic.

Peer-to-peer services overcode the intimate sphere with transactional relationships. Several years ago, after losing my housing, I stayed a few nights in an Airbnb room rented out to me by a young family. The house was modest, just outside city limits, and the room I had rented was across the hall from the parents' bedroom. On my way out one morning, I found the father feeding his toddler breakfast in the kitchen. I sipped coffee as he explained how renting out their spare room through Airbnb generated the necessary income that allowed the family to pay their mortgage in the hostile housing market of the Greater Vancouver area. This transaction was not unlike typical rent relationships except for the nature of the guests. The family hosting me accepted a different set of strangers into their home on a nightly basis – they continually shared their home with people they had not personally vetted or known in the slightest. My stay was one of many intrusions into their intimate sphere. I speculated that this kind of anonymous exchange occurred multiple times a week and risked subjection to considerable discomfort, and, at the very least, the underlying stress that comes with the loss of truly intimate, uninterrupted privacy.

For such intrusions into the intimate sphere to remain tolerable and continue, everyday life must undergo a kind of gradual de-eroticisation. The life instinct must be educated towards death, towards conformity to mechanical, polite modes of interaction. Deleuze and Guatarri famously identified that "what civilised modern societies deterritorialise with one hand they reterritorialise with the other."[56] The compulsion to enjoy – enjoy oneself, one's neighbour, enjoy one's exploitation – operates

56   Gilles Deleuze and Félix Guattari, *Anti-Oedipus: Capitalism and Schizophrenia*, trans. Robert Hurley, Mark Seem, and Helen R. Lane (London: Penguin Books, 1977), 257.

in response to an erosion of the symbolic and erotic dimension of collective life. Dissociation from the rhythms and emotion of the body and elevation of the mind to the site of all "motivation, competition, optimization and initiative"[57] effectively sanitises the libidinal economy of all its less governable attributes. That we manage to accommodate the intimate intrusions of technocratic survival labour so diligently implies our internalisation of capital's mandate to disregard interruptions of personal desire in favour of a more consistent, machinic sensibility. The body has been excluded in this formulation (an impossibility), but exists as an instrument, mediated through digital forms. It is here that we encounter a systematic reduction of desire to drive.

OnlyFans started as a digital platform designed to enable celebrities and influencers to share exclusive content with paying subscribers (one-to-one conversations, photos, videos). It quickly morphed into a platform selling exclusive access to content produced by sex workers. These workers noticed that OnlyFans offered a safe way to garner a following, receive payments for content, and avoid otherwise unsafe working conditions. In February 2020, the platform hosted the content of 200,000 creators. Over the course of the COVID-19 pandemic, migration of workers to the platform was exponential. In March 2020 alone, OnlyFans reported 3.5 million new signups, 60,000 of which were content creators.[58] By May 2020, the platform's chief operating officer announced that the site saw 200,000 new users sign up every 24 hours.[59] This movement occurred in step with labour's split between the work-from-home-crowd and the "essential workers." Naturally, precarious workers caught in the middle of this chasm searched for new income streams. Navigating the wave of uncertainty introduced by the pandemic, one content creator explained, "OnlyFans is the best way to make money, period right now, unless you have a normal 9 to 5 job that you're working from home."[60] What, then, does the labour of a content creator involve?

The content creator exemplifies the tenets of achievement subjectivity. Creators are rewarded highly for directing all libidinal investment towards self-objects. Posting and sending explicit images to subscribers requires dedicated and daily attention to your appearance, the messages in your phone from fans and, as one user explains, 45 minutes of prep (hair, makeup, etc.), a photo session of up to 300 photos (narrowed down to ten), and time strategising whom to send what to.[61] This form of

---

57   Byung-Chul Han, *Psychopolitics: Neoliberalism and New Technologies of Power*, trans. Erik Butler (NY: Verso Books, 2017), 39.

58   Annie Vainshtein, "Coronavirus Took Their Jobs Away. OnlyFans Let These Bay Area People Monetize Themselves," *San Francisco Chronicle*, April 4, 2020.

59   Otillia Steadman, "Everyone is Making Porn at Home Now. Will the Porn Industry Survive?" *Buzzfeed News*, May 6, 2020.

60   Vainshtein, Coronavirus Took."

61   Vainshtein, "Coronavirus Took."

sex work circumvents the possible transience, "rough treatment," and dependence on male authority characteristic of other forms of transactional intimacy.[62] Still, the exchange does not wholly liberate workers from economic insecurity nor does it offer any kind of labour protections. Digital sex workers share a fundamentally precarious structure of success based on a "never ending necessity of seducing the public and men anew" with all sex workers.[63] Moreover, digitally mediated sex work does not do away with intrusions of biopower in the slightest. While not imposing the exact extent of biopolitical control asserted by previous iterations of procurers, pimps, and madams, for example, OnlyFans, as a platform, exercises what Byung-Chul Han defines as smart power over its users by inviting them endlessly to share and participate in the generation of profit.[64] Work and life are indistinguishable – becoming a mingled stream of desirable output, an unending effort to concoct images to lure and sustain attention. OnlyFans takes a staggering 20% of all earnings generated by creators who depend on its infrastructure to host their content. Han explains that by operating as a permissive force, smart power intends to *guide* subjects' will rather than forbidding or depriving it.[65] It does this seductively, with the promise of pleasing and fulfilling subjects – smart power aims not to make subjects compliant but *dependent*.[66]

After witnessing two world wars, Simone de Beauvoir identifies in *The Second Sex* how the exchange of sexual services for money "only increases during wars and subsequent social disorders."[67] De Beauvoir points out that it is not any particular moral or psychological situation that makes sex work challenging to bear but the hostile material conditions – navigating the exploitation of pimps and madams, the spectre of poverty, and bodily risks – that make this kind of exchange most brutal.[68] She describes a specific form of sex work that is now, just as it was when she was writing, reserved for the most vulnerable and exploited classes. To highlight this fact, she opposes this hostile form of sex work with the exchanges undertaken by the hetaira, an ancient Greek courtesan much like the geishas of Japan. The hetaira endeavours to generate income and recognition for herself as a singularity – de Beauvoir uses this term to designate "all women who treat not only their bodies but their entire personalities as capital to be exploited."[69] Movie stars epitomised this category at the time of de Beauvoir's writing.[70] In a society dominated by self-enterprising and

62   Simone de Beauvoir, *The Second Sex*, trans. H. M. Parshley (NY: Vintage Books, 1974), 622.
63   De Beauvoir, *The Second Sex*, 635.
64   Han, *Psychopolitics*, 33.
65   Han, 33.
66   Han, 34.
67   De Beauvoir, *The Second Sex*, 623.
68   De Beauvoir, 629.
69   De Beauvoir, 631.
70   De Beauvoir, 630.

spectacle, the class of hetairas has been democratised. We are all invited to transform ourselves into living capital.

The synthesis of capital and persona embodied by the influencer culminates in the total monetisation of the subject. OnlyFans attracts influencers who already possess a large social media following and recognise the chance to monetise themselves at a significantly higher price point. As experts of the attention economy, the influencer "seeks to captivate the world for [their] own profit"[71] – given the tools afforded by the platforms that host them, influencers are incentivised to entrance a mass of anonymous admirers from whom they can extract a profit. Their cult of personality grows in step with their magnetic pull for brand partnerships.

The influencer is compelled to organise the day's activities in conformity to the performance principle. No intimate moment can remain uncaptured, wasted or unobserved – all is ripe with potential to stimulate interest and exact attention. The influencer exists as a digital canvas by integrating brand messages into a stream of intimate self-stylisations, not unlike websites that generate profit by selling ad space. Within this synthesis of capital and persona, life oscillates between work-like leisure and play-like work. The self is indistinguishable from objects of consumption – one's phone exists as a medium of entangled business correspondence, intimate exchanges, communicative capitalism and personal enjoyment. The economic conditions experienced by OnlyFans content creators exemplify the economic conditions that await workers in general. Economic relations of the future will exhibit similarly smooth, intimate transactional dynamics that incorporate the worker's whole being.

Parasocial jouissance

Transactions of digital intimacy are becoming more and more common.[72] The pandemic's restructuring of the libidinal economy accelerated the process of disinvestment from external objects (people, places, things) and intensified investment in digital self-objects. This process intensified the popularity of parasocial relationships. Parasocial relationships are nonreciprocal but involve two parties: a performer and an audience[73] – celebrity worship is considered the parasocial's

---

71   De Beauvoir, 632.

72   Consider the popularity of mental health apps like BetterHelp, an online counselling platform that simultaneously offers text message–based therapy while selling its users' data to Facebook. Thomas Germain, "Mental Health Apps Aren't as Private as You Think," Consumer Reports, March 2, 2021, https://www.consumerreports.org/health-privacy/mental-health-apps-and-user-privacy-a7415198244/.

73   Donald Horton and R. Richard Wohl, "Mass Communication and Para-Social Interaction: Observations on Intimacy at a Distance," Psychiatry 19, no. 3 (1956).

original form. Parasocial relations can be understood as reterritorialising attempts to inhabit the meaning and security afforded by the big Other by relating to another human being. Universal cravings for interpellation cause us to search for the presence of an Other who can, in a generalised, objectified way, confer symbolic identification onto us.[74] The big Other is precisely the object through which desire is coordinated and symbolic certainty is achieved – Žižek explains that this object functions as a "retroactive illusion," structuring social reality and masking "the contingency of the Real."[75] In flight from this traumatic void at the centre of subjectivity, the parasocial supports the fantasy of omnipotence on behalf of the performer and fosters a fantasy of belonging on behalf of the audience, producing a feedback loop of projection, satisfaction, and simulation – smooth interpellation with reduced interpersonal risk.

Parasocial relationships facilitate the development of an audience's attachment to an idolised object without any of the risk involved in intimate attachment to an other. The performer is attached to reflections of her own image – using the audience as a mirror through which she can refine and instrumentalise her image. From this perspective – of the streamer, podcaster, influencer, or poster – content produced is consumed and discussed by an anonymous mass.[76] Content creators vary in how they choose to address their audience. Some employ a register of affectation, some react with disdain or pity, and some express immense gratitude. Similarly, the attachment a follower has to a performer also varies. A follower may not admire or even like the person they follow. They might derive a kind of parasocial jouissance in the repetitive engagement with and curiosity about a performer to whom they feel magnetised.

Nonetheless, both parties enjoy this simulative relation, whose attachments are organised on purely projective terms. Parasocial dynamics serve as a primary mode through which human intimacy can be simulated and monetised. Through the parasocial, the isolated achievement subject, suffering in an "epidemic of loneliness," finds human conversation, humour, information, entertainment, and understanding. She can stand in relation to the other without sacrificing control over her image. She can *feel* seen without taking on the risk of *being* seen. Still, she possesses some awareness that this relationship is not complete. It falls short on the basis of stimulating drive by failing to fulfil desire.

Within the parasocial, we are at once both too close and too far away. This mode sharpens proximity and erases boundaries. The distance that characterised previous

---

74   Žižek, *For They*, 109.

75   Žižek, 71.

76   Referring to Twitch and other streaming platforms, podcasts with a large following like True Anon, Red Scare, Chapo Trap House or the Adam Friedland Show, Instagram, YouTube and other image-based apps, and Twitter, respectively.

iterations of the parasocial – celebrity worship, identification with a film or sports star – has been dissolved. Performers are no longer creative producers but exhibitionists and entrepreneurs of personality. Verging on a state of overproximity, the whole existence of the performer is sought after as a site of projection. One's habits, hobbies, products used, emotional life, inner world – every detail is rendered relevant and potentially monetisable. An influencer's "personal brand" might attract "brand collaborations" from mindfulness apps, clothing companies, meal delivery or online therapy services, audiobook apps, etc. Thus, her appearance, the food she eats, the entertainment she consumes, and the moods she feels are sites of value. Capital mediates the entire relationship between performer and audience. If it is not the more indirect insertion of brand advertisements into an influencer's photos and videos, it is the direct transaction of capital for subscriptions to exclusive content. The influencer must internalise the notion that in a parasocial culture, "creation of the self" functions as the most rewarded form of creativity.[77]

While the possibility for self-creation via constructing a "personal brand" may release the individual ego into a zone of freedom vis-à-vis commodification, these relations are organised based on projections that alienate and distract one from the truth of one's experience. While the subject's hyper-commodification under conditions of communicative capitalism may appear as aesthetic and expressive freedom in a permissive society, the limits of this freedom, contingent on the capitalist mode of production, dictate that true freedom of self-determination remains unavailable. The achievement subject is self-abandoning, compelled to generate economic obedience in a culture obsessed with the signification of achievement.

TFW no internal good objects

This economic model of libidinal organisation attracts and sustains the psychological structures that benefit it. In turn, it also reproduces and intensifies these structures through a system of rewards. With so much libidinal investment in self-objects, two dominant and complementary psychological structures prevail. The achievement model rewards narcissistic performance and accommodates schizoid states – these being two sides of the same coin. For decades, psychoanalysts, beginning with Freud, have speculated on the shared characteristics of schizoid and narcissistic structures. Freud begins his essay *On Narcissism* with comments about the paraphrenic's "withdrawal of libido from people and things in the external

---

77   Lasch, *The Culture of Narcissism*, 168.

world."[78] It is from these reflections that we have come to understand how the schizoid structure replaces external objects with internal objects.

A person operating from a schizoid position has "renounced objects" – objects that exist as internalisations of external objects perceived from the position of a "neutral observer" or "detached spectator."[79] This internalisation of object relations links narcissism to the schizoid condition. Object relations theorist Harry Guntrip affirms this link, listing narcissism as one of the key attributes of the schizoid type. As with narcissism, the schizoid's love objects exist inside himself.[80] We can think about narcissism more neutrally as simply "the ego itself cathected with libido"[81] – a plane of self-objects. These two structures, the narcissist and the schizoid, mirror one another and work together to produce a short-circuiting parasocial feedback loop that reinforces investments in the ego-libido. The parasocial exists as a kind of short-circuit in the libidinal economy, sustained on the promise of fame and belonging – a promise of love. Generated by the energy of drive, this relation is experienced as repetitive, addictive, empty, and inherently unsatisfying.

Positioned as an object to be incorporated into the schizoid's subjectivity, the narcissist prepares their "nervous system as an active receiving terminal for as much time as possible."[82] Podcasters, streamers, and Youtubers know that the more content they produce, the more engagement they receive and the more capital they accrue. The influencer or online performer reveals personal information, thoughts, ideas, and imagery to invite viewers into their inner world and, thus, to identify with them. To effectively sell a form of intimacy, the performer must also invest significant libidinal energy towards internal objects. The self is configured as a vessel of confession and disclosure – internal objects are commodities to seduce the attention of others.

Freud writes that the narcissist's charm exists in his "self-contentment and inaccessibility."[83] The narcissist wants to be loved – they crave the other's desire and validation not as an act of craving the other but as an effort to incorporate the other as a good internal object. Narcissistic desire aims towards adoration at a distance.

---

78   Referring to "paraphrenia," Freud's term for what Bleuler termed "schizophrenia." "Para" meaning "beside," "apart from," or "beyond," and "phrenia" meaning "mind." Similarly, we might interpret "parasocial" to mean "beyond the social" – a social relation that does away with the Real of the social to enter a zone of pure identification and projection – an Imaginary social. See Freud, *On Narcissism*, 546.

79   Harry Guntrip, *Schizoid Phenomena, Object Relations and the Self* (NY: International Universities Press Inc., 1969), 18.

80   Guntrip, 42.

81   Sigmund Freud, "Civilization and Its Discontents," in *The Freud Reader*, ed. Peter Gay, trans. James Strachey (NY: Norton, 1989), 753.

82   Berardi, *The Soul at Work*, 90.

83   Freud, *On Narcissism*, 555.

It functions best when faced with thousands, if not millions, of anonymous "follow-ers" with whom one interacts with on a purely generalised, imaginary basis. This simulation of intimate relating allows the performer to avoid the other's gaze – they are left gazing and speaking to their own image, directing their affectation towards an abstract base of admirers. They interact with an abstracted gaze, a mirror. The schizoid stares at his own reflection as well, relating to the performer as an object to be incorporated into the self. They stare in one another's direction but gaze past each other.

This can go on forever, but it does not lead to the process of individuation. It is by passing through the gaze of the other, encountering the negativity of the other, that we individuate. For example, if we did not receive the gaze of our mother, our first (caregiving) other, as infants, we spend considerable energy through the remainder of our lives searching for the mother's gaze in everything we encounter. We act out, entertain, seduce. We fix our efforts on attracting surrogate gazes – those abstracted gazes mediated by the spectacle. The endeavour ultimately fails to meet the need for recognition because it does not incorporate the negativity necessary to water the seeds of individuation.[84]

Just as the narcissist hunts for others to incorporate as internal objects, the schizoid searches for an object that excites him, that he can pursue and draw away from at will, should the object attempt to engulf him.[85] Both prefer to instru-mentalise the other to derive satisfaction from a comfortable distance. While the schizoid hungers after intimacy, he fears the loss of his ego (engulfment) and thus finds his ideal object in the "desired deserter" with whom he can withdraw when the threat of his desire (the object's desire) becomes overwhelming.[86] The schizoid is relatively content to incorporate the generalised, projected desire of performers into his internal landscape. His libidinal investments are concentrated and manipulated within the intimate object par excellence: the personal smartphone.

Parasocial dynamics are a response to a social field organised by competition, performance, and fragmentation. In varying degrees, we are all called to withdraw our libido from the external world to invest in digital self-objects. The compulsive online exchange of intimacy compensates but does not resolve a social-symbolic cri-sis of desire.

---

84   It is worth speculating on the impact of a father's absence here as well. The father's gaze also aids and guides the process of individuation. The father is a primary other, a social-symbolic avatar – perhaps his gaze is sought not so much for attention and affirmation of one's exis-tence but for his approval. While the mother's gaze affirms, "yes, you exist," the father's gaze may suggest, "I see you and you matter."

85   Guntrip, *Schizoid Phenomena*, 24.

86   Guntrip, 27.

The task of loving

In his essay on narcissism, Freud explains that we must begin to love so as to not fall ill.[87] Indeed, if we do not educate desire, turning it towards object-love, we are doomed to sickness. The psychoanalytic project resists the achievement imperative in its dedication to facilitating the movement from ego-libido to object-libido – a process of sacrificing one's narcissism for loving the other. Because the decline of symbolic efficiency so ruthlessly exposes us to the meaninglessness of flattened imaginary relations and the void of the Real, we must undertake this movement. We cannot survive the brutal objectivity of the Real without symbolic mediation – we cannot find social or spiritual satisfaction in the narcissism and one-dimensionality of the imaginary register. As we move from narcissistic love to object-love, we initiate the process of individuation. Through this process, we are invited to create and inhabit new symbolic formations that account for the mythological and narrative dimensions of collective experience. If the crisis of desire is simply a crisis of turning away from the external world, the external world must be reanimated as a symbolic field again. Our antidote can be found in reterritorialising with a curious, contemplative mode of attention. We can educate our desire to relate on terms that exceed purely transactional aims and engage the body in its most honest and expressive capacities.

As the libidinal glue of civilisation, the symbolic order must remain a constant negotiation between people at the level of physical, psychical and spiritual experience. Flight from the Real into the imaginary is inherently avoidant and unsatisfying as the imaginary register is sustained by internal, ephemeral, and performative relationships. To inhabit a symbolic system, we must inhabit our bodies. The removal of corporeality shelters us from the charge and complexities of jouissance. However, this sense of disembodied happiness is, Berardi states, "a naturally frigid and false one."[88]

Collective psychic and political futures depend on the extent to which we relearn to *weave the unconscious into lived social fields intentionally*. Intention sustains the movement towards love and waters seeds of individuation. Deleuze and Guattari remind us that desire is a problem for groups – to get where we want, we must know what we want and be unafraid to ask for it.[89] As we take responsibility for our desire – educate and socialise it – we begin to individuate and participate in a more significant social process of transindividuation. For Stiegler, transindividuation is "energy circulating as exclamation"; it is "the socialisation of the psychic ... the realisation of

---

87   Freud, *On Narcissism*, 553.
88   Berardi, *The Soul at Work*, 104.
89   Deleuze and Guattari, *Anti-Oedipus*.

sublimation"; it is our ability to remember and transform on a collective level.[90] This potential lies in the creative will to remythologise everyday life. We are tasked with finding ways to articulate collective desire and mobilise towards it – we are asked to symbolise, ritualise, and remember. Rich with the discomfort of change and charged with egoic resistance, this is the pathway to human intimacy. Our courage to love induces death pangs of a new world.

References

de Beauvoir, Simone. *The Second Sex*. Translated by H. M. Parshley. NY: Vintage Books, 1974.

Benach, Joan, Alejandra Vives, Marco Amable, Christoph Vanroelen, Gemma Tarafa, and Carles Muntaner. "Precarious Employment: Understanding an Emerging Social Determinant of Health." *Annual Review of Public Health* 35, no. 1 (2014): 229–253. https://doi.org/10.1146/annurev-publhealth-032013-182500.

Berardi, Franco. *The Soul at Work*. Translated by Francesca Cadel and Giuseppina Mecchia. Cambridge: MIT Press, 2009.

———. *And. Phenomenology of the End. Cognition and Sensibility in the Transition from Conjunctive to Connective Mode of Social Communication*. Helsinki: Aalto ARTS Books, 2014.

Debord, Guy. *Society of the Spectacle*. Oakland: Black & Red, 2010.

Deleuze, Gilles, and Félix Guattari, *Anti-Oedipus: Capitalism and Schizophrenia*. Translated by Robert Hurley, Mark Seem, and Helen R. Lane. London: Penguin, 1977.

Crary, Jonathan. *Late Capitalism and the Ends of Sleep*. NY: Verso, 2013.

Dean, Jodi. *Blog Theory: Feedback and Capture in the Circuits of the Drive*. Malden: Polity Press, 2010.

Fisher, Mark. *Capitalist Realism: Is There No Alternative?* NY: Zero Books, 2009.

Freud, Sigmund. *Civilization and Its Discontents*. In *The Freud Reader*, edited by Peter Gay, translated by James Stratchey. NY: Norton, 1989. First published 1930.

Freud, Sigmund. "On Narcissism." In *The Freud Reader*, edited by Peter Gay, translated by James Stratchey. NY: Norton, 1989. First published 1914.

Germain, Thomas. "Mental Health Apps Aren't as Private as You Think." Consumer Reports. March 2, 2021. https://www.consumerreports.org/health-privacy/mental-health-apps-and-user-privacy-a7415198244/.

Guntrip, Harry. *Schizoid Phenomena, Object Relations and the Self*. NY: International Universities Press Inc., 1969.

Han, Byung-Chul. *Psychopolitics: Neoliberalism and New Technologies of Power*. Translated by Erik Butler. NY: Verso, 2017.

---

90   Stiegler, *Symbolic Misery*, 155.

———. *The Burnout Society*. Stanford: Stanford UP, 2015.

Horton, Donald, and R. Richard Wohl. "Mass Communication and Para-Social Interaction: Observations on Intimacy at a Distance." *Psychiatry* 19, no. 3 (1956): 215–229. https://doi.org/10.1080/00332747.1956.11023049

Houellebecq, Michel. *Serotonin*. Translated by Shaun Whiteside. NY: Farrar, Straus and Giroux, 2019.

Lacan, Jacques. *Écrits*. Translated by Bruce Fink. NY: Norton, 2002.

———. *Seminar V: Formations of the Unconscious. July 2, 1958: You are the One You Hate*. Translated by Cormac Gallagher. London: Karnac Books, 2002.

Lasch, Christopher. *The Culture of Narcissism*. NY: Warner Books, 1979.

Lorey, Isabell. *State of Insecurity: Government of the Precarious*. London: Verso, 2015.

Marcuse, Herbert. *One-Dimensional Man*. London: Routledge, 1964.

Moshfegh, Ottessa. *My Year of Rest and Relaxation*. NY: Penguin Press, 2019.

Nietzsche, Friedrich. *Ecce Homo, The Portable Nietzsche*. Toronto: Penguin Random House, 1977.

Standing, Guy. *The Precariat: The New Dangerous Class*. London: Bloomsbury Revelations, 2011.

Steadman, Otillia. "Everyone is Making Porn at Home Now. Will the Porn Industry Survive?" *Buzzfeed News*, May 6, 2020.

Stiegler, Bernard. *The Lost Spirit of Capitalism*. Translated by Daniel Ross. Malden: Polity Press, 2014.

———. *Symbolic Misery, Volume 2: The Katastropē of the Sensible*. Translated by Barnaby Norman. Cambridge: Polity Press, 2015.

Reich, William. *Mass Psychology of Fascism*. NY: Farrar, Straus and Giroux, 1970.

Tomšič, Samo. *The Capitalist Unconscious: Marx and Lacan*. London: Verso, 2015.

Vainshtein, Annie. "Coronavirus Took Their Jobs Away. OnlyFans Let These Bay Area People Monetize Themselves." *San Francisco Chronicle*, April 4, 2020. https://www.sfchronicle.com/bayarea/article/Coronavirus-took-their-jobs-away-OnlyFans-let-15175650.php

Žižek, Slavoj. *For They Do Not Know What They Do: Enjoyment as a Political Factor*. NY: Verso, 1991.

———. *Looking Awry: An Introduction to Jacques Lacan Through Popular Culture*. Cambridge: MIT Press, 1999.

———. *The Ticklish Subject: The Absent Centre of Political Ontology*. London: Verso, 1999.

1/0: Structuring Freedom Through the Digital Binary

Matthew Flisfeder

Part 1: 1/0

On the digital binary

What follows extends a particular line of thinking from an argument I develop in my book, *Algorithmic Desire: Toward a New Structuralist Theory of Social Media*.[1] In that book, I aim to develop a "new structuralist" theory of social media, drawing largely on Lacanian-Žižekian insights into the subject's position as expressing a lack or a gap in existing social, political, cultural struggles. In *Algorithmic Desire*, I argue that social media helps us to grasp the resuscitation of the big Other's virtual agency in conditions of postmodern capitalism and the supposed end of ideology, end of history, or as Žižek calls it, the "demise of symbolic efficiency," an offshoot of Fredric Jameson's thesis that the postmodern can be grasped in Lacanian terms as a "breakdown of the signifying chain."[2] Near the end of the book, I draw on the Lacanian logics of sexuation (Lacan's formulas of masculine and feminine sexuation) to rethink and interpret the binary logic of digital coding, and vice versa. There, I also draw on Joan Copjec and Alenka Zupančič as they have rethought the logics of sexuation through the prism of German Idealism – most notably with Copjec (and Žižek) via the Kantian antinomies of pure reason.[3] In this chapter, I aim to take up again this line of inquiry by proposing that binary code, as in the digital, provides us with a helpful shorthand for thinking about our current moment, particularly in the context of the current crises that we face – from the economic to the environmental and, of course, crises of identity. The way to read the digital, I claim, concerns the logic of

---

1   Matthew Flisfeder, *Algorithmic Desire: Toward a New Structuralist Theory of Social Media* (Evanston: Northwestern UP, 2021).

2   See Slavoj Žižek, *The Ticklish Subject: The Absent Center of Political Ontology* (NY: Verso, 1999); Fredric Jameson, "Postmodernism, or, the Cultural Logic of Late Capitalism," *New Left Review* I 146 (1984).

3   See Joan Copjec, "Sex and the Euthanasia of Reason," in *Read My Desire: Lacan Against the Historicists* (Cambridge: MIT Press, 1994); Alenka Zupančič, *What is Sex?* (Cambridge: MIT Press, 2017).

the binary opposition and the way it provides a point of structural thinking tied not only to emancipatory politics and ethics but also to the libidinal attachments of the subject in its connection to enjoyment and freedom.

The binary, we might say, is a useful expression of crisis insofar as it represents a logic of conflict and struggle. Here, I am drawing from points made differently by media theorists such as Alexander Galloway and Roberto Simonowski. Digital logic, for them, is evidentiary of how we conceive of the semiotics of political struggle. This point indicates something close to the formal structures of emancipatory thinking. As Simonowski puts it, "the basic principle of the [online] filter bubble is antagonistic: someone or something belongs or doesn't belong. The opposition connotes inside/outside or us/them thinking."[4] Antagonism, he writes, is thus reminiscent of binary code. Platform struggles thus extend beyond the surface level of the interface or the platform. The filtering systems on the front end of a platform follow the logic of the interface's back end, designed by a binary polarisation of 1s and 0s. As a shorthand, binary code thus helps us to figure or represent the political's binary logic in structuralist terms.

In his book on Laruelle, Galloway writes similarly that the digital provides insights into philosophy and critical theory, which, according to him, is "*a digitization of the real* because it is predicated on the one dividing in two."[5] The digital, he writes, "is the basic distinction that makes possible any distinction at all. The digital is the capacity to divide things and make distinctions between them. Thus not so much zero and one, but *one and two*" (emphasis original).[6] Galloway, in his reading of the binary within the digital, sets out to examine it in a much more standard, positivist, or affirmationist way, whether in terms of the binary opposition as read, for instance, in deconstruction (i.e., the mark of the supplement; or the transcendental signified), or maybe even in the Maoist dialectic of the one dividing into two. However, I think it is far more productive to read the binary opposition as Simonowski does, where the one and the zero (1/0) represent the difference between the inside and the out, between the positive and the negative, or more appropriately between the affirmation and the negation.[7] Or, perhaps more appropriately, we can read the 1/0 logic not

---

4   Roberto Simanowski, *Waste: A New Media Primer* (Cambridge: MIT Press, 2018), 4.
5   Alexander Galloway, *Laruelle: Against the Digital* (Minneapolis: University of Minnesota Press, 2014), 12.
6   Galloway, *Laruelle*, xxix.
7   It is worth noting, of course, that this is also the way that Mao reads the dialectic and, following Stalin, resolves to eliminate the Hegelian negation of the negation, preferring instead to think an infinite process of negation–affirmation–negation–affirmation. For me, though, an emancipatory dialectic is nothing if it does not include the subjective dimension of the negation of the negation, which, far from aiming at the synthesis of opposites, is in fact the position from which the subject grasps its own place within the process. See Mao Zedong, "Talk on the Question of Philosophy," in *On Practice and Contradiction* (NY: Verso, 2007), 181.

only as the relation of the affirmation to its negation but as the self-relating negation of the 1 itself.

Lacanian discourse theory helps us out in reading the binary logic this way. For instance, in Lacan's discourse of the Master, the self-relating of the one is posited in terms of the opposition between the position of the battery of signifiers and the production of the Symbolic order (marked as the S_2 in the formula). The barred subject's ($\$$) position in the place of truth, below the Master-Signifier (S_1), represents the lack or gap, the signifier's self-relating that marks the contradiction within itself, rather than simply the opposition between itself and the Symbolic order:

$$\frac{S_1}{\$} \quad \frac{S_2}{a}$$

Read in this way, the binary opposition leads us to theorise, not the one and the two, but the *self-relating* of the one – of positing the one as the founding moment, however empty, of the structure. It posits a relating that takes precedence over the splitting into the two, which is the marker of its set: the chain of signification that flows from instituting a foundational signifier. In other words, the two's development is epiphenomenal, the result of the self-relating of the one to itself, and of a foundational forced choice of being over nothingness – of the affirmative instead of its self-negation.

While we encounter the binary between the affirmation and the negation, what really concerns us is the question of *what* is being affirmed or posited in this split. We can turn to a different register, beyond the digital, and back towards the ideological. Switching our point of reference towards the linguistic binary of the signifier, I think we can read the binary in a more traditional, structuralist way that grants us an avenue for thinking about the relationship between the binary and the libidinal economy. After all, positing the 1 ties it to producing the Lacanian object little a, the object-cause of desire, holding the one in its place as the structure's button tie (*point de capiton* or quilting point). Underlying the signifier's affirmation, in other words, is the fantasy framework of the negated choices not chosen in a foundational act of becoming, which binds us to the choice of the already-chosen signifier.

Structure/structurelessness

In rethinking the binary in this way, both politically and libidinally, I am drawing on the work of Anna Kornbluh. She proposes that formalisation or *structure* is a goal of both psychoanalysis and emancipatory politics.[8] Structure is not merely the place to

---

8   Anna Kornbluh, "States of Psychoanalysis: Formalization and the Space of the Political," *Theory & Event* 19, no. 3 (2016). See also Anna Kornbluh, *The Order of Forms: Realism, Formalism, and Social Space* (Chicago: University of Chicago Press, 2019).

begin our analysis; it is also the product of our critique. Put differently, every point of critique of the structure is also, and always, the production of a new one. Again, this only makes sense when we consider the structure of the analyst's discourse in Lacan, where the product is the creation or invention of a new Master-Signifier:

$$\frac{a}{S_2} \quad \frac{\$}{S_1}$$

According to Kornbluh, emancipatory politics, therefore, can follow psychoanalysis by taking formalisation as its goal. This goal is in stark contrast to much of radical politics today, which sees smashing structures, and states of structurelessness, as its goal.

Referring to what she calls "anarcho-vitalism," Kornbluh writes that formlessness and a destituent politics – "burn it all down" – has become

> the ideal uniting a variety of theories, from the mosh of the multitude to the localization of microstruggle and microaggression, from the voluntarist assembly of actors and networks to the flow of affects untethered from constructs, from the deification of irony and incompletion to the culminating conviction that life springs forth without form and thrives in form's absence.[9]

Contemporary critical theory, in other words, tends to privilege immediacy and transgression over production and dialectical reasoning, giving way to the *exploding* of binaries as its principle critical gesture. This is partly why the vague term "poststructuralism" makes sense: the Foucauldian turn to micropolitics, or the Deleuzo-Guattarian deterritorialisation, so admired by the accelerationists, also places the subject in the position of permanent critique, never aiming to build structures of emancipation.[10]

Against this orthodoxy, Kornbluh argues that a politics of universal emancipation needs to take "the instituting capacity of the material signifier" and the practice of institution – of *affirming*, but nevertheless *limiting*, a structure – as its central project.[11] As she puts it, "what psychoanalysis institutes is the thought and practice of a necessary but contingent *state*, that which stamps, that which is formed, that which facilitates existence."[12] I would add here, as well, that which facilitates apprehending enjoyment. This point is also echoed in Todd McGowan's Hegelian theory of emancipation.

---

9   Kornbluh, *The Order of Forms*, 2.
10   Cf. Benjamin Noys, *Malign Velocities: Accelerationism and Capitalism* (Winchester: Zero Books, 2014).
11   Kornbluh, *The Order of Forms*, 140.
12   Kornbluh, *The Order of Forms*, 140.

Just as Kornbluh describes, it is typical to imagine emancipatory politics as one of absolute and determinate negation. In the neo-vitalist sense, this logic gains its impulse from the Spinozan conception of the absolutely infinite, *a perspective much more analogous to the analogue as opposed to the digital*. The digital, after all, emphasises the cut. Likewise, for Hegel, we grasp freedom as the subject's capacity to negate constraints or limits *externally* imposed. However, as McGowan notes, a perverse logic is in place if all one can ever do is transgress or negate external limits. Such an ethic ultimately helps to ensure the longevity of existing power, propping up authority as that against which we can only transgress and negate as the sign of our freedom. An ethics of transgression is constantly in need of – requires even – some authority that it must attempt to subvert. Thus, a true sign of our freedom is not merely our capacity to negate an externally imposed limit but our power to impose and affirm our own limitations. In fact, we can read the Lacanian traversal of the fantasy as grasping the fact that we are the ones who have chosen the obstacles to our desire in the first place. In a foundational act of forced free choice, the subject chooses or affirms the one, the signifier, negating all other choices not chosen.

This logic applies in the psychoanalytic conception of the cure, where we come to acknowledge that enjoyment lies not in the beyond of the limit but in the fantasy itself. In fantasy, we imagine that if only we could acquire the prohibited object then we would achieve full satisfaction; psychoanalysis teaches us, however, that enjoyment is actually contained in the fantasy. The political ethics of psychoanalysis is such that the subject itself has the freedom and capacity to impose *its own* limitations as a condition of non-repressive enjoyment.[13] Following both Kornbluh and McGowan, my approach is to conceive the binary logic of the signifier similarly to Simonowski's schema of antagonism, as the 1/0, or in Lacanian terms, as the couple $S_1/\$$: the signifier, marking the affirmation, and the signifier of the barred subject, as the negation – the subject as marking the gap or lack in the structure.

My interest in thinking the binary in this way, thus, has to do in part with our current moment of relating to binary oppositions and structures of identity and culture, as in the sexual relationship (or, rather, as the non-relationship of the masculine and feminine sides of the logics of sexuation), but also in terms of the political antagonism of the class struggle.[14] It is reasonable to consider the parallel between the digital *moment*, as Galloway does, and critical theories of the binary opposition as a way to remap the central contradiction of our times. My objective, then, is to think about the relationship between emancipatory politics and ethics, and in this sense,

---

13   I am drawing particularly on two of McGowan's texts here: *Emancipation After Hegel: Towards a Contradictory Revolution* (NY: Columbia UP, 2019) and *Capitalism and Desire: The Psychic Cost of Free Markets* (NY: Columbia UP, 2016).

14   For more on this point, interested readers should read chapter six of *Algorithmic Desire*, "The Swiping Logic of the Signifier."

the role of enjoyment, but along the lines of our thinking of the binary opposition and its connection to the structural production of our freedom.

To put it bluntly, I agree with Kornbluh that, in contrast to some of the language in post-structuralist and postmodernist theory, we need to defend a particular kind of structure or form – rather than its elimination – as a goal for emancipatory politics. However, I would add that doing so also means recognising how social constructions establish *historically defined* forms of power. Acknowledging this need not mean that emancipation equals the destruction of all structures. Certainly, emancipatory politics requires negating particularly limiting structures, like capitalism, patriarchy, heteronormativity, and eurocentrism. There certainly seems to be an anti-normative bent in so much of the performative rhetoric of the anarcho-vitalist Left.

But to put the point differently, we can acknowledge that norms are absolutely constructed *socially*, but they are also necessary and established *historically*; and often, still organically even when "structurelessness," as Jo Freeman explains, is the apparent aim.[15] Reading from the perspective of feminist efforts at structureless organisation, Freeman argues that the idealism of structurelessness often and evidently bites back with the materially inherent construction of *informal* and *deceptive* forms or structured elitism, which can often become far more violent than avowed structures and hierarchies. As Freeman puts it, "a 'laissez faire' group is about as realistic as 'laissez faire' society." *Structurelessness* "becomes a way of masking power."[16]

Bringing this point back to the framework of the digital binary, Reza Negarestani notes that even in mapping the logic of artificial general intelligence, we see that structure becomes inherent in every effort to grasp consciousness. There is, as he explains, "no structure in the world without the structuring mind, there is no mind and no *unrestricted* world without the structuration of language and its unrestricted universe in discourse."[17] To mark my commitments even more clearly: the binary opposition with which I am most concerned here is that between the 1 and the 0, between the positive and the negative, or between the affirmation and the negation – the affirmation of norms, or the negation of norms, for instance. Nevertheless, it is with regard to the structures of social and cultural norms that I see an activation of desire and investments in libidinal economies. Analytically, our aim, then, should be one of grasping the historicising logic of the signifier in various conditions of antagonism and struggle, which is, in the end, what an immanent critique allows us to do.

---

15   Jo Freeman, "The Tyranny of Structurelessness," *Jacobin Magazine*, September 16, 2019, https://www.jacobinmag.com/2019/09/tyranny-structurelessness-jo-freeman-consciousness-raising-women-liberation-feminism.

16   Freeman, "The Tyranny of Structurelessness."

17   Reza Negarestani, *Intelligence and Spirit* (Windsor Quarry: Urbanomic, 2018), 71.

Materiality of the binary: The signifier falls into the signified

The difficulty with binary thinking, insofar as we conceive it in terms of the 1 and the 0, rather than the 1 and the 2, centres on its limitations in historical thinking. If we consider, for instance, how Copjec distinguishes between essentialist or dogmatic views of sex (sex as a purely natural/biological dimension of identity, that is, biological determinism) and the social constructionist or sceptical view of it (for her, represented by Judith Butler's approach in *Gender Trouble*), then what we should add is a *historical* dimension.[18] Hegel indicated this with his "negation of the negation" – we acknowledge the social constructionist perspective (the object, sex, as a discursive construct) and accept it. However, in the Hegelian procedure, we also recognise that, with every critique of a norm, we also equally produce and impose a new one – the one from which the critique finds its basis of comparison. In this way, we discover the inscription of a new *necessary*, albeit contingent, instituting signifier. Negation of the negation is not a mere synthetical combination; instead, it is a way of reading the immanent self-negation of the initial positing of the Master-Signifier or the 1. It is a way of reading the signifier against its own lack. Thus, the new master-signifier's production is the result of taking critique to the end. It is not arbitrary. It is, instead, produced by thinking contradiction to its endpoint, as in the Lacanian discourse of the analyst. However, by *sublating* the older framework, this new signifier institutes a new structure rather than destroying the structure as such. It is what gives structure its historical ebb.

We can read this, for instance, through Zupančič's description of the Lacanian logic of the signifier falling into the signified or of the Symbolic having an effect in the Real. She points out that every signifying structure is organised around a gap: "for the relational differentiality to exist and to function, the *one* (of the binary relation) has to be missing." This, she writes, makes all the difference since this is "Lacan's crucial addition which allows him to reintroduce the concept of the subject (of the unconscious) at the very highest point of the structuralist attacking of this notion." But then notes, "Lacan is quick to add that his point is 'to show how the signifier in fact enters the signified.'"[19] The subject's presence (the shift from a foundational negation to the negation of the negation), in other words, marks the presence of a gap or a lack in the structure, therefore providing a space for the subject to act to transform the structures in place. When the signifier falls into the signified, the materiality of the structure, rather than its mere contingency (the perspective of the social constructionists), is fully produced.[20]

---

18   See Copjec, "Sex and the Euthanasia of Reason."

19   Zupančič, *What is Sex?*, 59. Cf. Jacques Lacan, *Écrits: The First Complete Edition in English*, trans. Bruce Fink (NY: Norton, 2006), 417.

20   See Flisfeder, *Algorithmic Desire*, 173–175.

Whether because of our knowledge of the Real, produced via discourse, or our non- or unconscious knowledge of it, we are still capable of acting upon the world and changing it. However, knowledge (*connaisance*) as opposed to consciousness (*conscience*) in the analytical discourse is what makes us freer. Climate science is a parallel example. Coming to know nature through discourse makes it possible for us to act on it, for better or worse – but this still carries an effect.[21] Here, what changes is the register of the object in our frameworks of knowledge, allowing us to reflect upon and ask what type of effect we can produce.

This impact on the Real always refers to a foundational choice – a decision between an affirmative and a negative; between the affirmation and the negation. I argue that such a choice is fundamentally attached to the conditions of our enjoyment or to our libidinal economy, which nevertheless is organised, formed or structured, with reference to a socially or culturally determined object or signifier. Moving towards my conclusion, I want to expand on how the binary I am addressing is represented in the registers of Deleuze (a supposedly affirmationist theorist) and Lacan (a theorist of negation or the negative, that is, lack).

Part 2: Deleuzian affirmationism versus Lacanian lack

Analogue ethics and affirmative monism

Considering the preceding, it is noteworthy that so much of the contemporary critical-ideological discourse finds its inspiration in the Deleuzo-Guattarian disdain for the imperialism of the despotic signifier. We see this, for instance, in varieties of new materialism, neo-vitalisms, posthumanisms, and accelerationisms. These tendencies appear to privilege the analogue over the digital (as Galloway might put it), proceeding from the substance's capacity for structureless self-organisation or development.[22] From this perspective, introducing the signifier into the topology of the Real becomes that which erroneously produces a split or a cut, or what Aaron Schuster calls, referring to Deleuze, the *violence* of the negative.[23] In this sense, the split signifier *inscribes* negativity and contradiction by cutting into what is otherwise whole or substantial. Introducing the negative appears to be what produces

---

21   I take up this point in "From the Sublime to the Hysterical Sublime: Reading the End of the World Against the Singularity," in *Lacan and the Environment*, ed. Clint Burnham and Paul Kingsbury (NY: Palgrave Macmillan, 2021).

22   Anton Syutkin explores this point, looking at the Deleuzian influence on contemporary vitalist new materialisms. See Syutkin, "Gilles Deleuze Among the New Materialists: Dialectic versus Neovitalism," *Stasis* 7, no. 1 (2019): 408.

23   Aaron Schuster, *The Trouble with Pleasure: Deleuze and Psychoanalysis* (Cambridge: MIT Press, 2016), 45.

and creates a tyrannical or hierarchical structure, which at the same time denies an affirmative desire.

There is, thus, a sense in which new materialists of this sort aim for a return to a kind of immanence that breaks the shackles of an imposing signifier or obstacle. Although Deleuze does not appear to go directly for a Spinozan monism of the kind often ascribed to him, his project still seems to point at times towards what Syutkin calls an "affirmative monism," which "always presupposes the possibility of a return to vitalism."[24] But I believe we can still detect this in the way that Deleuze privileges the *affirmation* of difference and the multiple in various places, but also specifically in his book on Nietzsche. In that book, Deleuze even describes the force of the negative as affirming the will's opposing aggression.[25] The claim regarding Deleuze's affirmative monism makes sense to me when we reflect upon the relationship between the subject and the obstacle in Deleuzian theory. Indeed, the obstacle's position can help us distinguish between the Deleuzian project of emancipation and Lacan's project.

Reading the binary through Lacan, we see that the posited two – as in the two sexes in the heterosexual relationship, for instance – are never two, but rather more foundationally, the one and its lack: the signifier and the lack (1/0). I prefer to think of this division as the affirmation of the phallic signifier *of castration* and its negation, so that both positions still relate to the same signifier; however, *one* form of this relating remains limited (the masculine), whereas the other does not (the feminine). One relates to the signifier as the paradoxical affirmation of a castration, whereas the other relates to it in the form of its negation. Nevertheless, we still need to ask, *what* is this void, this lack?

The choice of the cut

We should read this lack as a foundational split within the subject itself, between the subject's self-positing affirmation, as well as its self-reflecting negation, or as immanent and dialectical negation of the negation. We should read this split from the position of what Žižek sometimes refers to as the foundational forced choice of being, since even here, with every choice that follows, the choice is simultaneously the product of a split between the affirmation and the negation. Every choice, at the same time, negates the unchosen. We might imagine it, sticking with the representational form of the digital, as something like the swiping logic of social media apps, such as Tinder or TikTok. Swipe left; swipe right. Swipe up; swipe down – affirmation; negation. With every choice made, we negate another (and fantasy, we might add, is the imaginary of the choices not chosen).

---

24   Syutkin, "Gilles Deleuze," 409.

25   Gilles Deleuze, *Nietzsche & Philosophy*, trans. Hugh Tomlinson (NY: Columbia UP, 2006), 9.

Whatever we affirm *simultaneously* negates some other content. I believe this is how we should understand symbolic castration in the Lacanian sense. The affirmation, the self-positing, of the signifier also negates that unmade (little) other choice. The unchosen other/object is thus the inverse side of the object chosen. The signifier chosen is the one for which, now, all others come to determine the subject, but still, on the inverse side of this choice exists the *lost* object. This lost choice is translated into the object-cause of the subject's desire – it is lack, objectivised. What gets produced in the subject, through the fantasy of attaining or acquiring this lost object, is the curvature of its desire: its libidinal economy. Hence, the binary opposition is productive of both the subject of the unconscious and its libidinal economy.

Todd McGowan is quite clever in relating the subject's desire to the logic of capital, or, more specifically, to the logic of commodity fetishism. In his book on capitalism and desire, he boldly claims that capital plays on the subject's desire because it systematically knows that what the subject desires – the way it invests into its libidinal economy – is not the object but the obstacle preventing its realisation. I should add that this was also one of the insights in Lyotard's *Libidinal Economy* and Deleuze and Guattari's *Capitalism and Schizophrenia*. On this point, I disagree with the reading of capitalism as schizophrenic – its formal discursive and libidinal shape is much closer to that of perversion. As Samo Tomšič puts it, capitalism is not itself perverse, but it *"demands* perversion from its subjects... [It] demands that subjects *enjoy* exploitation."[26] That is to say, it *"imposes* the perverse position on the subject," but how?[27]

It is important to specify here the relationship between knowledge and its disavowal on the part of the perverse subject, who may appear to avow the non-existence of the object but pursues it nonetheless (because that knowledge is disavowed). As McGowan puts it elsewhere, the subject can acknowledge "the hopelessness of consumption while simultaneously consuming with as much hope as the most naïve consumer."[28] But we might also read the subject's relationship to its desire under capital in the form of the obsessional neurotic, who constantly erects their obstacles to realising desire since enjoyment is procured through the chase. In either case, though, it is positing the *obstacle* that creates the conditions of possibility for enjoyment. But this, nevertheless, is a *self-positing* of the obstacle, and not merely its imposition from outside. There is then a paradoxical relation to the obstacle and to the structure for which it stands: there is a desire to negate the obstacle and its structure, since it appears to prevent access to our enjoyment; however, there is also a desire to affirm the obstacle and its structure since only within these coordinates

26   Samo Tomšič, *The Capitalist Unconscious: Marx and Lacan* (NY: Verso, 2015), 151.
27   Tomšič, 150.
28   Todd McGowan, *Out of Time: Desire in Atemporal Cinema* (Minneapolis: University of Minnesota Press, 2011), 29.

can the subject enjoy its failure to attain its object. Therein lies a critical difference between the libidinal economy in the Lacanian register and its interpretation in the Deleuzian one.

From the Deleuzian perspective, the obstacle can be read as an *external* force negating the positive, affirmative flows of desire. This is why it is crucial (contrary, perhaps, to what I said above) not to read Deleuze as a monist but as a dualist of a specific type – namely, one who still emphasises dialectic and antagonism, and conflict. In this way, the Deleuzian logic is the mirror reflection of capitalist desire, which also engages in an endless conversion from deterritorialisation to reterritorialisation; why not, even the Maoist dialectic of affirmation-negation-affirmation. If we can understand desire in the Lacanian register as a lack, as the negative, then in the Deleuzian one, it becomes an affirmative force, or, in the Spinozan sense, of determination by way of its negation. Everything depends on where we locate the site of the obstacle – is the obstacle imposed externally, by some oppositional or exploitative force, or is it self-imposed (self-posited) by the subject?

Whereas the Deleuzian ethic is one of deterritorialisation, we can locate the Lacanian ethic in the idea that the ends of analysis arrive once the subject avows the positing of its own presuppositions. The subject realises that it has posited the obstacle, on its own, as the only means for accessing enjoyment, and coming to terms with this fact requires not merely the negation of the obstacle but the negation of the negation. At the end of analysis, the analysand concludes that the source of enjoyment is the fantasy, not what appears to lie beyond it. The subject brings to consciousness the inevitability of the contradiction between the signifier and the lack, and its inability to transcend its positing as such. This awareness, however, brings the subject face to face with its own freedom: it has the freedom to posit its own presuppositions or impose its own obstacles or limits/limitations – the subject gives to itself the structure of its own freedom. But, still, how do we arrive at this position as an act of emancipation?

The binary logic of the true infinite

How might we read, in other words, Lacan's motto, do not give up on (or give ground towards) your desire? The first thing to do here is to *begin* with negation rather than affirmation. The subject is split by the desire to *transcend* the contradiction between the signifier at its lack, and the desire to nevertheless *pursue* this contradiction. We should, in other words, proceed with the negation as the starting point of choice, where freedom is the continuous act of saying "that's not it, I am not that" – or, even, the hysterical question, "why am I that? Why am I what you are saying that I am?"

Even in the political register, it is *necessary* to negate real material forces that do oppose from outside the subject's freedom. For instance, the structural contradictions of capital create genuine material barriers for subjects needing to access everyday resources. Certainly, we need to oppose such external forces. That is obvious. And freedom, here, surely is the result of a certain practice of negation. History, after all, is made by the masses but in conditions not of their choosing. Differently put, the base may determine the superstructure, but the revolutionary class can negate the base.

Here, freedom is produced as a negation of all the subject's determinations – biological, cultural, or political. Desire, here, should be read as the object-cause that initiates freedom through negation, which still aims towards a particular object. Here, we can see the splitting of the drive between its goal, which is its target, and its aim, which is to circulate around its goal. But at a certain point, as McGowan notes, negation can only prop up what it opposes, as what it negates. At a certain point, it must set its own limits, its determinations, and affirm whatever necessary, however contingent, structure is required to realise its freedom. Again, this is the perspective we arrive at through the negation of the negation, which does not merely affirm the new but grasps the position from which the new can be affirmed.

The Deleuzo-Guattarian ethic, in contrast, is one of seeking to affirm desire rather than structure, which gets inhibited by some *external* negating and contradictory force. Deleuze, in particular, draws on Nietzsche to assert this position against the Hegelian dialectical one:

> In Nietzsche the essential relation of one force to another is never conceived of as a negative element in the essence. In its relation with the other the force which makes itself obeyed does not deny the other of that which it is not, it affirms its own difference and enjoys this difference. The negative is not present in the essence as that form which draws its activity: on the contrary, it is a result of activity, of the existence of an active force and the affirmation of its difference. The negative is a product of existence itself: the aggression necessarily linked to an active existence, the aggression of an affirmation. As for the negative concept (that is to say, negation as a concept) "it is only a subsequently-invented pale contrasting image in relation to its positive basic concept – filled with life and passion through and through." For the speculative element of negation, opposition or contradiction Nietzsche substitutes the practical element of *difference*, the object of affirmation and enjoyment... The question which Nietzsche constantly repeats, "what does a will want, what does this one or that one what?", must not be understood as the search of a goal, a motive or an object for this will. What a will wants is to affirm its difference. It is essential relation with the "other" a will makes its difference an object of affirmation.[29]

The difference between freedom in the Deleuzian register and its place in the Lacanian one concerns the position of the obstacle. For Deleuze, desire is an affirmative

---

29   Deleuze, *Nietzsche & Philosophy*, 9.

force that gets thwarted by an *imposing* external obstacle – contradiction and nega-tion are imposed upon the subject, imposed upon the subject's positive substantial desire. For Lacan, desire is lack (the desire to avoid contradiction and the drive to pursue contradiction) – lack in objective form – and the obstacle is self-imposed as a limit: a limit that the subject self-posits rather than being imposed by the Other. We find here the difference between an absolute infinity of the kind we also find in Spinoza, and the Hegelian true infinity, which is premised, not on extension forever, as in a straight line that forever expands, or as an infinite self-division into an on-going multiple, but rather as the circular form of going through the process in order to arrive back at the beginning again, from the starting point, only with a new and different perspective on the problem we were pursuing in the first place. "As true in-finite, bent back upon itself," Hegel writes, "its image becomes that of a *circle*, the line that has reached itself, closed and wholly present."[30]

So to return to the problem of the binary opposition I started with, we see, first of all, we are speaking about the opposition between affirmation and negation; that the contradiction between them is vital to the interpellation of the subject; and that the subject's interpellation is at the same time the emergence of its libidinal econ-omy. Our question remains: must emancipation follow the path of destroying the limit/obstacle – aspiring towards structureless deterritorialisation – or of a legit-imate, self-imposed structure needed both in realising enjoyment in fantasy and universal freedom?

Building on arguments made by Kornbluh and McGowan, I propose that produc-ing a new master-signifier – producing a new historical norm – posits both the for-mal logic of emancipation and its enjoyment. This new arrives, in other words, not merely by some completely conscious choice of action, but by following our desire and thinking it all the way to its logical ends. This makes the dialectic of enjoyment, the dialectic of the binary, affirmation and negation, an emancipatory political fac-tor worth considering. The binary logic of the digital merely maps for us in represen-tational terms how we can think of this relation today. After all, the dominant media of every historical period give us points of entry for conceiving the dominant form of consciousness and the dominant ideology. It is, in this sense, appropriate for us to conceive the digital as a representational strategy for conceiving the libidinal and the political.

---

30   Georg Wilhelm Friedrich Hegel, *The Science of Logic*, trans. George Di Giovanni (Cambridge: Cambridge UP, 2010), 119.

References

Copjec, Joan. "Sex and the Euthanasia of Reason." In *Read My Desire: Lacan Against the Historicists*, 201–236. Cambridge: MIT Press, 1994.

Deleuze, Gilles. *Nietzsche & Philosophy*. Translated by Hugh Tomlinson. NY: Columbia UP, 2006.

Flisfeder, Matthew. *Algorithmic Desire: Toward a New Structuralist Theory of Social Media*. Evanston: Northwestern UP, 2021.

———. "From the Sublime to the Hysterical Sublime: Reading the End of the World Against the Singularity." In *Lacan and the Environment*, edited by Clint Burnham and Paul Kingsbury, 239–253. NY: Palgrave Macmillan, 2021.

Freeman, Jo. "The Tyranny of Structurelessness." *Jacobin Magazine*, September 16, 2019, https://www.jacobinmag.com/2019/09/tyranny-structurelessness-jo-free man-consciousness-raising-women-liberation-feminism.

Galloway, Alexander. *Laruelle: Against the Digital*. Minneapolis: University of Minnesota Press, 2014.

Hegel, Georg Wilhelm Friedrich. *The Science of Logic*. Translated by George Di Giovanni. Cambridge: Cambridge UP, 2010.

Jameson, Fredric. "Postmodernism, or, the Cultural Logic of Late Capitalism." *New Left Review I* 146 (1984): 53–92.

Kornbluh, Anna. "States of Psychoanalysis: Formalization and the Space of the Political." *Theory & Event* 19, no. 3 (2016). https://muse.jhu.edu/pub/1/article/62 3989

———. *The Order of Forms: Realism, Formalism, and Social Space*. Chicago: University of Chicago Press, 2019.

Lacan, Jacques. *Écrits: The First Complete Edition in English*. Translated by Bruce Fink. NY: Norton, 2006.

McGowan, Todd. *Out of Time: Desire in Atemporal Cinema*. Minneapolis: University of Minnesota Press, 2011.

———. *Capitalism and Desire: The Psychic Cost of Free Markets*. NY: Columbia UP, 2016.

———. *Emancipation After Hegel: Towards a Contradictory Revolution*. NY: Columbia UP, 2019.

Negarestani, Reza. *Intelligence and Spirit*. Windsor Quarry: Urbanomic, 2018.

Noys, Benjamin. *Malign Velocities: Accelerationism and Capitalism*. Winchester, UK: Zero Books, 2014.

Schuster, Aaron. *The Trouble With Pleasure: Deleuze and Psychoanalysis*. Cambridge: MIT Press, 2016.

Simanowski, Roberto. *Waste: A New Media Primer*. Cambridge: MIT Press, 2018.

Syutkin, Anton. "Gilles Deleuze Among the New Materialists: Dialectic versus Neovitalism." *Stasis* 7, no. 1 (2019): 390–414. https://doi.org/10.33280/2310-3817-2019-7 -1-390-414

Tomšič, Samo. *The Capitalist Unconscious: Marx and Lacan*. NY: Verso, 2015.

Zedong, Mao. "Talk on the Question of Philosophy." In *On Practice and Contradiction*, 169–185. NY: Verso, 2007.

Žižek, Slavoj. *The Ticklish Subject: The Absent Center of Political Ontology*. NY: Verso, 1999.

Zupančič, Alenka. *What is Sex?* Cambridge: MIT Press, 2017.

Deviant and Diseased: Metaphors of Crisis and the Sexual Semantics of Excess and Perversion

Jule Govrin

> Only a crisis – actual or perceived – pro-
> duces real change. When that crisis occurs,
> the actions that are taken depend on
> the ideas that are lying around. That, I
> believe, is our basic function: to develop
> alternatives to existing policies, to keep
> them alive and available until the politi-
> cally impossible becomes the politically
> inevitable.
> – Milton Friedman[1]

Crises as opportunities. Milton Friedman's catchphrase seems characteristic of capital's turmoil amid multiple crises, be they economic, political, ecological, or – at the
time of my writing – the COVID-19 pandemic crisis. The term "crisis" stems from the
field of medical semantics, indexing the turning point of a disease, thus pointing either to life or death. This medical etymology manifests in the metaphors of crisis. For
example, during the economic crisis that arose out of the COVID-19 crisis in 2020,
a typical headline read, "Some Jobs are Coming Back, but Economy Will Need Years
to Heal."[2] Another read, "U.S. Labor Market Healing; Businesses Boost Spending as
Profits Rebound."[3] Such titles are common in times of economic crisis, deploying

1   Milton Friedman, *Capitalism and Freedom: Fortieth Anniversary Edition* (Chicago: Chicago UP,
     2002), xiv.
2   David Lynch, "Some Jobs are Coming Back, but Economy Will Need Years to Heal," *The Wash-
     ington Post*, July 3, 2020, https://www.washingtonpost.com/business/2020/07/03/some-jobs
     -are-coming-back-economy-will-need-years-heal/.
3   Lucia Mutikani, "U.S. Labor Market Healing; Businesses Boost Spending as Profits Rebound,"
     Reuters, June 25, 2021, https://www.reuters.com/business/us-weekly-jobless-claims-fall-firs
     t-quarter-gdp-unrevised-64-2021-06-24/.

a familiar metaphor, depicting the economy as a sick body requiring remedies and cures. Yet whose bodies are implicated by this metaphor?

Semantics of health, immunity, and resilience are deeply interwoven with sexual semantics. This semantic intermingling has been increased by the modern medicalisation of desire, which defines the modern formation of sexuality, according to Michel Foucault. In the first volume of his history of sexuality, Foucault lays out how the emerging sexual sciences in the 19th century analysed sexuality in a secularised approach that differed enormously from the religious vocabulary of moral guilt and sins:

> Imbedded in bodies, becoming deeply characteristic of individuals, the oddities of sex relied on a technology of health and pathology. And conversely, since sexuality was a medical and medicalizable object, one had to try and detect it – as a lesion, a dysfunction, or a symptom – in the depths of the organism, or on the surface of the skin, or among all the signs of behavior. The power which thus took charge of sexuality set about contacting bodies, caressing them with its eyes, intensifying areas, electrifying surfaces, dramatizing troubled moments. It wrapped the sexual body in its embrace.[4]

Deviance was not only associated with delinquency, but perversions were also turned into pathological phenomena due to the modern medical discourses, which revolved around the differentiation of normal/anormal. From now on, the heteronormative bourgeois family was the centre of political, economic, medical, and juridical operations; it became an ideal image for a healthy society and economy, while persistently being problematised as a source of trouble that required measures of control. At this point, Foucault recalls the sexual panics of hysterical women or masturbating children who pose permanent threats to the moral purity within the family.[5] Next to these inner threats of the bourgeois family, as an outer threat appeared in those subjects diagnosed as homosexual, members "of the numberless family of perverts who were on friendly terms with delinquents and akin to madmen."[6] As much as the history of sexuality changes over time, and differs from context to context, normalising and naturalising tendencies of equating disease and illness persist up to the present. Sexual bodies are also embraced by metaphorical means, and I am interested in how the semantics of crisis link excessive economies to deviance and disease.

While crises of capital come up continuously, crises of desire are also repeatedly conjured. The eclipse of desire, the claim of confusion in the libidinal household, is a topic that frequently occurs in media debates. It often accompanies a critique of the

---

4   Michel Foucault, *History of Sexuality: An Introduction*, vol. 1 (NY: Pantheon Books, 1978), 44.

5   Foucault, 110–114.

6   Foucault, 40.

commodification of intimacy and sexuality. In recent years, such claims of a crisis of desire took a decisive reactionary turn: far-right, religious actors postulate such a crisis while attacking an alleged "gender ideology."[7] They argue that feminism, gender equality, diversity, and liberated sexualities put the desire for heterosexual family formations at risk. How is this rhetoric on desire in crisis connected to the endless cycles of capital's crises?

This chapter considers these questions while noting the following assumption. Crises of capital are often discussed with metaphors that display the pathologising semantics that link perversion to sickness. These metaphorical manoeuvres strengthen the appeal of security and safety associated with the heteronormative family. At the same time, claims of a crisis of desire seem to connect economic critique with matters of sexuality. As manifold, divergent, and even contradictory as these metaphors and semantics of crises may be, I suspect that they imply a distinction between a normal economy, on the one hand, and a perverted economy, on the other. As shown below, this distinction bears a long intellectual tradition, going back to Aristotle. Due to this distinction, economic crises may offer conservatives an opportunity to re-establish heteronormative family values. Yet, when it comes to metaphors that seek to depict economic crisis, my focus is not on the alleged individual intention of a speaker or author; my focus is on the semantic interplay that metaphors unfold. When it comes to reactionary movements and actors who claim a crisis of desire, I assume a concrete rhetorical strategy at work aiming to associate neoliberalism's hazards with queer bodies. Despite all their discursive difference, both narratives of crisis – of capital and desire – bear naturalising effects. They tend to naturalise capitalism and heterosexual family formations. This linkage may be traced in bodily metaphors deployed to describe a crisis. Through reference to an organic system, naturalising effects occur. These metamorphic bodies are not any body, but specific bodies depicted as sick and deviant. And I assume a strong correlation between these bodies that symbolise the crises and the bodies impacted the most by economic crises.

My analysis is informed by the theses of Gilles Deleuze and Félix Guattari on the entanglements of desire and economy. In their two volumes on capitalism and schizophrenia, Deleuze and Guattari opt for rethinking capitalism, assuming that desire and economy are ontologically connected. Moreover, production "constitutes a cycle whose relationship to desire is that of an immanent principle."[8] They thus

7   Roman Kuhar and David Patternotte offer an overview on the political usages of the term "gender ideology." See Roman Kuhar and David Patternotte, "'Gender Ideology' in Movement: Introduction," in Anti-Gender Campaigns in Europe. Mobilizing Against Equality, ed. Roman Kuhar and David Patternotte (London: Rowman & Littlefield, 2017).

8   Gilles Deleuze and Félix Guattari, Anti-Oedipus. Capitalism and Schizophrenia (Minneapolis: University of Minnesota, 1983), 5.

define desire as a productive force that creates new assemblages; therefore, desire bears transformative potential, as these new assemblages undermine socioeconomic orders. In this view, desire "produces reality, or stated another way, desiring-production is one and the same thing as social production."[9] Desire manifests materially – it moves bodies and makes them work. Hence, it is not a mere fantasy that lacks reality. It instead works as an ontological force that produces socioeconomic orders.[10] In its productivity, desire also appears as a driving force of capitalism. In this respect, economies must be broadly understood as economies of desire. Commonly, the economy is conceived as a system of rational choice; market rationality allegedly regulates economic processes. Against this naïve conception of capitalism as a pure sphere of reason, Deleuze and Guattari adhere to an intellectual lineage that revolves around the affective dynamics in capitalist processes, as in Friedrich Nietzsche, Georges Bataille, and Pierre Klossowski, among others. Pursuing this path, Deleuze and Guattari grasp economies as economies of desire – hence, desire works as the driving force of capital.[11]

Due to these ontological entanglements of desire and economy, my perspective is twofold: economies are driven by desire, and vice versa, desire is economised.[12] After laying out how capitalism is driven by desire, my second assumption requires further clarification. The economisation of desire hints at the fact that desire is organised to suit the economic order. For instance, Deleuze and Guattari point out that Sigmund Freud's model of Oedipal desire universalised the bourgeois family. In doing so, it served the requirements of Fordist societies because it is built on the figures of the masculine worker as breadwinner and the housewife as the unpaid provider of care work.[13] This linkage of economy, gender roles, and sexual relations is already inherent in the etymology of *oikonomia*: *Oikos* defined the household, and thus an administration of land that works through gendered and sexual roles. Shifting from the ancient *Oikos* to modern capitalism, the heteronormative organisation of gender and sexuality provides the basic ground for surplus extraction. Silvia Federici lays out how the gendered division of labour secures social reproduction:

---

9   Deleuze and Guattari, 29.
10   Deleuze and Guattari, 25.
11   Deleuze and Guattari, 239. Of course, not only Deleuze and Guattari offer this insight; authors also such as Luc Boltanski and Ève Chiapello – who remain sceptical to the formers' praise of productive desire – assume that as "a process of unlimited accumulation, capitalism must constantly stimulate tendencies to insatiability and activate different forms of desire for accumulation: amassing property; concentrating power." See Luc Boltanski and Ève Chiapello, *The New Spirit of Capitalism* (NY: Verso, 2005), 487.
12   Jule Govrin, *Begehren und Ökonomie. Eine sozialphilosophische Studie* (Berlin: de Gruyter, 2020).
13   Deleuze and Guattari, *Anti-Oedipus*, 51–57.

The expulsion of reproductive work from the spheres of economic relations and its deceptive relegation to the sphere of the "private," the "personal," "outside" of capital accumulation, and, above all, "feminine" has made it invisible as work and has naturalized its exploitation. It has also been the basis for the institution of a new sexual division of labor and a new family organization, subordinating women to men.[14]

All in all, this exploitation of gender inequality, like the formation of the heteronormative family as an economic unit, appears as an economisation of desire. These subjectivations operate through disciplining desire.

To grasp these entanglements of desire and economy, it is essential to inquire into their molecular, micropolitical and molar, macropolitical movements.[15] For this purpose, Deleuze and Guattari introduce the useful analytical tools of deterritorialisation and reterritorialisation. Deterritorialisation unbinds desire from socioeconomic hierarchies, whereas reterritorialisation binds desire back into these orders.[16] De- and reterritorialisation always go together because capital "axiomatizes the decoded flows," which means organising them according to the principle of accumulation, and simultaneously "reterritorializes the deterritorialized flows."[17] For example, the deterritorialising dynamics of financial speculation guided the economic crisis in 2008, and the subsequent state interventions and investments to save banks can be seen as reterritorialisation.[18] Capital's crises unfold deterritorialising dynamics, and these deterritorialisations manifest as dispossessions that intensify socio-political crises. The impacts of such socio-political crises stemming from accumulation through dispossession[19] are often addressed in terms of a crisis of de-

---

14   Silvia Federici, *Re-enchanting the World: Feminism and the Politics of the Commons* (Oakland, CA: PM Press, 2019), 17.

15   Deleuze and Guattari, *Anti-Oedipus*, 181–184.

16   Deleuze and Guattari, 35.

17   Deleuze and Guattari, 266.

18   Adam Tooze offers a profound analysis on the financial crisis of 2008: Adam Tooze, *Crashed. How a Decade of Financial Crisis Changed the World* (London: Alan Lane, 2018). Deleuze and Guattari deploy their twin terms of de- and reterritorialisation in an analytical approach and a normative approach. They understand deterritorialisation as a potentially transformative movement assuming capitalism could collapse by continuously exceeding its own limits. For them, the goal lies in "liberating the schizoid movement of deterritorialisation in all the flows, in such a way that this ... affects just as well the flows of labor and desire, of production, knowledge, and creation in their most profound tendency": Deleuze and Guattari, *Anti-Oedipus*, 321. About 50 years after the publication, and after five decades of neoliberalism, Deleuze and Guattari's assessment appears all too hopeful. Nowadays, the term "deterritorialisation" perfectly describes the transnational capital flows in a globalised world.

19   On accumulation through dispossession as main mechanism of capital, see David Harvey, *The New Imperialism* (Oxford: Oxford UP, 2005).

sire. For instance, right-wing forces frame the effects of globalisation as a crisis of the heterosexual family. This reactionary rhetoric summons sexual politics for affective mobilisation – a rhetorical twist that may be conceived as reterritorialising resentment.

I situate my approach in the field of feminist economics, following two impulses. First, Lucí Cavallero and Verónica Gago argue that a "feminist reading of debt proposes concrete bodies and narratives of its operation in opposition to financial abstraction."[20] Taking up their proposal, I pursue a bottom up approach for analysing the economy regarding its material impacts on and inscriptions in bodies. Second, Evangeline Hellinger offers a reading of precarious, popular economic practices such as trash picking in terms of metaphors of economic bodies. In doing so, she seeks to pluralise perspectives on economy. Following the ecofeminist author duo J. K. Gibson-Graham, Heilinger's approach aims at multiplying "the metaphor of body, using 'economic bodies' (rather than economic body) to counter powerful existing metaphors that promote the idea of a singular, unified, economic totality such as 'the body of Capitalism' and 'the Market.'"[21] She further aims to unveil the differential of power inscribed in bodies. All in all, her approach of using "metaphor of 'bodies' ... – rather than 'actor', 'economy', or 'economic actor'" seeks

(1) to pluralize and multiply economic systems; (2) to emphasize the vulnerability of the human bodies living and working under conditions of structural inequality; and (3) to utilize the power of metaphor to insert images of vulnerable economies in the minds of readers.[22]

Heilinger highlights that the

relationships of and between economic bodies can be understood only through engaging a radical analysis that incorporates intersectional analytics of power, including but not limited to gender, race/ethnicity, class, sexuality, nationality, embodiment, and other structural forms of power.[23]

Although her approach differs from mine, her insights about the socio-somatic[24] dimension of the economy and the economic dimension of bodies support analysing bodily metaphors of crisis. Nicky Marsh offers a similar approach in exploring the

20   Luci Cavallero and Verónica Gago, *A Feminist Reading of Debt* (London: Pluto Press, 2021), 5.
21   Evangeline Heilinger, "Queer Economies: Possibilities of Queer Desires and Economic Bodies (Because 'the Economy' is Not Enough)," in *Global Justice and Desire: Queering Economy*, ed. Nikita Dhawan et al. (NY: Routledge, 2015), 199.
22   Heilinger, 198.
23   Heilinger, 197.
24   Govrin, *Begehren und Ökonomie*, 142–144.

linguistics of crisis and its manifestation in metaphors of deviant and diseased bodies. She "focuses on the recurring deployment of bodily metaphors in moments of recent crisis, highlighting the ways in which they lay bare some of the contradictions inherent in neo-liberal conceptions of the economic corpus."[25] My consequent analysis relies on their studies to carve out the semantic interplay of narratives of economic crisis and narratives of a crisis of desire.

To pursue this endeavour, the first part of this chapter provides insights into the genealogical assemblage, which links bodies, economies, deviance, and disease in various metaphors. The second part focuses on bodily metaphors of financial crises. The third part discusses reactionary claims of a crisis of desire and, to conclude, I offer an outlook on the intermingling of virological and social immunisation amid the recent COVID-19 pandemic crisis.

Sane and straight economies versus diseased and deviant economies

The somatic metaphorisation of economy bears a long intellectual history, resulting from (nonmetaphorical) material linkages between economy and corporeality. In its most basic procedures, the economy organises bodily needs and thus provides the means for social reproduction and may thus be conceived as *body economic*.[26] Given this bodily basis of the economy, it becomes obvious why the body serves as such a prominent economic metaphor. Early attempts to describe economic organisation leans on the body and conceives of its organic processes as models to describe economic processes, thereby revealing that the body is literally the most proximate metaphor. Fundamental economic concepts, such as "homoestasis," are, in fact, former corporeal concepts that grasp the body's household. As persistent as such material and metaphorical linkages between economy and corporeality are, they are far from static, constantly shifting to other forms, expressions, and semantic fields. Like our understanding and perception of corporeality changes in the course of histories, approaches to economy change over time. As mentioned above, etymologically, economy (*Oikonomia*) defined the household. In contrast, the idea of the economy as a separate sphere is a modern phenomenon that emerged in the early Enlightenment philosophies of the 18th century, as J. K. Gibson-Graham observe. Even Adam Smith's conception of the market coins economy as a corporeal, organic system:

---

25   Nicky Marsh, "Desire and Disease in the Speculative Economy. A Critique of the Language of Crisis," *Journal of Cultural Economy* 4, no. 3 (2011): 301.

26   David Stuckler and Sanjay Basu, *Body Economic. Why Austerity Kills. Recessions. Budget Battles, and the Politics of Life and Death* (NY: Basic Books, 2013), 139.

the body economic is an organism, a modern paradigm of totality that is quite ubiquitous and familiar. The organismic totality emerged, by some accounts, with the birth of "the economy" as a discrete social location. When Adam Smith theorized the social division of labor as the most productive route to social reproduction, he laid the groundwork for a conception of "the economy" as a coherent and self-regulating whole. By analogy with the individual who labored to produce his own means of subsistence, thereby constituting a unity of production and consumption, Smith saw society as structured by a division of labor among quintessentially "economic" human beings laboring for their own good and achieving the common good in a process of harmonious reproduction.[27]

Still, for Gibson-Graham, this *body economic* is not a neutral but a gendered body that relies on the masculine conception of a self-regulating, strengthened organic system:

Man's body, constituted as an organism structured by a life force that produces order from within, became at this time the modern episteme, setting unspoken rules of discursive practice that invisibly unified and constrained the multifarious and divergent discourses of the physical, life, and social sciences. Modern economics is grounded in Man's body, finding the essence of economic development in man's essential nature – his labor (the struggle against nature and death), for example, or his needs and desires.[28]

One might argue against Gibson-Graham that the economic is depicted in various manners, and that different metaphorical figures symbolise divergent aspects of the economy, as Heilinger shows. Yet, Gibson-Graham hint at the overall conception of capitalism, and its most prominent discursive figure, the *homo economicus*. Even if its boundaries have become more permeable during capitalist history, in its discursive foundations, the homo economicus constitutes a masculinised figure defined by its self-sufficiency, passion for capitalist ventures, and entrepreneurial spirit. It is modelled in distinction to gendered and racialised alterity.[29] In this overarching, genealogical view, Gibson-Graham's analogy of the capitalist economy and the masculine body seems accurate.

This modern paradigm of the economic body that Gibson-Graham portray marks the theorising of capitalist economies as bodies. These economic bodies are regularly at risk due to disease but get revalorised to grow and prosper. Thus, there

---

27   J. K. Gibson-Graham, *The End of Capitalism (as We Knew It). A Feminist Critique of Political Economy* (Minneapolis: University of Minnesota Press, 2006), 98.

28   Gibson-Graham, 101.

29   A detailed study on the construction of the *homo economicus* in distinction to racialised and gendered alterity is provided by economist Friederike Habermann. See Friederike Habermann, *Der homo oeconomicus und das Andere* (Baden-Baden: Nomos, 2008).

is a double movement at play in corporeal metamorphoses of economic processes: first, steady tendencies for growth, and second, continuous cycles of crisis. Economy and society appear "as an organic structure that operates as a unity among harmoniously functioning parts," and considering this, "[c]apitalist history is portrayed as a succession of such structures, each one experiencing maturation and healthy functioning followed by sickness and death."[30] In the meantime, "growth and reproduction are the narrative constants of capitalism's story, revealing the hidden role of accumulation as its life force."[31]

Relying on Gibson-Graham's analysis, Heilinger stresses the importance of pluralising economic bodies. For in statements such as "the economy is sick," it becomes visible that it is mostly thought of as a singular body, shaped in terms of embodiments that "rely on a Western framework that values certain 'masculine-affiliated' qualities over 'feminine-affiliated' others."[32] In a similar vein to Gibson-Graham, Heilinger hints at "the gendered nature of economic discourse," yet the

> tendency to anthropomorphize "the economy" also serves to break down an image of the economy as singular: "the" economy is variously described as masculine, feminine, hard, soft, sick, dying, racialized, reproducing, and lazy. ... Each of these scenarios holds promise for imagining multiple, diverse economic bodies.[33]

As much as I sympathise with Hellinger's approach, I disagree with her assumption that an expression such as "the economy is sick" refers to singularity. I would argue instead that discourses pursuing a disease diagnosis of the economy tend to distinguish between a safe, sane, stable, and straight economy, on the one hand, and a deviant, diseased economy, on the other, associated with a plurality of precarised, perverted bodies. This leads us to corporeal metaphors of crises.

Crises, commonly coined in terms of disease and deviance, are depicted in bodily metaphors of ill and infectious bodies.[34] Kristoffer Klammer offers an historic-semantic analysis of economic crises.[35] His findings make clear that images of illness and sickened bodies do not only appear in the contexts of economic crises in the

---

30   Gibson-Graham, *The End of Capitalism*, 100.

31   Gibson-Graham, 100.

32   Heilinger, "Queer Economies," 203.

33   Heilinger, 203.

34   Another metaphorical strand is the semantic field of machines and mechanics, yet this appears minor in contrast to the strand of metaphors of disease and sick bodies, which may be explained by the fact that the metaphorisation of the economy as an organic system or as body politic has a much longer history. See Kristoffer Klammer, "Körper und Krankheit, Maschine und Mechanik. Formen und Funktionen von Metaphern in ökonomischen Krisendiskursen," *Jahrbuch für Wirtschaftsgeschichte* (2016): 416.

35   Klammer, "Körper und Krankheit," 410.

twentieth and twenty-first centuries. This metaphorisation goes back to the idea of the *body politic*, prominently depicted by Ernst Kantorowicz,[36] which presents social systems as organic systems. Gibson-Graham implicitly rely on the term "body politics," naming body metaphors of the economy as *"body economic."*[37]

Metaphors in general – and body metaphors in particular – bear political impact. They intervene in social imaginations, enabling new visions for more just societies. They can also limit imagination in established economic systems. As Heilinger comments:

> [M]etaphors influence our thinking whether or not we are explicitly aware of the metaphor's role in our decision-making process. [T]hose who consider all economic activities part of a singular, unified entity such as "the economy" will seek out economic solutions for a singular, unified economy, convinced these are the best solutions regardless of data. If the same people are willing to think of economies as bodies – as lots of different kinds of "people" moving through the world interacting with other "people" – they will look for economic solutions that meet the needs of diverse people who will function best by interacting with others to meet their needs.[38]

Her assessment can also be understood in a negative sense. When bodies marked as "other" are associated with economic practices from which one wishes to distance oneself, body metaphors may exclude economic alternatives and, at the same time, reinforce the stigmatisation of those bodies.

Even as metaphors differ with every crisis, there are common, characteristic features. Klammer roughly defines two fields of crisis metaphors: first, metaphors of disease and sickened bodies, and second, metaphors of medicine, cures, and treatments.[39] Metaphors of ill bodies usually point to a particular problem and offer a specific interpretation of this problem. In contrast, medical metaphors suggest ideas for a possible cure.[40]

There are numerous examples revolving around the financial crises or the economic crisis that arose from the COVID-19 pandemic, seen across the titles of books, newspapers, and other scholarly works – for example, *Financial Crisis and the Free*

---

36   Ernst Kantorowicz, *The King's Two Bodies. A Study in Medieval Political Theology* (Princeton: Princeton UP, 2016).

37   Gibson-Graham, *The End of Capitalism*, 98.

38   Heilinger, "Queer Economies," 199.

39   Klammer, "Körper und Krankheit," 410. In the context of corporal metaphors of illness, one must, of course, allude to the prominent essay by Susan Sontag, *Illness as Metaphor and AIDS and its Metaphors* (London: Penguin Books, 2002).

40   Klammer, "Körper und Krankheit," 410.

Market Cure, "There Will be No Easy Cure for a Recession Triggered by the Coronavirus," and "How the Sick Man Avoided Pneumonia: The Philippines in the Asian Financial Crisis."[41] Such metaphors warn against the hazards of specific economic practices – for instance, in 2008, against excessive, high-risk financial speculation. However, they also define the push to revitalise the economic body. A tendency becomes visible to naturalise certain conceptions of the economy as it is depicted as an organism that became sick, and thus needs recovery. This tendency connects with a long tradition that reaches back before the birth of capitalism.

Especially in metaphors which depict financial crises, we can spot a subtle distinction between a "normal" economy that seems stable and secure and an economy that turned bad by being too excessive. For instance, in the case of the financial crisis of 2008, it was the speculation with housing mortgages that upset a functional economy. Such subtle distinctions between natural and unnatural economies appear in Aristotle's writings.[42] He distinguishes between "wealth acquisition" and "household management."[43] Aristotle states that "there is a natural kind of property acquisition for household managers and statesmen."[44] He defines this natural sphere of acquisition and administration of good, as *Oikos*, as economy. He connects the household to natural reproductive cycles and portrays the *Oikos* in its stabilising effects that uphold social orders, ergo, the patriarchal order of the "master of the household." The master governs "his" wife and children as "his" slaves.[45] In contrast, "there is another

---

41   John Allison, *The Financial Crisis and the Free Market Cure: Why Pure Capitalism is the World Economy's Only Hope* (NY: McGraw Hill, 2018). Simon Jenkins, "There Will be No Easy Cure for a Recession Triggered by the Coronavirus," *The Guardian*, March 9, 2020, https://www.theguardian.com/commentisfree/2020/mar/09/cure-recession-coronavirus-economic-collapse-globalisation; Marcus Noland, "The Philippines in the Asian Financial Crisis: How the Sick Man Avoided Pneumonia," *Asian Survey* 40, no. 3 (2000): 401–12

42   Aristotle also links economy to medicine, even as he differentiates the tasks of a household manger and those of a doctor: "For one might be puzzled as to why wealth acquisition is a part of household management but medicine is not, even though the members of a household need health, just as they need life and every other necessity. And in fact there is a way in which it is the task of a household manager or ruler to see to health, but in another way it is not his task but a doctor's. So too with wealth: there is a way in which a household manager has to see to it, and another in which he does not, and an assistant craft does": Aristotle, *Politics*, trans. C. D. C. Reeve (Indianapolis: Hackett Publishing Company, 1998), 1258a.

43   Aristotle, 1256a.

44   Aristotle, 1256b.

45   Aristotle, 1255b. Aristotle embeds the household in natural cycles of reproduction: "It is evident that nature itself gives such property to all living things, both right from the beginning, when they are first conceived, and similarly when they have reached complete maturity. Animals that produce larvae or eggs produce their offspring together with enough food to last them until they can provide for themselves. Animals that give birth to live offspring carry food for their offspring in their own bodies for a certain period, namely, the natural substance we call milk": Aristotle, 1256b.

type of property acquisition which is especially called wealth acquisition";[46] it does not aim at the use-value of goods, but rather at their exchange value. "Take the wearing of a shoe, for example, and its use in exchange":[47] the practice of simply wearing shoes defines the household where all goods are used for subsistence; the exchange defines chrematistics, and thus deals to acquire more and more and transgress the proper use of a good. In short, shoes should be worn and not exchanged, according to Aristotle.

One may sympathise with Aristotle's decisive stance against any kind of economy in which exchange value transcends use-value, and thus does not aim at the good life but at accumulating goods. However, his distinction between economy and chrematistics involves difficult distinctions as he projects sociosexual norms onto economic practices. In contrast to the natural household, chrematistics is seen as unnatural, excessive, and a destabilising set of economic practices because "the part of wealth acquisition which is commerce does not exist by nature."[48] It is acceptable to exchange wine for wheat if needed, "for its purpose was to fill a lack in a natural self-sufficiency."[49] Yet, exchange that merely aims at acquiring and accumulating goods is morally wrong. In early medieval Europe, Thomas Aquinas, a neo-Aristotelian, reworked the concepts of chrematistics and strengthened its sexual associations. Aquinas characterises chrematistics as excessive, cannibalistic, unnatural, perverted, and sodomitical. He thus links it to sinful, sexual practices out of wedlock, while, in contrast, the household represents the "natural" economy incorporated by the patriarchal family.[50] Moreover, Aquinas' rhetoric undergoes an antisemitic twist. Christian ideology forbade credit. Meanwhile Jewish people were banned from working as farmers, artisans, shop owners, or millers. They were thus forced to conduct credit transactions and, in a blatant victim-perpetrator reversal, were treated with hostility and resentment for doing so. Hence, the modern antisemitic associations with finance stem from this early anti-Judaism and its stigmatising practices.

Even without examining these older ideas on natural and unnatural economy in detail, it already becomes apparent that economic metaphors of disease and illness rely on distinctions between a morally good and bad economy. These distinctions are actualised in discourses of crises.

---

46   Aristotle, 1256b.
47   Aristotle, 1257a.
48   Aristotle, 1257a.
49   Aristotle, 1257a.
50   Sabine Schülting, "Wa(h)re Liebe. Geldgeschfte und Liebesgaben in der Frühen Neuzeit," in *Imaginationen des Anderen im 16. und 17. Jahrhundert*, ed. Ina Schabert and Michaela Boenke (Wiesbaden: Harrassowitz, 2002).

Cycles of capitalist crises: Othering economies

Neoliberal economic policies are deeply intertwined with neoconservative family values. Early neoliberal pioneers and neoconservative politicians such as Margret Thatcher, Ronald Reagan, and Gary Becker were proponents of heteronormative family models. This approach is captured in Thatcher's catchphrase, "There's no such thing as society. There are individual men and women and there are families."[51]

Melinda Cooper outlines how early neoliberal policies came alongside claims of a family crisis – more precisely, the white, heterosexual, Fordist family.[52] Especially in the United States, economists blamed welfare state programs for supporting single mothers and thus increasing the disruption and divorce rates of heterosexual marriages – a deeply racialised debate, as Black single mothers were targeted as representatives for these allegedly misguided programs.[53] These appeals to re-establish white, bourgeois, christian, heterosexual family values and stable family structures thus served to sabotage social-state structures. As Wendy Brown stresses, neoliberal politics aims at a double privatisation: first, an economic privatisation of state structures, and second, a socio-political privatisation that deliberately sabotages the principles of public institutions.[54] In this approach to economic policies, the nuclear family becomes, economically and affectively, a privatised unit of care for the individual. The neoconservatives of Margaret Thatcher and Ronald Reagan's era in the 1980s framed these affective appeals to the family in terms of heteronormativity. Yet, as Melinda Cooper lays out, not every neoliberal economist shared these conservative family values; they "may well be in favor of the decriminalization of drugs, sodomy, bathhouses, and prostitution," still, "their apparent moral indifference comes with the proviso that the costs of such behavior must be fully borne in private."[55] For instance, in 1993, two Chicago economists, Richard Posner and Tomas Philipson, published their proposition on the HIV epidemic. Their text lacks any vocabulary of moral panics. According to the neoliberal approach, which conceives social spaces in the logics of markets, Posner and Philipson analyse sexual behaviour as economic transactions and assume that HIV infections are a result of

51   Douglas Keay, "Interview for *Woman's Own* ('No Such Thing as Society')," September 23, 1987, https://www.margaretthatcher.org/document/106689. David Harvey offers a concise overview of the history of neoliberalism. See David Harvey, *A Brief History of Neoliberalism* (Oxford: Oxford UP, 2007).

52   Melinda Cooper, *Family Values: Between Neoliberalism and the New Social Conservatism* (NY: Zone Books, 2017), 8.

53   Cooper, 32–40.

54   Wendy Brown, "Authoritarian Freedom in Twenty-First Century 'Democracies,'" in *Authoritarianism: Three Inquiries in Critical Theory*, ed. Wendy Brown, Peter Gordon, and Max Pensky (Chicago: University of Chicago Press, 2018), 18.

55   Cooper, *Family Values*, 174–175.

rational cost–benefit calculation of the respective actors.[56] This serves as an argument to privatise responsibility, and thus privatise the medical costs, which, in the end, means reducing public health programs. Moreover, their cynical conclusion is that the death of AIDS patients is more profitable for the state:

> Taking into account the limited life expectancy of AIDS patients in the early 1990s and the correspondingly foreshortened burden on public welfare programs such as Medicaid, they calculated that the AIDS crisis might in fact have saved the state money in terms of long-term Social Security payments. Those who were dying of AIDS in the greatest numbers tended on average to be young but poor and relatively unproductive (aside from being ill, many of them were drug users); the state therefore would have lost relatively little in terms of productive working years from their premature deaths.[57]

As much as this approach contrasts the moralistic arguments deployed by neoconservative politicians such as Thatcher or Reagan, both neoliberal strands share the tendency to privatise responsibility. Thus, they seek to deterritorialise the market, while reterritorialising social relation in the idea of the family as an intimate unit of care. After briefly outlining these tenets of neoliberal family policies, I turn now to economic crisis metaphors that conjure up sexual panic.

Nicky Marsh notes that metaphors of sex and disease intersect in discourses on financial crises. In crisis cycles that accompany the rhetoric of boom and bust, the "possibility of the bust is always contained within the figurative languages of the boom and images of degeneration and disease are never very far removed from these sexualised languages of masculine desire."[58] In the first decades of neoliberalism, the bodies of energetic managers – usually white, bourgeois, cisgender, and heterosexual – symbolised the successful entrepreneur, the venture capitalist whose joy for risk pushes the capitalist desire for creative destruction[59] or the dynamic manager, the creative CEO.[60] Commonly, these bodies traditionally symbolise the figure of the *homo economicus*, building the unmarked norm in contrast to bodies marked

56   Cooper, 168–170.

57   Cooper, 170.

58   Marsh, "Desire and Disease," 303.

59   The idea that capitalism is defined by a logic of progression that manifests as cycles of creation and destruction, thus in processes of creative destruction, originates from economist of Joseph Schumpeter. See Joseph Schumpeter, *Capitalism, Socialism and Democracy* (London: Routledge, 1994), 82–84. Teresa de Lauretis rightfully criticises that Schumpeter's view was much too optimistic, concealing the material destruction of work structures and social structures. See Teresa de Lauretis, *Freud's Drive. Psychonalysis, Literature and Film* (NY: Palgrave Macmillan, 2010), 93–95.

60   Boltanski and Chiapello, *The New Spirit*, 78–80.

by racialised and gendered differences. Yet, in times of crisis, certain manager, investor, and trader bodies, which usually represent growth and progression, must be put at a distance from economic policies. They must be defamed as unnormal, unnatural. Similarly, those economic practices that appear all too excessive and as a cause for crisis must be presented as an exception to the established economic system, which is presented in the image of a stable and natural economy. Marsh shows how, in contexts of currency crises, politicians who were very much in favour of neoliberal politics became eager to distance themselves from financial speculation. Hence, "heads of state, from Robert Nixon to Margaret Thatcher to Mahathir Mohamad, have repeatedly damned the willful opportunism and self-interest of currency traders."[61] In the 1990s, after the peak of the HIV crisis in Western Europe, the metaphorical field of infection was actualised: "The description of such traders as the 'AIDS of the world economy', attributed to Jacques Chirac, potently suggests how the healthy blood of speculation becomes infected in such instances, as it is turned against its host organism."[62]

There is no coherent metaphorisation of economy as a body, yet a strong heteronormative framing defines them, as the economy is imagined in the idea of heterosexual dynamics, as Gibson-Graham stress.[63] Still, these economic metaphors stuck in the heterosexual matrix differ enormously from one another. For instance, in discourses of financial specialisation, speculation is feminised, while the traders are characterised by masculinised striving to venture and to conquer. The dynamics that unfold between speculation and speculator are thus grasped as heterosexual seduction.[64] In times of crisis, economic metaphors often imply a separation between a "good economy" and an economy "gone bad." Of course, it is neither feasible nor desirable to draw a straight genealogical line from Aristotle and Aquinas to current metaphors. Still, they share the differentiation of two types of economies expressed in terms of deviance. To give another example, Gibson-Graham explain how the body of the industrial economy is depicted as a masculine body while labour runs like blood through the economy's veins – it is a robust body of constant, stable growth. "Social labor is pumped from the industrial heart of the economy and circulates through the veinous circuitry in its commodity, money, and productive forms. As it flows, it nourishes the body and ensures its growth."[65] Yet, in the Global North, this body is shaken by waves of deindustrialisation in the last decades of the

---

61   Marsh, "Desire and Disease," 305.
62   Marsh, 305. On metaphoric uses of AIDS and HIV, see Sontag, *Illness as Metaphors*, 93–184.
63   Gibson-Graham, *The End of Capitalism*, 101.
64   Urs Stäheli, *Spektakuläre Spekulation. Das Populäre der Ökonomie* (Frankfurt: Suhrkamp, 2007), 272–275.
65   Gibson-Graham, *The End of Capitalism*, 100.

20th century.[66] In the accelerated dynamics of economic globalisation, the new vital essence, the lifeblood, is not labour but finance capital. Its transitional, free-flow-ing, deterritorialised movements appear as a crisis in the double meaning suggested by Friedman: as a risk and an opportunity. According to Gibson-Graham, these am-bivalences inherent to finance capital become visible in vital metaphors – eventually, excessive flows are associated with semen. This association manifests most blatantly in the term *money shot* used in the porn industry. Gibson-Graham comment on the dangers posed by excessive capital flows as follows:

> Consider the seminal fluid of capitalism – finance capital (or money) – which has more traditionally been represented as the lifeblood of the economic system whose free circulation ensures health and growth of the capitalist body. As sem-inal fluid, however, it periodically breaks its bounds, unleashing uncontrollable gushes of capital that flow every which way, including into self-destruction. One such spectacle of bodily excess, a wet dream that stained markets around the globe, occurred in October 1987, when stock markets across the world crashed, vaporizing millions of dollars in immaterial wealth.[67]

Thus, financial speculation is imagined as an excess of flows that transgress bodily borders, rendering it porous, penetrable, erratic, and excessive.[68] The fear and dis-gust evoked by the metaphorical body manifests the homophobia inherent in the conceptualisation of the body economic.[69] This homophobic tendency is analysed by Gibson-Graham in quite abstract terms; they appear much more concretely in Chirac's quote calling traders "the HIV of the world." However, it also manifests in the infection metaphors that have circulated in discourses of economic crisis since the late 20th century. Marsh hints to the conjuncture of HIV and AIDS as a metaphor for economic danger and decline, feeding on the moral panics that orchestrated the stigmatising social discourses on HIV:

---

66   Gibson-Graham writes, "It is not hard to see lurking in the vicinity of economic and industrial policy a body engaged in a battle for survival. Couched in the language of the living body or machine, the economy is portrayed as an organism machine) whose endemic growth dy-namic (or mechanical functioning) is in jeopardy. Diagnoses usually focus upon two key areas of economic physiology, obstructions in the circulation system and/or malfunctioning of the heart. The faltering national economy is often compared to healthier bodies elsewhere, all poised to invade and deprive the ailing, or less fit, organism of its life force. Economic and industry policy is formulated to remove the internal, and create immunity to the external, threats to reproduction": Gibson-Graham, *The End of Capitalism*, 105.

67   Gibson-Graham, 135–137.

68   Gibson-Graham, 135.

69   Gibson-Graham, 137.

As a metaphor for financial bust ... the discourses of HIV/AIDS speak very pointedly to the tensions within the neo-liberal agenda. In replacing the ostensibly rational individual abstractions of financial risk with an emphasis on risk as a political and social phenomena the shift draws sceptical attention to the promise of tolerance that neoliberalism appears to hold out, requiring us to re-evaluate what kind of society this individualism produces.[70]

For instance, in "Britain in the mid-eighties HIV/AIDS emerged as a metaphor for the excesses of the financial market in ways that pointed precisely to the limitations of these ideals." Among others, a

parody published in *The Times Literary Supplement* in March 1987 ..., conflated the sexually celebratory languages of money with the fearful languages of AIDS in articulating a dream about "a deadly new ailment that was transmitted by money. The first people to go down with it were usurers and croupiers and everyone said 'serves them right', PAY PLAGUE: GOD'S PUNISHMENT FOR AVARICE: said the headlines; SERVE THE DIRTY BANKER'S RIGHT said the graffiti."[71]

In this manner, the image of the healthy economic body that got sick due to the excesses of financial speculation merges images of illness with denotations of deviance. As convincing as Marsh's reading can be of the metamorphotic linkages of HIV and speculation, disease, and deviance, her assumption that neoliberalism held out a promise of tolerance towards queer communities falls short. Even though Thatcher herself did not equate financial speculation and HIV as did British newspapers, she nevertheless nourished a deeply homophobic climate. In reaction to the growing LGBT movements claiming equal rights, Thatcher remarked in a speech at the 1987 Conservative Party conference, "Children who need to be taught to respect traditional moral values are being taught that they have an inalienable right to be gay. All of those children are being cheated of a sound start in life. Yes, cheated."[72] Consequently, in 1988, the Thatcher Government introduced Section 28, a law that censored queer publishing and prohibited public support in schools or local authorities.

These associations of capitalist crisis with disease and deviance reveal that neo-conservative politicians were well served by using metaphors depicting speculation gone bad, and linking this with the risk of infection caused by HIV. Such language

70   Marsh, "Desire and Disease," 306.
71   Marsh, 306.
72   Patrick Kelleher, "The Terrible History of Margaret Thatcher's Homophobic Section 28, 16 Years Since It was Repealed in England and Wales," *Pink News*, November 18, 2019, https://www.pinknews.co.uk/2019/11/18/section-28-homophobic-repealed-england-wales-history-margaret-thatcher/.

offered a possibility to praise their sound economic policies while distancing them from defamed economic practices such as speculation. It also allowed neoconservative politicians to reaffirm their heteronormative family values and create an aura of security and belonging promised by their politics. They thus rhetorically reterritorialise deterritorialised capital flows. As soon as they single out the economy's diseased and devious aberrations, the economy is renaturalised – and, in the meantime, queerness is denaturalised. A similar tendency seems to be at play in current reactionary movements.

Crisis of desire: Rhetoric of resentment and reactionary reterritorialisations

Claims of crises of desire come up regularly. They are primarily uttered in scandalising tones, embedded in media footage. For instance, in the mid-1990s, in the aftermath of the HIV crisis, sexologists diagnosed a decrease in libido. Such diagnoses of desire's decline persist in the 21st century. Yet, as Dagmar Herzog remarks, they are uttered so scandalously that it is impossible to decide if these claims bear any empirical basis.[73] Such a diagnosis often goes along with a fierce critique of May '68, highlighting how the liberalisation of sexuality led to its commodification. Even though it is hard to ascribe a clear-cut political position to such criticism, it often leads to reaffirming heteronormative family values. French author Michel Houellebecq, the self-entitled prophet of an "eclipse of desire,"[74] provides a compelling example. In his novels, the protagonists – white, bourgeois, heterosexual men in their midlife crises – attack the atomisation in late-capitalist society. Yet, the cause for all the suffering and assumed state of decadence lies for them in sexual liberalisation and gender equality. Houellebecq's protagonists prefigure the antifeminist rhetoric of current right-wing movements that attack feminism and movements for sexual emancipation for Western society's decline. What appears to be a critique of neoliberalism is an attack on gender equality and sexual rights.[75]

Houellebecq's novels and public statements provide only one of many examples. For instance, since 2013, the *Manif Pour Tous* – a far-right-wing, ultra-catholic movement – has protested legal gay marriage with similar rhetoric. This French movement has equivalents in other European countries, such as Germany and Italy. All de-

73   Dagmar Herzog, "Die 'Sexuelle Revolution' in Westeuropa und ihre Ambivalenzen," in *Sexuelle Revolution? Zur Geschichte der Sexualität im deutschsprachigen Raum seit den 1960er Jahren*, ed. Peter-Paul Bänziger et al. (Bielefeld: transcript, 2015), 636.

74   Jack Abecassis, "The Eclipse of Desire: L'Affaire Houellebecq," *MLN* 115, no. 4 (2000): 801–827.

75   For a detailed analysis of Houellebecq's reactionary rhetoric, see Jule Govrin, *Sex, Gott und Kapital. Houellebecqs Unterwerfung zwischen neoreaktionärer Rhetorik und postsäkularen Politiken* (Münster: Edition Assemblage, 2016).

ploy the same vocabulary and "corporate design." For example, they all use pink and blue as predominant colours to symbolise a strict gender dualism. Regarding the German equivalent, called *Demo für Alle*, Imke Schmincke outlines its main rhetorical manoeuvres:

> Instead of arguments, one only finds key concepts (i.e. discursive weapons) on their website, which are repeated and framed within a rhetoric of fear, loss and destruction. Marriage and the family are in danger; "gender ideology" is abolishing "natural" gender identities (male/female); parents' rights are in danger and must be defended; sexualization takes place in schools (via sex education), threatens children by violating their sense of shame; and indoctrination is underway (through sex education, "gender ideology," gender mainstreaming, "lobby groups" or LGBTIQ people).[76]

Queer bodies are targeted as hazards to society, hazards to children, hazards to families, and, finally, hazards to the economy. These bodies are associated with deterritorialising neoliberal policies. The French movement used anti-neoliberal rhetoric while protesting legalising gay marriage. They managed to associate the unpopular neoliberal policies of former French President François Hollande and his social-democratic government with homosexuality and rainbow families. They blame an alleged "gay lobby" or "LGBT lobby" for the precarisation and insecurity stemming from neoliberal state policies.[77] In the meantime, they advertise the heteronormative breadwinner family as a safe harbour against the dangers of economic globalisation. Hence, the bodies of gay and trans people depict the economic danger that threatens the wellbeing of so-called "common people." In the case of *Manif Pour Tous*, the movement managed to mobilise a platform for the far-right party *Rassemblement National* (formerly *Front National*). In the 2022 presidential elections, Marine Le Pen, party leader of *Rassemblement National*, prominently reached the ballot with centre-right neoliberal Emmanuel Macron for the second time in succession.

Associating queerness and neoliberalism is quite effective as a reactionary rhetoric strategy. It is particularly successful, as many neoliberal politicians have deployed a tone of tolerance towards sexual minorities since the 1990s, celebrating

---

76   Imke Schmincke, "Sexual Politics from the Right. Attacks on Gender, Sexual Diversity, and Sex Education," in *Right-Wing Populism and Gender. European Perspectives and Beyond*, ed. Gabriele Dietze and Julia Roth (Bielefeld: transcript, 2020), 64.

77   La Manif Pour Tous, "Une fois de plus, François Hollande méprise les familles," Press Release, July 1, 2016, https://www.lamanifpourtous.fr/actualites/une-fois-de-plus-francois-hollande -meprise-les-familles-communique-de-presse.

difference and diversity while increasing social inequality.[78] The anti-neoliberal and anti-globalisation rhetoric that right-wing actors use connects the crises of desire, conceived as a crisis of heterosexuality, with the threat of economic crisis. Broadly speaking, an alleged crisis of masculinity merges with the claim of national sovereignty. Thus, fixed gender roles are presented as a medical cure against the economic hazards of the present. For instance, Björn Höcke, a fascist politician in the *Alternative für Deutschland* (*AfD*), claimed, "We have to rediscover our masculinity. Only if we rediscover our masculinity will we be manful. And only if we are manful will we be able to become fortified; and we have to be able to become fortified, dear friends!"[79] Höcke also argues for a strict restriction of international experts and presents a higher reproduction rate as an opportunity to revitalise the economy in the German state of Thuringia, his electoral district.[80] In his perspective, a healthy economy is merely embodied by a white, German, patriarchal family. This volkisch-nationalist approach amalgamates the people's organic body (*Völkskörper*) with the economy's organic body (*Volkswirtschaft*), recalling the National Socialist regime's rhetoric in the 1930s and 1940s considering the economic crisis of 1929.[81]

The rise of such right-wing rhetoric resulted from the restructuring of work in the neoliberal decades, which strongly impacted gender roles. Analysing right-wing identarian politics, Brigit Sauer notes that "male labor became more precarious and the 'family income' declined as a consequence of neoliberal restructuring."[82] Still, instead of fighting the sources of social inequality, right-wing parties, such as Höcke's *AfD*, pursue a scapegoat logic. They blame migrants for the rising precarisation, and in so doing, conceal the economic causes of socio-political conflicts. While migrants, particularly Muslim migrants, function as an outer enemy, the inner enemies to attack include queers and feminists. They are associated with elites linked to finance – hence, antisemitic patterns are actualised.

Renaud Camus' conspiracy theory about "The Great Replacement" provides a paradigmatic example. Camus sets forth basic concepts for international right-wing politics today. He is not only closely connected to the French *Rassemblement*

---

78   In his autobiographical essay, Didier Eribon offers an intriguing analysis how these neoliberal politics reinforced right-wing parties, such as the *Rassemblemt National*. See Didier Eribon, *Returning to Reims* (Los Angeles: Semiotext(e), 2007).

79   Höcke translation by Birgit Sauer. See Birgit Sauer, "Authoritarian Right-Wing Populism as Masculinist Identity Politics. The Role of Affects," in *Right-Wing Populism and Gender. European Perspectives and Beyond*, ed. Gabriele Dietze and Julia Roth (Bielefeld: transcript, 2020), 29–31.

80   Dietmar Neuerer, "Landtagswahl Thüringens Wirtschaft warnt vor AfD-Wahl – DIW-Ökonom attestiert Partei wirtschaftsfeindliche Politik," *Handelsblatt*, October 21, 2019, https://www.handelsblatt.com/politik/deutschland/landtagswahl-thueringens-wirtschaft-warnt-vor-afd-wahl-diw-oekonom-attestiert-partei-wirtschaftsfeindliche-politik/25135846.html.

81   Klammer, "Körper und Krankheit," 410.

82   Sauer, "Authoritarian Right-Wing," 29.

National, but the German translation of his text was also published by *Antaois*, whose editor, Götz Kubitschek, is associated with Höcke and *AfD*. Camus' conspiracy theory claims that Muslim families and migrants had secretly replaced France's white population due to the French government's migration policies and the higher reproduction rate of Muslim families. Presenting a eugenic, biopolitical horror scenario that portrays migration in terms of stream and flood metaphors, he demands that national and cultural identity be bordered. He combines this claim of a clash of cultures with eugenic ideas of reproduction rates, thereby fusing aspects of cultural and biological racism. Moreover, Camus blames international elites in finance for secretly fostering the plan of exchanging populations – another clear-cut antisemitic narrative.

The sexual, gendered, racialised, religious other embodies the hazards of economic crises. Hence, while right-wing rhetoric often addresses economic inequalities, their aim does not lie in more just societies. To stick with the example of the *AfD*, their political programs do not aim at restructuring and redistributing property. Their anti-neoliberal and anti-globalisation rhetoric addresses the alleged crisis of masculinity and the decline of the patriarchal family. Sauer comments:

> The populist right frames the marginalization of working- and middle-class men as a "crisis of masculinity" and blames this crisis on female labor market integration, gender equality and, of course, migration policies. Instead of arguing for a new distribution of labor and time between men and women, the populist right channels the feelings caused by the deprived class status of "subordinated men" into hatred against well-educated women and against migrants.[83]

Sauer concludes that "the right-wing anti-gender discourse and the evocation of a 'crisis of masculinity' is another facet of the re-signification process of neoliberal social inequality, strategically confounding causes and consequences by interpellating 'wounded white men.'"[84] Such right-wing rhetoric often goes along with protectionist programs, like those promoted by former United States President Donald Trump, whose blatant sexism is embedded in the fairy tale of a hardworking, self-made man, thereby disavowing his wealthy family. Another example is Jair Bolsonaro, former president of Brazil, who presents a protectionist agenda while performing militarised masculinity and aggressively attacking and endangering queer communities. A more ambivalent example is Marine Le Pen, leader of *Rassemblement National*, who uses solid protectionist rhetoric and attempts to de-demonise her party by presenting herself as a strong, female leader while providing pro-gay and pro-feminist arguments – but only if she can use them to defame Muslims and

---

83   Sauer, "Authoritarian Right-Wing," 30.
84   Sauer, 30.

migrants. This protectionist rhetoric requires a separate analysis and hints at the differences within the field of current right-wing politics. At the same time, some shared characteristics of their rhetoric are already apparent.

Reactionary claims of crises of heterosexual desire and masculinity profit from neoliberal policies as they can address feelings of alienation and anger that stem from the increased inequality produced by neoliberalism's privatising and precarising policies. Instead of calling for market regulations, they call for a de-liberalisation of society and a return to a patriarchal order. In this regard, they draw on the two economies at work in metaphors of economic crisis: the natural and healthy body of the economy and, in contrast, the diseased and deviant body of the economy. Whereas white, Christian, heteronormative families depict the sane and safe national economy, queer bodies are associated with finance, trading, and venture capital – narratives that feed from patterns of antisemitic resentment. In this rhetorical realm, racialised bodies appear as a phantasmagorical threat of a cheap labour force that threatens employment and unregulated reproduction that threatens emasculated white men. These politics of fear and resentment do not challenge the causes of economic injustices but seek to deepen social inequalities by naturalising differences. As much as current reactionary positions and politics differ enormously from the neoconservative stance that Margaret Thatcher prominently represented, right-wing policies profit not only from the precarisation resulting from neoliberal policies but can also build on the neoconservative appeal to heteronormativity – praising the family as an affective nucleus amid the market sphere and social competition.

Even though current reactionary and neoconservative metaphors of crises differ tremendously, they share tendencies to naturalise the family by associating it with a healthy and stable economy. Meanwhile, the "bad" economy – the finance economy, embodied by trader figures in Thatcher's time and today – is depicted as diseased and deviant. In close connection with queer bodies and eventually racialised bodies, this excessive economy is othered and defamed as alien and abject. Hence, it is projected on the bodies of those who appear as a phantasmagorical threat to the white, christian family. They appear not only as embodiments of a perverted, unnatural, excessive economy but are also targeted as causes for capitalist crises, pursuing a rigorous scapegoat logic that covers the actual causes for capital's turmoil.

Conclusion: Metaphors of infection and immunisation in times of pandemic crisis

Economic crises conjure up disease metaphors often associated with deviance. These metaphorical manoeuvres traverse various discursive strands, although they cannot be conceived according to a linear coherence. Its manifestations are divergent and must not be reduced to individual intentions and expressions. There is no precise sequence of the semantics of crisis in the different sociohistorical contexts of Aristotle and Aquinas, Thatcher, and Trump. Still, they share tendencies of naturalising and denaturalising certain economies. Moreover, they unveil how crisis metaphors of disease strengthen social norms.

Instead of summarising the train of thought within this text at this point, a closer look at metaphors of infection and immunisation might be helpful. The metaphoric field of infection and immunisation is much too broad to outline in full.[85] Yet, a specific characteristic lies in the idea of social immunisation – immunising the social body means making it resilient against inner and outer enemies. This is a recurrent image that perhaps had its peak in times of National Socialism and its antisemitic appeal to an alleged organic unity of people (*Volkskörper*). Still, as we have seen in recent pandemic times, these metaphors alter when actual issues of infection and immunisation are at play. The COVID-19 pandemic, which shapes the present of my writing, radically shifts the perspectives on bodily metaphors of crisis and metaphors of immunisation.[86] It renders the material brutality of metaphors of social immunisation painfully perceptible. The bodies most exposed to the risk of COVID-19 infections are racialised, feminised bodies, which have few protections in associated workplaces – typically the highly precarious fields of care. In political discourse around the pandemic, social immunisation and virological immunisation often merge. For instance, Donald Trump rigorously employed the racist ascription of COVID-19 as the "Chinese virus" while constantly denying its dangers. Moreover, bodies marked as "other" are depicted as virological hazards. For example, many media images of herds of infections accompanied scandalising reports on migrant and Roma families in Berlin.[87] These families were called "clans" and stigmatised as irrational, irresponsible subjects spreading the virus.

In contrast, rural, white, more affluent, bourgeois villages – such as Berchtesgaden in Bavaria – that also turned out to be virus hotspots have not been similarly attacked. Such depictions not only reproduce racist logics of social immunisation but also conceal the real causes for infections – often economic inequality, manifesting in unprotected work environments and confined living conditions. At the same time, many lockdown restrictions revealed a narrow conception of familial

---

85   For a detailed analysis of social immunisation, see Roberto Esposito, *Immunitas. The Protection and Negation of Life* (Cambridge: Polity, 2011).

86   On the political dimensions of embodiment, and pandemic bodies, see Jule Govrin, *Politische Körper. Von Sorge und Solidarität* (Berlin: Matthes & Seitz, 2002).

87   Pascal Bartosz, "Polizei beobachtet Berliner Großfamilie: Clan-Hochzeit in Neukölln – trotz Corona-Maßnahmen," *Tagesspiegel*, March 31, 2021, https://www.tagesspiegel.de/berlin/po lizei-beobachtet-berliner-grossfamilie-clan-hochzeit-in-neukoelln-trotz-corona-massnah men/27056050.html; Berliner Zeitung, "Trauriger Spitzenreiter! Neukölln ist Deutschlands Corona-Hotspot," *Berliner Zeitung*, October 15, 2020, https://www.bz-berlin.de/berlin/neuko elln/trauriger-spitzenreiter-neukoelln-ist-deutschlands-corona-hotspot.

contacts, carrying old images of the bourgeois, heteronormative family living in one house, for example, in Bavaria.[88] This political focus on the family unfolds privatising effects: it denied the socioeconomic dimension of viral infection by defaming precarised subjects as irresponsible. In the broader picture, this appeal to self-responsibility hinders solidarity on a global scale – for instance, in the German federal government's refusal to release vaccine patents. Thus, to a certain degree, political discourses on the pandemic pursued a similar logic as crisis metaphors of disease and deviance: they projected ideas of social immunisation on virological immunisation and infection, often concealing the concrete virological routes of dissemination while undermining global measures against COVID-19.

In these pandemic times of crisis, a strong controversy about bodily self-determination is at stake. "Coronavirus deniers," as well as antivaxxers organising in right-wing contexts, tend to refer to bodily self-determination to protest basal solidaristic protections such as vaccinations and masks, even adapting and appropriating the feminist slogan "my body, my choice." They equate bodily self-determination with negative freedom and fully fail to recognise that our bodies are interdependent, reliant on mutual protection in a spirit of solidarity, just as the air we breathe is shared and cannot be divided into yours or mine. At the same time, these same right-wing contexts mobilise massively against the bodily self-determination of women and trans people, for example, through the illegalisation of abortion in the United States, or through the campaign against the human rights of trans people, who are currently the main target of right-wing attacks.

In terms of the body economic, the pandemic crisis has revealed clear winners and losers. The virus "has exposed, fed off and increased existing inequalities of wealth, gender and race." Consequently, over "two million people have died, and hundreds of millions of people are being forced into poverty while many of the richest – individuals and corporations – are thriving."[89] Indeed, crises offer opportunities. In this respect, Friedman is quite right. The cynicism of his statement is cruelly revealed by the COVID-19 pandemic just as in the multiple ongoing crises of our time.

---

88   Magdalena Müssig and Louka Goetzke, "Familismus in der Coronakrise," *Soziologie Magazin* (2020). https://soziologieblog.hypotheses.org/13599.

89   Esmé Berkhout et al., "The Inequality Virus. Bringing Together a World Torn Apart by Coronavirus Through a Fair, Just and Sustainable Economy," Oxfam International Policy Papers, January 25, 2021, https://www.oxfam.org/en/research/inequality-virus.

References

Abecassis, Jack. "The Eclipse of Desire: L'Affaire Houellebecq." *MLN* 115, no. 4 (2000): 801–827. https://doi.org/10.1353/mln.2000.0042

Allison, John, *The Financial Crisis and the Free Market Cure: Why Pure Capitalism is the World Economy's Only Hope*. NY: McGraw-Hill, 2018.

Aristotle. *Politics*. Translated by C. D. C. Reeve. Indianapolis: Hackett Publishing Company, 1998.

Bartosz, Pascal. "Polizei beobachtet Berliner Großfamilie: Clan-Hochzeit in Neukölln – trotz Corona-Maßnahmen." *Tagesspiegel*, March 31, 2021. https://ww w.tagesspiegel.de/berlin/polizei-beobachtet-berliner-grossfamilie-clan-hochz eit-in-neukoelln-trotz-corona-massnahmen/27056050.html.

Berkhout, Esmé, Galasso, Nick, Lawson, Max, Rivero Morales, Pablo Andrés, Taneja, Anjela, Vázquez Pimentel, Diego Alejo. "The Inequality Virus. Bringing Together a World Torn Apart by Coronavirus Through a Fair, Just and Sustainable Economy." Oxfam International Policy Papers, January 25, 2021. https://doi.org/10.2 1201/2021.6409.

Berliner Zeitung. "Trauriger Spitzenreiter! Neukölln ist Deutschlands Corona-Hotspot." *Berliner Zeitung*, October 15, 2020. https://www.bz-berlin.de/berlin/n eukoelln/trauriger-spitzenreiter-neukoelln-ist-deutschlands-corona-hotspot.

Boltanski, Luc, and Ève Chiapello. *The New Spirit of Capitalism*. NY: Verso, 2005.

Brown, Wendy. 2018. "Authoritarian Freedom in Twenty-First Century 'Democracies.'" In *Authoritarianism: Three Inquiries in Critical Theory*, edited by Wendy Brown, Peter Gordon, and Max Pensky, 7–45. Chicago: University of Chicago Press, 2018.

Cavallero, Lucí, and Verónica Gago. *A Feminist Reading of Debt*. London: Pluto Press, 2021.

Cooper, Melinda. *Family Values: Between Neoliberalism and the New Social Conservatism*. NY: Zone Books, 2017.

De Lauretis, Teresa. *Freud's Drive. Psychoanalysis, Literature and Film*. NY: Palgrave Macmillan, 2010.

Deleuze, Gilles, and Félix Guattari. *Anti-Oedipus. Capitalism and Schizophrenia*. Minneapolis: University of Minnesota, 1983.

Eribon, Didier. *Returning to Reims*. Los Angeles: Semiotext(e), 2007.

Esposito, Roberto. *Immunitas. The Protection and Negation of Life*. Cambridge: Polity Press, 2011.

Federici, Silvia. *Re-enchanting the World: Feminism and the Politics of the Commons*. Oakland, CA: PM Press, 2019.

Foucault, Michel. *History of Sexuality: An Introduction*. Vol. I. Translated by Robert Hurley. NY: Pantheon Books, 1978.

Friedman, Milton. *Capitalism and Freedom: Fortieth Anniversary Edition*. Chicago: University of Chicago Press, 2002.

Gibson-Graham, J. K. *The End of Capitalism (as We Knew It). A Feminist Critique of Political Economy*. Minneapolis: University of Minnesota Press, 2006.

Govrin, Jule. *Begehren und Ökonomie. Eine sozialphilosophische Studie*. Berlin: de Gruyter, 2020.

———. *Politische Körper. Von Sorge und Solidarität*. Berlin: Matthes & Seitz, 2022.

———. *Sex, Gott und Kapital. Houellebecqs Unterwerfung zwischen neoreaktionärer Rhetorik und postsäkularen Politiken*. Münster: Edition Assemblage, 2016.

Habermann, Friederike. *Der homo oeconomicus und das Andere*. Baden-Baden: Nomos, 2008.

Harvey, David. *A Brief History of Neoliberalism*. Oxford: Oxford UP, 2007.

———. *The New Imperialism*. Oxford: Oxford UP, 2005.

Heilinger, Evangeline. "Queer Economies: Possibilities of Queer Desires and Economic Bodies (Because 'the Economy' is Not Enough)." In *Global Justice and Desire: Queering Economy*, edited by Nikita Dhawan, Antke Engel, Christoph Holzhey, and Volker Woltersdorff, 195–213. NY: Routledge, 2015.

Herzog, Dagmar. "Die 'Sexuelle Revolution' in Westeuropa und ihre Ambivalenzen." In *Sexuelle Revoluton? Zur Geschichte der Sexualität im deutschsprachigen Raum seit den 1960er Jahren*, edited by Peter-Paul Bänziger, Magdalena Beljan, Franz Eder, and Pascal Eitler, 347–369. Bielefeld: transcript, 2015.

Jenkins, Simon. "There Will be No Easy Cure for a Recession Triggered by the Coronavirus." *The Guardian*, March 9, 2020. https://www.theguardian.com/commentisfree/2020/mar/09/cure-recession-coronavirus-economic-collapse-globalisation.

Kantorowicz, Ernst. *The King's Two Bodies. A Study in Medieval Political Theology*. Princeton: Princeton UP, 2016.

Keay, Douglas. "Interview for *Woman's Own* ('No Such Thing as Society')." September 23, 1987. https://www.margaretthatcher.org/document/106689.

Kelleher, Patrick. "The Terrible History of Margaret Thatcher's Homophobic Section 28, 16 Years Since It was Repealed in England and Wales." *Pink News*, November 18, 2019. https://www.pinknews.co.uk/2019/11/18/section-28-homophobic-repealed-england-wales-history-margaret-thatcher/.

Klammer, Kristoffer. "Körper und Krankheit, Maschine und Mechanik Formen und Funktionen von Metaphern in ökonomischen Krisendiskursen." *Jahrbuch für Wirtschaftsgeschichte* (2016): 397–422. https://doi.org/10.1515/jbwg-2016-0017

Kuhar, Roman, and David Patternotte. "'Gender Ideology' in Movement: Introduction." In *Anti-Gender Campaigns in Europe. Mobilizing Against Equality*, edited by Roman Kuhar and David Patternotte, 1–23. London: Rowman & Littlefield, 2017.

La Manif Pour Tous. "Une fois de plus, François Hollande méprise les familles." Press Release, July 1, 2016. https://www.lamanifpourtous.fr/actualites/une-fois-de-p lus-francois-hollande-meprise-les-familles-communique-de-presse.

Lynch, David. "Some Jobs are Coming Back, but Economy Will Need Years to Heal." *The Washington Post*, July 3, 2020. https://www.washingtonpost.com/business/2 020/07/03/some-jobs-are-coming-back-economy-will-need-years-heal/.

Marsh, Nicky. "Desire and Disease in the Speculative Economy. A Critique of the Language of Crisis." *Journal of Cultural Economy* (2011): 301–314. https://doi.org/1 0.1080/17530350.2011.586851

Müssig, Magdalena, and Goetzke. Louka. "Familismus in der Coronakrise." *Soziologie Magazin* (2020). https://soziologieblog.hypotheses.org/13599.

Mutikani, Lucia. "U.S. Labor Market Healing; Businesses Boost Spending as Profits Rebound." *Reuters*, June 25, 2021. https://www.reuters.com/business/us-weekly -jobless-claims-fall-first-quarter-gdp-unrevised-64-2021-06-24/.

Neuerer, Dietmar. "Landtagswahl Thüringens Wirtschaft warnt vor AfD-Wahl – DIW-Ökonom attestiert Partei wirtschaftsfeindliche Politik." *Handelsblatt*, October 21, 2019. https://www.handelsblatt.com/politik/deutschland/landtags wahl-thueringens-wirtschaft-warnt-vor-afd-wahl-diw-oekonom-attestiert-pa rtei-wirtschaftsfeindliche-politik/25135846.html.

Noland, Marcus. "The Philippines in the Asian Financial Crisis: How the Sick Man Avoided Pneumonia." *Asian Survey* 40, no. 3 (2000): 401–12. https://doi.org/10.2 307/3021153.

Sauer, Birgit. "Authoritarian Right-Wing Populism as Masculinist Identity Politics. The Role of Affects." In *Right-Wing Populism and Gender. European Perspectives and Beyond*, edited by Gabriele Dietze and Julia Roth, 24–40. Bielefeld: transcript, 2020.

Schmincke, Imke. "Sexual Politics from the Right. Attacks on Gender, Sexual Diversity, and Sex Education." In *Right-Wing Populism and Gender. European Perspectives and Beyond*, edited by Gabriele Dietze and Julia Roth, 58–74. Bielefeld: transcript, 2020.

Schülting, Sabine. "Wa(h)re Liebe. Geldgeschäfte und Liebesgaben in der Frühen Neuzeit." In *Imaginationen des Anderen im 16. und 17. Jahrhundert*, edited by Ina Schabert and Michaela Boenke, 263–285. Wiesbaden: Harrassowitz, 2002.

Schumpeter, Joseph. *Capitalism, Socialism and Democracy*. London: Routledge, 1994.

Sontag, Susan. *Illness as Metaphor and AIDS and its Metaphors*. London: Penguin Books, 2002.

Stäheli, Urs. *Spektakuläre Spekulation. Das Populäre der Ökonomie*. Frankfurt: Suhrkamp, 2007.

Stuckler, David, and Sanjay Basu. *Body Economic. Why Austerity Kills. Recessions. Budget Battles, and the Politics of Life and Death*. NY: Basic Books, 2013.

Tooze, Adam. *Crashed. How a Decade of Financial Crisis Changed the World*. London: Alan
    Lane, 2018.

The Renewed Desire for the Critique of Libidinal Economy: Pain, Stress, Flesh

Ben Gook

For US$160, an Australian company called LBDO will send you its Essensual De-Stress Bundle. It includes a vibrator ("colour of your choice"), 250g bath salts ("for solo or partnered baths"), a 120g massage candle ("melts down into a warming and sensual pool"), and a stylish LBDO tote bag to tout your essensuality. For an extra $37, you can upgrade to include their Vitality Vitamins – a 60-tablet course to create "a strong foundation to optimise your physical, mental and sexual wellbeing."[1] The LBDO bundle promises its buyers access to today's optimised, sexually competent body: a couple of hundred dollars lighter and ready for tranquil pleasure. Whatever the rise and fall of Freud's cultural currency over the past century, here he still haunts the contemporary economy with his notion of libido: the post-Freudian subject is sexually aware and unafraid to go to market to find what it needs. Distressed by interconnected social crises and their daily rhythms, they know just where to shop to de-stress.

LBDO, through its threefold pitch for wellbeing ("physical, mental and sexual"), sells the sexual stimulation of the individual body as an intervention against globalised stress. Nevertheless, from its vowelless name to its brand identity – warm, sensual images on social media with sex-positive phrases ("feel good about feeling good"), body-positive models and pro-pleasure self-care blog posts alongside its online shop – the Australian company aspires to connect its socially-conscious and sexually-awakened demographic to the capitalist market for what LBDO and its competitors now cannily sell as "sexual wellness." The company's direct-to-consumer deals encapsulate the commodity aesthetics and psychosocial status quo among at least one well-connected and culturally hypervisible corner of the west in these crisis times: stressed, horny, anxious; tired, wired, always online; sunk in the body and its failings but looking to connect; polymorphously perverse, polyamorously curious, enthusiastically consensual; self-diagnosing, self-administering, self-sooth-

---

1 https://web.archive.org/web/20231001190757/https://www.lbdo.com/blogs/the-talk/introd ucing-lbdo-vitality. They also note: "what makes LBDO Vitality different, is that we will not now, or ever claim to 'fix' your libido."

ing.[2] Yet even with its vowels plucked like unsightly body hair, can the libidinal be so frictionlessly joined with *pleasure* and *feeling good*? Equally, what is the gain of this term, libido, if it is merely interchangeable with Eros or the sexual?

In what follows, I want to keep an eye on how the circuits of the libidinal are imagined to be circuits of illness and cure, distress and wellbeing. LBDO is not alone in its pitch for ailing the distressed body via sexual pleasure. A whole suite of differently branded devices, increasingly marketed on street posters in cities and sold in mainstream department stores, are now on hand as sources of libidinal relief. Like LBDO, they also purport to provide self-care and optimised life: some new "sex tech" devices use sensors and AI, offering their users feedback via a dashboard of real-time and historic data, all with the promise of reaching untold heights of enjoyment. In this chapter, then, I return to the place of the sexual in the libidinal economy, as it is often passed over with some embarrassment. At the same time, I also note how libidinised enjoyment is conjured – and captured – in proximity to crisis situations. In the opening to this volume, I outlined Freud's understanding of libido before discussing its overlaps with, and distinctions from, related terms, such as desire. I also addressed the two other key terms in this collection: economy and crisis. Here, I resume the discussion of these terms in the context of contemporary debates and crises, while drawing on several authors who do not typically feature in the critique of libidinal economy, including Elaine Scarry and Paul B. Preciado. "The flesh" – as the jointure of the symbolic and real that comes to the fore in crisis – plays a prominent role in this chapter, as will a set of further examples drawn from libidinal investments in recent interconnected crises.

Tracking libidinal economic activity

In reaching the concluding pages of the book, we might now say that libidinal economy concerns the way that human beings manage and distribute their erotic attachments – desires, sources of enjoyment and suffering – in the world. As the preceding chapters have made clear, in our crisis-prone era, questions continually arise around how desires are shaped, modulated and guided by the leading institutions of capitalist economies. If the libidinal is de-natured, then this is another way of saying it comes to us – enters us, circulates within us – via the world or the social field. For most of the world today, this social field, this *socius*, this reigning form of life, is capitalist.[3] As it is in the broader economy, so it is with the libido: our desires

---

2   On sexuality and commodity aesthetics: Wolfgang Fritz Haug, *Critique of Commodity Aesthetics: Appearance, Sexuality and Advertising in Capitalist Society* (Cambridge: Polity, 1986).

3   On libidinal economies outside or adjacent to capitalist forms: Marinus Ossewaarde, "Socialism's Struggles with Eros: Politics of the Body in Cuba and China," *International Sociology* 31,

move within, and sometimes against, the capitalist economy's range of pleasures. A range of pleasures, it is worth underlining, that ideologists of capitalism hold up as distinctive and to be celebrated in their delivery – precisely as variety and choice – by this social and economic form; something that it, capitalism, does better than rival systems, which are less responsive to needs, wants and desires. The name attached to this superiority is "the market." This virtual entity – nowhere visible but always operative, always materialised in practices – offers all that one, that every subject of the market, could desire. This is a "site" earlier embodied in local economies by a space so designated, a *Marktplatz*, and still sometimes quaintly spatialised as a "marketplace," as if in a bazaar or medieval town square, yet, again, never truly seen or present in its entirety.[4] Leaving aside the fact that markets themselves are not inherently capitalist, one longstanding view propounded by capitalism's advocates is that the market is where coordination, distribution, value and production are given their ideal economic ordering. In this view, the market is the site to organise and enact desires and, thus, where an economy gets and takes its orders (buy this, sell that).[5] Ultimately, the market is an institution of economic administration – established and maintained by a state form – that attempts to order and price desire.

Yet the *capitalist* market is besieged, disordered, by crisis after crisis – as if the tumult of desire were the actual guiding principle. "While economic institutions and discourses try to administer and domesticate enjoyment," Ceren Özselçuk and Yahya Madra write, "they always fail since it is impossible to balance out, apportion or stitch together enjoyment."[6] Indeed, the libidinal marks out a field of enjoyment and pleasure with its unconscious operations; it denotes how enjoyment can be intrusive and involuntary for the subject, and how the pleasurable excesses of *jouissance* – Jacques Lacan's name for libidinal enjoyment, encompassing sexuality, suffering

---

no. 5 (2016): 525–32; Keti Chukhrov, *Practicing the Good: Desire and Boredom in Soviet Socialism* (Minneapolis: e-flux, 2020); Charlie Yi Zhang, *Dreadful Desires: The Uses of Love in Neoliberal China* (Duke UP, 2022); Perry Johansson, *The Libidinal Economy of China: Gender, Nationalism, and Consumer Culture* (Lanham: Lexington Books, 2015); Bogdan G. Popa, *De-Centering Queer Theory: Communist Sexuality in the Flow during and after the Cold War* (Manchester: Manchester UP, 2021).

4   Even in the bazaar or marketplace, we would often find another marketplace – that of raw goods and so on – effectively hidden behind the site where the market sits; so "the market" has never been anything but another iteration of the economy's part-whole relation, as I explored in the opening chapter.

5   Keith Tribe, *Strategies of Economic Order: German Economic Discourse, 1750–1950* (Cambridge: Cambridge UP, 1995). Roffe points out that "not every social form includes [a market]. The strange, ahistorical, cultish view of societies past promulgated by economics, in which the market has always existed in immature, kernel forms (circumscribed by the famous barter illusion), precisely excludes this recognition" (*Abstract Market Theory* (NY: Palgrave, 2015), 50).

6   Ceren Özselçuk and Yahya M Madra, "Enjoyment as an Economic Factor: Reading Marx with Lacan," *Subjectivity* 3, no. 3 (2010): 335.

and satisfaction beyond the rational ego, identities, and normative institutions –
emerge and recede, sometimes chased by pain or in admixtures of both.[7] If those
critiquing libidinal economy focus on *jouissance* as excessive, sacrificial, destructive
of self and others and ultimately unstable, this is because it negates economic func-
tionalism or reproductionism – namely, countering those images of the economy "in
which the practices of consumption, production and distribution are glued snugly
together in a systemic cycle of social equilibrium and crisis."[8] Human subjectivity in
the libidinal political economy of capitalism can be "understood as the fluctuating
outcome of an individual's attempts to negotiate self-coherency while immersed in
the instituted practices of the market."[9] At the same time, the subjective grammar
of libidinal economy and the structural grammar of capitalist political economy are
mutually supportive. The economic actor seen as a subject of libidinal economy will
act less on the basis of conscious rationality than unconscious anxiety and enjoyment, including pleasure in the suffering, subordination and failure of others.[10]

---

7   Derek Hook, "Jouissance as Tool of Psychosocial Analysis," in *The Palgrave Handbook of Psy-
     chosocial Studies*, ed. Stephen Frosh, Marita Vyrgioti, and Julie Walsh (Cham: Springer, 2020),
     1–27. As Hook points out, commenting on Frank Wilderson III's claim about enjoyment in
     anti-Black violence: *Jouissance* "is not a free-floating or merely individual moment of intensity
     (an isolated instance, for example of the pleasure of hating). It is, by contrast, a sanctioned
     excess which ensures the maintenance of a sociopolitical structure, a formation of power, (or,
     in Wilderson's terms, a 'regime of violence') and that anchors a broader *weltanschauung* and
     its associated libidinal community." In essence, the claim is: "any system of domination nec-
     essarily entails a particular libidinal economy, that is, a particular distribution of *jouissance*"
     (12). If we follow Hook's proposed method for understanding libidinal identifications – that
     is, the process of understanding such distributions – the following questions can help the
     analysis: "What are the shared instances of transgressive-enjoyment that enable the forma-
     tion of communities of entitlement? What accumulative 'micro-enjoyments' make subjects
     into stakeholders of a particular libidinal economy? Consider how instances of enjoyment
     contradict – or exist in tension with – professed ideals, symbolic values, or imaginary iden-
     tifications. Lastly: How are particular identifications consolidated by means of a hatred of an
     other's jouissance?" (25).
8   Özselçuk and Madra, "Enjoyment as an Economic Factor," 335. Darian Leader suggests we
     could "divide up" a list of jouissances "between those of the real body, those linked to how
     we perceive the Other's subjectivity and its claims on us, how we act on ourselves and on
     the Other to negate these claims, and those linked to the virtual, to points of inaccessibility,
     generated retroactively by symbolic structures" (*Jouissance: Sexuality, Suffering and Satisfaction*
     (Cambridge: Polity, 2021), 133). The jouissance concept is notoriously – sometimes produc-
     tively, sometimes unproductively – amorphous, and Leader speculates about what Lacanians
     like himself would do if, from time to time, they left "jouissance" aside in favour of "thinking
     more carefully about how we inhabit and are inhabited by the body and by language" (132).
9   Earl Gammon, "Narcissism, Rage, Avocado Toast," in *Clickbait Capitalism: Economies of Desire in
     the Twenty-First Century*, ed. Amin Samman and Earl Gammon (Manchester: Manchester UP,
     2023), 22.
10   Kapoor et al., *Global Libidinal Economy* (Albany: SUNY Press, 2023), 10.

It is, of course, psychoanalysis's *modus operandi* to focus on what is excluded from discourses and practices – the repressed, disavowed, foreclosed – and how what is excluded returns and is efficacious despite its ostensible elimination. Even in everyday terms, the ideological associations of capitalist market activity with equilibrium, fairness, and measure are met with their equally well-known underside of exploitation, crisis and chaos. A libidinal political economy sees economic beliefs and behaviours as shaped by the unconscious, such that "what is rational in the sphere of political economy is contextual, and ostensibly irrational behaviours commonly indicate a conflict between unconscious demands and what is socially expedient."[11] Excess, irrationality, immoderate compulsions – all this "libidinal stuckness," in the words of the authors of *Global Libidinal Economy*, "helps explain both the intensity and extensity of contemporary global capitalism – why it is able to reach everywhere, mesmerize everyone, and continuously reproduce itself, even (and perhaps especially) in the face of obstacle or crisis."[12]

Again, the heights of the economy disavow this enjoyment and stuckness, often depicting economic management as tendentially dry, calculating, boring; as so many graphs, trading terminals and spreadsheets that lead to rational decision-making. Yet every discourse, even this economic one of apparently bloodless analysis and allocation, is a discourse of enjoyment: "enjoyment is articulated like a discourse," Samo Tomšič writes, "it is an inevitable product of linguistic, economic, religious, epistemic and other types of symbolic bonds, which affect the human body."[13] Popular culture offers us a countervision of this in its libidinally-charged depictions of financial traders, avatars from capitalism's ideological apex – for example, in the films *Wall Street* (1987) to *American Psycho* (2000) to *Wolf of Wall Street* (2013) to *The Big Short* (2015) to the TV series *Billions* (2016–23) and on, all of them circulating from the heart of the global economic hegemon in the neoliberal era.[14] Notably, these also depict financial elites in various modalities of manic enjoyment and breakdown,

---

11   Gammon, 24.

12   Ilan Kapoor et al., *Global*, 158.

13   Samo Tomšič, *The Labour of Enjoyment: Towards a Critique of Libidinal Economy* (Cologne: August Verlag, 2019), 10.

14   Alberto Toscano and Jeff Kinkle, *Cartographies of the Absolute* (Winchester: Zero Books, 2014); Clint Burnham, *Fredric Jameson and The Wolf of Wall Street* (NY: Bloomsbury, 2016); Calum Watt, *Derivative Images: Financial Derivatives in French Film, Literature and Thought* (Edinburgh: Edinburgh UP, 2022); Alasdair King, *The Financial Image: Finance, Philosophy and Contemporary Film* (Cham: Springer, 2024); J. D. Connor, *Hollywood Math and Aftermath: The Economic Image and the Digital Recession* (London: Bloomsbury, 2018). The German production *Bad Banks* (2018–20) depicts this scene from a different angle: the commanding heights of the European economic regime – Frankfurt am Main, London and Luxembourg plus a fintech and start-up interlude in Berlin.

brought undone either by an exploitative social field, typically euphemised as "inequality," or the pleasure traduced by the castrating governmental bogeyman of "regulation."

With its eyes trained on what falls out of the standard accounts of economic life, the critique of libidinal economy is one wing of politico-existential or psychosocial inquiry that has tried to make sense of the contemporary conjuncture. "In virtually all this work," as Emily Apter and Martin Crowley write, summarising what they call the *economies of existence*, "the emphasis on financial outcomes, predictive processing, and quant-think typically found in professional economics is displaced by the investigation of their psychic and phenomenological fallout, often diffuse and hard to measure."[15] So one appeal of "libidinal economy" is this sense that by discussing it rather than "quant-think," we immediately challenge a picture of people as the rational, utility-maximising and pleasure-seeking individuals of dominant economic theories. That is to say, in the relation of an expansive financialisation in everyday life, the libidinal – like the "affective" – is taken to be the antithesis of measured value: "that which is incalculable (by means of rational choice), unaccountable, noncapitalized, non-optimized, non-transcendent, non-equivalent or untranslatable as a measure of economic, political and existential value."[16]

This claim for an antithetical relation to quantity is ironic, given that Freud had hoped that the libido would *someday* be measurable. It is also slightly caricaturing, as utilitarianism and its adherents in economics pay attention to pleasure, pain, happiness and so on – although they suggest we answer difficulties in measuring these experiences through a *calculus*, bringing it back to the rational. Nevertheless, the turn to the libidinal is more complicated than a quasi-vitalist strategy of resistance, siding with the pulsations of "life" against reigning "systems." After all, what

---

15   Emily Apter and Martin Crowley, "Economies of Existence," *Diacritics* 47, no. 1 (2019): 6. To crib their list of responses: "Georges Friedmann (machinism), Pierre Bourdieu (symbolic capital, the wages of social suffering), Luc Boltanski and Ève Chiapello (post-Fordist, network-based capitalism), Bernard Stiegler (the symbolic misery of the hyper-industrial epoch), Jonathan Crary (time measurement in the attention economy), David Harvey (accumulation by dispossession), Thomas Piketty (r > g), Achille Mbembe (the racial subsidy), Antoinette Rouvroy (algorithmic governmentality), Maurizio Lazzarato (debt as the basis of social life), Roberto Finelli (the ontology of real abstraction), Arlie Hochschild (affect management), Frédéric Lordon (willing slaves of capital), Randy Martin (the social logic of derivatives), Mark Fisher (capitalist realism), Nick Srnicek and Alex Williams (accelerationist economics), Michael Hardt and Antonio Negri (immaterial labor), Karen Gregory (subjectivity and digital labor), Yann Moulier Boutang (cognitive capitalism), Antonio A. Casilli (the microlabor of machinic taskers like Amazon Mechanical Turk or Clickworker), Keller Easterling (infrastructure as a space of extrastatecraft), Ivan Ascher (the portfolio society), Tiziana Terranova (free labor), Harmut Rosa (social resonance as anti-alienation)" (5). See also John Roberts, *Capitalism and the Limits of Desire* (NY: Bloomsbury, 2022).

16   Apter and Crowley, "Economies of Existence," 3.

complicates this position of libidinal resistance are the complex ways that capitalist societies have, in some realms, invoked rational maximisers while, in others, they have not been shy about provoking libidinal attachments to institutions, people and commodities – or, indeed, joining the two by establishing an affective attachment to rationality, good measure, markets and so on. For Bernard Stiegler, this investment by capital in the libidinal drains our sexual reserves.[17] Stiegler describes contemporary social conditions as exhibiting a *libidinal dis-economy* with devastating psychopathological and sociopathological consequences. This threatens community disintegration, economic ruination and destruction of a well-lubricated capitalist libidinal economy. Stiegler will call this our contemporary "symbolic misery," his response to compounding contemporary crises, as capital raids our subjective and collective reserves, cannibalising these resources just as it has with others.[18]

An era of polymorphous crises

In what looks and feels like an era of everlasting crisis – that is to say, crises that are multiple, diverse and not clearly time-bound – the question of how capitalist economies survive, die or stumble on seems to be posed in radically different ways. Equally, the populist political moment of recent years has thrown into broadsheet columns and social media feeds a thousand wild discussions of the ids, egos and superegos – the unchecked desires and passions – of voters and leaders. And the pervasiveness of climate anxiety and doom, alongside apathy and inaction, have had many reaching for explanations in the unconscious. While Stiegler proposes a dis-economy, economists themselves struggle to describe what is occurring in the contemporary political-economic field. Prediction, equilibrium and measure all seem ineffective, delivering a crisis of and for the discipline. Economists seem hard-pressed or unable – epistemologically – to answer what is going on and going wrong in

---

17   See also Dominic Pettman, *Peak Libido: Sex, Ecology, and the Collapse of Desire* (Cambridge: Polity, 2021).

18   "Symbolic misery is the way that the exploitation of libidinal energy tends to exhaust it, with the result that, when this process approaches its conclusion, libidinal energy is replaced by the unleashing of drive-based tendencies. Only when it reaches this point is it expressed as spiritual misery. The binding force that was libidinal energy, as the premier energy of capitalism, then becomes an unbound force, decomposing the drives that were bound by libidinal energy, the latter no longer being able to contain them because it has been destroyed" (Bernard Stiegler, *The Lost Spirit of Capitalism* (Cambridge: Polity, 2014), 7). Stiegler is partly aiming at the idea of a "new spirit" of capitalism: Bernard Stiegler, *The Re-Enchantment of the World: The Value of Spirit against Industrial Populism* (London: Bloomsbury, 2014); Bernard Stiegler, *For a New Critique of Political Economy* (Cambridge: Polity, 2010); Daniel Ross, "Translator's Introduction to Bernard Stiegler's 'Pharmacology of Desire: Drive-Based Capitalism and Libidinal Dis-Economy,'" *New Formations* 72 (2011): 146–49

these crisis times. After all, the modern financialised and globalised economy "is attempting to come to grips with the world it has created in its image." The difficulty economists face is both real and hermeneutic: "the science of economics has spent the last three hundred years creating the very economic facts it is now struggling to decipher."[19]

If this rings true for recent financial crises, it is also true of crises in other areas of social life. The prevailing understanding and representation of the world today is one of cascading crises: polycrisis and omnicrisis are currently two popular terms. This understanding is efficacious. Once a society is said to be in crisis by prominent voices, it has been altered by its self-perception of crisis conditions: the crisis is operative within it.[20] Crisis talk is immanent, performative and nonneutral. As Sara Ahmed notes:

> to declare a crisis is not "to make something out of nothing": such declarations often work with real events, facts or figures (as we can see, for example, in how the rise in divorce rates is used to announce a crisis in marriage and the family). But the declaration of crisis *reads* that fact/figure/event and transforms it into a fetish object that then acquires a life of its own, in other words, that can become the grounds for declarations of war against that which is read as the source of the threat.[21]

By noticing this fetishisation, by making this analytic move to a reflexive level, we are prompted to consider precisely what "crisis" is, and how crisis talk often gets deployed *strategically* rather than baldly describing the state of, among other things, the global market, the household, earth systems, sex and libido, asylum seeking, the "white race," and so on.[22] That is, we can remind ourselves to halt at the point of

---

19   Joseph Vogl, *The Specter of Capital*, trans. Joachim Redner and Robert Savage (Stanford: Stanford UP, 2015), x. Writing almost a century earlier, Georg Lukács made a similar point: "the very success with which the economy is totally rationalised and transformed into an abstract and mathematically orientated system of formal 'laws' ... creates the methodological barrier to understanding the phenomenon of crisis. In moments of crisis the qualitative existence of the 'things' that lead their lives beyond the purview of economics as misunderstood and neglected things-in-themselves, as use-values, suddenly becomes the decisive factor. (Suddenly, that is, for reified, rational thought.) Or, rather: these 'laws' fail to function and the reified mind is unable to perceive a pattern in this 'chaos'" (*History and Class Consciousness: Studies in Marxist Dialectics*, trans. Rodney Livingstone, (Cambridge: MIT Press, 1976), 105).

20   Andrew Simon Gilbert, *The Crisis Paradigm: Description and Prescription in Social and Political Theory* (Cham: Palgrave, 2019), 9.

21   Sara Ahmed, *The Cultural Politics of Emotion*, 2nd ed. (Edinburgh: Edinburgh UP, 2014), 77.

22   Stuart Hall et al., *Policing the Crisis: Mugging, the State and Law and Order*, 2nd ed. (London: Palgrave, 2013); Achille Mbembe and Janet Roitman, "Figures of the Subject in Times of Crisis," *Public Culture* 7, no. 2 (1995): 323–52; Janet Roitman, "The Stakes of Crisis," in *Critical Theories of Crisis in Europe: From Weimar to the Euro*, ed. Poul F. Kjaer and Niklas Olsen (London: Rowman

glibly invoking crisis, and notice, instead, in whose social, political and economic interests such a crisis may be declared. This crisis terminology has been routinised in recent years, in discussions of all political stripes – giving us even more reason to be mindful of its use. This caution can be advised, even as we might wish to affirm the account, partially or wholly, that it offers of the facts – of the state of global heating or the misery of certain "surplus" populations and so on.

Crisis was imported into social inquiry from predominantly medical and military uses, which privilege technical expertise, licensing those who diagnose and act. It offers the chance for description and proscription. Janet Roitman writes that crisis is "an observation that produces meaning," responding to a given (bad) condition.[23] As Ahmed and others make plain, crises are simultaneously *objects*, referring to states in the world, and *demands*, asking for a decision or resolution. They seek to establish empirical validity in their *descriptions*, and normative, existential, or political force in their *proscriptions*. Crisis theory draws its authority from its claim to bring chaotic events under conceptual control and ordering.[24] In this sense, crisis is bound up in processes of power and hegemony, even as it offers countervailing forces the prospect of providing a new frame and intervention. It is, as Reinhart Koselleck puts it, a *Kampfbegriff*, "a concept designed for combat ... used by both sides against each other."[25] In recent decades, we have seen how, once a crisis has been declared and broadly recognised, no shortage of jockeying begins for control of futures – be they economic, planetary or sexual. This jockeying is visibly true of status quo elites in high offices, as well as a reactionary right and an emancipatory left. The left, in particular, has found crisis to be "an invaluable historical hermeneutic, compelling us to anticipate limits, to imagine alternatives, to welcome collapse, and thus to resist the 'end of history' triumphalism characteristic of late capitalist ideology in boom times."[26] For Karl Marx and Friedrich Engels, the term had a positive political valence, even if born from economic misery. "This crisis," Engels wrote to Marx in 1857, "will make me feel as good as a swim in the ocean."[27]

& Littlefield International, 2016), 17–34; Joseph Vogl, Sven Fabre, and Arne Vanraes, "The History of the Notion of Crisis," in *Critical Theory at a Crossroads: Conversations on Resistance in Times of Crisis*, ed. Stijn de Cauwer (NY: Columbia UP, 2018), 61–74.

23   Janet Roitman, *Anti-Crisis* (Durham: Duke UP, 2014), 82.

24   Gilbert, *Crisis Paradigm*, 9, 217.

25   Reinhart Koselleck, "Crisis," trans. Michaela W. Richter, *Journal of the History of Ideas* 67, no. 2 (2006): 376.

26   Annie McClanahan, *Dead Pledges: Debt, Crisis and the Twenty-First-Century Culture* (Stanford: Stanford UP, 2017), 15.

27   Quoted in Koselleck, "Crisis," 394.

In our era, swimming in the sea of crisis talk feels less energising. "Whoever speaks of 'crisis' today," Nancy Fraser warns, "risks being dismissed as a bloviator."[28] Consequently, some have suggested the term is now demobilising or outright reactionary: fascism, too, is a politics of crisis. Koselleck, in his conceptual-historical work over several decades, already issued this diagnosis and warning:

> The concept of crisis, which once had the power to pose unavoidable, harsh and non-negotiable alternatives, has been transformed to fit the uncertainties of whatever might be favored at a given moment. Such a tendency towards imprecision and vagueness, however, may itself be viewed as the symptom of a historical crisis that cannot as yet be fully gauged. This makes it all the more important for scholars to weigh the concept carefully before adopting it in their own terminology.[29]

As Annie McClanahan suggests, part of the current efficacy of "crisis" consists in how it is both "ambient context and the manifest content of much cultural production, social experience and economic life." This has "transformed our sense of personhood … and our experience of social belonging."[30] Or, as Lauren Berlant puts it, "the way we live now" is a "survival in the present of an ordinary collective life suffused with a historic and historical crisis to which we are always catching up."[31] Berlant describes a "crisis ordinariness," a paradox marking the banality of the apparently exceptional. They note that "crisis is not exceptional to history or consciousness but a process embedded in the ordinary that unfolds in stories about navigating what's overwhelming."[32] These mark the "intensities of a situation that spreads into modes, habits, or genres of being."[33] Indeed, it is often these ordinary and everyday conditions – the fallout of stuttering economies and societies – that clinical psychoanalysts find themselves addressing today: climate anxieties and loss, for example, or ramifying inequality and its attendant anxieties, as these turn up in the day-to-day suffering of subjects forced to navigate them.[34]

---

28   Nancy Fraser, *The Old Is Dying and the New Cannot Be Born: From Progressive Neoliberalism to Trump and Beyond* (London: Verso, 2019), 7.

29   Koselleck, "Crisis," 399–400.

30   McClanahan, *Dead Pledges*, 15.

31   Lauren Berlant, *Cruel Optimism* (Durham: Duke UP, 2011), 59. See also Anne Allison, *Precarious Japan* (Durham: Duke, 2013).

32   Berlant, *Cruel*, 10.

33   Berlant, 81.

34   Sally Weintrobe, ed., *Engaging with Climate Change: Psychoanalytic and Interdisciplinary Perspectives* (London: Taylor & Francis, 2012); Sally Weintrobe, *Psychological Roots of the Climate Crisis: Neoliberal Exceptionalism and the Culture of Uncare* (London: Bloomsbury, 2021); Elissa Marder, "The Shadow of the Eco: Denial and Climate Change," *Philosophy & Social Criticism* 49, no. 2 (2023): 139–50; Tad DeLay, *Future of Denial: The Ideologies of Climate Change* (London: Verso,

Pounds of flesh

Bodily experiences of suffering become a ground in moments of crisis and its discourses.[35] Elaine Scarry makes this point in her study of the body in pain. "When there is within society a crisis of belief," she writes, "when some central idea or ideology or cultural construct has ceased to elicit a population's belief either because it is manifestly fictitious or because it has for some reason been divested of ordinary forms of substantiation," then, she continues, "the sheer material factualness of the human body will be borrowed to lend that cultural construct the aura of 'realness' and 'certainty.'"[36] Scarry is writing about torture and war, and how human pain – the liveness of tissue – is "borrowed" to verify and substantiate the symbolic authority of institutions. Many other feelings can be faked, but pain always seems to be true: even phantom pain is *pain*.

Pain for Freud was what allowed the body to attain "its special position among other objects in the world of perception."[37] Psychoanalysis will, of course, want to introduce questions of pleasure amid pain – the common-enough experiences of sadomasochism, self-harm, addictions and so on. In other words, all the ways the apparent biological program of avoiding pain and suffering comes up against enjoyment, relief and pleasure. In "Psychoanalysis and Medicine," a speech given in 1966, Lacan suggests the body is made to *jouir*. But in this context, he goes on to define *jouissance* in particular terms: "in the register of tension, of forcing, of expenditure [*dépense*], indeed of the exploit." He adds that "there is incontestably *jouissance* at the level where pain begins to emerge, and we know that it is only at this level of pain that a whole dimension of the organism can be felt which would otherwise remain veiled."[38] Pain reveals something in us – the organism – while also pointing to something vital outside ourselves. Those who specialise in the study of pain agree: it is

---

2024). From the opposite angle, this has also seen climate crisis thinkers and activists come to see the relevance of psychoanalytic theory: Andreas Malm, "The Future Is the Termination Shock: On the Antinomies and Psychopathologies of Geoengineering. Part One," *Historical Materialism* 30, no. 4 (2022): 3–53; Andreas Malm, "The Future Is the Termination Shock: On the Antinomies and Psychopathologies of Geoengineering. Part Two," *Historical Materialism* 31, no. 1 (2023): 3–61

35   This is true in the following examples but also in another sense explored in Marina Vishmidt, "Bodies in Space: On the Ends of Vulnerability," *Radical Philosophy* 2, no. 8 (2020): 33–46.

36   Elaine Scarry, *The Body in Pain: The Making and Unmaking of the World* (Oxford: Oxford UP, 1985), 14. Scarry limited her understanding of pain to the physical, even as she acknowledged the accuracy of also talking about pain in mental suffering, such as grief or depression.

37   Sigmund Freud, *The Standard Edition of the Complete Psychological Works of Sigmund Freud*, 24 vols. (London: Hogarth Press, 1953), XIX: 25. Freud describes the bodily ego as a surface that is also a projection of a surface, ruptured by wounds, palpitating with organ pain.

38   Translated from the French in Leader, *Jouissance*, 54–55.

never private but socially and publicly formed.[39] Psychoanalysis always intervenes here, positioning itself between body and language.

The mediation of bodily pain by language can be among the causes of distress. Alongside feelings of certainty, pain can instil in the sufferer a striking feeling of dependency and loneliness – no one else can directly feel the sensations and thoughts. This often leads to a retreat to the body as the here-and-now becomes the locus of attention. But the difficulty of communicating the experience can also breed pressurised speech. Pain can dominate the sufferer's conversation, just as the site of pain pushes other sensations below awareness, and the painful present marginalises past and future. This over-presence of pain can set in motion a concurrent alienation from other people.[40] As Scarry writes, for the person in pain, the perception is "so incontestably and unnegotiably present ... that 'having pain' may come to be thought of as the most vibrant example of what it is to 'have certainty,' while for the other person it is so elusive that 'hearing about pain' may exist as the primary model of what it is 'to have doubt.'" She concludes, "thus pain comes unsharably into our midst as at once that which cannot be denied and that which cannot be confirmed."[41] Part of the sufferer's sense of abandonment amid the uncertainty of others derives from the fact that pain also comes to resist language. Expressions of pain regularly slip back "before" language to infantile cries, sobs and howls. While these express the suffering, as objectifications – as extensions into the world – they also attest to pain's factualness, little cries from the real that short-circuit the linguistic alienations of the symbolic, underwriting a realness that can be borrowed by ideologies. In other words, for those going through it, pain is incontestably real and this quality of realness can be conferred on whatever brought it into being.[42]

There is, thus, apparent certainty in pain and injury. The injured body is a piece of the real that provides the ultimate support or backing of a symbolic order – the national sacrifice of "our fallen and wounded," for example, will prop up, via the bodies of the injured, a national ideology's senses of valued belonging and worthy collective endeavour. Such injuries make the social facts constituted within the space of representation feel real – vital – rather than virtual. Scarry discusses the "intricacies of the process of transfer that make it possible for the incontestable reality of

---

39   Joanna Bourke, *The Story of Pain: From Prayer to Painkillers* (Oxford: Oxford UP, 2014)

40   Scarry, *The Body in Pain*, 55.

41   Scarry, *The Body in Pain*, 4. Later (54–55) she writes, "pain begins by being 'not oneself' and ends by having eliminated all that is 'not itself.' . . . It eventually occupies the entire body and spills out into the realm beyond the body, takes over all that is inside and outside, makes the two obscenely indistinguishable, and systematically destroys anything like language or world extension that is alien to itself and threatening to its claims. Terrifying for its narrowness, it nevertheless exhausts and displaces all else until it seems to become the single broad and omnipresent fact of existence."

42   Scarry, *The Body in Pain*, 27.

the physical body to now become an attribute of an issue that at that moment has no independent reality of its own."[43] The dead and injured are evidence that the nation and its cause ever existed. This is, then, an account of the body as ground and source of verification and substantiation of institutional, symbolic authority – and thus an account of how this becomes a crucial site for the working through and out of crisis. This can include authoritarian paths out, using the lure of "resurrecting a more visceral, less careful form of power, that could settle matters of life and death in public, and give vent to anger," as William Davies has described. Authoritarianism, for instance, offers an imaginary of simple solutions with recourse to the body and feeling states: "Guilt should mean pain, innocence should mean comfort, and then justice is finally done."[44]

Bodily pain is a source of verification – and of information and power in the modern world. Feeling, sentiment and experience have moved to the centre of data capture, communication and, hence, to value creation. Many of these techniques come from the "real-time intelligence" technologies of the military-industrial complex. An emphasis on real-time knowledge has bled from military operations to digital platforms to market algorithms to smart-home sensors to public CCTV systems to smartwatches and even, as I noted earlier, to sex toys. In this context, Davies has accounted for a generalised war footing: from this spread of onetime military technology in everyday life (real-time intel on imminent cardiovascular attacks) to geopolitical cyberwarfare to the quasi-militaristic frames of contemporary politics (culture wars, wars on terror, and wokeness) and social problems (wars on drugs, obesity, addiction).[45] During the COVID-19 pandemic, leaders deployed slogans such as "we are at war" to galvanise the population to stay at home, telecommute and maintain total vigilance over their bodies and those nearby. Attending to the past decade's political economy and crisis tendencies, Davies accounts for how the

---

43   Scarry, *The Body in Pain*, 124–25. Santner (*The Royal Remains: The People's Two Bodies and the Endgames of Sovereignty* (Chicago: University of Chicago Press, 2011), xvi) leaps off this mention of "transfer" to discuss "transference" in psychoanalytic terms, which is not precisely what Scarry meant in her phrase. Nevertheless, Santner considers transference a social phenomenon, a source of verification and a mode of perception. In psychoanalysis, transference is the process by which the subject transfers or projects their libidinal attachments, fantasies, and expectations onto another person, usually the analyst, who comes to represent a figure of authority or influence in the subject's life. Santner suggests that transference can also be understood as a way of transferring the reality and certainty of the physical body onto a cultural construct or a symbolic order that lacks independent reality or legitimacy. Hence, in the current discussion, transference figures one way of coping with the crisis of belief or the lack of fit between the human subject and the social field.

44   William Davies, *Nervous States: Democracy and the Decline of Reason* (NY: Norton, 2020), 93.

45   Davies, *Nervous States*. The war on terror was the first war waged on an emotion: Lauren Berlant, "The Epistemology of State Emotion," in *Dissent in Dangerous Times*, ed. Austin Sarat (Ann Arbor: University of Michigan Press, 2005), 46–78.

time of combative, pervasive wars on multiple fronts manifest the characteristics of the current conjuncture: deepening inequalities, environmental degradation, and political polarisation. War is, like crisis, a pronouncement with effects. But war is also a symptom of crisis that only deepens its causes and effects – splitting the population, instilling aggression, foreclosing debate, and so on. This describes a breakdown of a fundamental modern distinction – ideal as it always was – between wartime and peacetime. This breakdown has produced individuals and governments existing in a state of near-constant heightened alertness, combativeness and a feeling of being "under siege," which leads to twitchy nervous states in subjects, leaders and bodies politic.

Beyond their role in value creation – outside the military, chiefly in the *ressentiment* machines of the social industry[46] – the libidinal circuit here concerns the pleasures, pains and suffering instilled by warlike relations with others. We might recall here a passage from Lacan's seminar on Edgar Allan Poe's *Purloined Letter*:

> Every human drama ... is founded on the existence of established bonds, ties, pacts. Human beings already have commitments which tie them together, commitments which have determined their places, names, their essences. Then along comes another discourse, other commitments, other speech. It is quite certain that there'll be some places where they'll have to come to blows. All treaties aren't signed simultaneously. Some are contradictory. If you go to war, it is so as to know which treaty will be binding.[47]

Lacan here outlines the inevitable conflicts around commitments, names, places, and bonds.[48] If we live in a period characterised by generalised war, as Davies characterises it, then, if we follow Lacan, this means that the regular "going to war" in cultural and political life indicates we are in a crisis of contradictory or unsettled symbolic pacts, bonds, and ties; or, put differently, crises and their discourses indicate the battle over the settlement of what bonds, ties, and titles come to reign for the next phase of some putative crisis-free political and libidinal economy. Such

---

46   Joseph Vogl, *Capital and Ressentiment: A Short Theory of the Present*, trans. Neil Solomon (London: Polity, 2023); Richard Seymour, *The Twittering Machine* (London: Indigo, 2019).

47   Jacques Lacan, *The Seminar of Jacques Lacan. Book II: The Ego in Freud's Theory and in the Technique of Psychoanalysis*, trans. Sylvana Tomaselli (Cambridge: Cambridge UP, 1988), 197.

48   In the circuit of the economic, we can even consider the conjunction of *war* and *bonds* in those debt securities issued under that very name. The "war bond" emerged in the twentieth century partly to channel consumer spending into patriotic duty. In WWI, these were called "liberty bonds" in the US; elsewhere, they were sometimes called "victory bonds." These bonds are paradigmatic for understanding national belonging as a macroeconomic and identificatory endeavour, tying individual (financial) fates to national fates. If all goes well, then the surplus of victory is apportioned and enjoyed. Lizabeth Cohen, *A Consumer's Republic: The Politics of Mass Consumption in Postwar America* (NY: Knopf, 2003), chap. 2.

are the promises of homeostasis and anxiety-free futures offered by combatants in these dramas – dramas that stage battles for hegemony. These battles are, among other things, about the tying together – the binding – of subjects to projects, places, names, and essences, when subjects otherwise feel themselves adrift.

We have seen throughout this volume that, for the human to come into their social being and be distinguished from the nonhuman, libidinal implication in the space of the cultural (i.e., the representational, the world of symbolic roles, mandates, titles, exchanges) is necessary. Our enjoyment is tied to these signifiers, titles, and entitlements; our erotic attachments in the world are born from our existence within a matrix of signifying representations. Scarry's work suggests that in crises of representation (such as those of democracy and politics) and the world (such as those of climate, precarity and health), the body becomes an unrivalled veridical instrument, valorised and prized for its apparent immediacy and vulnerability. The body will shift individuals and social orders away from crisis and back to senses of normality. In other words, in crises of the spaces of representations and accompanying social being (subjectivity), the flesh becomes vitally enlisted in attempts to renew the underwriting, or rewriting, of social facts and orders. The flesh – "the bit of the real," Eric Santner proposes, "that underwrites the circulation of signs and values"[49] – represents the site where the personal and the political intersect, always already entangled with the social and symbolic orders that structure our world.

The flesh, in its somatic-discursive entanglements, captures the material and affective dimensions of the capitalist libidinal economy – a different sort of body language. *Flesh* is something in the body that is more than the body, the symbolic order's subject-matter – which is to say, the subject's matter, the stuff, that they offer up and work on in the name of the social. Flesh is not only a biological substance, then, but also a medium of the historical and political forces that shape the libidinal economy. It is a substance that "forms at and as the unstable jointure of the somatic and the normative dimensions of human life."[50] It is also one that, across history, forms at an oscillation between the transcendent (holy) and sinful (profane), or the physical (material) and scriptural (biblical), or the particular (enfleshed races and genders) and universal (humanity per se). Santner explores how flesh becomes a site of suffering, resistance, and transformation in crisis: as a social medium, the flesh and its functions can be most apparent when it starts registering breakdowns.

The contemporary doxa that you ought to "listen to your body" has a certain value here. Psychologists and medical professionals, after Freud's initial interest in the psychosomatic, have been sceptical about "conversion disorder." Conversion is associated with concerns at the border of the bodily and psychic: classically, conversion

---

49   Santner, *Royal*, xv.

50   Eric L. Santner, *The Weight of All Flesh: On the Subject-Matter of Political Economy*, ed. Kevis Goodman (Oxford: Oxford UP, 2016), 238.

disorder names the symptomatic traffic of psychic and somatic distress.[51] Jamieson Webster comments in her recent book on the topic that, after a decade in private practice and the intimacy it offers ("after hours and hours of listening to patients – mostly women"), not a single patient escapes "touching the realm of so-called conversion disorder."[52] She writes:

> if I survey my practice, everyone is troubled by what it means to have a body, having a series of bodily symptoms that define their life…. They take pressures and pains and protests in the body personally, meaning that they assume a kind of guilt in relation to their existence…. From within *this stagnant economy of culpability* (one that easily reverses into blame at other moments) you can find the deep longing for a way out, for another way of life, including a way to find the conviction to pursue something other than what has been offered – this I also want to name conversion.[53]

In a striking passage, Webster records what she hears in these recent analytic encounters with forms of conversion disorder:

> The threat of symptomatic pains that write themselves on [the patient's] flesh: strange autoimmune diseases; obscure aches; a litany of possible diseases; with medications on offer, some taken; and the infinite number of people at your disposal that you can pay to treat weary flesh. A body between the cracks. Please touch me. Tell me where it hurts. With these healers of various sorts, she is given a place to know herself in some other way, to have herself again, as a body in pain but attended to by others. We are still living in the nineteenth century. Hydrotherapy and sanatoriums have other names, including the recourse to seaside vacation or energy work or massage. On the less privileged end, it is somewhat the same as it was; the barbaric institutions of psychiatric facilities or prison are tempting, a solution to an inequitable and counterproductive fight for protection and stability.[54]

---

51   Jamieson Webster, in the introduction to her *Conversion Disorder: Listening to the Body in Psychoanalysis* (NY: Columbia UP, 2019), draws out a definition from the APA's 2013 *DSM-V* diagnostic manual: "'conversion disorder' is a diagnosis that is part of the subgroup 'somatic symptoms and related disorders,' which includes hypochondria, pain disorder, and somatic symptom disorder (APA 2013). Conversion requires a neurological evaluation of symptoms that can range from dizziness to loss of consciousness to changes in motor or sensory functions, from difficulty seeing, smelling, and touching to paralysis, weakness or numbness in the body, and even difficulty speaking or swallowing. The diagnosis gives a nod to psychoanalytic history, the link between the first conception of psychoanalysis and the vicissitudes of neurology" (12–13).

52   Webster, 54.

53   Webster, 14, emphasis added.

54   Webster, 47.

The massage room and the psychiatric cell are places, among others, "where one can hide for a time from the demands of efficiency and productivity leveled at one's body." Later, Webster writes that "the body rebels first" against the dictates of assimilating to regimes of work, lifestyle, authentic experience and so on.[55] The appeal of the bodily retreat or the masseur's thumbs pressing into knotted shoulders suggests how and why the flesh is also the focus of attempts to right the social order. A fix in the body will right the crisis, bring it to an end, and ease the suffering – or so the fantasy goes. As Santner puts it, in moments of symbolic crisis, a "bottoming out of symbolic function on … the flesh becomes urgent."[56] The body – whether in pleasure or pain or both – is essential to these symbolic, ideological operations, a material substrate of our desires and fantasies, and a source of both vitality and vulnerability.

Amid the abstractions of contemporary capitalism, the flesh returns us to creaturely life – something firm if not meaty – only to inscribe this in yet another set of valuations and symbolisations. In moments of crisis, this attempt to recapture the fugitive desires for something valuable can appear absurd, incongruous, and incommensurate. As Benjamin Noys points out, the key texts in the critique of libidinal economy represent a "striking attempt to come to terms with capitalism's capacity to subsume the most seemingly outré elements of human behaviour to the value-form."[57] That these practices keep returning to the body and its libidinal circuits leads us to what I consider in the remainder of the chapter: a set of explicitly sexualised responses to crisis. This time they concern the climate crisis and the pandemic, where forms of relief and bodily pleasure are central to value and reinscribing enjoyment – or types of (libidinal) economic stimulus.

Here, coincidentally, as with LBDO, we find another Australian sex toy company taking the lead. In late 2019 and early 2020, shortly before COVID-19 rushed through the boarding gates of the world's airports, Australia endured devastating bushfires across thousands of kilometres. These fires killed an unfathomable number of animals, including the beloved and distinctive koalas, kangaroos, and wallabies. Amid this disaster, Geeky Sex Toys raised funds for wildlife with its Down-Under Donation Dildo – a silicone toy in the green-and-gold colours of native wattle trees and Australia's sporting teams, set on a base in the shape of the continental landmass. It also featured an image of a koala, a resonant victim of the fires. In recent years, the koala has become a singular and potent object in mourning Australia's accelerating

55   Webster, 47.

56   Here Santner is extending Scarry in his *Royal*, xvi.

57   Benjamin Noys, "'We Are All Prostitutes': Crisis and Libidinal Economy," in *Credo Credit Crisis*, ed. Aidan Tynan, Laurent Milesi, and Christopher John Muller (London: Rowman & Littlefield International, 2017), 170.

climate disasters. The koala is, after all, a form of commodified kitsch in the Australian and international imagination of the country. Such cute figures, for Sianne Ngai, aestheticise powerlessness, which comes to the fore when they are perceived as injured, disabled or attacked.[58] Ngai argues that "the cute," which the koala globally embodies, is strongly associated with commodity-oriented aesthetics. "Cuteness" is also linked with the infantile, feminine and unthreatening, and, partly through anthropomorphising, often demands an emotional and caring response; ultimately, the koala looks like a sleepy, slightly grumpy human baby.

"I just care so much about the motherfucking koalas," singer Lizzo famously exclaimed when visiting Australia around the time of the fires.[59] Her statement encapsulates a generalised libidinal attachment in the expansive sense indicated by Freud's understanding of the libido, its economy and the way it can "stick" to particular objects in circulation. The commodification of koalas concerns their role in a lucrative tourist economy, where this libidinal attachment enters the capitalist economy: not only is their likeness exploited on key rings, hats and media imagery, but also by visitors "buying" the privilege of holding them and posing for sanctuary selfies. Cuteness unveils the spectrum of feelings – or the complex libidinal relationship – individuals have toward objects within capitalism, including not only tenderness but also aggression towards these ostensibly subordinate and unthreatening creature-commodities. Yet, despite deceptively cuddly appearances, they might also threaten us: as Evie Kendal points out, given the koala population's "struggle with high rates of chlamydial infections, it may not have been the best choice for a sex toy."[60]

Sexually transmitted diseases aside, a symptomatic response is legible in mobilising the cute koala amid the catastrophe. As Elissa Marder has argued, in the context of "ecocide" (a "primordial crime scene" that augurs "egocide"), climate change presents a unique challenge to the human psyche. The inexorable unfolding of eco-crises threatens the establishment of a rational relation to reality. Given the monumental scale of climate change, individuals often resort to personal actions to manage feelings of guilt and helplessness. After all, climate change challenges conventional perceptions of time, forcing a re-evaluation of the subject's relation to this horizon: "the traumatic temporality of climate change," Marder points out, "unfolds as an unprogrammable future that bears within it the belated, unknowable and incalculable effects of past actions and inactions that are beyond repair."[61] Recognis-

---

58   Sianne Ngai, *Our Aesthetic Categories: Zany, Cute, Interesting*, 1st edition (Cambridge: Harvard UP, 2015)

59   Emily McAvan, "'I Just Care so Much About the Koalas,'" *Angelaki* 28, no. 5 (2023): 21–38.

60   Evie Kendal, "Horny for COVID: The Growth of Coronavirus Erotica," *Extrapolation* 63, no. 1 (2022): 64.

61   Marder, "The Shadow of the Eco," 144.

ing irreparable damage to the planet prompts existential questions about human responsibility and the limitations of individual agency – and ultimately, forms of mourning and pre-mourning.

Just after WWI, in an essay titled "On Transience," Freud gives a short rendition of his work on melancholia and mourning, written around the same time. The libido ("our capacity for love") attaches to objects "which are thus in a sense taken into our ego." When these are "destroyed or ... lost to us," the libido "is once more liberated," and it can then "take other objects instead," he concludes.[62] This passage suggests the interchangeability of objects and, in this context, how mourning concerns the difficulty of renouncing libidinised objects of care, investment and longing. It also intimates the turn to fantasy and imagination in response to death. Closing the short essay – which is a stylised recollection of dialogue with Rainer Maria Rilke and Lou Andreas-Salomé on natural beauty and, fittingly enough, extinction – Freud commented that although the conversation "took place in the summer before the war," the landscape they contemplated had been subsequently ruined. Freud could be describing the great ravages of human-induced wildfire, and climate catastrophe more generally, when he writes:

> [war] destroyed ... the beauty of the countrysides through which it passed and ... also shattered our pride in the achievements of our civilization.... It tarnished the lofty impartiality of our science; it revealed our instincts in all their nakedness and let loose the evil spirits within us, which we thought had been tamed forever by centuries of continuous education by the noblest minds.... It robbed us of very much that we had loved, and showed us how ephemeral were many things that we had regarded as changeless. We cannot be surprised that our libido, thus bereft of so many of its objects, has clung with all the greater intensity to what is left to us, that our love of our country, our affection for those nearest us and our pride in what is common to us have suddenly grown stronger.[63]

The ambivalence here about human civilisation and science – equally the bringer of social advances and extinction – is not unfamiliar in our time. Given the nationalistic overtones in Freud too, we might observe how the Geeky Sex Toy proffers a new libidinal object for subjects in distress: clinging, like a koala in a eucalypt, to the figure of national pride, even as habitat loss from fossil capital drives it to an alarming level of threat. In Australia's case, this is a sort of manic mourning stitched into a national libidinal economy amid a mining-rich national political economy. Freud writes that, however painful mourning may be, it ultimately "comes to a spontaneous end. When it has renounced everything that has been lost, then it has consumed itself, and our libido is once more free ... to replace the lost objects by fresh ones, equally or still

---

62   Freud, *SE*, XIV: 306.
63   Freud, 307.

more precious."[64] In the context of wildfire and its affectively overwhelming devastation – its total consumption of whole regions – the Geeky Sex Toy was a way to, all at once, honour the dead, enjoy the charitable ecological crisis response and briefly dissipate the stress of 21st century doom through benevolence, humour and sexual pleasure.

Around the same time as the charity sex toy was offered for sale, PornHub, the world's biggest video porn site, launched its "Sexstainable" series of videos. Under the slogan, "let's f*ck the planet right," they asked, "is there anything sexier in today's world than a person who cares about the future of our planet?" Sounding uncertain, they replied, "probably not." They then announced their new initiative: "to educate and inspire more people to start acting sustainably, PornHub, in partnership with 2030 or Bust, has created an entirely new genre of porn: Sexstainable Jerk Off Instructions." Their other slogan promoted this as "the most pleasurable way of caring for the environment." Indeed, they ultimately defined their neologism – "sexstainable" – as "the act of deriving pleasure from taking action towards a better environment."[65] These are the realms that Dominic Pettman, in his book *Peak Libido*, covered under the subtitle of "sex, ecology, and the collapse of desire."[66] What Pettman and others have observed are debates about how the climate emergency has depressed libido, either through psychic symptoms, such as anxiety and depression, or physical effects, such as microplastic pollution or radiation and other potential causes of impotence and declining Western birthrates. With "sexstainability," the leading brand name in internet pornography and one of the most prolific producers of CO_2 on the planet, looked to ruefully counteract the flagging libido amid crisis, just as the LBDO package gives you a little "me time" in an unendingly stressful era, and the sex toy stages a vigil for the coming and current mass extinction events.[67]

These examples may perhaps be overly explicit in conjoining the sexual and the social. Yet, in their nakedness, in their subsumption of the once outré to commodification, they underline just how commonly and openly libido and money are linked

---

64   Freud, 307. Several authors have turned to this essay to consider climate change, including Jonathan Lear, *Imagining the End: Mourning and Ethical Life* (Cambridge: Harvard UP, 2022).

65   https://web.archive.org/web/20210127123905/https://www.pornhub.com/sexstainability. Asterisk in the original. Their "tips" included innuendo-laden suggestions for helping the planet: go easy on the meat; get turned on by dark fantasies; go "au naturel"; always go for a full load; screw the mile-high club; use a second hand; spread your seed; swallow all of it; use me over and over again.

66   Pettman, *Peak Libido*.

67   In 2019, *New Scientist* reported that watching online "pornographic videos generates as much CO2 per year as is emitted by countries such as Belgium, Bangladesh and Nigeria." PornHub, as the largest platform by some margin, takes an outsized share of these emissions. https://web.archive.org/web/20190701000000*/https://www.newscientist.com/articl e/2209569-streaming-online-pornography-produces-as-much-co2-as-belgium/

today. This plainness differs from Freud's time: he pointed out in his guide for analysts beginning an analysis that setting a fee needed to be done plainly, as "money matters are treated by civilized people in the same way as sexual matters – with the same inconsistency, prudishness and hypocrisy." The analyst, by speaking matter-of-factly, demonstrates "that he himself has cast off false shame on these topics," and the analyst understands that, with money, "powerful sexual factors are involved in the value set upon it."[68] (In many ways, it may be easier in our time to speak plainly about one's private sexual arrangements than it is to speak without shame about one's financial investments and inheritances.) Nevertheless, the examples here also suggest how powerful money matters are involved in the value set upon libido. Or, put differently, these examples suggest how easily libido and crisis are linked today – and how openly a price can be put upon them.

In the cases I have outlined, it is almost as if the manifold corporeal immiserations could be removed – or at least forgotten about – by direct, pleasurable, fleshly interventions. This contrasts with what Scarry noted as the role of the body, pain and mental life in crisis. But it also ostensibly inverts the mortification of the flesh in the Christian tradition. Namely, those forms of ritual and practice to deaden sinful nature – the human's concupiscence – via a humbling self-denial or inflicting pain on the body: self-flagellation, abstinence and wearing of irritating hairshirts; all are reminders of the need to repent.[69] Perhaps what we see in the contemporary recourse to fleshly pleasure is how the proximity of what is happening in acute crisis phases – billions of dead animals, flooded cities, overwhelmed emergency services

---

68   Freud, *SE*, XII: 131. Elsewhere, Freud (XVIII: 91) remarked on the offence taken by "educated people" to his focus on sex: "In psychoanalysis … love drives (a *potiori* and because of their origin) are referred to as sexual drives. Most 'educated people,' finding this nomenclature offensive, have taken their revenge by saddling psychoanalysis with the charge of 'pan-sexualism'. Anyone who considers sexuality as something shameful and degrading to human nature is at liberty to use the more genteel expressions 'Eros' and 'eroticism.' I might have done so myself from the outset and spared myself much opposition. However, I chose not to, being keen to avoid concessions to faintheartedness. There is no knowing where such an avenue will lead; one gives way first in words, and then little by little in substance too. I cannot see that anything is gained by being ashamed of sexuality; after all, the Greek word 'Eros,' which apparently softens the offence, is quite simply the translation of our German word *Liebe* [love], and ultimately, the man who can wait need make no concessions."

69   The Bible paragraphs that undergird this theology include: "for if you live according to the flesh you will die; but if by the Spirit you put to death the deeds of the body, you will live" (Romans 8:13); "put to death … whatever belongs to your earthly nature: sexual immorality, impurity, lust, evil desires and greed, which is idolatry" (Colossians 3:5); "those who belong to Christ Jesus have crucified the flesh with its passions and desires" (Galatians 5:24); "blows and wounds scrub away evil, and beatings purge the inmost being" (Proverbs 20:30). Anthropologists have noted versions of some similar painful bodily practices occur in indigenous communities, which have a clear symbolic function during rites of passage.

– draws the subject to coping mechanisms of disinhibited self-soothing alongside visions and experiences of pain and torture. These are ways of temporarily putting to death the deeds of a crisis ridden world. For this soothing, we find the market provides no shortage of services and objects to smooth the path away from pain – and some of these, where they raise funds for charitable causes, even offer the chance of buying indulgences and a little repentance.

The libidinal exploit

In 2020, amid pandemic-induced fear and anxiety, public health measures shaped intensive libidinal investments in mask wearing, crowds, social distancing, mandated shutdowns, and, ultimately, conspiracies and scapegoats. These were all challenges to the notion of control over the external world and the human body, or the porous edges of the body and self.[70] Porn producers, ever the avant-garde in the culture industry and always tuned into fluctuations in the libidinal economy, began uploading content tagged as "COVID" or "quarantine" to porn sites in the pandemic's first month. Widely circulating elements of political and medical discourse – personal protective equipment, nurses, doctors, homes in lockdown – took on a fascination as users, morbidly curious about the risks, engaged in fantasies of proximity to what threatened them and the world.

PornHub saw itself as a first responder on the scene of the crisis, or perhaps even as a partisan of the mutual aid networks that flourished in the first phrase of the pandemic. It offered free "premium content" to people in self-isolation and quarantine. In this role, it presumably hoped to help stymie a zombie-like urge for the infected to roam the streets looking for means to discharge libidinal energy. Erotica also emerged during the early pandemic, notably in the four-part ebook series, *Kissing the Coronavirus* by M. J. Edwards. As the title suggests, this entails dalliances with the sentient virus itself ("I want to be inside as many people as possible. I must spread my seed"); the virus is the character-subject of desire in the series.[71] Other contributions to the genre featured global leaders of 2020 – such as British Prime

---

70   Preciado ("Learning from the Virus," *Artforum*, June 2020) writes: "the management of epidemics stages an idea of community, reveals a society's immunitary fantasies, and exposes sovereignty's dreams of omnipotence – and its impotence." Many conspiracy theories alternate between wild fantasies of sovereigns who are either omnipotent or impotent. This exposure of the sovereign seems to be precisely what conspiracy thinking cannot bear, hence the intensity of such thinking in periods of crisis.

71   For a close reading of the series, see Kendal, "Horny for COVID." Other self-published works, largely appearing online at fandom site Archive of Our Own, include *Courting the Coronavirus: A Positively Viral Love Story* (2020) and *Scissoring the Coronavirus: A Sickeningly Erotic Lesbian Sex Story* (2020).

Minister Boris Johnson and US President Donald Trump – in stories of man-virus love. Across the mutating variants of COVID-erotica, we find "speculative fiction, body horror, fantasy, fan, and slash fiction," mixing "stories of sexual adventure during isolation and quarantine, cybersex, medical fetishism, handwashing and other cleanliness kinks, and their abject counterparts."[72] This is a long way from the imagined normative ideal of sex. But it reflects the rapidity with which desire can introduce new elements from the world and thereby take new shapes – up to and including the virulent, hot green beasts of this erotica, presumably unknown to fantasy life before January 2020.

In the global COVID-19 crisis, the libidinal, in all its plasticity, charted the fixations of populations enduring a rising mix of anxiety, boredom and isolation.[73] Overall, porn traffic spiked upwards during the lockdowns, as the PornHub response suggested. This increase prompted the "porn wars" of earlier decades to be rapidly re-enacted in media and scholarly outlets, now articulated with some prepandemic discourse about sexual ethics, harassment and abuse (e.g., #MeToo).[74] Debates about broader internet addiction and "over-consumption" appeared in psychiatric and public health journals, suggesting a disturbance in the libidinal economy that needed swift medical redress. However, the moral panic around a "porndemic" was misplaced as website usage dropped after the initial explosion in the freighted first half of 2020. What seems to have occurred is a porn-Prozac effect: self-dosing with erotics to quell or alleviate the intense uncertainty of the early pandemic period. As many white-collar workers settled into working-from-home habits, pornography returned to being a mundane feature of their day, either for heightened reminders

---

72   Kendal, "Horny for COVID," 56.

73   For many women, this isolation equalled violence. On femicide and the threat of the feminine for masculinised subjects during the pandemic, see Jacqueline Rose, *The Plague*, Ebook (London: Fitzcarraldo, 2023). Rose writes that women "are being punished – paying with their lives – for a death that has become too keenly felt. As defences start to crumble, the phobic core of being human explodes. Even as the pandemic seems to diminish in its force, this violence against women has continued, as if the felt fragility of life had released into the atmosphere a new, ugly – and seemingly unstoppable – permission to engage in violence. The numbers of sexual offences are soaring.... Domestic violence has become more visible, but the renewed attention has not reduced the prevalence of sexual crime – if anything the opposite" (n.p.). A poster she sees around London encapsulated the pandemic experience for women locked down in violent situations: "abusers always work from home."

74   For recent accounts of the porn wars: Amia Srinivasan, *The Right to Sex: Feminism in the Twenty-First Century* (London: Bloomsbury, 2022); Nancy Bauer, *How to Do Things with Pornography* (Cambridge: Harvard UP, 2015); Lorna N. Bracewell, *Why We Lost the Sex Wars: Sexual Freedom in the #MeToo Era* (Minneapolis: University of Minnesota Press, 2021). Meanwhile, some research showed that COVID-19 infection caused "sexual dysfunction" and what one paper calls "prolonged libido problems": Issam Nessaibia et al., "The Way COVID-19 Transforms Our Sexual Lives," *International Journal of Impotence Research* 34, no. 2 (2022): 117–19.

of selfhood or the desired loss of it. Porn content was now "essential for work" rather than "not safe for work." From the other side of the screen, during the COVID-19 pandemic, porn labourers were doing "essential work," to use the terminology of the time. After all, "every porn scene is a record of people at work."[75] Sex workers collectively laboured throughout the pandemic to produce an indispensable component of capitalism – enjoyment.

Paul B. Preciado has described the contemporary capitalist era as "pharmaco-pornographic."[76] Following Preciado's theorisation, we can say that online pornography has a firm place in the global libidinal economy and – at least during the pandemic – national governance. During the pandemic's height, pornography offered not purely private, commodified pleasures but overlapped with techniques for managing the national (cum global) libidinal economy. Some governments introduced curfews to prevent nocturnal gatherings and promoted masturbation instead of casual sex, all in the name of "stopping the spread" and "flattening the curve" of infection. People's searches for pleasure, they intimated, needed to measure up to the reality of the global situation.

In *Civilisation and Its Discontents*, Freud wrote that if the pleasure principle determines the purpose of life, then it is nevertheless at odds with the whole world, which seems to oppose happiness. Faced with this reality, people temper their claim to happiness, he suggests, being content to escape unhappiness and prevent suffering. Among the ways we "regulate our constitution" is with self-administered pleasures, such as pornography and "intoxicants," about which Freud wrote that their effect "in the struggle for happiness and keeping misery at a distance is seen as so great a boon that not only individuals, but whole nations, have accorded them a firm place in the economy of the libido." Similar to the depletions figured in Stiegler's libidinal dis-economy, Freud warned that, while yielding a positive effect on pleasure and desired independence from the world's reality at certain times ("drowning our sorrows"), the desired aid of intoxicants also makes them "dangerous and harmful. In some circumstances, they are responsible for the futile loss of large amounts of energy that might have been used to improve the lot of mankind."[77] In an early let-

75   Heather Berg, *Porn Work: Sex, Labor, and Late Capitalism* (Chapel Hill: University of North Carolina Press, 2021).

76   Paul B. Preciado, *Testo Junkie*, trans. Bruce Benderson (NY: The Feminist Press, 2012). Despite a glancing similarity, Preciado's analysis, as we will see, differs considerably from US anti-pornography campaign groups such as Fight the New Drug. Such groups suggest pornography is analogous to a drug and public health crisis. These campaigns have been effective: by 2020, 14 US states had non-binding resolutions declaring pornography a public health hazard. See Emily F. Rothman, *Pornography and Public Health* (Oxford: Oxford UP, 2021), 7.

77   Freud, *SE*, XXI: 78. Translation altered. The German is "Die Leistung der Rauschmittel im Kampf um das Glück und zur Fernhaltung des Elends wird so sehr als Wohltat geschätzt, daß Individuen wie Völker ihnen eine feste Stellung in ihrer Libidoökonomie eingeräumt

ter to Wilhelm Fliess, Freud connects addiction, masturbation and intoxicants: "the insight has dawned on me that masturbation is the one major habit, the 'primary addiction,' and it is only as a substitute and replacement for it that the other addictions – to alcohol, morphine, tobacco, and the like – come into existence."[78]

The current global model of political economy is, in a certain sense, also addicted to masturbation, particularly in the guise of pornography. Preciado's theory of "pornpower" describes the intricate relationship between sex, pornography, and desire within larger economic structures. A play on Michel Foucault's conception of "biopower," Preciado's term points to discourses of pleasure that ground contemporary power. These discourses and practices emotionally engage individuals, generating economic value by harnessing work discipline and pleasure discipline. With internet pornography, a new form of work and labour emerges for capital, "an economy of ejaculation."[79] Precisely tracked by online data gathering to identify broad trends and micro fluctuations of interest (when porn users skip, pause, re-watch, like, favourite, share), it is the "culture industry" model at its zenith: an industry of precisely targeted production and precisely dosed pleasure. Indeed, Preciado suggests that the porn industry is the model of efficient profitability, excitation and affective impact in the current market: "minimum investment, direct sales of the product in real time in a unique fashion, the production of instant satisfaction for the consumer."[80] Developments since *Testo Junkie*, such as entrepreneurial porn subscription platforms (e.g., OnlyFans), have simply increased the level of niche consumption and illustrated the imbrication with logics of capital: they have added parasocial elements from celebrity and social media culture to increase affective attachments; many "amateur" profiles are now overseen by dedicated brand management companies with teams of people, often offshore in low-

---

haben." The noun "Völker" can indicate either "peoples" in a generic sense or "nations" in a more bounded sense.

78   Sigmund Freud, *The Complete Letters of Sigmund Freud to Wilhelm Fliess, 1887–1904*, trans. Jeffrey Moussaieff Masson (Cambridge: Belknap, 1986), 287. The depletion has its description in these letters to Fliess, too. As summarised by Jamieson Webster: "Neurasthenic melancholia – languor, malaise, boredom – Freud ties to excessive masturbation, namely, too much terminal discharge of sensation, creating an overall weakening of one's system. This is what we might think of as the vicissitudes of addiction and the problems of indulgence that eventually induce anesthesia. Here, depression follows an excess, but one that creates an inability to maintain any store of energy or pleasure that might amount to anything other than a demand for total discharge. Your system is spent. You've blown your load too many times – the result of a reified love object that you infinitely consume because it is not separate from yourself, tied into the external world" (*Conversion Disorder*, 80).

79   Preciado, 293. Berg's argument in *Porn Work* suggests how sex workers are always at the vanguard of changes in economic and labour relations, both in creating new possibilities and responding to harsh legal regimes.

80   Preciado, *Testo*, 39.

wage centres such as the Philippines, ventriloquising the models and responding to private messages 24/7, typically to extract cash from wealthy subscribers for purportedly exclusive content.[81]

Preciado's book *Testo Junkie*, a self-described "body-essay," sketches a "new cartography" of how, during the past century, sexuality and the body became subjects of meticulous governmental and industrial management – and source of economic value. He uses "pharmacopornographic" because "these management techniques function no longer through the repression and prohibition of sexuality, but through the incitement of consumption and the constant production of a regulated and quantifiable pleasure."[82] Pharmacological consumption, pornographic representation, and sexual services are the characteristic vectors of economic growth. Notions of libido – alongside psyche, consciousness, gender, sexuality – have been transformed into tangible realities by technoscience, manifest in commercial chemical substances, molecules and fungible technological goods. These entities are managed by multinationals, their goods listed on government-administered health care schedules and their value traded in shares: depression ↔ Prozac, masculinity ↔ testosterone, (non)erection ↔ Viagra, reproduction ↔ the Pill, HIV ↔ tritherapy. The bidirectional arrows indicate that once discovered, these open potentials that individuals *must* seize upon – with Viagra, you *can*, therefore, you *must*.[83] This confers a set of expectations and understandings of "the problem" (fertility, impotence, dysmorphia) that cannot but be read back into it. The opioid crisis in the US over the past decade has further evidenced the role of prescription and illicit drugs in the search for profit amid pleasure (and dependency and despair).[84] Here again, as we saw earlier, finding relief for the body in pain becomes the site of intervention

---

81   On the economic implications of these platforms, see Gwyn Easterbrook-Smith, "OnlyFans as Gig-Economy Work: A Nexus of Precarity and Stigma," *Porn Studies*, 2022, 1–16. On the marketing and management companies, see Ezra Marcus's report from 2022 in *NY Times*: https://www.nytimes.com/2022/05/16/magazine/e-pimps-onlyfans.html

82   Preciado, "Learning."

83   Slavoj Žižek, "'You May!,'" *London Review of Books*, March 18, 1999. As Žižek writes: "The superego inverts the Kantian 'You can, because you must' in a different way, turning it into 'You must, because you can.' This is the meaning of Viagra, which promises to restore the capacity of male erection in a purely biochemical way, bypassing all psychological problems. Now that Viagra can take care of the erection, there is no excuse: you should have sex whenever you can; and if you don't you should feel guilty."

84   Max Haiven, *Revenge Capitalism: The Ghosts of Empire, the Demons of Capital, and the Settling of Unpayable Debts* (London: Pluto, 2020); Jesse Proudfoot, "The Libidinal Economy of Revanchism: Illicit Drugs, Harm Reduction, and the Problem of Enjoyment," *Progress in Human Geography* 43, no. 2 (2019): 214–34; John L. Fitzgerald, *Life in Pain: Affective Economy and the Demand for Pain Relief* (Singapore: Springer, 2020). Fitzgerald points out that illicit drug strategies attempt to inflict pain and death on drug users, as in the drug death squads of Rodrigo Duterte's Philippines. These were a point of sadistic pride for the leader and his followers.

into social ills, a *pharmakon* in Derrida's sense, undecidably on the cusp of cure and poison.

Preciado's work describes this contemporary libidinal economy without placing it in that particular tradition.[85] He proposes "*potentia gaudendi*" – the inherent capacity to produce and experience pleasure, desire and affects within the human body – as the raw material exploited in current regimes. This *potentia* encompasses both physical sensations (such as desire, arousal, and orgasm) and mental experiences related to pleasure: products such as Viagra are marketed to promise enhanced and managed bodily pleasure; aids such as poppers are used to cause euphoric highs and enhance sexual pleasure; pornography is offered as a failsafe route to pleasure via managed doses of representation and fantasy; and, practically folding all of these together, online communities such as "gooners" aspire to marathon, hours-long, trance-like masturbation sessions using poppers and looping porn videos. To get a grip on this conjuncture, we might propose joining Santner's "flesh" with the psychiatric language of addiction and speak of a "substance use disorder" of a different type – the fleshy substance, the subject-matter, of global libidinal economy, the substantialisation of the object as, and in, pleasure. If the use of the substance in such regimes is ostensibly disordered, then Preciado's work suggests – in age of disorganised capitalism that cashes in on this disordered enjoyment – there might nevertheless be a certain senseless or compulsive order to this disorder.

If we follow Preciado, then at this stage of global capitalism, any baroque vision of economic disturbance via sexual excess – the fantasy of earlier libidinal liberationists, bursting through repression and economic rationality, an eruption of the libidinal in the factory or office cubicle or delivery van – does not seem to capture the smooth functioning of porn consumption (and porn production and sex work) within the workaday realities of the contemporary economy. Today, the widespread accessibility of porn is no longer taken to be the "filthy commerce with oneself" denigrated by anti-masturbation campaigners of earlier centuries, but a salve for loneliness and boredom in conditions of antisocial capitalism.[86] Pornography use has

---

85   Preciado has a complicated relationship with psychoanalysis, explicitly distancing himself from it but also drawing on elements despite himself. As Webster argues, his project and the critique of libidinal economy are not really at odds: "Somato-Militancy: A New Vision for Psychoanalysis in the Work of Paul B. Preciado," *Paragraph* 46, no. 1 (2023): 124–41; "Memento Mori: The Book as a Cut," *Studies in Gender and Sexuality* 17, no. 1 (2016): 14–18.

86   Here, we can acknowledge the contemporary "no fap" anti-masturbation movement as a marginal cultural formation, born precisely as a reaction to porn's quasi-sanctioned mainstream availability. We can note their pleasure in renouncing pleasure, a formal similarity with the religious movements associated with earlier anti-masturbation campaigners that often see the two groups compared. These cultural movements overlook the achievements of masturbatory pleasure in Darian Leader's estimation: "we learn how to use phantasy quite early on in life, as we coordinate our daydreams to manipulation of the body. It's quite a feat,

become more mundane, less exceptional. As Mari Ruti pointed out before the pandemic, the common practice of using internet porn to "take a break" from work and other demands – that is, "to recharge one's ability to tackle the next task or to endure the dullness of the day" – is maximally efficient: "you take your break, you satisfy your desire while neatly sidestepping the (potentially time-consuming) tangles of intersubjectivity, and then you go right back to 'producing.'"[87] This recalls, unexpectedly, a passage from Plato's *Symposium* in which Aristophanes speaks about the functional role of homosexual intercourse in that era: "when a man embraced a woman, he would cast his seed and they would have children; but when a male embraced a male, they would at least have the satisfaction of intercourse, after which they could *stop embracing, return to their jobs, and look after their needs in life*."[88] In these examples, the sexual release is used to prop up the Other, enabling participation in social and professional functions, living up to expectations and perhaps supporting the identifications that keep the subject up and running in its roles (e.g., a good and productive worker).

In opening a browser window to a wall of fleshy thumbnail images ready to be stirred into action with a click, the user's libido is not repressed or delayed in its sexual gratification. As Preciado sees it, the excitation-frustration chain is ultimately slackened and temporarily returned to quiescence – yet at that moment, capital derives its surplus and readies for the next round, following the rhythmic circuit "excitation-capital-frustration-excitation-capital," echoing Marx's general formula for endless capital accumulation: "money-commodity-money."[89] Preciado notes this as a model of post-Fordist consumption in general (other industries have "porn envy") and a specific mode of production, "a masturbatory temporization of life," the "ultra-rapid diffusion of information, a continuous mode of desiring and resisting, of consuming and destroying, of evolution and self-destruction."[90] Frustration and loss are hallmarks of the libidinal – and porn's purpose, as Preciado sees it, is producing

---

after all, to make a significant moment in a story we are picturing coincide with an orgasm. This requires a very complex set of cognitive and physical skills, and it has even been described as a milestone in sensorimotor development, like learning how to write or tie one's shoelaces. As we learn how to build and use masturbatory stories, we are also learning how to identify with characters, how to be other people, which is arguably something we need in order to read and relate to the world more generally" (*Is It Ever Just Sex?* (London: Penguin, 2023), 183).

87   Mari Ruti, *Distillations: Theory, Ethics, Affect* (NY: Bloomsbury, 2018), 105.
88   Quoted in Alenka Zupančič, *The Odd One in: On Comedy* (Cambridge: MIT Press, 2008), 188. Emphasis added.
89   Preciado, *Testo*, 271–72.
90   Preciado, 41, 271.

"frustrating satisfaction" or, to quote multihyphenate artist and sometime experimental porn actor Lydia Lunch: "I sell frustration, not relief."[91]

As Freud theorised, sexual drives initially find satisfaction in the subject's own body (autoeroticism). They are delayed in finding an object, which means they can lead to a closer relationship between sexual drive and fantasising – where the circulation of pornography offers itself as a medium of libidinal gratification, a smorgasbord of niche and privately enjoyed content. Studies of online porn users suggest they interrupt one video and replace it with another, shuffling fantasy worlds to find their path to climax. What might be at stake for subjects in this widespread take-up of such material? "Fantasizing about intensified feeling can be a way of imagining the thrill of sexual or political control or its loss, or," Berlant writes, "conversely, a way of overwhelming one's sexual ambivalence or insecurity with a frenzy of representation."[92] Berlant here puts pornography in dialogue with the chaste romance plot in popular culture, suggesting viewers of both have multifarious purposes connected with fantasy life and desire, navigating between reality and pleasure principles.

Freud's concern about intoxicants, particularly in situations of addiction, was that they gave free rein to the pleasure principle over the reality principle. As Freud sees it, a contradiction stems from these two principles of mental functioning. The "pleasure principle" seeks to eliminate tension by fulfilling our desires. For example, when we are hungry (a state of unpleasure), we eat to satisfy our hunger and experience pleasure. However, if we constantly fulfil all our desires (if the buffet never closes), we will be stuck in a cycle of excitement and exhaustion, making it difficult to accomplish anything. This is where the second principle, the "reality principle," comes into its own: it involves delaying gratification and conserving energy to manage the tasks of life. The more we internalise this principle – the more we sit in the state of frustration – the more control we have over ourselves and the world. Freud describes how, when libidinal energy reaches a certain level (unpleasure), this can be satisfied either autoerotically, as modelled in those early stages of life, or by finding an external object, which will entail some reality testing. Fantasising, however, is exempt from reality testing, thereby obeying the pleasure principle. Reflecting on these principles, Jamieson Webster suggests that "we try to master ourselves, self-regulate our access to pleasure, defend against pleasure that has grown too intense" but find ourselves in "a losing game."[93] Indeed, moment by moment, day in, day out, this is a lot of psychic work.

Religious myths about renouncing earthly pleasures for future rewards, such as those in the Protestant ethic, echo the apparent transition from Freud's "pleasure

---

91   Preciado, 304, 265.
92   Lauren Berlant, *Desire/Love* (NY: Punctum, 2012), 96–97.
93   Webster, *Conversion Disorder*, 31.

principle" to the "reality principle."[94] Although often presented in this way, as if the pleasure principle was a primitive compulsion checked by the later development of the reality principle or – in some accounts of libidinal liberation – as if pleasure and reality are opposed, the point is that they exist in dialectical tension, in a relationship of dependency.[95] At the same time, the relation between pleasure and reality principles is not fixed and ontological but historical, which means it is social, changeable, and analysable in these terms: that is, as "an historical becoming of the relation between pleasure and desire."[96] This further implies that – in tracing a development of pleasure and desire – drives and the libido are changeable and subject to historical modification.

The contemporary porn industry's precise online data gathering, for instance, produces a welter of proprietary research about people's access to pleasure. "Year in review" stats from PornHub consistently show over recent years that the two busiest periods on the site are those of the postprandial lull (1 pm–6 pm) and after dark (9 pm–2 am); other appetites are presumably fed between 6 pm and 9 pm. If for the sake of argument we assume the site's users work ordinary business hours, then those enjoying after dark are following a traditional, morally severe Protestant ethic: the subject should focus on performing productive tasks throughout the workday rather than taking the pornographic detour, which can instead be the delayed gratification of a day's work, perhaps even following other imperatives to "de-stress" and aid insomnia or sleep anxieties.[97] The midafternoon porn browser, by contrast, is the one

---

94   Freud, *SE*, XII: 213–226.

95   Stiegler, *Lost Spirit*, 45.

96   Stiegler, 46. Herbert Marcuse, for example, names the "performance principle" as the reigning reality principle of the twentieth century. It includes the pay-off for the readiness to always perform the functions desired by and for capital: "under its rule society is stratified according to the competitive economic performances of its members. It is clearly not the only historical reality principle: other modes of societal organization not merely prevailed in primitive cultures but also survived into the modern period." Nevertheless, "the performance principle, which is that of an acquisitive and antagonistic society in the process of constant expansion, presupposes a long development during which domination has been increasingly rationalized: control over social labor now reproduces society on an enlarged scale and under improving conditions" (*Eros and Civilization: A Philosophical Inquiry into Freud* (London: Routledge, 2023), 33). The sacrifice in Marcuse is not to "civilisation" as Freud put it, but rather to specific economic interests and instrumental rationality.

97   Max Weber quoted the Puritan minister Richard Baxter to encapsulate the ethos: "keep up a high esteem of time; and be every day more careful that you lose none of your time, than you are that you lose none of your gold or silver. And if vain recreation, dressings, feastings, idle talk, unprofitable company, or sleep be any of them temptations to rob you of any of your time, accordingly heighten your watchfulness" (*The Protestant Ethic and the 'Spirit' of Capitalism and Other Writings*, ed. and trans. Peter Baehr and Gordon C. Wells (London: Penguin, 2002), 231n14).

"drawn into the neoliberal game of keeping up with a multitude of practical, psychic, emotional, and work-related pressures."[98] Overworked by work and more besides, this is close to a capitalist consumer ethic, a type of impulse shopping: "spending not saving, self-gratification not self-denial, the pleasures of consumption rather than the dignity of labour."[99]

In the reality principle of rational asceticism and self-command central to the earlier capitalist spirit described by Max Weber and Adam Smith, emotional suppression was required for future goals to be prioritised over an urgent desire.[100] Yet those goals, in contemporary crisis times, can be difficult to glimpse or, in the case of climate change, can be outright terrifying. Goals, whether collective or individual, become more challenging to commit to and it becomes more difficult to believe in the worth of self-denial in the present; the desperate spectacles of self-denying fitness influencers and tech entrepreneurs only attest to the crisis of mass investment in the old mythos. The ascetic denial of satisfaction via consumption recedes with this missing horizon; gratification collapses into the present or near future. Objectively – which is to say, following the reality principle – accumulation and hope through the subject's denial no longer seem to be wise bets. Agentive futures feel barred. What is the subject's sacrifice, foresight, industry, application, constant effort and purpose for, if, beyond the passing esteem and recognition of a job well done, or the transient power and recognition of wealth, all are hostages to the fortune of a grim future in which even the wealthy will burn with the koalas, jobs are all gig work and the prospects of economic growth, on which so much is premised, are serially revised down?

To take the question from the other side of the ledger, what, in the end (times), is the economic utility of all this libidinal enjoyment? In recent years, human resources researchers have empirically investigated this topic. As the true libidinal economists of our time, they concluded: "employees experience a 5% increase in mood at work the next day for each time they engaged in sex the previous evening."[101] The contem-

98   Ruti, *Distillations*, 106.

99   David Bennett, *The Currency of Desire: Libidinal Economy, Psychoanalysis and Sexual Revolution* (London: Lawrence & Wishart, 2016), 44. "Spending" was the Victorian-era metaphor for orgasm. The colloquial "I'm spent" also carries this implication.

100   Jack Barbalet, *Weber, Passion and Profits: "The Protestant Ethic and the Spirit of Capitalism" in Context* (Cambridge: Cambridge UP, 2008), 117.

101   Keith Leavitt et al., "From the Bedroom to the Office: Workplace Spillover Effects of Sexual Activity at Home," *Journal of Management* 45, no. 3 (2019): 1185–86. Amusingly in this context, they also write that "an editorial commentary in the *Academy of Management Journal* titled 'What Makes Management Research Interesting, and Why Does It Matter?' notes that sex and stock options are topics that immediately generate interest" (1174). Of course, "sex" and masturbation with pornography are different activities. These researchers focus on married couples and "intercourse," by which they seem to mean penetrative sex as they oppose this to "oral sex or other forms of stimulation" (1177). They are largely interested in the mood and

porary awareness of libido and its impacts at work is not the upshot of our especially enlightened, liberal, sexually positive 21st century. Henry Ford, the factory boss of 20th-century American capitalism, suggested that when married working-class couples have a good sex life, workers become more productive and easier to manage.[102] Centuries earlier, political economists such as Bernard Mandeville pointed out how sexual vices and self-interest were compatible with the common good of economic development – (female) prostitution, for example, was a vice and an urban blight but was ultimately helpful to business.[103] What emerges here, in elite libidinal economic management, "is the link between exploitation and enjoyment, the reproduction of the relations of domination by means of the production of enjoyment." This is the exploitative nexus of *power-enjoyment*: "in their seemingly private enjoyment, subjects work for the system."[104]

While sexuality's imbrication with the market is not new, what has changed is its intensity and scale, as Preciado suggests. After all, our era is one in which global infrastructures – such as undersea cables and 5G technologies – have been built up in part to support porn consumption at the highest possible definitions with minimum lag and the ostensibly unwelcome frustrations of buffering. Sexual markets, commodification and consumption are now vast, involving millions of people around the globe in production and circulation – and millions more in their consumption. As capitalism faces roiling crises and capitalists go hunting for commodities to create surplus-generating inputs, markets linked to sexual products and services are a continuing zone of profit. These are multifarious, selling: *relationships* (dating apps, forced marriages, sex tourism); *expertise* (sex therapy and self-help); *objects* (drugs and sex toys); *representations* (pornography and advertising); *bodies* (sex work); *people* (sex trafficking); and *life* or *contraception* (reproductive technologies – IVF to birth control to offshore surrogacy). All this commerce is worth hundreds of billions of US dollars annually. All of it has been criticised on multiple fronts, including its elements of economic exploitation, sexual oppression, capital accumulation, organised

---

physiological (hormonal) responses of this interpersonal intimacy. As Leader (*Is It?*, 7) points out, in pornography, characters typically do not show loyalty to others. There's a lack of prior commitments or emotional connections, which contrasts with relationships where loyalty and emotional bonds are significant factors; even the brief hook-up at a party or organised by app (etc.) carries an extra dimension that is not present in screen-based recorded media – a dimension of bodies colliding with bodies, sometimes physically, always affectively.

102   Antonio Gramsci, *Selections from the Prison Notebooks of Antonio Gramsci* (London: Lawrence & Wishart, 1971), 296. This is from the section on "Americanism and Fordism," which includes several fascinating passages about sexuality and gender.

103   Dana Kaplan and Eva Illouz, *What Is Sexual Capital?* (Cambridge: Polity, 2022), 50–51.

104   Tomšič, *Labour*, 15

crime, forced migration, and unequal development, as well as racism and gendered violence.[105]

This generalised commodification of sex and bodies – "the finest consumer object"[106] – only confirms critics' longstanding warnings about capitalism's grip on increasing areas of human intercourse. The point Lacanian critiques have offered of contemporary sexualities is that whenever we most consider ourselves to be liberated in comparison to previous generations, we are being directed to desire in line with the desire of the symbolic (or big Other), both through the direct monetisation of our desire via goods and the indirect monetisation of our desire through increased productivity.[107] Historically, some have traced "sexual liberalism" – not liberation – to the era that began in the 1960s in many Western countries. This new regime encouraged a liberal sexual subject, particularly among men. Literature and popular culture were decensored, while pornography came to be viewed as a source of sexual knowledge. These liberal subjects embraced sexual pleasure and sexual consumerism: seeking self-fulfilment and self-actualisation, they became self-educators, bettering themselves through the sexual encounter. This liberalism spread, shaping gender norms and consumer behaviour, despite challenges from feminist and LGBTI+ movements that sought to counter the reinforcement of traditional gender roles and promotion of individualistic attitudes towards sexuality.[108] The "sexual wellness" devices with which I opened this chapter offer twenty-first-century visions of this sexual liberalism: typically marketed to individual women as forms of sexual education, enlightenment and pleasure, they offer, via what the brand Lioness calls "sexperiments," biofeedback and machine learning optimisation to improve – or have "smarter" – orgasms. This image of both reification and utopia, of capital and new frontiers of pleasure, only reiterates the point that the human is the libidinal creature that subjects its sexual pleasure to cultures of (quasi-)scientific reflection but also to data capture – to a melange of wellness, science and venture capital.

---

105   This paragraph draws from the expert summary and reference list in Ken Plummer, "Sexual Markets, Commodification, and Consumption," in *The Blackwell Encyclopedia of Sociology*, ed. George Ritzer (Oxford: Wiley, 2017), 1–4. We could add here the spate of twenty-first century reality TV franchises (*Love Island, Too Hot to Handle, FBOY Island, Dating Naked, Naked and Afraid, Naked Attraction* and so on) organised around competitive relationships, frustration, titillation and moralism – the winning capitalist mix of prurience and puritanism.

106   Jean Baudrillard, *The Consumer Society: Myths and Structures* (London: Sage, 1998), chap. 8.

107   Ruti, *Distillations*, 106.

108   See Ben Mechen's work: "'Instamatic Living Rooms of Sin': Pornography, Participation and the Erotics of Ordinariness in the 1970s," *Contemporary British History* 36, no. 2 (2022): 174–206; "Dirty Magazines, Clean Consciences: Men and Pornography in the 1970s," in *Men and Masculinities in Modern Britain*, ed. Matt Houlbrook, Katie Jones, and Ben Mechen (Manchester: Manchester UP, 2024), 253–68

In the capitalist universe, it often seems "there are only commodified plea-sures."[109] For some, however, this contemporary sexual-cum-libidinal variety still marks a liberation, despite capital's role. These are tensions long explored in fem-inist, queer and gender studies: the difficult tangle of repression and progress, co-optation and radicality, market and deviance, pleasure and exploitation – all of this under the bigger question of sexuality as a site of politics, or the expanding and contracting of pleasures in exchange societies (aka "the capitalist paradox").[110] In the French (male) tradition of libidinal economy – Pierre Klossowski, Georges Bataille, Jean-François Lyotard, Gilles Deleuze and Félix Guattari – this tension con-cerns whether it is possible to "render libidinal economy as a counter-economy."[111] For Lyotard, no counter-economy exists in global capitalism. Whoever "does not want to recognize that political economy is libidinal," Lyotard writes, "reproduces in other terms the same phantasy of an externalized region where desire would be sheltered from every treacherous transcription into production, labour and the law of value." He suggests this is the "phantasy of a non-alienated region."[112] For Lyotard, this is at once a spatial, psychic and physical truth in his polemic against Western philosophy, anthropology and sociology: there is no spot for us to retreat to, withdraw to or celebrate for its nonalienation or its shelter for free, direct libidinal expression.

Lyotard and others in the line of libidinal economy ultimately question what is generated in a capitalist matrix of exchange and, by implication, what might escape that matrix. It is a matrix in which, Noys writes, "living bodies become the mate-rial which capital posits as its ground and [which] play an unstable role as a recalci-

---

109   Tomšič, *Labour*, 188.

110   To indicate a few recent works that have taken up these questions again: Srinivasan, *The Right to Sex*; Kaplan and Illouz, *What Is*; Nona Willis Aronowitz, *Bad Sex: Truth, Pleasure, and an Un-finished Revolution* (NY: Plume, 2022); Jayne Swift, "Toxic Positivity? Rethinking Respectabil-ity, Revaluing Pleasure," *South Atlantic Quarterly* 120, no. 3 (2021): 591–608; Angela Jones, "Sex Positivity: A Black Feminist Gift," in *Introducing the New Sexuality Studies*, ed. Nancy Fischer, Laurel Westbrook, and Steven Seidman, 4th ed. (NY: Routledge, 2022); Bracewell, *Why We Lost*; Berg, *Porn Work*; Lauren Berlant and Lee Edelman, *Sex, or the Unbearable* (Durham: Duke UP, 2014) For a classic collection covering the "capitalist paradox" of pleasure's dilation: Ann Barr Snitow, Christine Stansell, and Sharon Thompson, eds., *Powers of Desire: The Politics of Sexuality* (NY: Monthly Review Press, 1983).

111   Noys, "'We Are All Prostitutes,'" 176. Another French iteration of the libidinal economy debate is the feminist one around Irigaray and Cixous, which concerns the question of an economy of generosity rather than scarcity. For example, the scarcity thesis in Freud contributes to his un-derstanding of abnormal narcissism as an overallocation of libido to the self, leaving less for outward investment. See Teresa Brennan, *The Interpretation of the Flesh: Freud and Femininity* (London: Routledge, 2002), 75.

112   Jean-François Lyotard, *Libdinal Economy*, trans. Iain Hamilton Grant (Bloomington: Indiana UP, 1993), 107.

trant and problematic 'base.'" In other words, living bodies are turned into sources of value, an operation resting on the flesh and materiality of sex.[113] So the problem of the critique of the libidinal economy remains: namely, imagining "a liberation that interrupts rather than replicates a capitalist logic," the logic that everywhere transforms "the body from mere material into a mere resource for exploitation."[114]

Continued collective conceptual labour

The usual charge *against* psychoanalytic cultural and social theory is that it is not viable to generalise from the individual to the collective, the clinic to the social. But this misunderstands the task of such an approach, which is, rather, to "show how individuals get initiated, drawn into, 'seduced' by, the ways in which historical forms of life have – always precariously and provisionally – come to terms with fundamental impasses plaguing human flourishing more generally."[115] In this chapter, we have seen that late capitalism has a certain shamelessness in extracting value from the lustful, drawing from and on the libidinal impasses of its subjects in crisis times – including their pains and their attempted remedies at the level of the flesh. In the other chapters, we have also seen the regular seesaw from the *libidinal* economy to the libidinal *economy*. I have touched on some of the ways the libidinal is capitalised upon, while many other contributors to this volume have explored how capital is (always already) libidinised.

In closing, I want to recall that the impetus for this edited volume came from noticing the term "libidinal economy" – or variations on it, such as "psychic economy" – had popped up again, partly in response to the Global Financial Crisis of 2007–8 and the subsequent interest in debt and finance. This re-emergence suggested the appeal of such concepts to deal with the ever-starker crisis tendencies and their subjective implication and fallout in capitalist societies. That the idea of the libidinal economy might be doing some interesting new work was apparent in its appearance in writing of various sorts in recent times: critical political economy; re-engagements with Lyotard's infamous text, particularly in the cultural politics of the accelerationists; Lacanian psychoanalytic critique; queer theory; critical accounts of sex work; afropessimism / antiblackness; cultural criticism's fascination with affect; libidinal "ecology."[116] There has been a whole sweep of thinking, then,

---

113   Noys, "'We Are All Prostitutes,'" 180.

114   Noys, 180.

115   Santner, *Royal*, 73.

116   In addition to those already cited, see, for example: Amin Samman and Stefano Sgambati, "Financial Eschatology and the Libidinal Economy of Leverage," *Theory, Culture & Society* 40, no. 3 (2023): 103–21; Angus Cameron, Anastasia Nesvetailova, and Ronen Palan, "Wages of Sin?: Crisis and the Libidinal Economy," *Journal of Cultural Economy* 4, no. 2 (2011): 117–35; Earl

about bodies, the flesh and desire, or the psychic life of the economy. This has joined a renewed and reinvigorated interest in the psychosocial impacts of capitalism's current regimes, and a desire for a revenant critique of libidinal economy. The conference in Berlin aimed to weave together these threads to see what patterns would emerge. Inevitably, not all the critiques of libidinal economy could be addressed in the conference, or this book, and those included here have skewed towards the Lacanian, Deleuzian and Lyotardian versions of the term. Equally, some have explored conceptual and philosophical lineages that are precursors of this libidinal economic thought – Spinoza, Cavendish, Ibn Sina, Marx and more.

The work on these realms continues, with two other books published shortly before this one: the first, from a similarly titled conference that ran in the UK a year or so after the Berlin event; the second, a co-authored volume proposing a theory of global libidinal economy.[117] As such, the current collection can be seen as contributing to a broader, collective conceptual labour on libidinal economy that emerged after 2007 and that continues a decade and a half later, just as the crises continue apace. The present volume has been curious about the most fruitful inquiries in these various fields, remaining committed to theoretical pluralism to explore this manifold and nebulous category – hence, too, the plural "economies" in the title. It

Gammon and Duncan Wigan, "Libidinal Political Economy: A Psycho-Social Analysis of Financial Violence," in *Global Political Economy: Contemporary Theories*, ed. Ronen Palan, 2nd ed (NY: Routledge, 2013), 205–16; Maureen Sioh, "Manicheism Delirium: Desire and Disavowal in the Libidinal Economy of an Emerging Economy," *Third World Quarterly* 35, no. 7 (2014): 1162–78; Frank B. Wilderson, *Red, White & Black: Cinema and the Structure of U.S. Antagonisms* (Durham: Duke UP, 2010); Frank B. Wilderson, *Afropessimism* (NY: Liveright, 2020); Ashley Woodward, "'White Skin': Lyotard's Sketch of a Postcolonial Libidinal Economy," *Journal of the British Society for Phenomenology* 51, no. 4 (2020): 337–51; Aaron Schuster, "One or Many Antisexes? Introduction to Andrei Platonov's 'The Anti-Sexus,'" *Stasis* 4, no. 1 (2016); André L. Brock, *Distributed Blackness: African American Cybercultures* (NY: NYU Press, 2020); Barbara Markowska, "Homo Libidinous and the Economy of Desire: Reading Simmel's *The Philosophy of Money* after Freud," *Polish Sociological Review*, no. 4 (2018): 485–98; Bara Kolenc, "Voyeurism and Exhibitionism on the Internet: The Libidinal Economy of the Spectacle of Instanternity," *Filozofski Vestnik* 43, no. 3 (2022); Alessandra Campo, "Pierre Klossowski's Libidinal Economy," *Vestigia* 3, no. 2 (2022): 7–21; Ilan Kapoor, ed., *Psychoanalysis and the Global* (Lincoln: University of Nebraska Press, 2018); David Hancock, *The Countercultural Logic of Neoliberalism* (London: Routledge, 2019); Jordan Osserman, "'Gay Culture Rampant in Hyderabad': Analysing the Political and Libidinal Economy of Homophobia," in *New Voices in Psychosocial Studies*, ed. Stephen Frosh, Studies in the Psychosocial (Cham: Springer, 2019), 179–93; Mark Fisher, *Postcapitalist Desire: The Final Lectures*, ed. Matt Colquhoun (London: Repeater, 2021); Luce DeLire, "Full Queerocracy Now!: Pink Totaliterianism and the Industrialization of Libidinal Agriculture," *E-Flux*, no. 117 (2021); Fredric Jameson, "Schematizations, or How to Draw a Thought," *Critical Inquiry* 50, no. 1 (2023): 31–53.

117   Kapoor et al., *Global Libidinal Economy*; Amin Samman and Earl Gammon, eds., *Clickbait Capitalism: Economies of Desire in the Twenty-First Century* (Manchester: Manchester UP, 2023).

has also been intrigued by the sources of libidinal economy's return, while moving beyond the basic observation that the fallout of the financial crisis is the sole cause of interest in the idea. Something is afoot, but we do not quite know what it is. As the preceding has explored, the libidinal economy in capitalist crises touches on areas of deep significance for understanding contemporary life. The chapters in this volume have continued that exploration of life in all its pleasures and pains.

References

Ahmed, Sara. *The Cultural Politics of Emotion*. 2nd ed. Edinburgh: Edinburgh UP, 2014.

Allison, Anne. *Precarious Japan*. Durham: Duke, 2013.

Apter, Emily, and Martin Crowley. "Economies of Existence." *Diacritics* 47, no. 1 (2019): 3–15. https://doi.org/10.1353/dia.2019.0007.

Barbalet, Jack. *Weber, Passion and Profits: "The Protestant Ethic and the Spirit of Capitalism" in Context*. Cambridge: Cambridge UP, 2008.

Baudrillard, Jean. *The Consumer Society: Myths and Structures*. London: Sage, 1998.

Bauer, Nancy. *How to Do Things with Pornography*. Cambridge: Harvard UP, 2015.

Bennett, David. *The Currency of Desire: Libidinal Economy, Psychoanalysis and Sexual Revolution*. London: Lawrence & Wishart, 2016.

Berg, Heather. *Porn Work: Sex, Labor, and Late Capitalism*. Chapel Hill: University of North Carolina Press, 2021.

Berlant, Lauren. *Cruel Optimism*. Durham: Duke UP, 2011.

———. *Desire/Love*. NY: Punctum, 2012.

———. "The Epistemology of State Emotion." In *Dissent in Dangerous Times*, edited by Austin Sarat, 46–78. Ann Arbor: University of Michigan Press, 2005.

Berlant, Lauren, and Lee Edelman. *Sex, or the Unbearable*. Durham: Duke UP, 2014.

Bourke, Joanna. *The Story of Pain: From Prayer to Painkillers*. Oxford: Oxford UP, 2014.

Bracewell, Lorna N. *Why We Lost the Sex Wars: Sexual Freedom in the #MeToo Era*. Minneapolis: University of Minnesota Press, 2021.

Brennan, Teresa. *The Interpretation of the Flesh: Freud and Femininity*. London: Routledge, 2002.

Brock, André L. *Distributed Blackness: African American Cybercultures*. NY: NYU Press, 2020.

Burnham, Clint. *Fredric Jameson and The Wolf of Wall Street*. NY: Bloomsbury, 2016.

Cameron, Angus, Anastasia Nesvetailova, and Ronen Palan. "Wages of Sin?: Crisis and the Libidinal Economy." *Journal of Cultural Economy* 4, no. 2 (2011): 117–35. https://doi.org/10.1080/17530350.2011.563066.

Campo, Alessandra. "Pierre Klossowski's Libidinal Economy." *Vestigia* 3, no. 2 (2022): 7–21.

Chukhrov, Keti. *Practicing the Good: Desire and Boredom in Soviet Socialism*. Minneapolis: e-flux, 2020.

Cohen, Lizabeth. *A Consumer's Republic: The Politics of Mass Consumption in Postwar America*. NY: Knopf, 2003.

Connor, J. D. *Hollywood Math and Aftermath: The Economic Image and the Digital Recession*. London: Bloomsbury, 2018.

Davies, William. *Nervous States: Democracy and the Decline of Reason*. NY: Norton, 2020.

DeLay, Tad. *Future of Denial: The Ideologies of Climate Change*. London: Verso, 2024.

DeLire, Luce. "Full Queerocracy Now!: Pink Totaliterianism and the Industrialization of Libidinal Agriculture." *E-Flux*, no. 117 (2021). https://www.e-flux.com/jo urnal/117/386679/full-queerocracy-now-pink-totaliterianism-and-the-industri alization-of-libidinal-agriculture/.

Easterbrook-Smith, Gwyn. "OnlyFans as Gig-Economy Work: A Nexus of Precarity and Stigma." *Porn Studies* 10, no. 3 (2022): 252–267. https://doi.org/10.1080/2326 8743.2022.2096682.

Fisher, Mark. *Postcapitalist Desire: The Final Lectures*. Edited by Matt Colquhoun. London: Repeater, 2021.

Fitzgerald, John L. *Life in Pain: Affective Economy and the Demand for Pain Relief*. Singapore: Springer, 2020.

Fraser, Nancy. *The Old Is Dying and the New Cannot Be Born: From Progressive Neoliberalism to Trump and Beyond*. London: Verso, 2019.

Freud, Sigmund. *The Complete Letters of Sigmund Freud to Wilhelm Fliess, 1887–1904*. Translated by Jeffrey Moussaieff Masson. Cambridge: Belknap, 1986.

———. *The Standard Edition of the Complete Psychological Works of Sigmund Freud*. 24 vols. London: Hogarth Press, 1953.

Gammon, Earl. "Narcissism, Rage, Avocado Toast." In *Clickbait Capitalism: Economies of Desire in the Twenty-First Century*, edited by Amin Samman and Earl Gammon, 21–40. Manchester: Manchester UP, 2023.

Gammon, Earl, and Duncan Wigan. "Libidinal Political Economy: A Psycho-Social Analysis of Financial Violence." In *Global Political Economy: Contemporary Theories*, edited by Ronen Palan, 2nd ed., 205–16. NY: Routledge, 2013.

Gilbert, Andrew Simon. *The Crisis Paradigm: Description and Prescription in Social and Political Theory*. Cham: Palgrave, 2019.

Gramsci, Antonio. *Selections from the Prison Notebooks of Antonio Gramsci*. London: Lawrence & Wishart, 1971.

Haiven, Max. *Revenge Capitalism: The Ghosts of Empire, the Demons of Capital, and the Settling of Unpayable Debts*. London: Pluto, 2020.

Hall, Stuart, Chas Critcher, Tony Jefferson, John Clarke, and Brian Roberts. *Policing the Crisis: Mugging, the State and Law and Order*. 2nd ed. London: Palgrave, 2013.

Hancock, David. *The Countercultural Logic of Neoliberalism*. London: Routledge, 2019.

Haug, Wolfgang Fritz. *Critique of Commodity Aesthetics: Appearance, Sexuality and Advertising in Capitalist Society*. Cambridge: Polity, 1986.

Hook, Derek. "Jouissance as Tool of Psychosocial Analysis." In *The Palgrave Handbook of Psychosocial Studies*, edited by Stephen Frosh, Marita Vyrgioti, and Julie Walsh, 1–27. Cham: Springer, 2020.

Jameson, Fredric. "Schematizations, or How to Draw a Thought." *Critical Inquiry* 50, no. 1 (2023): 31–53. https://doi.org/10.1086/726275.

Johansson, Perry. *The Libidinal Economy of China: Gender, Nationalism, and Consumer Culture*. Lanham: Lexington Books, 2015.

Jones, Angela. "Sex Positivity: A Black Feminist Gift." In *Introducing the New Sexuality Studies*, edited by Nancy Fischer, Laurel Westbrook, and Steven Seidman, 4th ed. NY: Routledge, 2022.

Kaplan, Dana, and Eva Illouz. *What Is Sexual Capital?* Cambridge: Polity Press, 2022.

Kapoor, Ilan, ed. *Psychoanalysis and the Global*. Lincoln: University of Nebraska Press, 2018.

Kapoor, Ilan, Gavin Fridell, Maureen Sioh, and Pieter de Vries. *Global Libidinal Economy*. Albany: SUNY Press, 2023.

Kendal, Evie. "Horny for COVID: The Growth of Coronavirus Erotica." *Extrapolation* 63, no. 1 (2022): 55–73. https://doi.org/10.3828/extr.2022.6.

King, Alasdair. *The Financial Image: Finance, Philosophy and Contemporary Film*. Cham: Springer, 2024.

Kolenc, Bara. "Voyeurism and Exhibitionism on the Internet: The Libidinal Economy of the Spectacle of Instanternity." *Filozofski Vestnik* 43, no. 3 (2022). https://doi.org/10.3986/fv.43.3.09.

Koselleck, Reinhart. "Crisis." Translated by Michaela W. Richter. *Journal of the History of Ideas* 67, no. 2 (2006): 357–400. https://doi.org/10.1353/jhi.2006.0013.

Lacan, Jacques. *The Seminar of Jacques Lacan. Book II: The Ego in Freud's Theory and in the Technique of Psychoanalysis*. Translated by Sylvana Tomaselli. Cambridge: Cambridge UP, 1988.

Leader, Darian. *Is It Ever Just Sex?* London: Penguin, 2023.

———. *Jouissance: Sexuality, Suffering and Satisfaction*. Cambridge: Polity, 2021.

Lear, Jonathan. *Imagining the End: Mourning and Ethical Life*. Cambridge: Harvard UP, 2022.

Leavitt, Keith, Christopher M. Barnes, Trevor Watkins, and David T. Wagner. "From the Bedroom to the Office: Workplace Spillover Effects of Sexual Activity at Home." *Journal of Management* 45, no. 3 (2019): 1173–92. https://doi.org/10.1177/0149206317698022.

Lukács, Georg. *History and Class Consciousness: Studies in Marxist Dialectics*. Translated by Rodney Livingstone. Cambridge: MIT Press, 1976.

Lyotard, Jean-François. *Libdinal Economy*. Translated by Iain Hamilton Grant. Bloomington: Indiana UP, 1993.

Malm, Andreas. "The Future Is the Termination Shock: On the Antinomies and Psychopathologies of Geoengineering. Part One." *Historical Materialism* 30, no. 4 (2022): 3–53. https://doi.org/10.1163/1569206x-20222369.

———. "The Future Is the Termination Shock: On the Antinomies and Psychopathologies of Geoengineering. Part Two." *Historical Materialism* 31, no. 1 (2023): 3–61. https://doi.org/10.1163/1569206x-20232430.

Marcuse, Herbert. *Eros and Civilization: A Philosophical Inquiry into Freud*. London: Routledge, 2023.

Marder, Elissa. "The Shadow of the Eco: Denial and Climate Change." *Philosophy & Social Criticism* 49, no. 2 (2023): 139–50. https://doi.org/10.1177/01914537221150455.

Markowska, Barbara. "Homo Libidinous and the Economy of Desire: Reading Simmel's *The Philosophy of Money* after Freud." *Polish Sociological Review*, no. 4 (2018): 485–98. https://doi.org/10.26412/psr204.05.

May, Rollo. *The Meaning of Anxiety*. Rev. ed. NY: Norton, 1977.

Mbembe, Achille, and Janet Roitman. "Figures of the Subject in Times of Crisis." *Public Culture* 7, no. 2 (1995): 323–52. https://doi.org/10.1215/08992363-7-2-323.

McAvan, Emily. "'I Just Care so Much About the Koalas.'" *Angelaki* 28, no. 5 (2023): 21–38. https://doi.org/10.1080/0969725X.2023.2243156.

McClanahan, Annie. *Dead Pledges: Debt, Crisis and the Twenty-First-Century Culture*. Stanford: Stanford UP, 2017.

Mechen, Ben. "Dirty Magazines, Clean Consciences: Men and Pornography in the 1970s." In *Men and Masculinities in Modern Britain*, edited by Matt Houlbrook, Katie Jones, and Ben Mechen, 253–68. Manchester: Manchester UP, 2024.

———. "'Instamatic Living Rooms of Sin': Pornography, Participation and the Erotics of Ordinariness in the 1970s." *Contemporary British History* 36, no. 2 (2022): 174–206. https://doi.org/10.1080/13619462.2022.2051486.

Nessaibia, Issam, Raffaello Sagese, Leo Atwood, Zihad Bouslama, Luigi Cocci, Tarek Merad, and Abdelkrim Tahraoui. "The Way COVID-19 Transforms Our Sexual Lives." *International Journal of Impotence Research* 34, no. 2 (2022): 117–19. https://doi.org/10.1038/s41443-021-00494-9.

Ngai, Sianne. *Our Aesthetic Categories: Zany, Cute, Interesting*. Cambridge: Harvard UP, 2015.

Noys, Benjamin. "'We Are All Prostitutes': Crisis and Libidinal Economy." In *Credo Credit Crisis*, edited by Aidan Tynan, Laurent Milesi, and Christopher John Muller, 169–84. London: Rowman & Littlefield International, 2017.

Osserman, Jordan. "'Gay Culture Rampant in Hyderabad': Analysing the Political and Libidinal Economy of Homophobia." In *New Voices in Psychosocial Studies*, edited by Stephen Frosh, 179–93. Cham: Springer, 2019.

Ossewaarde, Marinus. "Socialism's Struggles with Eros: Politics of the Body in Cuba and China." *International Sociology* 31, no. 5 (2016): 525–32. https://doi.org/10.1177/0268580916655750.

Özselçuk, Ceren, and Yahya M Madra. "Enjoyment as an Economic Factor: Reading Marx with Lacan." *Subjectivity* 3, no. 3 (2010): 323–47. https://doi.org/10.1057/sub.2010.13.

Pettman, Dominic. *Peak Libido: Sex, Ecology, and the Collapse of Desire*. Cambridge: Polity, 2021.

Plummer, Ken. "Sexual Markets, Commodification, and Consumption." In *The Blackwell Encyclopedia of Sociology*, edited by George Ritzer, 1–4. Oxford: Wiley, 2017.

Popa, Bogdan G. *De-Centering Queer Theory: Communist Sexuality in the Flow during and after the Cold War*. Manchester: Manchester UP, 2021.

Preciado, Paul B. "Learning from the Virus." *Artforum*, June 2020. https://www.artforum.com/print/202005/paul-b-preciado-82823.

———. *Testo Junkie*. Translated by Bruce Benderson. NY: The Feminist Press, 2012.

Proudfoot, Jesse. "The Libidinal Economy of Revanchism: Illicit Drugs, Harm Reduction, and the Problem of Enjoyment." *Progress in Human Geography* 43, no. 2 (2019): 214–34. https://doi.org/10.1177/0309132517739143.

Roberts, John. *Capitalism and the Limits of Desire*. NY: Bloomsbury, 2022.

Roffe, Jon. *Abstract Market Theory*. NY: Palgrave Macmillan, 2015.

Roitman, Janet. *Anti-Crisis*. Durham: Duke UP, 2014.

———. "The Stakes of Crisis." In *Critical Theories of Crisis in Europe: From Weimar to the Euro*, edited by Poul F. Kjaer and Niklas Olsen, 17–34. London: Rowman & Littlefield International, 2016.

Rose, Jacqueline. *The Plague*. Ebook. London: Fitzcarraldo, 2023.

Ross, Daniel. "Translator's Introduction to Bernard Stiegler's 'Pharmacology of Desire: Drive-Based Capitalism and Libidinal Dis-Economy.'" *New Formations* 72 (2011): 146–49.

Rothman, Emily F. *Pornography and Public Health*. Oxford: Oxford UP, 2021.

Ruti, Mari. *Distillations: Theory, Ethics, Affect*. NY: Bloomsbury, 2018.

Safatle, Vladimir. "Affects and Politics." In *The Palgrave Handbook of Psychosocial Studies*, edited by Stephen Frosh, Marita Vyrgioti, and Julie Walsh, 1–17. Cham: Springer, 2020.

———. "Freud as a Thinker of the Political Body: Fear and Distress as Political Affects." New York, 2016.

Samman, Amin, and Earl Gammon, eds. *Clickbait Capitalism: Economies of Desire in the Twenty-First Century*. Manchester: Manchester UP, 2023.

Samman, Amin, and Stefano Sgambati. "Financial Eschatology and the Libidinal Economy of Leverage." *Theory, Culture & Society* 40, no. 3 (2023): 103–21. https://doi.org/10.1177/02632764211070805.

Santner, Eric L. *The Weight of All Flesh: On the Subject-Matter of Political Economy*. Edited by Kevis Goodman. Oxford: Oxford UP, 2016.

———. *The Royal Remains: The People's Two Bodies and the Endgames of Sovereignty*. Chicago: University of Chicago Press, 2011.

Scarry, Elaine. *The Body in Pain: The Making and Unmaking of the World*. Oxford: Oxford UP, 1985.

Schuster, Aaron. "One or Many Antisexes? Introduction to Andrei Platonov's 'The Anti-Sexus.'" *Stasis* 4, no. 1 (2016). https://doi.org/10.33280/2310-3817-2016-4-1-20-35.

Seymour, Richard. *The Twittering Machine*. London: Indigo, 2019.

Sioh, Maureen. "Manicheism Delirium: Desire and Disavowal in the Libidinal Economy of an Emerging Economy." *Third World Quarterly* 35, no. 7 (2014): 1162–78. https://doi.org/10.1080/01436597.2014.926106.

Smail, David. *Origins of Unhappiness: A New Understanding of Personal Distress*. London: Karnac, 2015.

Snitow, Ann Barr, Christine Stansell, and Sharon Thompson, eds. *Powers of Desire: The Politics of Sexuality*. NY: Monthly Review Press, 1983.

Srinivasan, Amia. *The Right to Sex: Feminism in the Twenty-First Century*. London: Bloomsbury, 2022.

Stiegler, Bernard. *For a New Critique of Political Economy*. Cambridge: Polity, 2010.

———. *The Lost Spirit of Capitalism*. Cambridge: Polity Press, 2014.

———. *The Re-Enchantment of the World: The Value of Spirit against Industrial Populism*. London: Bloomsbury, 2014.

Swift, Jayne. "Toxic Positivity? Rethinking Respectability, Revaluing Pleasure." *South Atlantic Quarterly* 120, no. 3 (2021): 591–608. https://doi.org/10.1215/00382876-9423071.

Tomšič, Samo. *The Labour of Enjoyment: Towards a Critique of Libidinal Economy*. Cologne: August Verlag, 2019.

Toscano, Alberto, and Jeff Kinkle. *Cartographies of the Absolute*. Winchester: Zero Books, 2014.

Tribe, Keith. *Strategies of Economic Order: German Economic Discourse, 1750–1950*. Cambridge: Cambridge UP, 1995.

Vishmidt, Marina. "Bodies in Space: On the Ends of Vulnerability." *Radical Philosophy* 2, no. 8 (2020): 33–46.

Vogl, Joseph. *Capital and Ressentiment: A Short Theory of the Present*. Translated by Neil Solomon. London: Polity Press, 2023.

———. *The Specter of Capital*. Translated by Joachim Redner and Robert Savage. Stanford: Stanford UP, 2015.

Vogl, Joseph, Sven Fabre, and Arne Vanraes. "The History of the Notion of Crisis." In *Critical Theory at a Crossroads: Conversations on Resistance in Times of Crisis*, edited by Stijn de Cauwer, 61–74. NY: Columbia UP, 2018.

Watt, Calum. *Derivative Images: Financial Derivatives in French Film, Literature and Thought*. Edinburgh: Edinburgh UP, 2022.

Weber, Max. *The Protestant Ethic and the 'Spirit' of Capitalism and Other Writings*. Edited and translated by Peter Baehr and Gordon C. Wells. London: Penguin, 2002.

Webster, Jamieson. *Conversion Disorder: Listening to the Body in Psychoanalysis*. NY: Columbia UP, 2019.

———. "Memento Mori: The Book as a Cut." *Studies in Gender and Sexuality* 17, no. 1 (2016): 14–18. https://doi.org/10.1080/15240657.2016.1135663.

———. "Somato-Militancy: A New Vision for Psychoanalysis in the Work of Paul B. Preciado." *Paragraph* 46, no. 1 (2023): 124–41. https://doi.org/10.3366/para.2023.0422.

Weintrobe, Sally, ed. *Engaging with Climate Change: Psychoanalytic and Interdisciplinary Perspectives*. London: Taylor & Francis, 2012.

———. *Psychological Roots of the Climate Crisis: Neoliberal Exceptionalism and the Culture of Uncare*. London: Bloomsbury, 2021.

Wilderson, Frank B. *Afropessimism*. NY: Liveright, 2020.

———. *Red, White & Black: Cinema and the Structure of U.S. Antagonisms*. Durham: Duke UP, 2010.

Willis Aronowitz, Nona. *Bad Sex: Truth, Pleasure, and an Unfinished Revolution*. NY: Plume, 2022.

Woodward, Ashley. "'White Skin': Lyotard's Sketch of a Postcolonial Libidinal Economy." *Journal of the British Society for Phenomenology* 51, no. 4 (2020): 337–51. https://doi.org/10.1080/00071773.2020.1732580.

Zhang, Charlie Yi. *Dreadful Desires: The Uses of Love in Neoliberal China*. Duke UP, 2022.

Žižek, Slavoj. "'You May!'" *London Review of Books*, March 18, 1999. https://www.lrb.co.uk/the-paper/v21/n06/slavoj-zizek/you-may!

Zupančič, Alenka. *The Odd One in: On Comedy*. Cambridge: MIT Press, 2008.

Authors

Adriana Zaharijević is Principal Research Fellow at the Institute for Philosophy and Social Theory, University of Belgrade.

Alexis Wolfe is a psychotherapist working on the west coast of Turtle Island.

Ben Gook is Senior Lecturer in Cultural Studies at the University of Melbourne.

Benjamin Noys is Professor of Critical Theory at the University of Chichester.

Christopher Chamberlin is the Marie Skłodowska-Curie Postdoctoral Fellow in the Department of Psychosocial and Psychoanalytic Studies at the University of Essex.

Daniel Tutt teaches philosophy at several institutions, including George Washington University and the Global Center for Advanced Studies, and convenes Study Groups on Psychoanalysis and Politics.

Jason Read is Professor of Philosophy at the University of Southern Maine.

Jule Govrin is a philosopher and political writer. Their research is situated at the intersection of Social Philosophy, Feminist Philosophy, Political Theory and Aesthetics, with a focus on Feminist Political Economy and issues of desire, bodies and equality.

Julie Gaillard is an Assistant Professor in French at the University of Illinois.

Luce deLire is a ship with eight sails and she lays off the quay.

Matthew Flisfeder is an Associate Professor of Rhetoric and Communications at the University of Winnipeg.

Samo Tomšič is Professor of Philosophy/Aesthetics at the University of Fine Arts Dresden.

Todd McGowan is a Professor in English at the University of Vermont.

Vladimir Safatle is a Professor in the Department of Philosophy and the Department of Psychology at the University of São Paulo.

Acknowledgements

Thanks to contributors for sticking with the project despite pandemic challenges and other delays. These crisis times have also affected this volume's diversity among contributors and topics. Among those initially involved in the conference, then the plans for the volume, it was primarily women and people of colour who had to drop out along the way. This reflects a sociological fact about the pandemic. While I offered further time or formats to stay involved, accumulating demands meant that many had no choice but to drop out and focus on core teaching and social reproductive work, amid home-schooling, caregiving and precarious positions. It would be at once shameless and shaming to name those who had to drop out, but I acknowledge their time and put on the record that I hoped for their involvement.

In Berlin, Joseph Vogl generously offered funds for the conference at Acud Macht Neu and support for the idea; Samo Tomšič offered intellectual and other comradeship; Sabine Imhof and Stephan Brändle provided crucial practical support for the event; Ada Favaron designed great posters; Eva von Redecker connected me with excellent thinkers, including Adriana Zaharijević, a dear lockdown fellow traveller; and Jakob Horstmann generously proposed the idea for the book and shepherded it through to completion. Thanks also to Annika Linnemann at Transcript for final production work. Funds from the Alexander von Humboldt Stiftung supported the event and publication. In Melbourne, thanks to Knox Peden and Justin Clemens for reading various chapters; Vincent Lê for research assistance work; Cynthia Troup and Bonnie Reid for their comments on various chapter drafts; and the Head of School fund in the School of Culture & Communication at the University of Melbourne. And, lastly, thanks to Camille for infinite patience.

GPSR Authorized Representative: Easy Access System Europe, Mustamäe tee
50, 10621 Tallinn, Estonia, gpsr.requests@easproject.com

www.ingramcontent.com/pod-product-compliance
Lightning Source LLC
Jackson TN
JSHW011810260325
81483JS00004B/94